critique confronts the world. Without dogma, without new principles, it refuses to conform and instead demands insurrection of thought. It must be ruthless, unafraid of both its results and the powers it may come into conflict with. Critique takes the world, our world, as its object, so that we may develop new ways of making it.

influence is a step from critique toward the future, when effects begin to be felt, when the ground becomes unstable, when a movement ignites. These critiques of the state of our world have influenced a generation. They are crucial guides to change.

change is when the structures shift. The books in this series take critique as their starting point and as such have influenced both their respective disciplines and thought the world over. This series is born out of our conviction that change lies not in the novelty of the future but in the realization of the thoughts of the past.

These texts are not mere interpretations or reflections, but scientific, critical, and impassioned analyses of our world. After all, the point is to change it.

TITLES IN THE CRITIQUE INFLUENCE CHANGE SERIES

Reclaiming Development
An Alternative Policy Manual
by Ha-Joon Chang and Ilene Grabel

Realizing Hope
Life Beyond Capitalism
by Michael Albert

Global Governance and the New Wars
The Merging of Development and Security
by Mark Duffield

Capitalism in the Age of Globalization
The Management of Contemporary Society
by Samir Amin

Ecofeminism
by Maria Mies and Vandana Shiva

Debating Cultural Hybridity
Multicultural Identities and the Politics of Anti-Racism
edited by Pnina Werbner and Tariq Modood

Deglobalization
Ideas for a New World Economy
by Walden Bello

A Fundamental Fear
Eurocentrism and the Emergence of Islamism
by Bobby S. Sayyid

Grassroots Post-modernism
Remaking the Soil of Cultures
by Gustavo Esteva and Madhu Suri Prakash

Patriarchy and Accumulation on a World Scale
Women in the International Division of Labour
by Maria Mies

ABOUT THE AUTHOR

Mark Duffield is emeritus professor at the Global Insecurities Centre, University of Bristol. He has taught at the universities of Khartoum, Aston and Birmingham and held fellowships and chairs at Sussex, Leeds and Lancaster. Mark is currently a member of the Scientific Board of the Flemish Peace Institute, Brussels, and a fellow of the Rift Valley Institute, London and Nairobi. Outside of academia, during the 1980s he was Oxfam's country representative in Sudan. Duffield has advised government departments, including DFID, EU (ECHO), the Swedish Ministry of Foreign Affairs and the Swedish International Development Cooperation Agency (SIDA), and non-governmental organisations, such as CAFOD, International Alert, Comic Relief and Oxfam, along with UNICEF, UNOCHA, UNDP and UNHCR.

GLOBAL GOVERNANCE AND THE NEW WARS

THE MERGING OF DEVELOPMENT AND SECURITY

MARK DUFFIELD

WITH A FOREWORD BY

ANTONIO DONINI

Zed Books
London & New York

Global Governance and the New Wars: The Merging of Development and Security
was first published in 2001 by Zed Books Ltd, 7 Cynthia Street, London N1 9JF, UK
and Room 400, 175 Fifth Avenue, New York, NY 10010, USA

This edition was published in 2014.

www.zedbooks.co.uk

Designed and set in 9.6 / 12 pt Palatino by Long House, Cumbria, UK
Cover designed by www.alice-marwick.co.uk
Printed and bound by TJ International Ltd, Padstow, Cornwall, UK

Distributed in the USA exclusively by Palgrave Macmillan, a division of St Martin's
Press, LLC, 175 Fifth Avenue, New York, NY 10010, USA

A catalogue record for this book is available from the British Library
Library of Congress Cataloging in Publication Data available

ISBN 978 1 78032 560 6

For Roberta

Contents

Acknowledgements   xi
List of abbreviations   xiii
Foreword by Antonio Donini   xv
Preface to the critique influence change edition   xix

1. Introduction: The New Development–Security Terrain   1
2. The Merging of Development and Security   22
3. Strategic Complexes and Global Governance   44
4. The New Humanitarianism   75
5. Global Governance and the Causes of Conflict   108
6. The Growth of Transborder Shadow Economies   136
7. Non-Liberal Political Complexes and the New Wars   161
8. Internal Displacement and the New Humanitarianism:
   Displacement and Complicity in Sudan (Part 1)   202
9. Aid and Social Subjugation: Displacement and Complicity
   in Sudan (Part 2)   230
10. Conclusion: Global Governance, Moral Responsibility
    and Complexity – Internal Displacement and the
    New Humanitarianism   257

Bibliography   266
Index   280

Acknowledgements

This book has taken a long time to come to fruition. Its germ formed in the 1980s while I was working as Oxfam's Country Representative in Sudan. This experience established an appreciation of war as a forcing-house for new systems of international governance and regulation. For most of the 1990s, I was at the School of Public Policy, University of Birmingham. Because the School encourages practical assignments and consultancy, it provided a singular opportunity to explore further the governmental relationship between aid policy and conflict. Creating a space for systematic analysis, however, was not easy. I would like to thank Alan Murie and Richard Batley for doing all they could to help. In 1999, I moved to the Institute for Politics and International Studies at the University of Leeds. The generous granting of sabbatical leave at the start of my employment provided the first real opportunity to take stock and pull things together. In retrospect, the book has probably benefited from the wait. The conflict and governance field continues to evolve at a rapid pace with new departures and interconnections occurring every few months. Trying to form a sober view of such developments and uncover the forms of mobilisation that drive the system has benefited from the passage of time. It has also meant, however, that my debt to friends and colleagues is a long-standing and varied one.

Help and support in writing this book has come in many different forms and from numerous directions. Mentioning everyone is a difficult and, in the end, impossible task. Nevertheless, I would like to thank Mark Bradbury, Ray Bush, David Keen, Nick Stockton and Susan Woodward for their support and critical comments on the draft chapters. I am also indebted to David Campbell, Mick Dillon and Jenny Edkins who, through their participation in the Emerging Political Complexes Group, helped me take what I had a step further. Over the years, I have been encouraged, challenged and variously aided and abetted by Philippa Atkinson, Aldo Benini, John Borton, Matthew Carter, Bob Deacon, James Fennell, Jonathan Goodhand, Fiona Fox, John Hammock, Ankie Hoogvelt, Barbara Hendrie, Susan Jaspars, Wendy James, Douglas Johnson, Sue Lautze, Iain Levine, John Mackinlay, Joanna Macrae, Andy Mawson, David Moore, Angela Raven-Roberts, Jemera Rone, John Ryle, Carl-Ulrik Schierup, Hugo Slim, David Sogge,

Finn Stepputat, Paul Stubbs, Alex de Waal and Helen Young. As is usual in these circumstances, I would like to point out that any errors or misconceptions in the following pages are entirely my own. Finally, I would like to thank Jean. Without her support, patience and understanding, nothing would be possible.

Abbreviations

ACP	African, Caribbean and Pacific countries
CARE	Cooperative for American Relief Everywhere
CBI	Confederation of British Industry
CCHA	Committee for the Coordination of Humanitarian Assistance
CIA	Central Intelligence Agency
CIMIC	Civil–Military Cooperation
CMOC	Civil–Military Operations Centre
CNPL	China National Petroleum Company
DFID	Department for International Development (UK)
DHA	Department of Humanitarian Affairs (UN)
DSL	Defence Services Limited
DTAP	Democracy Transition Assistance Programme
DUP	Democratic Unionist Party (North Sudan)
ECHO	European Commission Humanitarian Office
ECOSOC	Economic and Social Commission (UN)
ECRE	European Council on Refugees and Exiles
ELC	Environmental Liaison Committee
EU	European Union
FAF	Federation of Bosnia-Herzegovia Armed Forces
FPA	Framework Partnership Agreement
HAC	Humanitarian Aid Committee
HH	household
ICVA	International Council of Voluntary Agencies
IDC	International Development Committee (UK)
IDP	internally displaced person
IFI	international financial institution
IFRC	International Federation for Red Cross and Red Crescent Societies
IGAD	Intergovernmental Agency for Development
IGO	intergovernmental organisation
ILO	International Labour Organisation
IRC	International Rescue Committee
MSF	Médecins Sans Frontières
MinOps	Minimal Operating Standards
MPLA	People's Movement for the Liberation of Angola
MPRI	Military Professional Resources Incorporated

MSP	military stabilisation programme
mt	metric tonnes
NATO	North Atlantic Treaty Organisation
NGO	non-governmental organisation
NIEO	New International Economic Order
NPFL	National Patriotic Front of Liberia
OAU	Organisation for African Unity
OCHA	Organisation for the Coordination of Humanitarian Assistance
OECD	Organisation for Economic Co-operation and Development
OHCHR	Office of the High Commissioner for Human Rights
OLS	Operation Lifeline Sudan
OPEC	Organisation of the Petroleum Exporting Countries
OSCE	Organisation for Security and Cooperation in Europe
PMC	private military company
PSC	private security company
RUF	Revolutionary United Front (Sierra Leone)
SCF	Save the Children Fund
SCHR	Steering Committee for Humanitarian Response
SPLA	Sudanese People's Liberation Army
UN	United Nations
UNCTAD	United Nations Conference on Trade and Development
UNDP	United Nations Development Programme
UNHCU	United Nations Humanitarian Co-ordination Unit
UNICEF	United Nations Children's Fund
UNITA	National Union for the Total Independence of Angola
UN/WIDER	United Nations and the World Institute for Development Economics Research
VOICE	Voluntary Organisations in Cooperation in Emergencies
WFP	World Food Programme
WHO	World Health Organisation

Foreword

Antonio Donini

Ours is an era of rapid and far-reaching change but the book that you are holding is no less relevant than when it was first published. Zed Books have done well to bring it out again with a new hard-hitting preface by its author. Unlike the many books on development, humanitarianism and international relations that come and go after an initial academic or media flourish, this one has remained – and for good reason. This was and is a ground-breaking book that has shaped a generation of practitioners, policy-makers and academics. It explains what lies behind the fog of development and the pale sun of humanitarianism. It provides the theoretical software that allows us to understand – with our eyes wide open – the key relationship between Western aid policies and security. The picture that Mark Duffield so eloquently provides is a sobering one: he convincingly unpacks the functions that development assistance and humanitarian action perform in a globalised world. His findings may be inconvenient to some, but they are unavoidable for anyone who seeks to understand the darker side of Western modernity.

Three issues stand out.

The first is the tight fit between aid and what Duffield calls the promotion of liberal peace. His book was written before 9/11, but it is visionary in its analysis that a wave of political and military interventionism was in the offing after the collapse of the ideological and structural certitudes of the Cold War. The revolutionary push for decolonisation and modernisation after the Second World War has morphed into what is euphemistically called global governance – the falsely technocratic politicisation and militarisation of development that serves to incorporate the restive peripheries into the globalised web of liberal peace. That the terms of this incorporation are imposed from outside and that the outcomes of the interventionist wave of the last fifteen years is neither liberal nor peaceful only reinforces the continuing relevance of Duffield's analysis.

The second is the devastating critique of 'new humanitarianism', that is, the instrumental use of the language and tools of humanitarian action to achieve political objectives through the supposedly 'moral' foreign policies of Western states. Pressed by their donors, and sometimes by their own arrogance, countless actors in the humanitarian aid establishment wittingly or unwittingly have accepted the notion that in addition to working *in* conflict they should also work *on* conflict and bring the tools of their trade to bear in solving what they thought were 'humanitarian' crises but were in reality what Duffield calls 'emerging political complexes'. The road to Afghanistan, Iraq and Sri Lanka is paved with the carcasses of such misguided good intentions. The humanitarian act, traditionally and fundamentally, is about saving and protecting lives *in extremis* in the here and now. That is what everyone who claims to be humanitarian is duty bound to do. As Duffield points out, the intrusion of the consequentialist ethics of a better tomorrow, as a price worth paying for suffering today, has corrupted the very essence of humanitarianism. He reminds us that the uncritical subordination of humanitarianism to the 'magicians and sorcerers' of peace enforcement and development can result in the 'normalisation of violence' and even 'complicity with its perpetrators'.

The third is about the new wars that Duffield describes as non-territorial network wars, where the objective is not the subjugation of the enemy's subjects, so much as the reconfiguration of the system to the victor's benefit. That is not to say that today's asymmetrical conflicts are less ugly than their antecedents. They are even more likely to result in the destruction of development assets, widespread violence against civilians and the devastation of the social fabric. Duffield observed in early 2001 that 'organised violence may no longer take the earlier form of short but world-shattering outbursts'. Conflict now appears to assume more systemic, intrusive and non-controllable forms. 'From security-conscious airline operators to armed African cattle herders, in different ways the threat or actuality of pervasive violence now affects all of us most of the time' (p. 257). The fact that these new wars can impact directly on the North underpins Duffield's prescient conclusion that the 'reinvention of development as conflict resolution' was bound to fail. Linked to growing transborder 'shadow' economies, these often illiberal political complexes may be perceived as rational responses to the exclusions and compartmentalisation of the neoliberal version of globalisation. He illustrates how emerging political complexes, which we in the West usually saw as aberrations on the highway to peace and development, are in fact important durable phenomena that need to be understood in their own right.

What, then, lies ahead? If crises are the new normal and the interventionist network power of the North is increasingly in conflict with the network wars in the borderlands, what of the plight of the vulnerable populations caught in this violent and never-ending purgatory? Duffield tells us that the humanitarian project is in more serious trouble than is widely understood or acknowledged and that the hopes that politicised humanitarianism would contribute to global governance, that is, to a world ordered for and by the North, were misplaced.

I am doubtful that the current love affair of Western/Northern states with humanitarian action will continue deep into the twenty-first century. This love affair is currently based on two notions: that humanitarian action is functional to the security interests of the countries that are its traditional funders and therefore seek to shape the humanitarian enterprise; and that the current political economy of humanitarian action will continue to be dominated by like-minded Northern and Western-driven values, behaviours and styles of management. Clearly, these assumptions no longer hold in an emerging multi-polar world; the humanitarian enterprise, and its Northern donors, must quickly come to grips with a new and rapidly changing global reality in which a multiplicity of actors – state and non-state, private and public, local and global – will define an environment of action that will no longer be the preserve of the North.

Humanitarianism, as traditionally framed and implemented, may well come to occupy a smaller place -on the international screen, relegated to crises with low political profile in which the strategic interests of the major powers are not perceived to be at play. The assistance and protection needs of the Afghanistans, Somalias and Syrias will continue to pose major challenges. Needs in such high-profile conflicts seem likely to be addressed increasingly, if at all, by an array of non-traditional actors, including international or regional military forces, private contractors and shady non-state actors, rather than by card-carrying humanitarian agencies.

Over the past decade and a half, the humanitarian agenda has expanded to encompass an array of transformative activities, such as advocacy on social and human rights issues, rehabilitation, peace-building and development, while at the same time a preoccupation with material assistance has frequently ignored or exacerbated the protection problems of crisis-affected communities. Some would say that humanitarianism has drifted away from its traditional moorings and its primary focus on lives in immediate danger. An evolution towards a more modest humanitarianism that is delimited in scope, objectives and actors would not be an entirely negative development. It would reflect a realisation that current global trends that generate a need for humanitarian action can be neither redirected nor significantly contained by the humanitarian enterprise itself. This does not mean that humanitarians are less committed than before to a more compassionate, just and secure world, but rather that they are realistic in recognising that their first obligation is to be effective in saving and protecting lives that are at imminent risk.

Humanitarian action is about injecting a measure of humanity into situations that should not exist. It is not about changing the world. Buffeted by strong crosswinds, the flickering light of humanitarianism continues to shine. It lights a narrow path strewn with obstacles and compromises. Not all will be overcome. Vigilance is in order, as Duffield reminds us in his preface, to ensure that the human in the humanitarian relationship is not held hostage to excessive institutionalisation, distance technologies and bunkerisation. Holding the line of principle, working wherever the needs are most urgent and looking for opportunities to push back partisan agendas continues to be a fundamentally necessary and worthwhile activity despite, or perhaps because of, the challenges identified in this book.

Preface to the critique influence change edition

Published in 2001, *Global Governance and the New Wars* provides the reader with an analysis of the relationship between the civil wars that erupted into public view with the end of the Cold War and the international humanitarian system that transformed itself within the space of this new post-nuclear threat to international security. It was framed by experience gained first as a doctoral student studying West African migration and settlement in Sudan and subsequently as Oxfam's country representative for Sudan during the latter half of the 1980s, the early days of the aid industry's 'fantastic invasion'. At that time, the SPLA's growing encirclement of the towns in South Sudan was, together with the civil war in Ethiopia, laying the foundations of the emerging system of liberal global governance and the strategic role of humanitarian action within it. During the expansionary 1990s, consultancies for the United Nations, non-governmental organisations and donor governments in the Balkans, the Horn of Africa, southern Africa and Afghanistan built on and nurtured this experience.

Being an anthropologist by background, and having experienced the actually existing politics of humanitarian aid, *Global Governance and the New Wars* is not bogged down with the academic fascination that international relations has for the state. It focuses more on the political economy of network war and how, through exploiting the opportunities of globalisation to cast off Cold War dependencies, the new wars announced the emergence of self-provisioning, armed non-state actors on the world stage. Drawing on complex emergent systems-thinking, it understands the new wars through their autonomous non-state dimensions and the implications of this threat complex for a similarly networked and emergent global governance. The link between the new wars and the expanding humanitarian system is examined in relation to the remix of the development-security nexus under post-Cold War conditions. While non-state violence had served the interests of earlier superpower rivalry, liberal interventionism was quick to pronounce it as now unacceptable. With a new ability to work in ongoing conflict, NGOs, multilaterals, donors, private companies and UN agencies transformed themselves and grew in the new spaces of ongoing conflict and permanent emergency.

The pacificatory effects of UN humanitarian and peace-building programmes rejuvenated the transformational vision of international aid. Under the rubric of human security, through their NGO implementers, donor governments were now able to bypass erstwhile client states and work directly at the level of communities, households and individuals. This remix pushed aid beyond the long-standing liberal goal of creating self-reliance to embrace that of conflict resolution with its promise of reordering societies using soft power harnessed to the interests of peace. Within the new development spaces created by the end of the Cold War, international aid quickly became a tool of NGO-led social intelligence and community-level counterinsurgency.

Global Governance and the New Wars charts both the initial expansionary phase of liberal interventionism and the beginning of the redundancy of the post-Cold War security–development remix and increasing recourse to state-led enforcement. Relatively speaking, much of the 1990s was a time of UN radicalism. The UN was able to negotiate humanitarian access directly with non-state actors. In places it established a system of ground rules regulating the relationship between humanitarian and armed actors. It was a time when negotiated access was thought synonymous with the creation of shared platforms for confidence-building among warring parties. While this worked in a few places, such as Mozambique, the fragility of negotiated access underpinned a more general period of a growing crisis of humanitarian-access denial. By the end of the 1990s, the formal merging of aid and politics within the creation of the UN integrated mission marked the subordination of international aid to Western foreign policy goals. Rather than operational neutrality, a donor-led new humanitarianism, involving taking sides in ongoing conflict to enforce liberal peace, had moved to the political foreground. The easy recourse to liberal violence as a necessary security restorative, preferably but not necessarily sanctioned by the UN, led inexorably to the debacles in Iraq and Afghanistan.

The continuing relevance of *Global Governance and the New Wars* lies in the presentation of its subject matter as unfinished business, that is, as an assemblage of trends and possibilities rather than a fixed entity.

Published just before 9/11, the book anticipates the growing aid-industry adaptation and co-option into the now state-led counterinsurgency role that, in many respects, it had already created for itself. However, the foreign policy disasters in Iraq and Afghanistan helped reveal that violent liberal interventionism not only leaves countries more rather than less politically fragmented, it also actively contributes to their de-development. One after another, from the Balkans to the Middle East, relatively industrialised countries with modern scientific credentials have had their critical infrastructure trashed while being rediscovered anew by an astonished but vindicated West, as adding to the list of irrevocably ethicised and tribalised societies. The War on Terror dealt a mortal blow to the expansionary post-Cold War remix of the development–security nexus. The overt politicisation of aid has resulted in increasing attacks on aid workers by armed actors that no longer recognise the neutrality of the UN or ICRC. By the end of the 1990s, the initial post-Cold War optimism had died, with the increasing withdrawal of international aid workers into the aid world's expanding archipelago of gated complexes and fortified aid compounds. The reassertion of state authority, access denial and growing risk-aversion among international actors has resulted in a growing physical remoteness of aid managers from the societies in which they work.

The dead end of post-Cold War development–security as a tool of foreign policy is illustrated in relation to the Sudan(s). With the pumping of oil from the late 1990s, Sudan's core–periphery relations have progressively consolidated as respective boom and gloom economies of liberal frontier. While the former, based on energy, telecommunications, import-substitution industries, irrigated land-leasing and real estate, has oriented itself towards the emerging markets of the Middle East and Asia, Western influence has been progressively confined, to a large extent by self-selection, to the disaster zones of Darfur and South Sudan. The West now widely finds itself occupying the role of humanitarian custodian for fragile states and ungoverned space. In a rebalancing world, this lock-out has debilitating consequences.

While exacerbated by the bunkerisation of aid workers, the growing crisis of ground-truth goes beyond the international aid industry. Private security advisers and the insurance industry now effectively rate the risk of university research. For security and ethical reasons, it is now hard to field research students beyond the ramparts of Fortress Europe. Reflecting the increasing difficulty of assessing aid impact in challenging environments, university area-research has become schematic and dependent on remote methodologies. Outside the safe

parts of their capital cities, fragile states increasingly present themselves as ethnographic voids emerging out of the spaces once known
through the sentiments of anthropologists, both professional and
amateur. The retreat from encounter has coincided with a major shift in
aid policy. Earlier distinctions between relief and development had
been blurring since the 1990s. The wholesale embrace of disaster
resilience has completed this process. While self-reliance has been a
long-standing aim of liberal development, in fulfilling the politics of
austerity, resilience brings a new emphasis: self-reliance through
constant adaptation to permanent emergency within post-security
landscapes where state and corporate social responsibility has effectively absented itself.

In managing disaster resilience, the view from the bunker is one of
pioneering new forms of remote management through accessing commercial geospatial technologies, computer-based mapping tools and
the mining of Big Data. The aim is to reconnect with aid beneficiaries
and disaster-affected populations digitally and thus usher in the latest
booster remix of McLuhan's global village. Led by the UN, the first
tentative steps to visualise refugee camps in the late 1990s has morphed
into, for example, aid agencies accessing commercial satellite imagery
to interrogate other remote socio-economic datasets, thereby gaining
insight into the wealth-distribution effects of pirate ransoms in Somalia,
or using social media metadata to access in near real time the changing
moods and sentiments of selected populations as they respond to
economic, health or environmental shocks.

The rise of machine-based interpretations of the visual human
terrain signals a new age of humanitarian remote management. Driven
by an uncritical cyber-optimism, these Net-driven technologies
promise much. However, their military success in overcoming successive terrestrial access and disclosure obstacles has normalised the
problem of growing physical distance, the problem that first called
forth these remote technologies. Moreover, the increasing effectiveness
of mapping, modelling and simulation tools not only questions the
absolute need for ground-truth, it also has the ability to render much of
the terrestrial archipelago of humanitarian infrastructure redundant,
making field-based professional and research skills, such as needs
assessment, victim testimony or humanitarian rescue, increasingly
surplus to technological requirements.

Cyber-humanitarianism, with its conflicting progressive and regressive hyper-bunker tendencies, will shape the aid debate over the
coming decade. Regarding regression, terrestrial forms of aid partnership have long been critiqued as masking unequal power relations. The

retreat from encounters to remote face-to-screen relations will give the politics of inequality a whole new dynamic. The new technologies create the conditions of possibility for hyper-bunkered aid managers to provide value-added feedback to communities tasked with constantly adapting to permanent emergency as a mark of their fitness and resilience. In cases of a validated exception, that is, requiring material assistance, commercial technology now exists to support in-region drone-based delivery mechanisms that fully comply with current risk insurance and ethical best-practice regimes. Following the largely unopposed spread of food banks in the global North, as it takes on a déjà vu character, this scenario looks less science fiction by the day.

The above concerns should not conceal the fact that the new technologies also support progressive and emancipatory tendencies. They connect people in new ways, making novel forms of intercourse and exchange possible. However, as machine interpretation replaces human sentiment, one cannot assume that progressive benefits will be easy to find in a world shaped by private and corporate enclosure of the portals and platforms and the sense-making algorithms that now seek to reshape global governance for the Network Age. If they are to fulfil their promise and not deepen a polarising world, the technologies now working the system demand democratic oversight and the demilitarisation of their operational logic. Without maintaining ground-truth, achieving such a political realisation is all the more difficult. With this is mind, one important lesson that can be drawn from *Global Governance and the New Wars* is that during the relative openness of much of the 1990s, it was possible to draw state and non-state actors into negotiation and dialogue while ameliorating the humanitarian effects of conflict. While difficult and contested, rather than turning our backs on that experience, it calls out for renewal and reanimation.

Mark Duffield
Sedgley
23 October 2013

1

Introduction
The New Development—Security Terrain

The optimism of the early post-Cold War years that the world was entering a new era of peace and stability has long since evaporated. It has been swept aside by a troubled decade of internal and regionalised forms of conflict, large-scale humanitarian interventions and social reconstruction programmes that have raised new challenges and questioned old assumptions. During the mid-1990s the need to address the issue of conflict became a central concern within mainstream development policy. Once a specialised discipline within international and security studies, war and its effects are now an important part of development discourse. At the same time, development concerns have become increasingly important in relation to how security is understood. It is now generally accepted that international organisations should be aware of conflict and its effects and, where possible, gear their work towards conflict resolution and helping to rebuild war-torn societies in a way that will avert future violence. Such engagement is regarded as essential if development and stability are to prevail. These views are well represented in the policy statements of leading intergovernmental organisations;[1] international financial institutions;[2] donor governments;[3] United Nations agencies;[4] influential think-tanks;[5] international NGOs;[6] and even large private companies.[7] At the same time, the literature on humanitarian assistance, conflict resolution and post-war reconstruction has burgeoned,[8] new university departments and courses have sprung up, and practitioner training programmes have been established. Conflict-related NGOs have emerged, while existing NGOs have expanded their mandates. In addition, donor governments, international financial institutions (IFIs), intergovernmental organisations (IGOs) and the UN have all created specialist units and committees. Linking these developments, dedicated multidisciplinary and multisectoral fora and networks have multiplied.

This book is a critical reflection on the incorporation of war into development discourse. The shift in aid policy towards conflict resolution and societal reconstruction is analysed not merely as a technical system of support and assistance, but as part of an emerging system of global governance. In order to frame this approach, the introduction has two main parts. First, the changing nature of North–South relations is described in broad terms. In particular, it is argued that the capitalist world system is no longer a necessarily expansive or inclusive complex. Since the 1970s, formal trade, productive, financial and technological networks have been concentrating within and between the North American, Western European and East Asian regional systems at the expense of outlying areas. On the basis of raw materials and cheap labour alone, the inclusion of the South within the conventional global economy can no longer be taken for granted. The second part of the introduction builds on this reconfiguration and focuses particularly on its association with the reinterpretation of the nature of security. Today, security concerns are no longer encompassed solely by the danger of conventional interstate war. The threat of an excluded South fomenting international instability through conflict, criminal activity and terrorism is now part of a new security framework. Within this framework, underdevelopment has become dangerous. This reinterpretation is closely associated with a radicalisation of development. Indeed, the incorporation of conflict resolution and societal reconstruction within aid policy – amounting to a commitment to transform societies as a whole – embodies this radicalisation. Such a project, however, is beyond the capabilities or legitimacy of individual Northern governments. In this respect, the changing nature of North–South relations is synonymous with a shift from hierarchical and territorial relations of government to polyarchical, non-territorial and networked relations of governance. The radical agenda of social transformation is embodied within Northern strategic networks and complexes that are bringing together governments, NGOs, military establishments and private companies in new ways. Such complexes are themselves part of an emerging system of global liberal governance.

From a capitalist to a liberal world system

The nation state was a political project based upon a logic of expansion, inclusion and subordination. It was also closely associated with the growth of a capitalist world system. Until the 1970s, this system was widely perceived as a geographically expanding and spatially deepening universe (Wallerstein 1974). A broad consensus held that capitalism

2

had grown over several hundred years from its European origins to span the globe by the end of the nineteenth century. Indeed, contrary to some of the current views on globalisation, a few writers have even argued that the world economy reached a peak of interdependence and openness in the early years of the twentieth century that has not been equalled since (Hirst and Thompson 1996). While such detail is contested, in capitalism's seemingly inexorable forward march other social systems fell before it and, for better or worse, found themselves subordinated to its logic. Even the peripheral areas of the world system were valued for their raw materials and cheap labour and were typically incorporated through colonial or semi-colonial relations of tutelage (Rodney 1972). In the capitalist core areas, bureaucratic, juridical and territorially based state systems developed. Through the emergence of widening forms of legal, political and economic protection, state actors forged inclusive national identities from the disparate social groups that lay within state borders.[9] On the basis of the growing competence of the nation state, citizens were expected to be loyal and defer to its normative structures and expectations (Derlugian 1996).

The 1970s are widely regarded as signalling a profound and historic change in the nature of the capitalist world system and with it the nation state. From this period, while market relations have continued to deepen in core areas, the future of capitalism as a globally expansive and inclusive system has been increasingly questioned (Hopkins and Wallerstein 1996). Contrary to popular views of globalisation which often portray capitalist relations as redoubling their penetration and interconnection of all parts of the globe (for examples see Waters 1995), the core regions of what could now be termed the liberal world system appear to be consolidating and strengthening the ties between them at the expense of outlying areas. In a review of the existing quantitative information, Hoogvelt (1997: 69–89) has argued that in broad terms the loci of economic power and influence in the world have remained remarkably stable for the past several hundred years. The one major exception is the relatively recent emergence of a number of East Asian countries to join Japan in confirming that region, together with the North American and Western European systems, as one of the core areas of an emerging global informational economy (Castells 1996).

If globalisation has a meaning in this context, it is the consolidation of several distinct but interrelated regionalised economic systems as the core of the formal international economy. Moreover, rather than continuing to expand in a spatial or geographical sense, the competitive financial, investment, trade and productive networks that link these regionalised systems have been thickening and deepening since the

1970s. Although there are, of course, many differences that separate them, these core regionalised systems of the global informational economy are here figuratively described as the 'North'. Correspondingly, the areas formally outside or only partially or conditionally integrated into these regional networks are loosely referred to as the 'South'. The inclusion of the South within the conventional economic flows and networks of the global economy – even when raw materials and cheap labour are available, even as unequal and exploited subjects – can no longer, as in the past, be taken for granted.

> The architecture of the global economy features an asymmetrically interdependent world, organised around three major economic regions and increasingly polarized along an axis of opposition between productive, information-rich, affluent areas, and impoverished areas, economically devalued and socially excluded. (Castells 1996: 145)

In the case of Africa, for example – with the exception of South Africa and, beyond it, a certain number of prized raw materials, niche tropical products and adventure tourism – commercial investment has collapsed since the 1970s. In much of the former Soviet Union a similar lack of interest exists, as evidenced by relatively low levels of Western investment in all fields except energy and a number of valuable raw materials. Manuel Castells (1996, 1998) has argued that global capitalism no longer operates on the basis of expansion and incorporation but on a new logic of consolidation and exclusion (see also Hirst and Thompson 1996: 68–9).

There are numerous instances of the logic of exclusion informing North–South relations, including the increasing restriction of immigration from the South since the 1970s and the hardening of the international refugee regime (UNHCR 1995). Indeed, the present refugee regime can best be described as one of return rather than asylum. Although some views of globalisation stress interconnection and integration, the movement of poor people from the South to the North, and even across international boundaries in the South itself, is becoming more difficult and contested. Writing in a similar vein, Robert Cox has argued that the irrelevance of much of the world's population in relation to the formal global economy is manifest in the shift from attempts to promote economic development in the South 'in favour of what can be called global poor relief and riot control' (Cox 1995: 41). Restriction, in many cases, has been matched by a system concordance geared to attempting to develop methods of population containment. During the first half of the 1990s, for example, a key response to the new wars of the post-Cold War era was the emergence of system-wide UN humanitarian opera-

4

tions. Largely through negotiating access with warring parties, in Africa and the Balkans, for example, aid agencies developed the means of providing humanitarian assistance directly to populations within their countries and areas of origin (Duffield 1997). Such operations, together with related 'safe area' policies, had the effect of encouraging war-affected populations, with varying degrees of success, to remain within conflict zones and to avoid crossing international borders.

The idea of exclusion, however, should not be understood too literally. As well as a closing of doors or severing of relationships, exclusion is also a subordinating social relationship embodied in new relations of connection, interaction and interdependence. In other words, the concept of exclusion encompasses both new types of restriction and emergent and subordinating forms of North–South integration.

The ambivalence of Southern exclusion

Political economy has largely understood Southern exclusion in terms of the ambivalence of its present economic position within the global economy. On the one hand, evidence suggests that the South has been increasingly isolated and excluded by the dominant networks of the conventional global informational economy. Many traditional primary products are no longer required or are too low-priced for commercial exploitation, investment is risky, the available workforce lacks appropriate skills and education, markets are extremely narrow, telecommunications inadequate, politics unpredictable, governments ineffective, and so on. Regarding much of Africa, Castells has argued that liberal economic reform has revealed its 'structural irrelevance' for the new informational economy (Castells 1996: 135). At the same time, however, formal economic exclusion is not synonymous with a void, far from it. The South has effectively reintegrated itself into the liberal world system through the spread and deepening of all types of parallel and shadow transborder activity (Bayart *et al.* 1999). This represents the site of new and expansive forms of local–global networking and innovative patterns of extra-legal and non-formal North–South integration.

Not only does exclusion imply both isolation and subordinating forms of interaction, the terms North and South also require some qualification. They are no longer regarded as relating to just spatial or geographical realities. They are now as much social as they are territorial.[10] Under the impact of market deregulation and the increased ease with which finance, investment and production can cross borders, although North–South distinctions are still geographically concentrated, they also reflect important non-territorial social modalities. While the gap in *per capita* income between Northern and Southern countries has been widening for generations (Hoogvelt 1997; UNDP 1996), similar gaps between the richest and poorest sections of the population in the North have also grown. Castells (1996: 145) describes as 'an enduring architecture and variable geometry' this qualified consolidation of historic North–South geographic divisions, accompanied at the same time by a growing non-territorial fluidity of the social modalities involved. Thus, within the networks and flows of the global economy, the North now has a 'variable geometry' of pockets of impoverishment, redundant skills and social exclusion, just as within 'the enduring architecture' of the South even the poorest countries usually have small sections of the workforce connected to high-value global networks. Indeed, such connections are important in understanding the new wars. They reflect the points at which the control of markets and populations, together with their selective integration into the networks of global governance, are often contested.

In studying the new wars, one is largely reliant on the contribution of political economy and anthropology. However, the literature has yet to make up its mind. Indeed, much of the work on global political economy avoids any serious analysis of the South.[11] Moreover, in relation to political economy, where the South is discussed, there is a major division between viewing the new wars as social regression or, in contrast, as systems of social transformation. That is, there is a distinction between seeing conflict in terms of having causes that lead mechanically to forms of breakdown, as opposed to sites of innovation and reordering resulting in the creation of new types of legitimacy and authority. This contrast, moreover, relates not only to political economy. It is a generic division that characterises the literature on the new wars in general. Most donor governments and aid agencies, for example, tend to see conflict as a form of social regression. For political economy, while its analysis of the exclusionary logic within global liberal governance contains a number of useful insights, much of this work has not translated into a credible theory of the new wars. Manuel Castells, a key figure in the analysis and documentation of the changing global political economy, well illustrates this failure. There is a risk in arguing that the new system logic results in the exclusion of the South from the dominant networks of the global economy, which it appears to do. The danger is to overstate the case and follow through with an implied void of scarcity that, it is assumed, leads to growing resource competition, breakdown, criminalisation and chaos. For Castells, the declining investment in Africa has led to a heightened competition for control of the remaining resources, including the state:

6

INTRODUCTION

[B]ecause tribal and ethnic networks were the safest bet for people's support, the fight to control the state … was organised around ethnic cleavages, reviving centuries-old hatred and prejudice: genocidal tendencies and widespread banditry are rooted in the political economy of Africa's disconnection from the new global economy. (Castells 1996: 135)

Castells has subsequently developed this argument in relation to the 'black holes of informational capitalism' (Castells 1998: 161–5). Due to self-defeating spirals of decline, poverty and breakdown, populations entering these black holes usually end up reinforcing their own social exclusion. The result has been that

a new world, the Fourth World, has emerged, made up of multiple black holes of social exclusion throughout the planet. The Fourth World comprises large areas of the globe, such as much of Sub-Saharan Africa, and impoverished rural areas of Latin America and Asia. But it is also present in literally every country, and every city, in this new geography of social exclusion. (*Ibid*.: 164)

Consistent with the logic of this view – that exclusion leads to the breakdown of normative order – Castells has argued that the only export from the global black holes that rivals the informational economy in terms of its innovation and networked character is the 'perverse' connection of a global criminal economy (*ibid*.: 166–205). In this respect, the Castells viewpoint well reflects current concerns that have led to the reinterpretation of the nature of security. The focus of new security concerns is not the threat of traditional interstate wars but the fear of underdevelopment as a source of conflict, criminalised activity and international instability. This reinterpretation, moreover, means that even if the system logic is one of exclusion, the idea of underdevelopment as dangerous and destabilising provides a justification for continued surveillance and engagement.

The internationalisation of public policy

The logic of exclusion informs and shapes public policy in many ways. In this respect, one should not forget that exclusion also implies the existence of criteria of *inclusion*. Unlike the more general logic of inclusion and subordination that existed when the capitalist world system was geographically expansive, however, inclusion under global liberal governance is more discerning and selective. Southern governments, project partners and populations now have to show themselves fit for consideration. That is, they have to meet defined standards of behaviour and normative expectations. In the case of governments, this could

7

mean following neoliberal economic prescriptions, adhering to international standards of good governance or subscribing to donor-approved poverty reduction measures. Through relations of fitness and normative benchmarking the logic of exclusion manifests itself in direct and indirect ways. In particular, it has allowed a stratified system of engagement to emerge. This ranges from forms of exclusion, such as the sanction regimes presently encompassing so-called rogue states, to conditional types of partnership and inclusion for authorities with whom the North feels able to do business. Indeed, the more extensive and significant application of an exclusionary logic is contained in the nuanced and complex interface of partnership, cooperation and participation through which the North now engages and selectively incorporates the South.

The politics of liberal governance are associated with the transformation of nation states in both the North and the South 'from being buffers between external economic forces and the domestic economy into agencies for adapting domestic economies for the exigencies of the global economy' (Cox 1995: 39). This transformation has been achieved through the emergence of new cross-cutting governance networks involving state and non-state actors from the supranational to the local level. The growth of such networks is associated with the attenuation of the ability of state incumbents to govern independently within their own borders. Governments now have to take account of new supranational, international and even local constituencies. However, this does not mean that states have necessarily become weaker (although many have, especially in the South); it primarily suggests that the nature of power and authority has changed. Indeed, contained within the shift in aid policy towards conflict resolution and societal reconstruction, Northern governments have found new methods and systems of governance through which to reassert their authority.

Governance networks create horizontal North–North flows and exchanges as well as enmeshing institutions and systems along a vertical North–South axis. However, there is a difference in the nature and character of these flows and networks. Those creating North–North linkages are primarily of an economic, technological, political and military character (Held et al. 1999). They reflect new forms of regionalisation and embody the North's dominant position. Such networks have been thickening noticeably since the 1970s. The governance networks linking North and South, however, largely reflect the internationalisation of public policy and reflect the South's subordination (Duffield 1992; de Waal 1997; Deacon et al. 1997). As the formal North–South economic linkages have narrowed and shrunk, the compensating

8

networks of international public policy have thickened and developed new organisational forms. To a certain extent, using Cox's imagery, the conflict resolution and post-war reconstruction concerns of liberal governance could be seen as the 'riot control' end of a spectrum encompassing a broad range of 'global poor relief' activities including, for example, NGO developmental attempts to encourage self-sufficiency in relation to food security and basic services. Such public welfare initiatives now complement the economic prescriptions of structural adjustment. The internationalisation of public policy has filled the vacuum, as it were, resulting from the marked process of debureaucratisation and attenuation of nation-state competence that has been deepened in the South by liberal economic reform (Reno 1998).

In terms of the international North–South flows and networks, there is a noticeable duality. While patterns are uneven and great differences exist, the shrinkage of formal economic ties has given rise to two opposing movements. Coming from the South, there has been an expansion of transborder and shadow economic activity that has forged new local–global linkages with the liberal world system and, in so doing, new patterns of actual development and political authority – that is, alternative and non-liberal forms of protection, legitimacy and social regulation. Emerging from the North, the networks of international public policy have thickened and multiplied their points of engagement and control. Many erstwhile functions of the nation state have been abandoned to these international networks as power and authority have been reconfigured. The encounter of the two systems has formed a new and complex development–security terrain. Concerns with stability and the new wars represent an extreme and particular form of engagement within this much broader framework. The networks and actors involved define the points of greatest tension and open confrontation within the encounter. At the same time, however, this violent engagement crystallises and reflects the logic of the system as a whole.

Liberal peace

The new development–security terrain remains underresearched and its study has yet to establish its own conceptual language.[12] One can, however, make a few preliminary remarks. In terms of methodology, a useful distinction is that between mechanical and complex forms of analysis. This difference sets apart Newtonian physics from the emerging complexity sciences such as quantum theory, non-linear mathematics, biotechnology and cybernetics (Dillon 2000). It can be summarised as the difference between seeing the world as a machine and seeing it as a living system or organism. The Newtonian view of the cosmos is that of a vast and perfect clockwork machine governed by exact mathematical laws. Within this giant cosmic machine everything can be determined and reduced to a scientific cause and effect. The material particles that make it up, and the laws of motion and forces that hold or repel them, are fixed and immutable. Set in motion at the birth of the cosmos, this huge mechanism has been running ever since. While having earlier origins, by the mid-twentieth century the Newtonian world view had been superseded. From quantum theory, for example, a new physics has emerged (Capra 1982). Rather than mechanical precepts, this is based on organic, holistic and ecological principles. What is suggested is not a mechanism made up of different basic parts but a unified and determining whole created from the relations between its separate units. The new physics represents a shift from the study of objects to that of interconnections.

A concern with interconnections defines a systems approach. Systems are integrated wholes that cannot be reduced to their separate parts. Instead of concentrating on basic elements, systems analysis places emphasis on the principles of organisation (*ibid.*: 286). From this perspective, a number of distinctions can be made between machines and systems. Machines are controlled and determined by their structure and characterised by linear chains of cause and effect. They are constructed from well-defined parts that have specific functions and tasks. Systems, on the other hand, are analogous to organisms. They grow and are process-oriented. Their structures are shaped by this orientation and they can exhibit a high degree of internal flexibility. Systems are characterised by cyclical patterns of information flow, non-linear interconnections and self-organisation within defined limits of autonomy. Moreover, using the analogy of an organism, a system is concerned with self-renewal. This is important, since while a machine carries out specific and predictable tasks, a system is primarily engaged in a process of renewal and, if necessary, self-transformation. It is a central contention in this book that aid policy, both generally and in relation to the new wars, continues to exhibit a Newtonian or mechanical view of the world. In developing a critique of aid policy as embodying emergent forms of liberal governance, and in analysing the new wars themselves, a systems orientation has been adopted: one that emphasises complex holistic systems in which interconnection, mutation and self-transformation are key characteristics.

Examining aid policy as an expression of global governance – as a political project in its own right – demands attention to its particular forms of mobilisation, justification and reward. The idea of *liberal peace*, for example, combines and conflates 'liberal' (as in contemporary liberal economic and political tenets) with 'peace' (the present policy predilection towards conflict resolution and societal reconstruction). It reflects the existing consensus that conflict in the South is best approached through a number of connected, ameliorative, harmonising and, especially, transformational measures. While this can include the provision of immediate relief and rehabilitation assistance, liberal peace embodies a new or political humanitarianism that lays emphasis on such things as conflict resolution and prevention, reconstructing social networks, strengthening civil and representative institutions, promoting the rule of law, and security sector reform in the context of a functioning market economy. In many respects, while contested and far from assured, liberal peace reflects a radical developmental agenda of social transformation. In this case however, this is an international responsibility and not that of an independent or single juridical state.

During the first half of the 1990s the main concern of the international community regarding conflict was that of humanitarian intervention: developing new institutional arrangements that allowed aid agencies to work in situations of ongoing conflict and to support civilians in war zones (Duffield 1997). Partly due to the limited success of these interventions and the difficulties encountered, since the mid-1990s the policy focus has shifted towards conflict resolution and post-war reconstruction. This change of emphasis does not mean that conflicts have necessarily reduced in number or lessened in terms of their seriousness. Rather, it is policy that has changed. Instead of revolving around humanitarian assistance *per se*, the new humanitarianism has invested developmental tools and initiatives with ameliorative, harmonising and transformational powers that, it is hoped, will reduce violent conflict and prevent its recurrence. While the initiatives that make up liberal peace are usually understood as being a response to specific needs and requirements, liberal peace is a political project in its own right.[13] The aim of liberal peace is to transform the dysfunctional and war-affected societies that it encounters on its borders into cooperative, representative and, especially, stable entities.

While states remain important, since the 1970s, under the influence of what is commonly known as globalisation, they have been drawn into multi-level and increasingly non-territorial decision-making networks that bring together governments, international agencies, non-governmental organisations, and so on, in new and complex ways. Consequently, there has been a noticeable move from the hierarchical, territorial and bureaucratic relations of government to more poly-archical, non-territorial and networked relations of governance (Held *et al.* 1999). While clearly they have deeper historical roots, relations of governance have come to shape and dominate political life over the past several decades. In this respect, liberal peace is not manifest within a single institution of global government; such a body does not exist and probably never will. It is part of the complex, mutating and stratified networks that make up global liberal governance. More specifically, liberal peace is embodied in a number of flows and nodes of authority within liberal governance that bring together different *strategic complexes* of state–non-state, military–civilian and public–private actors in pursuit of its aims. Such complexes now variously enmesh international NGOs, governments, military establishments, IFIs, private security companies, IGOs, the business sector, and so on. They are strategic in the sense of pursuing a radical agenda of social transformation in the interests of global stability. In the past, one might have referred to these complexes as representing the development or aid industry; now, however, they have expanded to constitute a network of strategic governance relations that are increasingly privatised and militarised.

The networks of liberal peace achieve their greatest definition on the borders of global governance, where its strategic actors confront systems and normative structures that are violently different from its own (Dillon and Reid 2000). In mainstream policy terms, these shifting border areas are usually described as constituting a complex emergency or, since the mid-1990s, a complex political emergency (Edkins 1996). Among UN agencies, a complex emergency is understood as denoting a conflict-related humanitarian disaster involving a high degree of breakdown and social dislocation and, reflecting this condition, requiring a system-wide aid response from the international community (Weiss 1999a: 20). The widespread upheaval and social displacement associated with Somalia and Bosnia during the early part of the 1990s, for example, typifies this condition. In requiring a system-wide response, these emergencies have made it necessary for UN agencies, donor governments, NGOs and military establishments to develop new roles, mechanisms of coordination and ways of working together. While the transformational aim of liberal peace now describes the political content of such system-wide operations, attempts to establish a liberal peace have been subject to controversy, marked unevenness and increasing patterns of regional differentiation and hierarchies of concern. Where complex emergencies are encountered, however, some form of strategic complex involving thicker or thinner networks of state–non-state actors is usually involved. This can range from what amounts to global governance's best efforts at social reconstruction, as presently found in the Balkans, to what Boutros-Ghali once referred to as Africa's orphan wars.

The new wars

In relation to the new post-Cold War conflicts, the conventional approach is to look for causes and motives and, rather like Victorian butterfly collectors, to construct lists and typologies of the different species identified. Ideas based on poverty, communication breakdown, resource competition, social exclusion, criminality and so on are widely accepted among strategic actors as providing an explanation. At the same time, various forms of collapse, chaos and regression are seen as the outcome. While such causes and outcomes may well exist, in terms of advancing our understanding of the new wars the search for causes is of limited use. The approach adopted here is to regard war as a given: an ever-present axis around which opposing societies and complexes continually measure themselves and reorder social, economic, scientific and political life. Apart from being a site of innovation, this process of restructuring is also one of imitation and replication (van Creveld 1991). If opposing societies or complexes are not to suffer compromise or defeat, they must match or counter the innovations that each is liable to make. Not only is war an axis of social reordering, historically it has been a powerful mechanism for the globalisation of economic, political and scientific relations (Held *et al.* 1999). In this respect, the development of the modern and centralised nation state has been closely associated with the restructuring and globalising effects of war.

When the competence of nation states begins to change and they become qualified and enmeshed within non-territorial and networked relations of governance, one can assume that the nature of war has also changed. This relates not only to the way the new wars are fought, in this case beyond the regulatory regimes formally associated with nation states, but also to the manner in which societies are mobilised, structured and rewarded in order to address them. A major contention in this book is that the strategic complexes of liberal peace, that is, the emerging relations between governments, NGOs, militaries and the business sector, are not just a mechanical response to conflict. In fact, they have a good deal in common, in structural and organisational terms, with the new wars. For example, strategic complexes and the new wars are both based on increasingly privatised networks of state–non-state actors working beyond the conventional competence of territorially defined governments. Through such flows and networks each is learning how to project power in new non-territorial ways. With contrasting results, liberal peace and the new wars have blurred and dissolved conventional distinctions between peoples, armies and governments. At the same time, new systems of reward and mobilisation, especially associated with privatisation, have emerged in the wake of the outmoding of such divisions. Liberal peace and the new wars are also both forms of adaptation to the effects of market deregulation and the qualification and attenuation of nation-state competence. In many respects, the networks and complexes that compose liberal peace also reflect an emerging liberal way of war.

In the case of the new wars, market deregulation has deepened all forms of parallel and transborder trade and allowed warring parties to forge local–global networks and shadow economies as a means of asset realisation and self-provisioning. The use of illicit alluvial diamonds to fund conflicts in West and Southern Africa is a well-known example of a system that has a far wider application. Rather than expressions of breakdown or chaos, the new wars can be understood as a form of non-territorial *network war* that works through and around states. Instead of conventional armies, the new wars typically oppose and ally the trans-border resource networks of state incumbents, social groups, diasporas, strongmen, and so on. These are refracted through legitimate and ille-gitimate forms of state–non-state, national–international and local–global flows and commodity chains. Far from being a peripheral aber-ration, network war reflects the contested integration of stratified markets and populations into the global economy. Not only can the forms of innovation and state–non-state networking involved be com-pared to those of liberal peace; more generally, they stand comparison with the manner in which Northern political and economic actors have similarly adapted to the pressures and opportunities of globalisation. In this respect, as far as it is successful, network war is synonymous with the emergence of new forms of protection, legitimacy and rights to wealth. Rather than regression, the new wars are organically associated with a process of social transformation: the emergence of new forms of authority and zones of alternative regulation.

Instead of complex political emergencies, global governance is encountering *emerging political complexes*[14] on its borders. Such com-plexes are essentially non-liberal. That is, they follow forms of economic logic that are usually antagonistic towards free-market prescriptions and formal regional integration. At the same time, politically, the new forms of protection and legitimacy involved tend to be socially exclusive rather than inclusive. However, for those that are included, such political complexes nonetheless represent new frameworks of social representation and regulation. In other words, political complexes themselves are part of a process of social transformation and system innovation, a characteristic that embodies the ambiguity of such forma-tions. While their economic and political logic can find violent and disruptive expression, in many cases such complexes are the only forms of existing or actual authority that have the powers to police stability. This ambiguity, however, pervades the general encounter of the new wars with the strategic complexes of liberal peace. The aid agencies, donors and NGOs involved also reflect and embody ideals of protection, legitimacy and rights. They also have transformational aims – in this case, however, liberal ones.

Global governance and the emerging political complexes are in competition in relation to the forms of authority and regulation they wish to establish. This competition establishes a fluctuating border area that is as much social as territorial across which a range of transactions, confrontations and interventions are possible. At its most general, it is the site of numerous discursive exchanges and narratives. The symbolic role of privatisation is a good example. Among many of the strategic actors of liberal governance, privatisation denotes a move towards a sound economy and the prospects of development. Among state actors and local strongmen, however, it can represent an innovative way to further the non-liberal political logic of the complex concerned. At the same time, at various points along this border, competition turns into antagonism and the site of more direct forms of intervention. If the Cold War represented a Third World War, then the contested, uneven and differential confrontation between the strategic complexes of liberal peace and the political complexes of the new wars is the site of the Fourth.

The merging of development and security

That liberal peace contains within it the emerging structures of liberal war is suggested in the blurring and convergence during the 1990s of development and security. The transformational aims of liberal peace and the new humanitarianism embody this convergence. The commitment to conflict resolution and the reconstruction of societies in such a way as to avoid future wars represents a marked radicalisation of the politics of development. Societies must be changed so that past problems do not arise, as happened with development in the past; moreover, this process of transformation cannot be left to chance but requires direct and concerted action (Stiglitz 1998). Development resources must now be used to shift the balance of power between groups and even to change attitudes and beliefs. The radicalisation of development in this way is closely associated with the reproblematisation of security. Conventional views on the causes of the new wars usually hinge upon their arising from a developmental malaise of poverty, resource competition and weak or predatory institutions. The links between these wars and international crime and terrorism are also increasingly drawn. Not only have the politics of development been radicalised to address this situation but, importantly, it reflects a new security framework within which the modalities of underdevelopment have become dangerous. This framework is different from that of the Cold War when the threat of massive interstate conflict prevailed. The question of security has almost gone full circle: from being concerned with the biggest economies and war machines in the world to an interest in some of its smallest.

In most of the policy statements mentioned above (see footnotes 1 to 7) there is a noticeable convergence between the notions of development and security. Through a circular form of reinforcement and mutuality, achieving one is now regarded as essential for securing the other. Development is ultimately impossible without stability and, at the same time, security is not sustainable without development. This convergence is not simply a policy matter. It has profound political and structural implications. In relation to the strategic complexes of liberal governance it embodies the increasing interaction between military and security actors on the one hand, and civilian and non-governmental organisations on the other. It reflects the thickening networks that now link UN agencies, military establishments, NGOs and private security companies. Regarding NGOs, the convergence of development and security has meant that it has become difficult to separate their own development and humanitarian activities from the pervasive logic of the North's new security regime. The increasingly overt and accepted politicisation of aid is but one outcome.

The encounter of the strategic complexes of liberal peace with the political complexes of the new wars has established a new development–security terrain. It is developmental in that liberal values and institutions have been vested with ameliorative and harmonising powers. At the same time, it represents a new security framework since these powers are being deployed in a context in which the modalities of underdevelopment have become dangerous and destabilising. This contested terrain, which looks set to deepen and shape our perceptions over the coming decades, remains underresearched and is not captured in conventional and increasingly prescriptive and policy-oriented development and international studies. It is comprised of complex relations of structural similarity, complicity and, at the same time, new asymmetries of power and authority.

In terms of similarity, both liberal peace and the new wars have blurred traditional distinctions between people, army and government and, at the same time, forged new ways of projecting power through non-territorial public–private networks and systems. Along the social border between these two complexes, relations of accommodation and complicity are common and find many forms of expression. Rather than eliminating famine, for example, aid agencies have been charged with obstructing this aim (de Waal 1997). The international hierarchy of concern that exists also denotes a susceptibility within global liberal governance to normalise violence and accept high levels of instability as an enduring if unfortunate characteristic of certain regions. This new development–security terrain also contains marked asymmetries of power. Indeed, it tends to reverse and upset traditional notions of what power is and where it lies. It is a terrain where, in confronting new challenges, the authority of the major states is in a process of reconfiguration. While the growth of increasingly privatised and non-territorial strategic complexes reflect new ways of projecting liberal power, the effectiveness of these forms of authority is still an open question – especially when they confront political actors who have a strong sense of right and history, despite being part of economically weaker systems. Whether donor governments, militaries, aid agencies and the private sector can secure a liberal peace remains an open question. One thing, however, is perhaps more clear. It is difficult to imagine that the increasingly privatised and regionally stratified strategic complexes of liberal governance will be able to deliver the geographically and socially more extensive patterns of *relative* security that characterised the Cold War years. Understanding this new terrain should therefore be a priority for us all.

The organisation of this book

Chapter 2 analyses the convergence of development and security. It does so by first describing the different view of instability that existed when capitalism was still an expansive and inclusionary world system. Third Worldism and dependency theory, for example, saw the problems of the South in terms of an unequal and exploitative international trade system. With the growing regionalisation of the global economy and the triumph of neoliberal prescriptions, such views have all but disappeared. They have been supplanted by a representation of conflict as stemming, essentially, from internal developmental causes. During the course of the 1990s, this representation underpinned the radicalisation of the politics of development: the commitment, in policy terms at least, to transform societies as a whole, including the attitudes and beliefs of their members. The politicisation of development is also related to the changing perception of security. Rather than interstate conflict being the main threat to world stability, the factors of underdevelopment now occupy this position.

Chapter 3 examines the emerging strategic complexes of liberal governance. The convergence of development and security is embodied in the expansion of international relations of governance involving state and non-state actors. The chapter describes the changing nature of loyalty and sacrifice that underpins such networks, particularly the emergence of more direct and pecuniary forms of reward associated with increasing public–private networking. It also looks at some of the adaptations and connections emerging within and between NGOs, military establishments, the commercial sector, IGOs and donor governments in relation to securing the aims of liberal peace.

Chapter 4 continues the analysis begun in Chapter 2 concerning the radicalisation of the politics of development, in this case by examining the new or principled humanitarianism that has emerged. This is discussed in relation to the policy of linking relief to development that underpins it. In terms of governance relations, the linking debate has provided Northern governments with new contractual tools, planning mechanisms and monitoring regimes necessary to extend their authority through non-state actors. The new humanitarianism represents a government-led shift from humanitarian assistance as a right to a new system framed by a consequentialist ethics. That is, humanitarian action is now only legitimate as long as it is felt to do no harm and generally support the conflict resolution and transformational aims of liberal peace. From helping people, policy has shifted towards supporting processes.

Chapter 5 analyses how strategic actors understand the causes of conflict. Reflecting the logic of exclusion and isolationism, global governance is confronted with the problem that the popular understanding of the new wars emphasises the reappearance of ancient tribal hatreds and other forms of biocultural determinism. Faced with this isolationist challenge, strategic actors have used conflict to reinvent development. Conflict is portrayed as deepening poverty and weakening social and cultural cohesion. In this way, violence is seen as creating a level playing field on which the possibilities of development have been renewed and reinvigorated. At the same time, through forms of analysis that delegitimise and criminalise the leadership of the new wars, the way is cleared for a radicalised development to attempt to change societies as a whole.

Chapter 6 begins an extended analysis of the new wars. It examines how market deregulation and structural adjustment have encouraged the expansion and deepening of all forms of parallel and shadow trans-border trade. Although excluded from the conventional economy, the South is now widely integrated into the global marketplace through shadow networks. While the parallel economy is extensive and a lifeline for millions of people, it is not reflected in official statistics or orthodox economic models. The chapter concludes by examining the non-liberal nature of transborder trade, that is, its tendency towards protectionism, extra-legal mechanisms and exclusive forms of social control.

Chapter 7 analyses the new wars in terms of their representing emerging forms of political complex in the South. The reintegration of the South through stratified shadow economic networks has facilitated this process. In particular, it has allowed the appearance of overlapping centres of political authority associated with market reform. The multi-plication of nodes of non-liberal authority in various relations of com-petition, complementarity and complicity with state actors has blurred the boundaries of legality and legitimacy. Rather than looking for causes, the chapter proceeds to analyse the new wars in terms of the organisational effects of a growing demand for private protection. Subaltern and non-state forms of protection and regulatory authority are examined, together with how they articulate with state forms. The demand for protection among state incumbents is discussed in relation to the Russian mafia and the growing involvement of private military companies in Africa. The chapter concludes with an analysis of the new wars as forms of network war. It examines the characteristics of such wars, the merging of war and peace, the selective incorporation of Southern economies within the global marketplace and, importantly, the high levels of commercial complicity necessary for such wars to develop.

Using the example of war-displaced Southerners in Sudan, chapters 8 and 9 provide a case study of the new development–security terrain. This study argues that donor governments and aid agencies have rein-forced the relations of violence they oppose. Chapter 8 examines this complicity in relation to the construction of an internally displaced person (IDP) identity. Reflecting how strategic actors understand con-flict, the IDP identity is a de-ethnicised construct based on an economic self-sufficiency model of development. Represented as having lost all assets through war and displacement, it is assumed that with a minimum input of economic resources (and avoiding dependency-creating food aid), IDPs will once more become self-provisioning. Even the development of a rights-based approach by NGOs has not altered this basic model; de-ethnicised liberal self-management has been redefined as a 'right'. The IDP identity represents the displaced as autonomous and self-contained households and ignores the wider relations of exploitation and oppression within which displaced Southerners are enmeshed in Northern Sudan.

Chapter 9 takes this analysis further by showing the effects of strategic complicity for displaced Southerners. At the same time, it serves to indicate the ambiguity of the political complexes that are emerging. The networks that have formed in western Sudan between merchants, commercial farmers and the military represent local forms of authority and legitimacy. At the same time, they are oppressive and exploitative in relation to Southerners. Attempts by aid agencies to promote development in this context have reinforced their subjugation. Cuts in food aid, in order to encourage Southerners into the wage economy, have resulted in their becoming further enmeshed in non-remunerative forms of bonded labour. At the same time, the development resources given to the displaced to promote their self-sufficiency have invariably ended up in the hands of the surrounding groups and networks. A decade of such assistance has resulted in the wretched condition of Southerners in Northern Sudan improving little if at all.

In drawing the book together, the Conclusion reinterprets the development–security terrain linking liberal peace and the new wars as a complex and shared system of moral responsibility. In this respect, it details the lacuna in our knowledge and the forms of research that are required if we are to understand the nature of this new terrain and the opportunities and dangers that it presents. In particular, if liberal peace is not to transform into liberal war, rather than searching for technical solutions and more informed analysis, the most pressing issue is that of understanding the organisational dynamics involved, including our own.

NOTES

1 OSCE 1995; EU 1996; DAC 1997; OECD 1998.
2 World Bank 1997b; World Bank 1997a.
3 Pronk and Kooijmans 1993; ODA 1996; DFID 1997; MFA 1997; IDC 1999.
4 Boutros-Ghali 1995 (original 1992); UNDP 1994; UNHCR 1995.
5 Carnegie Commission 1997; World Bank and Carter Center 1997.
6 ActionAid 1994; Cottey 1994; IFRCS 1996.
7 PWBLF 1999.
8 See the following bibliographies: Fagen 1995; Masefield and Harvey 1997; Gundel 1999.
9 For a discussion of the development of constitutional liberalism prior to universal suffrage in the West, see Zakaria 1997.
10 Cox 1995: 40; Castells 1996: 147; Hoogvelt 1997: 66.

11 A good example is the recent and substantial work by Held, McGraw, Goldblatt and Perraton (1999) on *Global Transformations*. While their work has been praised as exhaustive and comprehensive by commentators, the authors nonetheless consciously exclude the effects of globalisation on the South from their study.

12 In developing the critical concepts used in this book, I am greatly indebted to Mick Dillon, Department of Politics and International Relations, University of Lancaster. Coming, respectively, from development and security backgrounds, the telling surprise was to find that we were talking about similar things.

13 For an example of this approach to development, but one that mainly deals with the situation during the Cold War, see Escobar 1995.

14 This organisational rectification was first coined by Mick Dillon at a conference on 'The Politics of Emergency' in the Department of Politics, University of Manchester, May 1997.

2

The Merging of Development and Security

This chapter examines the radicalisation of the politics of development – the willingness within mainstream policy to contemplate the transformation of societies as a whole. At the same time, this radicalisation is intimately connected with the reproblematisation of security. The radicalisation of development derives its urgency from a new security framework that regards the modalities of underdevelopment as dangerous. The merger of development and security in this way reflects the transformation of the capitalist world system from an inclusionary to an exclusionary logic. Untroubled by viable alternatives to global liberal governance, the transformation of societies to fit liberal norms and expectations now reflects the selective, regionally differentiated and conditional interface linking North and South.

The demise of alternatives to liberal governance

Third Worldism as an oppositional movement
At least until the 1970s, in contrast to the dominance of global liberal governance today, alternative state-based models of modernity existed in the South. The opposition of international socialism, and the resulting Cold War system of superpower rivalry and geopolitical alliance, is well known. At the same time, while never achieving the ideological clarity or organisational consistency of international socialism, a loose and changing constellation of Third World opinion also frequently challenged the legitimacy of Western interests within the international economic system. It is easy to lose sight of the fact that both international socialism and Third Worldism sought to offer a different view of how wealth should be redistributed and the international system

organised. For Third Worldism, arguing that development and under-development were organically connected and a reflection of each other was an important part of shaping an oppositional position that has now all but disappeared from development discourse. Indeed, this disappearance is part of the move from an inclusionary to an exclusionary economic and political logic. It is important to resurrect this debate briefly since the passing of the Third World alternative is directly related to the liberal reproblematisation of underdevelopment as dangerous.

Emerging in the 1950s and lasting until the 1970s, the initial post-colonial development regime was mainly concerned with reducing poverty in the South through the promotion of economic growth based on investment and the application of science and technology. This was to be achieved through planning, state intervention and economic redistribution. The left critique of the discipline of development economics that grew up around this model was provided by dependency theory.[1] Development economics current at the time tended to see underdeveloped countries as so-called dual societies composed of culturally distinct modern and traditional sectors. These sectors, one forward-looking and scientific and the other conservative and custom-ary, were usually understood as existing independently of each other and being in a benign or even beneficial relationship. In relation to labour migration, for example, the existence of the modern sector allowed subsistence farmers the opportunity to earn extra cash as occasion demanded (Berg 1961). For dependency theory, however, the relationship was far from beneficial. Important for this perspective was the argument that Southern raw materials and labour power were being purchased below their true cost by Northern companies and related interests (Frank 1967). The traditional sector, rather than being unconnected with the modern or commercial areas of the economy, helped meet some of the subsistence needs of household members engaged in the modern sector. The activities of peasant farmers, for example, producing food crops for family consumption, satisfied a pro-portion of the physical and social reproductive costs of the household. This represented a saving for anyone purchasing such labour or its produce. Hence the existence of the subsistence sector meant that wages and labour costs could be paid below their real value.

The process of turning cheap Southern raw materials and labour power into Northern manufactured goods allowed this subsistence or traditional subsidy to be realised as added value. The capitalist enter-prise was therefore accorded high levels of profitability by operating in the South. For dependency theorists, the persistence of poverty and underdevelopment in the South was not an accident or failure of development policy: it was a necessary attribute of the production of wealth in the North (Rodney 1972). In other words, the underdevelopment of the periphery of the world system was seen as a function of the development of its centre. The two conditions were historically linked and mutually reinforcing (Wallerstein 1974). Unlike liberal discourse, which sees wealth and poverty as unconnected, the latter arising from a complex network of relative causes, dependency theory sees poverty as a direct consequence of the manner in which wealth is produced. At an international level, this highly exploitative relationship was said to be maintained by an inequitable system of world trade dominated by Northern interests and structured around relations of unequal exchange (Emmanuel 1972).

The utility of the traditional sector for capitalist development led a number of dependency theorists to argue that while traditional society was changed in a number of ways through its encounter with international capitalism, its subsistence structure was maintained as a source of cheap labour (Laclau 1971; Wolpe 1972). Southern economies were seen as skewed towards and dependent on the interests of a narrow range of metropolitan countries and their needs. Because of this subordinate and deformed character of the periphery, the idea of dependency was attached to the economies and ruling elites of the countries concerned. Regarding the latter, owing to the comprador role they played in the global economic system they were politically dependent on support from the metropolitan North. Consequently, they were regarded as incapable of initiating an independent or democratic development strategy.

Dependency theory has received its fair share of critique and counter-argument. In many respects, for example, it is a restatement of the dualism and economic orthodoxy that it set out to contest (Duffield 1982). In retrospect, however, whatever one's reservations, it was describing a capitalist world system that was still conceived in terms of expansion and inclusion. At the same time, many of the ideas and assumptions that informed it were reflected in the attempts to shape the Third World as a collective political identity (Hoogvelt 1997: 48–9). In other words, it was part of a Southern political discourse and its echo could be heard in many of the demands of Third World rulers throughout the 1960s and 1970s – for example, in the frequent agitation for the reform of the international trade system and a better return for Southern commodities and raw materials. This included demands for better terms of trade; preferential economic mechanisms; import substitution; infrastructural improvement; and the expansion of international organisations and representative structures the better to express Third World opinion. The ultimately unsuccessful demand in the mid-1970s for a New International Economic Order (NIEO), for example, was symptomatic of this mood (Adams 1993). Donor governments and institutions, even if they did little to act on Third World concerns, were at least forced to acknowledge them. The 1975 Lomé Convention linking the EU with its African, Caribbean and Pacific (ACP) partners, for example, reflected Third World pressure for preferential arrangements and access to European markets (Brown 1997). At the same time, one should not forget that the national liberation struggles of the period – Vietnam, Ethiopia, Angola, Mozambique, and so on – were a forceful expression of the rhetoric of anti-colonial critique, international trade reform and economic independence. That the socialist bloc countries also appeared to offer an alternative system to rival that of Western capitalism helped maintain the view that there were alternative paths to modernity.

Colonial patterns of world trade – a circular process of importing raw materials from Southern countries and exporting manufactured goods to them – remained significant for many Northern economies until the 1970s. The persistence of this structure gave both Third World demands and dependency theory a good deal of credence. Paradoxically, however, despite dependency theory's concerns about unequal exchange, many Southern countries achieved a level of general prosperity that has not been seen since this time. The aim of most national liberation movements, for example, remained that of gaining control of the state. Despite an inequitable trade system, the economies they inherited were still seen as going concerns. At the same time, Third World countries were not entirely powerless. To the extent that they controlled strategic commodities and could marshal collective action, they were able to exert some leverage on the North. This ability is much less marked today. One of the best examples concerns the Organisation of Petroleum Exporting Countries (OPEC). Formed in 1960, OPEC is a cartel of largely Middle Eastern oil exporters created as a means of maintaining price levels. In the early 1970s, its ability to introduce a fourfold increase in the price of oil, together with further increases at the end of that decade, had a significant impact on Northern economies. Indeed, it is held to have accentuated the economic downturn in the North and thus helped bring about the end of the long post-war boom (Wallerstein 1996) – a closure that helped to dissolve the remaining colonial patterns of trade and to introduce a new wave of technological innovation and the thickening of the networks linking the core areas of the conventional global economy to the exclusion of the South.

From inclusion to underdevelopment becoming dangerous

Third Worldism reached its apogee in the mid-1970s. Within a decade, it had ceased to exist as an independent or discernible political expression. Apart from views on the inequity of the global economic system, Third World and socialist leaders also had a position on the causes of conflict and political instability. These views were given clear expression in 1980 on the occasion of the UN's first 'root causes' debate on the origin of refugee flows. The impetus for this debate came from a growing crisis within the UNHCR. Initially formed after the Second World War in response to the European refugee problem, the UNHCR had seen its mandate and responsibilities progressively increase. In the early 1960s, conflicts and instability associated with African decolonisation had greatly added to the number of refugees and resulted in the organisation expanding its mandate to address problems arising from wars of liberation. By the mid-1970s, however, a fresh wave of refugee-producing instability had emerged 'relating to the internationalisation of revolutionary or ethnic liberation struggles in the developing world' (Suhrke 1994: 14). This involved Southern Africa, the Horn, Vietnam and, for the first time, major refugee flows in Latin America. The decade peaked with the Soviet Union's invasion of Afghanistan, from where 5 million people would eventually cross into neighbouring countries.

> This … crisis posed distinct, new problems for the international community. A growing number of the refugees appeared destined to remain indefinitely in camp or legal limbo. Conditions in the homeland rarely permitted repatriation, either because the new regime or social order became entrenched, or because war continued. The strain on first asylum countries mounted, leading to large-scale denial of protection in southeast Asia. In the affluent, industrialised countries, economic recession and popular fears of being flooded by developing country refugees – added to already large numbers of migrants – resulted in greater restrictions on asylum seekers. (*ibid.*: 14–15)

The ensuing 1980 debate within the UN's Special Political Committee on the causes of such refugee flows showed a division between Western and Third World/socialist opinion. The West and its anti-communist allies tended to blame internal abuse and the violation of human rights in the countries refugees were fleeing. Third World and socialist opinion, however, echoing dependency theory, pointed to problems associated with colonialism, global inequality, growing balance of payments problems and deteriorating terms of trade – issues

26

that had been cited in the earlier NIEO debate. This division roughly translated into the North's arguing the case for internal or domestic causes, while the South pressed the importance of the external or international environment. The difference was such that two separate UN reports were produced from this debate. The last, not published until 1985, emphasised Southern concern with issues of global inequality. The earlier report, produced in 1981 by Sadruddin Aga Khan, was more influential. That it gave more weight to the internal explanations favoured by the North was itself a reflection that, by this time, Third World opposition was rapidly losing coherence.

The Aga Khan report argued that refugee outflows resulted from political processes associated with such things as nationalism in the transition from feudal-tribal societies to modern nation states, the ready supply of arms, state formation within the heritage of colonialism, prolonged liberation struggles, high population growth, unemployment, desertification or rapid urbanisation. Moreover, such factors were compounded by

> the inability of many governments to create conditions in which the population as a whole can expect to enjoy – quite apart from civil and political rights – the economic, social and cultural rights set out in the Declaration of Human Rights. (Aga Khan, quoted by Suhrke 1994: 16)

The view expounded in this report – of conflict and population displacement resulting from the interplay of multiple and largely internal factors, including problems of political transition in the context of poverty, scarcity, ready access to arms, and weak government institutions – has been very influential. Indeed, it has shaped the conventional understanding of the new wars for the past couple of decades. The 1981 Aga Khan report was one of the first clear expositions of the now dominant view that conflict is ultimately a reflection of a developmental malaise affecting the countries concerned. While the language is more modern, this position is well represented, for example, in a recent OECD report.

> As a general rule, a society endowed with a good balance and distribution of solid social and economic resources, as evidenced in high human development indicators, is able to manage tensions with less risk of institutional and social breakdown than a society marked by destabilising conditions, such as pervasive poverty, extreme socio-economic disparities, systematic lack of opportunity and the absence of recourse to credible institutions to resolve grievances. (OECD 1998: 19)

For most aid practitioners, this statement no doubt appears as self-evident – an unproblematic recounting of safe, received wisdom. The reproblematisation of underdevelopment as dangerous, however, which this understanding reflects, is not an impartial act of social analysis; it is a historic and political construct. Internalising the causes of conflict and associating them with the modalities of underdevelopment and poor governance occurred in the context of political rivalry with Third Worldism and international socialism. At least until the end of the 1970s, this competition was a defining feature of the international system. It would be an ill-judged use of time to attempt to argue for or against external or internals views on the causes of conflict. All forms of discourse contain certain truths. Third Worldist arguments concerning inequality and exploitation within the global system, on one hand, and views that focus on domestic failings and inadequacies, on the other, both reflect valid aspects of distinct but interconnected realities. It is in the nature of discourse, however, to rework discrete truths and partial reflections into connected and coherent world views, forms of know-ledge that are simultaneously expressions of power. In redefining underdevelopment as dangerous, from its position of dominance liberal discourse has suppressed those aspects of Third Worldism and international socialism that argued the existence of inequalities within the global system and, importantly, that the way in which wealth is created has a direct bearing on the extent and nature of poverty. The new logic of exclusion is reflected in the relativisation and internalisa-tion of the causes of conflict and political instability within the South. At the same time, the main burden of responsibility for solving these problems has been placed on Southern actors.

The triumph of the market
It was the end of West's long period of robust post-war economic growth in the early 1970s that set in train a reconfiguration of its influence in both Africa and the European East. In the case of the former, the West enjoyed a growing ability to shape government policy after the relative autonomy of the early postcolonial period. In the case of the latter, it was able to rekindle relations of influence following varying periods of socialist autarchy. The engine of this change was the attraction of Western credit followed by the taskmaster of debt. By the 1970s, the attempts by Third World and socialist rulers to chart alterna-tive paths of modernity were coming under increasing strain in relation to the tremendous advances in the West during the early post-war decades. OPEC's oil price increases during the 1970s helped reduce the overall rate of global economic expansion. At the same time, however, it also left Western banks with huge investment deposits of petro-

dollars. The banks were more than willing to recycle these deposits as loans to the Third World and, as a result of détente, to socialist countries as well.

In many parts of Africa, borrowing money became one way of attempting to address a variety of problems ranging from declining food production to the decreasing competence of the nation state. Attempts to increase export production to meet growing balance of payments problems and declining terms of trade were a common response in many countries. In a number of places attempts were made to mechanise and intensify agricultural production, thereby shifting output towards commercial and non-staple export crops (Duffield 1991). Economies that had been geared to internal consumption became increasingly externally orientated. In the European East, meanwhile, by the 1970s many countries were experiencing the weaknesses and rigidities of 'actually existing socialism' (Bahro 1978). While the need for reform was well known, taking Western loans became a widespread means of attempting to delay or put off this process (Verdery 1996). As loans turned to debts during the 1980s, few of the original problems for which the debts had been incurred had been solved. Indeed, they had deepened. The ensuing crisis in both Africa and the European East resulted in an increasing loss of economic sovereignty through the growing ability of the West's international financial institutions to insist on structural adjustment and economic reform programmes (Walton and Seddon 1994).

It was President Reagan's 'magic of the market' speech at the North–South conference in Cancun in 1981, the same year as the publication of the Aga Khan report on the root causes of refugee flows, that publicly signalled the international shift to a neoliberal development strategy (Escobar 1995: 83). A number of influential World Bank reports quickly followed, outlining the new strategy. During the 1980s, neoliberalism increasingly became the dominant economic paradigm among the Southern elite as well. Statist and redistributive economic programmes were replaced by trade liberalisation, privatisation and stabilisation under the auspices of the IMF. Public spending on health and education declined. In this new context, Third Worldism rapidly lost coherence and expression. Beginning in the 1970s, many East Asian countries embarked on a rapid process of economic expansion, pulling away from Africa and other underdeveloped regions. As a consequence, they distanced themselves and hence weakened earlier collective aspirations (Harris 1987). Under the impact of structural adjustment, elites abandoned the pursuit of collective international goals owing to the growing pressure of debt repayment and the increasing acceptance of

GLOBAL GOVERNANCE AND THE NEW WARS

the need to focus on domestic issues (Westlake 1991). By the end of the 1980s, the attenuation of nation-state competence in the South had begun to extend from the economic to the political sphere, with the appearance of various forms of aid conditionality (ODI 1992). That is, development aid was increasingly tied to not only to progress with economic liberalisation but to the creation and support of democratic and pluralistic institutions as well.

During the 1980s Third Worldism and international socialism became redundant within the global system. Both of these alternative visions of modernity retained the state as their main agent and executor, albeit in the case of Third Worldism in a more economically mixed form compared to the socialist party–state model. Their demise was an important precondition for increased globalisation based on a renewed wave of free market expansion and, importantly, the associated consolidation of the networks of global liberal governance. In different and sometimes complementary ways, both Third Worldism and the socialist party–state attempted to maintain sovereign independence and alternative social and economic systems. It could be argued that their passing was a result of their ineffectiveness and unsuitability – indeed, that many of the corrupt and patrimonial regimes concerned had clearly failed their citizens and had therefore suffered a fate they deserved. While this may be the case, it has created a situation in which, with the possible but increasingly debatable exception of East Asia, there is no credible international alternative to global liberal governance and the economic and political structures that it favours. This demise has radically altered the view of what development is and how it should be achieved. Rather than requiring the reform of the international system, it has been redefined in terms of the radical transformation of Southern societies in order to make them fit into this system. Financial deregulation has made increasingly complex and opaque forms of transaction and ownership possible. At the same time, the notion that underdevelopment may be a function of the structural relationship between rich and poor countries has been more or less erased from policy discourse (Hoogvelt 1997: 162–5). While the dominant neoliberal model of macroeconomic management is often regarded as harsh or even unjust (Cornia 1987), and therefore still requiring some adjustment, it is nevertheless now accepted as the optimal model for maximising global welfare. Development has become a process of self-management within a liberal market environment. Through attempts to transform expectations and approaches, the tasks of social development (including transition in the European East) have become those of helping people to change and better adapt to this new system.

30

New imperialism or liberal peace?

In relation to conflict and its effects, most international aid agencies usually cite the humanitarian consequences and high social cost of internal war as the reason for their involvement; indeed, as the basis of their organisational existence. In other words, the predominant self-image is that of responding to need. If there were no needs, there would be no reason for aid agencies to be involved. At the same time, however, this type of justification tends to take for granted and thereby overlook an important factor: Northern organisations are now able to operate in a manner, and in countries, regions or areas of the South that even a decade ago would have been inaccessible to them. While their involvement has often been contested, Northern agencies have established a political and organisational competence to help the victims of violence on all sides of an ongoing conflict. Moreover, unlike during the Cold War, this competence is not necessarily dependent on the formal consent of recognised and involved governments. In reflecting on the revolutionary changes involved, a senior UN administrator described the position as follows.

> In many ways, it is the intervention itself that should be seen as the new defining element in the post-bipolar world, rather than conflict, which of course existed throughout the previous era whether in the form of wars by proxy or in resistance to superpower hegemony. Thus, recent years have witnessed a kind of double lifting of inhibitions that had been largely suppressed by the Cold War's rules of the game: *the inhibition to wage war and the inhibition to intervene.* (Donini 1996: 7, emphasis added)

Many former socialist countries, for example, have only recently opened their doors to outside aid agencies, social institutions and commercial companies. At the same time, the end of the Cold War has removed many of the international constraints previously placed in the way of providing humanitarian assistance in rebel or politically contested areas. Provided that access could be negotiated on the ground, during the course of the 1990s, in both Africa and the Balkans it was not uncommon to find NGOs and UN agencies providing relief assistance to all sides in a number of ongoing conflicts (Duffield 1997). This represents a radical departure with the past and suggests that the growing ability of agencies to respond to need should not be taken as a simple, unproblematic fact. It is part of a wider and complex process of globalisation involving the qualification of nation-state sovereignty, the growing intrusion of international relations of governance and the demise of Southern political alternatives.

A number of critics have interpreted the enhanced ability of Northern institutions to intervene in new ways in the South as a reworking of imperialism (Furedi 1994; Chomsky 1999). The reproblematisation of underdevelopment as dangerous, for example, can be seen as part of a moral rearming of the North. It both confines the causes of conflict to the South and helps provide the legitimation for outside involvement. From the new imperialism perspective, Northern aid agencies have tended to disqualify Southern political projects as inadequate, lacking or backward. NGOs are regarded as moral missionaries, playing a similar role to their nineteenth-century counterparts in providing the justification for domination (Crawford 1994). UNICEF's Declaration on the Rights of the Child, for example, allows aid agencies to present themselves as leading a civilising mission of enlightenment in the South. Whole societies can be placed beyond the pale according to how children are treated. In Bosnia, Northern insistence on a human rights dimension within the Dayton peace process is said to have effectively disenfranchised legitimate nationalist concerns in the region (Chandler 1997), transforming the fact that in successive polls voters have expressed clear nationalist preferences into a form of social pathology. Such delegitimation, it is argued, provides a rationale and moral justification for the growing influence of NGOs and aid agencies in the South – they have become the frontline actors of modern imperialism.

The new imperialism argument has made a number of important contributions. It has been particularly successful, for example, in deconstructing forms of representation that do indeed act as a means of organisational self-justification by delegitimising Southern actors. There are, however, a number of weaknesses. To the extent that Northern aid agencies represent Southern relations as problematic, the advocates of a new imperialism usually overcompensate in the opposite direction. That is, there is a tendency to place the South beyond reproach and to regard the emerging political complexes as if they lacked ambiguity. The result is usually an absence of any analysis of Southern relations or institutions – at least, in a critical depth similar to that levelled against Northern aid agencies. At the extreme, one encounters examples of denial and refutation that anything unacceptable or equivocal exists.

A good example of this is the celebrated attempt by the magazine *Living Marxism*, an exponent of the new imperialism thesis, to present the infamous pictures of emaciated Bosnian Muslims staring through the barbed wire of the Bosnian Serb camp at Trnopolje in August 1992 as a deliberate fake (Deichmann 1997). In 1994, the same magazine used the visit of the Archbishop of Canterbury, Dr George Carey, to Sudan to accuse Northern governments of an unfounded moral crusade against the country's Islamic regime. In relation to the accusations of human rights abuse levelled at the regime, it was remarked that 'the strange thing is that nobody has highlighted the absence of any hard evidence to support the charges against Sudan' (Crawford 1994: 24). What is really strange is that such a statement could be made when, since the mid-1980s, human rights organisations covering Sudan such as Human Rights Watch, Amnesty International and African Rights, between them, have probably published enough detailed situation reports, witness testimonies, and so on, to fill several bookcases – material, it should be added that, paradoxically, the 'moral crusade' of the international community has largely ignored. In this respect, one could argue that aid agencies in Sudan are complicit with state designs rather than opposing them (see Chapter 8). In many respects, the new imperialism thesis reflects a now outmoded solidarity politics, exchanging critical analysis for silent faith. Within this faith, the relations and institutions of the South represent the archetypal victim of Northern manipulation and oppression. As such, they are sanctified and placed beyond criticism.

Another weakness of the new imperialism thesis is the very attempt to understand the emerging structures of global liberal governance through the concept of imperialism. It denotes an inability to imagine that the nature of power and authority may have changed radically. For critics of the new imperialism, what we are seeing in humanitarian intervention is just another reworking of old formulas and established relations; in other words, an unchanging reality. Chomsky's analysis of the role of the West in the recent Kosovo war is a good example of this intellectual fixation.

> With the Soviet deterrent in decline, the Cold War victors are more free to exercise their will under the cloak of good intentions but in pursuit of interests that have a very familiar ring outside the realm of enlightenment. (Chomsky 1999: 11)

Unfortunately, short of a predilection, indeed, a consuming passion for conspiracies, using dubious evidence, applying Western values in a selective manner and a liking for making things worse rather than better, Chomsky is not able to provide a convincing explanation of what exactly those old and familiar motives are in relation to Kosovo. Moreover, regarding the shift in the logic of the capitalist world system from one of inclusion to exclusion regarding the South, the critics of the new imperialism thesis are silent. This is not to say, however, that stratified and hierarchical forms of power and authority no longer characterise the international system. The power concerned, however, is liberal power rather than imperial power.

The current concern of global governance is to establish a liberal peace on its troubled borders: to resolve conflicts, reconstruct societies and establish functioning market economies as a way to avoid future wars. The ultimate goal of liberal peace is stability. In achieving this aim, liberal peace is different from imperial peace. The latter was based on, or at least aspired to, direct territorial control where populations were ruled through juridical and bureaucratic means of authority. The imperial power dealt with opposition using physical and juridical forms of pacification, sometimes in an extreme and violent manner. Liberal peace is different; it is a non-territorial, mutable and networked relation of governance. The aim of the strategic state–non-state complexes that embody global governance is not the direct control of territory. Ideally, liberal power is based on the management and regulation of economic, political and social processes. It is power through the control and management of non-territorial systems and networks. As a result, liberal strategic complexes are usually averse to the long-term costs and responsibilities that controlling territory implies and have only been drawn reluctantly, and conditionally, into reconstruction operations such as those in the Balkans (Von Hippel 1999). The history of such interventions shows that the political consensus required is extremely fragile, subject to constant tensions and demands for periodic renewal.

Liberal peace aspires to secure stability within the political complexes that it encounters on its shifting borders through the developmental principles of partnership, participation and self-management. People in the South are no longer ordered what to do – they are now expected to do it *willingly* themselves. Compared to imperial peace, power in this form, while just as real and disruptive, is more nuanced, opaque and complex. Partnership and participation imply the mutual acceptance of shared normative standards and frameworks. Degrees of agreement, or apparent agreement, within such normative frameworks establish lines of inclusion and exclusion. Liberal peace is a system of carrots and sticks where cooperation paves the way for development assistance and access to the wider networks of global governance, while non-cooperation risks varying degrees of conditionality and isolation. Liberal peace is geared to a logic of exclusion and selective incorporation. Given this structure, it should be no surprise that an interest in the ethics of aid and the decisions that aid workers make is currently expanding (Slim 1997; Gasper 1999: 26–7).

The reproblematisation of security

Since the inception of development discourse at the end of the 1940s, global poverty and the threat of insurrection have always been closely linked. President Truman, for example, in setting out the basis of what became know as the Truman Doctrine, argued in 1947 that half of the world's population was living in a miserable condition. Their poverty was 'a handicap and a threat to both them and the more prosperous areas' (quoted by Escobar 1995: 3). In the mid-1970s, E. F. Schumacher, a leading figure in the creation of modern development studies, claimed that the prospects of a full and happy life for two-thirds of the world's population were slight, if not declining. Moreover, unless development was made appropriate and directly reached down to poor people, there was little chance that things would get better.

> But if the rural people of the developing countries are helped to help themselves, I have no doubt that a genuine development will ensue, without vast shanty towns and misery belts around every big city and without the cruel frustrations of bloody revolution. (Schumacher 1974: 171)

While such statements were often voiced in the past, the political conditions of the Cold War prevented the effective incorporation of the security implications of poverty and underdevelopment into aid policy. Development assistance was politicised during the Cold War in line with a dominant security strategy that demanded the establishment and maintenance of pro-Western political alliances among Third World countries. Aid flows tended to reflect the requirements of this strategy, and were largely unconnected with the degree to which countries were poor or not (Griffin 1991). This was a source of concern for many aid practitioners and created a tension within development policy. The primacy accorded the formation of political alliances, for example, meant that unsavoury domestic relations, including human rights abuse, were often overlooked in the pursuit of realist goals. The end of the Cold War, in removing the foundations of the existing security architecture, has allowed development discourse to re-establish earlier concerns with poverty and conflict. At the same time, security policy has reinvented itself and, among other things, has come to share the terrain of development. In the past, while development and security policy were clearly associated, compared to now the relationship was more opportunistic, geared to national interests and often covert. The current merger of development and security is much more inclusive, organic and transparent. The growing strategic networks linking

35

development and security actors – academics, military establishments, NGOs, private security companies and so on – is a good indication of the open and increasingly networked status of the association.

Since the mid-1960s the issues surrounding economic and political instability in the South have been slowly yet increasingly internation-alised. The last wave of conventional national liberation struggles in the mid-1970s added to this process. Growing refugee flows over most of this period were the main catalyst in shaping emerging Northern concern. At the same time, the internationalisation of the consequences of instability in the South has stood in contrast to the increasing tendency towards various forms of regional economic and political integration in the North. The deepening of EU cooperation since the mid-1980s is one pertinent example. In many respects, the Cold War overlay these trends and subordinated their security implications. With its passing, the reproblematisation of security has reconnected with many such pre-existing trends. Security threats to the North are no longer seen solely in terms of traditional forms of interstate conflict to be approached through the politics of alliance and nuclear deterrence. At the same time, the demise of political alternatives in the South, together with the declining remit of nation-state competence, has further internation-alised the effects of instability. Reflecting much of the 1980 UN debate around the root causes of refugee flows, especially the Western pre-dilection for attributing these to internal causes, recent opinion has re-inforced the view that the modalities of underdevelopment themselves represent a security issue. A Swedish government report, for example, argues that the 'threats to our own security today are assumed to be associated, inter alia, with global population trends, combined with slow economic development and social justice' (MFA 1997). A country's ability to manage the multiple problems of underdevelopment and transition (poverty, resource competition, unemployment, population growth, crime, environmental degradation and so on) and, especially, to resolve antagonisms peacefully, is now a central concern within the new or wider security framework.

> The 'new' conflicts are about identities and the status, culture and values of various groups. They are enacted in the social sphere rather than in arenas familiar to traditional security policy. As a complement to the concepts that are the common currency of traditional power politics ('high politics'), such as security guarantees and arms control, we must now introduce concepts appropriate to the community level ('low politics'), which have to do with preventing crises, enhancing stability and reducing the element of unpredictability in the system. (*Ibid.*: 16)

36

This line of security thinking now shares the same terrain as development discourse. It also represents the received wisdom within the major industrialised countries (OECD 1998). It is felt that the increasing interconnectedness of the global system has magnified the threat of the internationalisation of instability in the South. This relates not only to refugee flows but to an enhanced ability to disrupt commercial activity and, through supporting the spread of related terrorist and criminal networks, to impact more directly on the North (George 1992). From this perspective, remedial development is not only a moral right, but can be justified as a form of enlightened self-interest. Indeed, given the strong isolationist tendencies in the North, calls for enlightened self-interest are now an established part of mobilising the strategic complexes of liberal peace.

> There are two reasons above all why we should embrace the objectives of international development. First, because it is right to do so. Every generation has a moral duty to reach out to the poor and needy to try to create a more just world. Second, because we have a common interest in doing so. Global warming, land degradation, deforestation, loss of biodiversity, polluted and over-fished oceans, shortage of fresh water, population pressures and insufficient land on which to grow food will otherwise endanger the lives of everyone – rich and poor, developed and developing. (DFID 1997: 16)

The association of conflict with underdevelopment, together with the propensity of instability to communicate its effects more widely in an interconnected world, have served to blur security and development concerns. Hence, 'helping strengthen the capacity of a society to manage conflict without violence must be seen as a foundation for sustainable development' (DAC 1997). In other words, the promotion of development has become synonymous with the pursuit of security. At the same time, security has become a prerequisite for sustainable development.

The radicalisation of development

Within present discourse, not only are poverty and underdevelopment associated with conflict, but conflict itself, because it destroys development assets and social capital, is regarded as complicating poverty and deepening underdevelopment.

> Violent conflict generates social division, reverses economic progress, impedes sustainable development and frequently results in human rights violations. Large population movements triggered by conflict threaten the security and livelihood of whole regions. (DFID 1997: 67)

37

There is a compelling mutual reinforcement within this imagery. Underdevelopment is dangerous since it can lead to violence; at the same time, conflict entrenches and deepens that danger. Societies are left not only worse off, but even more prone to outbreaks of instability. Such commonly held sentiments have provided the rationale for the widespread incorporation into official aid policy during the mid-1990s of a commitment to conflict prevention and conflict resolution activities. This incorporation lies at the heart of the radicalisation of the politics of development. A commitment to conflict resolution denotes a major shift of official donor policy towards interventionism. At the same time, in so far as it is widely held that humanitarian and rehabilitation assistance can help restart development in a war-affected country, it is now also accepted among Northern governments that any such intervention is not concerned with restoring the *status quo ante*. The current aid policy of the EU in conflict situations is a good example. As a multilateral donor, in many respects the EU is a rather conservative institution. Nevertheless, since the mid-1990s, it has held that the reason for conflict in the first place would suggest that earlier social conditions were not conducive to sustainable development. Conflict is very often 'the result of the interaction of political, economic and social instability, frequently stemming from bad governance, failed economic policies and inappropriate development programmes which have exacerbated ethnic or religious differences' (EC 1996b: iii).

Because development is largely understood as an economic process, the unequal distribution of resources or other benefits between social groups and, especially, the absence of formal political mechanisms to peacefully reconcile such differences frequently exacerbate conflict. Re-establishing the development process is therefore a non-linear exercise that will often require the creation of new institutions and forms of social organisation. Among other things, the EU argues that development programmes, as well as promoting sustainability, will have to address the social and political dimensions of instability as well. Development instruments now need to take into account

> their potential for balancing the interests and opportunities of different identity groups within a state, for encouraging democratic governments that enjoy widespread legitimacy among the population, for fostering consensus on key national issues ... and for building mechanisms for the peaceful conciliation of group interests. (EC 1996a: 4)

Besides sustainable economic development, the wider social and political impacts of development programmes are now part of a new security framework. This emphasis on promoting direct social change in the South is acknowledged as representing a new departure for EU development programmes (EC 1996b: 20). Programme design should consider who are the main beneficiaries and losers in the development process and, if necessary, be prepared to shift the balance of power and opportunities within societies (EC 1996a). Such considerations were included, for example, in the November 1995 amendment of the Lomé Convention. Following the collapse of political alternatives in the South, development policy now directly engages the broad process of social and political change within recipient countries.

This represents a marked radicalisation of the politics of development. Development assistance is no longer concerned with helping support an often conservative pro-Western alliance of Southern elites; it is now in the business of transforming whole societies. Conflict resolution epitomises the radicalisation of development. The need to change behaviour and attitudes, especially in relation to violent conflict, has been clearly stated and widely accepted in this context – as demonstrated by a World Bank and Carter Center report on conflict resolution (the dual emphasis in the original is reproduced below).

> First, *behaviour* must be altered from the application of violence to more peaceful forms of dispute settlement; second, a transition from wartime to a peace *mentality* needs to occur; third, the *system of risks and rewards* should encourage peaceful pursuit of livelihoods, rather than intimidation, violence and rent-seeking; fourth, *adversaries* must come to view each other as members of the same society, working toward a common goal, a peaceful and prosperous future; and fifth, *structures and institutions* must be amended to support these new peaceful transformations. (World Bank and Carter Center 1997: 3–4)

It should be noted that, since the inception of development discourse at the end of the Second World War, development has always had as its aim the modernisation and transformation of the societies that it encounters. While NGOs have often been more radical in the past, until the mid-1990s the transformational aim of official development policy was usually regarded as a natural outcome of development policy; something that would follow of its own accord from the main activity of supporting economic growth. The incorporation of conflict into mainstream development policy has significantly changed this order of priorities. Given the new freedom of movement following the end of the Cold War, social change can no longer be left to the hoped-for synergies of modernising projects and market reform: effecting social transformation is itself now a direct and explicit policy aim. In a recent lecture, the former Senior Vice President and Chief Economist of the

World Bank, Joseph Stiglitz, described with some candour the failure of fifty years of development to make a significant impact on world poverty. Moreover, those countries in East Asia that had made major development advances had done so by mainly ignoring official development advice (Stiglitz 1998). In putting forward a 'new development paradigm', it was argued that earlier official development strategies, including the so-called Washington consensus based on structural adjustment and market reform, had failed because 'they viewed development too narrowly' (*ibid.*: 1), that is, as simply a matter of getting the economy right. The desired social change was expected to follow naturally from this. Instead, dual societies composed of entrenched traditional and modern sectors have emerged. Unlike the benign and functionalist views that one encountered regarding dualism a generation ago, the continuing existence of conservative and customary traditional values was itself a testimony to the failure of development and the inability 'of more advanced sectors to penetrate deeply into society' (*ibid.*: 3). A new development paradigm must, from the start, aim for 'catalysing change and transforming *whole* societies' (*ibid.*: 3, emphasis in original).

> This vision needs to include a view of the transformation of institutions, the creation of new capacities, in some cases to replace traditional institutions that will inevitably be weakened in the process of development. (*ibid.*: 11)

Such a radical process of social change, however, cannot be imposed. It is recognised that you might be able to make someone say or do something they do not believe in; you cannot, however, get someone to think what they do not accept. Social change, therefore, has to be based around a wide-ranging and liberal process of 'consensus building' that encourages ownership and participation.

> What is required … is participation in a process that constructs institutional arrangements, including incentives. Institutions, incentives, participation, and ownership can be viewed as complementary; none on its own is sufficient. (*ibid.*: 15)

Interestingly, not until the concluding remarks of the lecture was the central question posed: 'transformation to what kind of society, and for what ends?' (*ibid.*: 29) – a question that Stiglitz raises only to leave unanswered. Indeed, it is perhaps because global liberal governance has yet to answer that question convincingly that the issue of 'values' has come to the fore: as something that appears to provide a solution but in fact does not. The issue of values relates to the envisioned liberal future of the societies being transformed being challenged by the often contrary values and attitudes indigenous to those same societies. Commenting on the growing attempts by the EU to promote change among its Southern partners, it has been argued that systemic transformation in these regions

> is motivated by the positive experience of Western political systems based on law, human rights, pluralist government and the market economy. All of these Western values culminate in liberal democracy which, in the view of the EU and its Member States, has an in-built quality of peaceful conflict resolution, a respect for minorities and a comparatively high potential for popular participation in public policy. (Rummel 1996: 21)

Given that humanitarian assistance is usually a key factor in EU assistance in unstable areas, this too has been reinterpreted as an important part of the European value system.

> Commissioner Bonino [former Commissioner for humanitarian assistance] has often stated that humanitarian aid is not a 'policy' but a shared European value. Although not a 'policy', it is however an integral part of Europe's external identity, and all the more so in parts of the world where it is not possible to deploy other instruments. (ECHO 1997a: 2)

During the recent Kosovo conflict (February–May 1999) much was made of the claim that NATO was 'fighting not for territory but for values' (Blair 1999). The intervention was presented as a principled endeavour by a Western political and humanitarian alliance to end the violent attempt by Serbian aggressors to impose ethnic cleansing on Albanian Kosovars in the region. Using the occasion of the fiftieth anniversary of the Council of Europe in May 1999, the British Foreign Secretary Robin Cook put the case in the following way:

> There are now two Europes competing for the soul of our continent. One still follows the race ideology that blighted our continent under the fascists. The other emerged fifty years ago out from behind the shadow of the Second World War. The conflict between the international community and Yugoslavia is the struggle between these two Europes. Which side prevails will determine what sort of continent we live in. That is why we must win. (Cook 1999)

The Kosovo conflict was represented as a struggle to uphold the values of 'modern Europe'. It provided a good opportunity for the airing of this new morality that, indeed, found significant public support. As the above discussion suggests, however, the conceptual basis of such wars of value had already been established in theory in the radicalisation of development policy and the reproblematisation of security during the course of the 1990s. Regarding Kosovo, it is more a question of existing theory requiring a practical outlet than of events shaping or initiating new policy. At the same time, however, the Kosovo conflict does indicate a key feature of the operationalisation of the new development–security complex. That is, it is mainly beyond the power and influence of individual Northern governments or multilateral agencies. Today's wars of value are only possible through strategic complexes linking state and non-state political, development, humanitarian and private actors.

Concluding remarks

In less than a generation, the whole meaning of development has altered significantly. It is no longer concerned with promoting economic growth in the hope that development will follow. Today, it is better described as an attempt, preferably through cooperative partnership arrangements, to change whole societies and the behaviour and attitudes of the people within them. In attempting to promote direct social change, development has increasingly come to resemble a series of projects and strategies to change indigenous values and modes of organisation and replace them with liberal ones. Ideas of empowerment and sustainability are largely refracted through a lens of behavioural and attitudinal change. Whether this relates to the formation of community groups, cooperative forms of working, promoting the role of women, managing small loans or conflict resolution, the emphasis is on using participatory methods to change the way people do things and what they think. For many NGOs, changing behaviour is intrinsically related to the attempt to create new and egalitarian forms of social organisation. In other quarters, this process is synonymous with a change from traditional to modern values. The mid-1990s incorporation of conflict into mainstream aid policy has played a catalytic role in this radicalisation of development. In this process, development and security have increasingly merged. Representing underdevelopment as dangerous not only demands a remedial process of social transformation, it also creates an urgency and belief ensuring that this process is no longer trusted to chance.

NOTE

1 Dependency theory should not be confused with the popular meaning that dependency has acquired among aid agencies. Since the 1980s, there has been a concern

that food aid and, more recently, humanitarian assistance, since they represent free goods, create economic disincentives and market distortions that tend to discourage independent productive activity among recipients. This then encourages a dependence among aid beneficiaries on continuing free handouts. For dependency theory, on the other hand, dependence related to the subordinate position of Southern elites and economies within a neocolonial international system. Because of the comprador role they played, elites were dependent on support from the North. At the same time, markets and economies were distorted in order to satisfy the needs of a few metropolitan countries on which they remained dependent for technology and market outlets (see Frank 1967).

3
Strategic Complexes
and Global Governance

Global governance does not reside in a single powerful institution with
a clear international mandate, bureaucratic competence and recognised
regulatory authority. Such an organisation does not exist and is
unlikely to do so. Although it never aspired to become a global government, the changing fortunes of the UN are instructive in this respect.
The initial optimism surrounding its future following the end of the
Cold War, for example, has now dissipated and been replaced by a
growing emphasis on regional security arrangements, mandated subcontracting and other forms of authority delegation (Smith and Weiss
1998). This is not to say, however, that global governance does not have
a reality or substance. It resides in such processes of decentralisation
and burden sharing. Commenting on the increasing number of movements, groups and institutions emerging in relation to environmental
management, Georgi Derlugian has argued that the

> closely knit web of international and major nation-state bureaucracies,
> both scientific and managerial, public and private, may seek to legitimise
> themselves by assuming the functions of global management and
> security. (Derlugian 1996: 173)

Global governance has a reality not in a single institution but in the
networks and linkages that bring together different organisations,
interest groups and forms of authority in relation to specific regulatory
tasks. Moreover, the dominance of the liberal paradigm means that in
relation to such networks we should talk more accurately of global
liberal governance (Dillon and Reid 2000). While establishing durable
structures and relationships, global governance is also fluid, mutable
and non-territorial. New relations of governance can emerge in response to changing perceptions and assessments of risk. Global liberal

44

governance is an adaptive and selectively inclusive system. It is a radical project that thrives on creating networks that bridge traditional boundaries, specialisms and disciplines. Its rationale is that of information sharing, comparative advantage and coordination. While governance networks form around specific issues as problems mutate, discrete networks themselves can link and integrate their activities. In response to the new wars and the merging of development and security, innovative strategic complexes – linking state and non-state actors, public and private organisations, military and civilian organisations, and so on – have emerged. Such strategic complexes are the operational basis of liberal peace and an important and formative nexus of global governance.

Regarding the new wars, the massed armies, complex weapons systems and political blocs developed during the Cold War no longer represent an adequate response (van Creveld 1991). In their place, strategic complexes linking state and non-state actors have expanded. It is interesting to note that this response tends to imitate the nature of the new wars themselves, as in the blurring of conventional distinctions between people, army and government, and the intermingling of such actors. The liberal analogue includes the increasing interconnection between military and civilian organisations such as NGOs and private companies, together with the growing influence of the latter with regard to official government policy. In many respects, the organisations and linkages that make up liberal peace also constitute a liberal way of war. The merging of development and security has been essential for such strategic complexes to emerge. Among other things, in defining conflict as a social problem, that is, as underdevelopment becoming dangerous, it has allowed new and non-traditional networks to be mobilised in the cause of security. War is no longer a Clausewitzian affair of state, it is a problem of underdevelopment and political breakdown and, as such, it requires development as well as security professionals to conjoin and work together in new ways. Not only does this require new strategic networks going beyond the state, it also demands a reworking of what we understand to be loyalty and the conditions under which people are willing to sacrifice their lives. Payment or other non-patriotic forms of inducement increasingly motivate participation.

The merging of security and development has been institutionally facilitated by the privatisation and subcontracting of former state development and security responsibilities. Innovative networks linking governments, NGOs and the business sector have begun to emerge and consolidate. These strategic complexes, while dedicated to the cause of liberal peace are, simultaneously, the new war-fighting organisations that van Creveld (1991: 192) perceptively predicted would emerge in response to the challenge of the new wars. Given that conflict is highly imitative, in many respects the organisational forms of liberal peace and the new wars are similar. They are both based on new, mutable and increasingly privatised local–global linkages and networks. In the case of the North, liberal strategic complexes are assuming responsibility for securing peace on the borders of global governance. This chapter examines some of the conditions necessary for the emergence of such complexes, indicates the types of linkage that are developing between the strategic actors involved, and discusses a few of their characteristics.

The qualification of nation-state competence

Transforming whole societies in the South is beyond both the ability and the legitimacy of individual Northern governments. Not only does this require partnership with the South but, increasingly, this responsibility has been taken over by the North's emerging strategic complexes linking state and non-state actors. In understanding the nature of such networks, we have to consider briefly the issue of globalisation and how it relates to the changing competence of the nation state. The term globalisation has a number of different and even conflicting meanings. Within the international financial institutions (IFIs) and among free market economists, for example, globalisation is largely understood in terms of a world-wide economic and political convergence around liberal market principles and the increasing real-time integration of business, technological and financial systems (Held *et al*. 1997). Based on an expansion and deepening of market competition, globalisation is argued to be synonymous with an irresistible process of economic, political and cultural change that is sweeping all national boundaries and protectionist tendencies before it. Indeed, for a country to remain outside this process is now tantamount to its marginalisation and failure. The Introduction has already sketched a very different view of this essentially neoliberal conception of globalisation. In distinction, it can be argued that the growth of the informational economy and market liberalisation has had an ambiguous impact on the economies of the South. On the one hand, much of the South's conventional economic activity has become redundant in relation to the nodes and networks of the core areas of the global economy. On the other hand, as discussed in Chapter 6, the South has reintegrated itself into the liberal world system through the deepening and expansion of a wide range of transborder shadow economies.

The concept of globalisation has a more general and less ambiguous utility in relation to political rather than economic factors: the changing domestic competence of the nation state and the forms of public administration that international market liberalisation compels governments to follow. While their abilities to respond differ, in broad terms this is a phenomenon affecting both North and South. The modern nation state emerged in the mid-seventeenth century in the context of a long period of transborder religious wars. After three centuries of growth and institutional deepening, it is regarded as having reached its apogee during the so-called 'golden age' of world capitalism from the end of the Second World War until the early 1970s (Hopkins and Wallerstein 1996). While exceptions and differences in depth existed, the tone of this post-war period was one of nation-state competence and effectiveness. It was a time of comprehensive welfare provision, macroeconomic management, government regulation and unprecedented social engineering to combat the public ills of want, ill health and ignorance. In a phrase, it represented the triumph of modernity. Moreover, this development was not confined to the market economies of the West. While their legitimacy was weak, the socialist party states of the Second World reached the peak of their economic performance (Arrighi 1991). As for the Third World, state-led models of development, in theory at least, also reigned supreme. Even the national liberation struggles of the period did not seek to abolish the nation state. Their task was to drive out its bourgeois and comprador usurpers and proclaim a 'people's' state. Looking back to the 1960s with a hint of eulogy, Derlugian observes

> the state everywhere expanded, expansive, and in its full glory. The long-term process of state formation and state expansion appeared to culminate in an unprecedented triumph. The whole globe was covered in sovereign states, and these appeared to be working in a quite satisfactory manner. For the first time there were almost no merely 'nominal governments' that could rule outside the capital cities only thanks to the support of local non-state and parastatal authorities (warlords, strongmen, sheikhs, tribal chiefs). (Derlugian 1996: 159)

In retrospect, this success appears to have been partial and short-lived; a couple of decades after several centuries of formative growth. From the early 1970s, the competence of the nation state began to erode. Less than a decade later it would be widely accepted that it had reached the limits of its ability to manage social and economic change (*ibid.*: 170).

In both the North and the South, globalisation has become synonymous with pressures that are changing the architecture of the nation state and forcing a reworking of public policy and cutbacks in domestic welfare expenditure. While true economic and technological integration may characterise only Northern regions, in most places globalisation has brought growing income disparities and polarised life chances. In this respect, a number of broad North–South similarities exist. The authority of the nation state lay in its general social competence, including its ability to maintain effectively the provision of public goods such as employment, education, health and pension provision, and to uphold international commitments (Cerny 1998). Of special importance was the nation state's independent ability to plan and redistribute wealth and public goods within its juridical borders. Since the 1970s, states have been slowly losing their national competence in this respect.

States are no longer able to assure national living standards through the pursuit of domestic policies alone. Growing public indebtedness has led to insurmountable pressures to cut public expenditure and reduce state welfare provision. As a cheaper alternative, the privatisation of public goods and services has been promoted as the state has progressively withdrawn from anything that could be construed as commercial activity. Where it has proven unfeasible to privatise a public service, the trend has been towards marketisation, the introduction of private sector accounting and management techniques. In some cases, public institutions have been corporatised and run as if they were capitalist enterprises. At the same time, changes in industrial and commercial policy, plus rapid technological innovations that have improved the viability of transnational business, have encouraged a process of economic regionalisation and internationalisation (Morales and Quandt 1992). Increasingly, national economic strategy has shifted towards domestic budgetary restraint coupled with global trade liberalisation. By the beginning of the 1980s, this model had assumed a dominant position among OECD countries and, through the efforts of the World Bank and IMF, has become the template in the South as well. In the North, unable to maintain their competence through domestic policies alone,

> political authorities have sought to maximise economic growth through technical innovation and industrial specialisation with risk alleviation based on an expansive global system of intra-industry trade, international financial liberalisation and aggressive pursuit of cross-border corporate investment. (Dogan and Pugh 1997: 5)

The liberalisation of global markets has greatly increased the power and influence of transnational capital in relation to that of nation states

(Cox 1995). Importantly, liberalisation has given large companies a new degree of choice regarding where they operate. In other words, political authorities have become increasingly aware that inward investment is threatened by national policies that conflict with transnational interests. In an attempt to maintain living standards, this has generated pressures to keep public services and welfare commitments economically competitive. Globalisation in this sense – international market liberalisation and the growing influence of transnational capital – has encouraged a relatively consistent pattern of domestic social and economic policies to emerge. A sizeable international consensus now exists on the need for national economic regulation to be liberal, non-discriminatory and market-centred. Domestic policies of this type have been defended by politicians as synonymous with a country's international competitive position and essential for the welfare of its citizens. Privatisation, marketisation and internationalisation have emerged as the defining characteristics of what, since the mid-1980s, has been known as new public policy (Dogan and Pugh 1997) – the necessary tools of public administration to achieve economic growth in a deregulated and competitive global economic environment.

Pressures towards privatisation and internationalisation have tended to qualify and attenuate nation-state competence in a number of ways. New actors and intermediaries have arisen at supranational, international and subnational levels (Morss 1991). Although sovereignty remains important, it has been drawn out and qualified from 'above' and 'below', as it were. Concerning supranational intermediaries, not only has the significance of international financial institutions (IFIs) and transnational capital increased, but so has the influence of inter-governmental organisations (IGOs), regional bodies and international NGOs. At the subnational level, processes of privatisation and volun-tarisation have also attenuated state competence. Private companies and voluntary organisations have increasingly taken over the provision of public goods and services formally associated with states. Single-issue and identity politics have also grown at the expense of formal parties. The attenuation of state competence through the inclusion of new supranational, international and subnational actors within decision-making processes has significantly altered the nature of political authority (Demirovic 1996). Complex cross-cutting linkages between state and non-state actors characterise the present system. Political authority has become increasingly multi-levelled and, compared to the nation-state ideal, asymmetrical. The growing importance of networks and cross-cutting linkages is central to the transition from hierarchical structures of government to the more polyarchical and networked patterns of governance, with the emergence of 'cooperative network-like types of negotiation and bargaining' (ibid.: 4).

While states and governments remain important, and will continue to do so, increasingly they exercise their authority through complex international, national and subnational governance networks linking state and non-state actors. This is a common feature of political instrumentality in both the North and the South. Regarding the latter, however, the qualification of nation-state competence has been particularly marked. Indeed, in some places, nation-state competence in any traditional meaning of the term has all but disappeared (Reno 1998). More generally in the South, this attenuation can be seen in the largely uncontested ability of the IFIs to determine the macroeconomic policy of a country. The recent wave of democratisation and multi-party elections during the 1990s, for example, took place after the international community had already decided the macroeconomic and trade policy of most of the countries concerned. Such issues can no longer be left to chance and effectively have been elevated above the democratic process. At the same time, as state competence has declined in relation to the provision of public goods, international NGOs have greatly expanded their operations in the South (de Waal 1997). Indeed, growing linkages between NGOs, IFIs and donor governments have given the emerging strategic complexes of global liberal governance the ability to shape not only the economic policy of a country but its welfare and social policy as well (Deacon et al. 1997).

Liberal strategic complexes

The changing nature of loyalty and sacrifice
Analysing the effects of the new public policy on security issues in the North, in this case the trend towards privatisation and marketisation within military establishments, Dogan and Pugh (1997) have argued that these policies have not always been welcomed by politicians. While new public policy offers states a strategy for economic growth, 'this is secured through mechanisms which involve a significant diminution of national political autonomy' (ibid.: 8). Moreover, this reduction of authority is not captured within the language and concepts of traditional international studies. The concern of Dogan and Pugh is that the logic of the new public policy 'actually destroys the state's physical capability to act alone – the Emperor is not naked, but he is wearing hired clothes' (ibid.: 9). Besides direct pressures towards the privatisation and marketisation of security responsibilities, there

are also more indirect consequence of these policies that relate to a state's inability to act alone. In particular, its increasing reliance on civilian or non-state actors raises issues of loyalty, reward and sacrifice. Addressing the change in the nature of war, van Creveld (1991) has argued that the

> most important single demand that any political community must meet is the demand for protection. A community which cannot safeguard the lives of its members, subjects, citizens, comrades, brothers, or whatever they are called is unlikely to command their loyalty or to survive for very long. The opposite is also correct: any community able and, more importantly, willing to exert itself to protect its members will be able to call on those members' loyalty even to the point where they are prepared to die for it. (*ibid.*: 198)

Protection not only involves physical security from dangers such as violence and crime. It also includes the integrity of the family, freedom from economic insecurity, upholding value systems, cultural mores and the generally maintaining the quality of life. From this perspective, in many ways globalisation has eroded the ability of a state to protect its citizens. While domestic budgetary restraint and trade liberalisation may be one way to establish international economic competitiveness, it simultaneously erodes and places national identities and loyalties under strain. Few people – including, one would guess, those that support such measures – are prepared to die for a flexible labour market or to sacrifice their lives so that multinational companies can invest or disinvest in countries as they please. War and liberal consumer societies do not mix well. This paradox of modern life is clearly evident in the paranoia of Northern states regarding the possibility of their suffering military casualties in the new wars. Some states have created professional armies as one way of addressing the changing demands on loyalty and sacrifice. The new wars, however, with their mixture of peace-keeping and peace-enforcement activities are not popular with such armies (Weale 1999). They do not represent a 'cause' in the traditional sense. They are ragged, unpredictable and dirty. Moreover, while humanitarianism may play an important mobilising role, eventually all sides usually end up shooting at the peace makers.

The new strategic complexes of state and non-state actors offer one solution to the growing problem of loyalty, reward and sacrifice. They have cultivated new forms of allegiance to complement and replace the patriotism traditionally associated with the nation state. Apart from the increasing professionalisation of military establishments, the growing involvement of NGOs and private companies has changed and broadened our understanding of such matters. The humanitarian, developmental and charitable ethos of NGOs, for example, also encompasses ideas of duty and sacrifice. Many aid workers, both expatriate and national staff, have been killed in the new wars. Between 1992 and 1999, for example, within the UN system alone, 175 personnel have been killed and a similar number taken hostage (Hammock 1999). If one added other aid agency staff, journalists, and so on, the number would be greatly increased. Besides the humanitarian impulse, the profit motives of private companies and the pecuniary interests of individuals also provide powerful incentives for attempting to construct a liberal peace. Monetary return or material gain are becoming increasingly important as a means of mobilising the strategic complexes of global governance (van Creveld 1991: 212). While issues relating to legitimacy and regulation remain, the growing crisis of loyalty and sacrifice is a defining reason why the role of international private security companies will continue to grow. This is discussed more fully below. However, compared to the spirit of sacrifice involved with the defence of one's homeland, identity or livelihood that frequently animates emerging political complexes in the new wars, such an amalgam of often competing liberal loyalties is complex, mutable and fickle.

The Centre for Defence Studies, King's College, London, has identified five communities 'that need to be coordinated in order for future responses to complex emergencies to be successful' (Von Hippel 1999: 151). These are NGOs, donor governments, multilateral agencies, military establishments and the corporate sector. Excepting the omission of academics, these communities are the main actors that have come together in new and innovative ways in pursuit of liberal peace. The post-Cold War ability to work in situations of ongoing conflict has been an important catalyst in the formation of such strategic complexes. The emergence of these networks, however, takes the form of a complex institutional history. In adapting to the new security environment of the 1990s, the relevant parts of each of these communities have been subject to major processes of change and adaptation. This is not only in terms of internal organisational and policy change. Under the influence of the merging of development and security and the privatisation of these responsibilities, cross-cutting linkages and networks uniting these communities have been consolidated, or else new forms of collaboration have grown. Actors, organisations and institutions that were previously relatively autonomous now find new forms of synergy, overlap and mutual interest. New institutions have emerged, existing ones have changed their mandates and found new ways of interaction. Here it is only possible to provide an indicative and selective sketch of the extensive, underresearched and complex institutional history that forms the basis of liberal peace. The following is a general description of the types of changes occurring among strategic actors and, especially, the linkages that are forming between them.

Non-governmental organisations

In the institutional history of global liberal governance, international NGOs have a central place. Since the 1970s, predating official commitments to direct forms of social transformation by a couple of decades, NGOs have been increasingly important as hands-on developmental actors. Indeed, this early and, at the time, non-conventional engagement has given NGOs a radical and innovative ethos; a view that has only begun to wane in recent years as the complexity of their position has become apparent (Edwards and Hulme 1995; Hulme and Edwards 1997). In relation to the discussion of strategic complexes, two issues relating to international NGOs will be mentioned: subcontracting and networking.

Funding and subcontracting
While some international NGOs can trace their origins to the early and mid-twentieth century, the last two or three decades have seen a remarkable expansion in both their number and strategic influence. Most of the growth in Southern NGOs has also taken place during the 1990s. In the mid-1990s, for example, it has been estimated that almost 29,000 international NGOs (operational in more than three countries) were active. Most of these were from the North. During the same period, estimates for Southern NGOs were many times in excess of this figure (Weiss 1999a: 28–9). For example, those local organisations eligible within the UN system to receive external funding numbered 50,000 alone. The total amount of aid to the South going through NGOs now exceeds that being disbursed through the UN system. At $10–12 billion, this represents about 13 per cent of all development assistance and at least half of all humanitarian aid. Since this sum excludes food aid, the actual proportion of aid being channelled through NGOs is probably higher. While the absolute numbers of NGOs are high, it is also the case that there are great differences in size among them. Some of the well-established international NGOs, for example, now rival and exceed many of the UN specialist organisations in terms of their incomes. In the mid-1990s, for example, it was estimated that just 20 American and

European NGOs accounted for 75 per cent of all relief expenditure (Weiss and Collins 1996).

While the importance of NGOs as aid implementers is now well established, this was not always the case. Until the early 1980s, for example, government-to-government (or IGO-to-government) development assistance was the predominant pattern. From this period onwards, however, donor governments have increasingly channelled development and humanitarian assistance through NGOs (Clark 1991). During the 1980s, the basic form of subcontracting involved donor governments funding NGOs to implement aid projects. In turn, NGOs reported back to donors when projects were complete and used their growing influence to lobby for more effective assistance. In many respects, it was an arm's-length form of subcontracting, having relatively few conditions. From the end of the 1980s, not only has the number and scale of NGO operations grown, but a type of competitive aid market has emerged where none existed before. At the same time, however, it is not a pure free market. Donor governments usually fund their own national NGOs preferentially. However, with the increasing role of IGOs in negotiating access to unstable regions and, especially, their acting as a multilateral funding conduit for NGOs, funding sources have moved beyond states. With the growth of UN and EU subcontracting, for example, while the national link between donor governments and NGOs remains strong, the aid market now has a more global existence. The enlargement of the aid market has been synonymous with the expansion of complex donor/UN/NGO welfare safety nets and human-dimension projects first in the Third World and then in Eastern Europe and the former Soviet Union. The post-Cold War ability to work in situations of ongoing conflict has been a major contributing factor to this growth and the increasing complexity and depth of contractual relations.

In general terms, the main developments during the 1990s have been a major expansion of NGO relations with UN agencies and military establishments, and a growing formalisation of relations with donor governments. In relation to the UN, the growth of UN humanitarian operations in African and the Balkans during the first part of the 1990s served to expose the UN's lack of operational capacity (Weiss 1998). UN and NGO relations developed new forms as not only NGOs took on responsibilities for implementing UN programmes but, as in the case of Sudan and Bosnia, the UN became responsible for negotiating access for NGOs working in war zones (Duffield 1997). The ability of NGOs to work in ongoing conflict also saw new working relations emerging between NGOs and military establishments (Weiss 1999a). In relation to donor governments, subcontracting relations with NGOs have grown in depth and comprehensiveness. Compared to the 1980s, more stringent project guidelines, monitoring mechanisms and performance targets now exist (Hulme and Edwards 1997). This increasing regulation is examined in more detail in the following chapter in relation to the governance implications of the debate surrounding the need to link relief to development in conflict situations.

Networking and advocacy

Not only has the number of international NGOs grown in the last twenty years but, in order to be effective, they have also tended to cluster into networks and representative structures. Such networks have been the primary means whereby NGOs have gained access to national and international decision-making processes. At the same time, in relation to policy formation, NGOs have established their own international conference fora.[1] Many international organisations now have special committees or other forms of institutional linkage with international NGOs, such as UNICEF's NGO Committee. Similar committees also advise the UN's Economic and Social Commission (ECOSOC), Inter-Agency Standing Committee and Organisation for the Coordination of Humanitarian Assistance (OCHA). At the World Bank, the Operation Policy Group is involved in NGO liaison. There are also numerous NGO platforms at the national level that, in various ways, advise Northern governments on humanitarian and development policy. In Germany, for example, the Committee for the Coordination of Humanitarian Assistance (CCHA) has been set up within the Foreign Ministry. For many NGOs, such involvement with political institutions has not been free of anxiety that their role as advocates of international reform may be compromised (Topçu 1999). In this respect, the forma-tion of networks and representative platforms has been regarded as helpful. Because they allow the pooling of resources and the develop-ment of common positions, rather than direct co-option, networks are regarded as better enabling NGOs to act as institutional counterparts to international organisations and, especially, governments.

Many NGO international networks and platforms now exist and cover the whole field of relief and development. To give some idea of their scope and linkages, a few examples will be given of European networks that relate to humanitarian assistance.

INTERNATIONAL COUNCIL OF VOLUNTARY AGENCIES (ICVA)
Established in 1962, ICVA now has a membership of over 100 interna-tional NGOs. It provides a forum for cooperation, information sharing

and consultation. It also liaises with other NGO networks, donor governments and multilateral organisations. While ICVA is non-operational, it has played a role, for example, in the development and dissemination of voluntary codes of conduct relating to the role and responsibilities of NGOs in conflict situations. ICVA has consultative status with a number of UN organisations including ECOSOC, the International Labour Organisation (ILO), the UN Conference on Trade and Development (UNCTAD) and UNICEF. A similar relationship exists with the Council of Europe. It has cooperative ties with the Organisation of African Unity (OAU), the OECD, the World Bank and the International Federation of Red Cross and Red Crescent Societies (IFRC), together with a number of UN agencies including OCHA, the UN Development Programme (UNDP), the UN High Commissioner for Refugees (UNHCR), the World Food Programme (WFP) and the World Health Organisation (WHO). ICVA is also a member of the African Environmental Liaison Committee (ELC) International, the European Council on Refugees and Exiles (ECRE) and the Geneva-based Federation of Semi-Official and Private International Institutions.

STEERING COMMITTEE FOR HUMANITARIAN RESPONSE (SCHR)
The SCHR brings together eight of the largest European-registered international NGOs working in the field of humanitarian assistance.[2] Many of these organisations are themselves networks of sister organisations. The SCHR exists to further cooperation among its members and to project a common position on key policy and operational issues to donor governments, UN agencies and other NGO networks.

LIAISON COMMITTEE OF DEVELOPMENT NGOS TO THE EUROPEAN UNION
The Committee brings together 15 national platforms of over 880 NGOs working in the field of relief and development. It operates as an interface between these national platforms and international networks lobbying at an EU level. It represents its members in political dialogue with several EU institutions, including the Commission.

VOLUNTARY ORGANISATIONS IN COOPERATION IN EMERGENCIES (VOICE)
VOICE was established in 1992 as part of the Liaison Committee structure (see above) specifically focused on humanitarian assistance. It is the interface between its 65 members and the EU, especially the European Commission Humanitarian Office (ECHO), which is a key provider of relief assistance. Among its other activities, VOICE has been involved in the production of ECHO Global Plans for specific countries and in helping revise the Framework Partnership Agreement

(FPA), the contractual agreement between ECHO and implementing NGOs. VOICE also has ties with other NGO networks, including the IFRC and the US platform InterAction.

These few examples indicate the type and scope of the networks that now function among NGOs. Many more exist, including large denominational networks that span the globe. They indicate one way in which NGOs have become integrated and increasingly influential within international decision-making processes. In this respect, the aid market is a two-way process. While many NGOs are dependent on government and IGO funding, their ability to monopolise local access and control information has given NGOs a strong role in policy formation. NGOs, for example, have been at the forefront in pushing for a human emphasis in development and the reorientation of aid towards civil society issues (ODI 1995). Donor governments, reflecting the predominance of neoliberal economic thinking, have incorporated the NGO critique of state-led development and have shifted funding away from recipient governments and towards NGOs. During the early 1990s, NGOs were a strong voice calling for humanitarian intervention. Since the mid-1990s, they have also been part of the donor-led shift towards supporting conflict resolution as a central aim of development policy.

Military establishments

The changing role of the North's military establishments is a central part of liberal peace. The adaptations involved clearly reflect the move away from the traditional view of war as an affair of state to the need to address conflict through the creation of more collective and inclusive civil–military networks. The Gulf War in 1991 represented a major turning point in this respect (Weiss and Campbell 1991). The allied post-conflict intervention in northern Iraq to protect the Kurds and allow the delivery of humanitarian assistance marked a major shift in the public perception of the limits of sovereignty (Boutros-Ghali 1995). At the same time, it reinforced the urgency of rethinking UN–military relationships. During the Cold War, the UN seldom intervened in ongoing conflicts. When it did, it was usually in the context of policing an agreed ceasefire. Moreover, troops from NATO countries were largely absent from such operations. The so-called 'second-generation' peacekeeping operations that emerged from the end of the 1980s reflected new demands and requirements (Goulding 1993). Between 1988 and 1994, not only did peacekeeping operations multiply, but compared to the past they were intrusive and multi-levelled, requiring the creation of new forms of interaction between the military and civilian actors, especially aid agencies. At the same time, troops from NATO countries have tended to predominate. The classic literature on civil–military relations focused on the appropriate relations with the highest political authorities. Today, the main concern is relations between the North's military establishments and civil society as a whole.

The new wars, with their disregard for conventional distinctions between people, army and government, have created a new environment for peacekeeping operations: either one of ongoing conflict or, in many cases, an inconclusive and contested peace. Reflecting on the UN peacekeeping operations during the first half of the 1990s, one commentator has remarked that the troops involved

> were neither armies of occupation, nor were they waging war against the local population. Instead, they found themselves working first with civilians *within* the mission (colleagues in the UN and its agencies); second, with civilians on the *fringes* of the mission (the NGO community); and third, with civilians *outside* the mission (the local population). Officers were expected to broker diplomatic deals, shelter the displaced, protect human rights, supervise the return of refugees, organise and monitor elections and support civil reconstruction. (Williams 1998: 14, emphasis in original)

Given the commitment of donor governments to conflict prevention, the rationale of the contemporary civil–military interface could be described as follows: regarding the new wars, the military is expected to create the necessary conditions to allow aid agencies to get on with the task of conflict resolution and social reconstruction (Freedman 1995). Stated in another way, since the end of the Cold War, the focus of civil–military relations has changed from that of planning civil support for military operations to that of providing military support for civil peace-building operations (Zandee 1998: 64–5). While the rationale is clear, it should be noted that throughout the 1990s it has proved difficult to operationalise. Moreover, as discussed below in relation to the commercial sector, part of the complexity of the civil–military interface concerns the growing trend to privatise some erstwhile military responsibilities.

One indication of the difficulties surrounding civil–military co-operation is the decline since the mid-1990s of UN-led consent-based peacekeeping operations. These have tended to be replaced by the growing role of regional alliances, such as NATO in the Balkans, and *ad hoc* political 'coalitions of the willing' (Smith and Weiss 1998). UN troop deployment reached a post-Cold War peak of around 70,000 in 1994.

This had dropped to 12,000 by 1998 (Williams 1998: 15). One reason that has been offered for the decline in UN peacekeeping operations is the poor civil–military relations that characterised the UN interventions in Angola, Bosnia and Somalia. While the UN has a structure for civil–military relations, it was shown to be inadequate in terms of the demands of 'second generation' peacekeeping. In the New York-based UN Secretariat and Security Council, mission conception, planning and implementation were poor and lacking sufficient military advice and input. Command and control arrangements were inadequate for the size and complexity of the mission concerned. In particular, the Security Council found it difficult to express a unified position on peacekeeping operations since its members hold different and some-times conflicting views. In relation to Bosnia, for example, the result was a series of ill-conceived and changing mandates. The failure of the 'safe area' policy – in particular, the massacre in 1995 of Muslims at Sebrenica under the eyes of Dutch UNPROFOR troops – tragically reflected this general problem.

While attracting some controversy, NATO's involvement in the Balkans since 1995[3] has arguably corrected some of the military weak-nesses of earlier UN peacekeeping operations. In the case of the Kosovo conflict in 1999, the alliance only belatedly sought UN approval for its decision to intervene. NATO operations have allowed the military greater initial involvement and, as a security organisation, it has a more robust command and control system than its UN equivalent. However, regarding civil–military relations NATO structures are more *ad hoc* than those of the UN. In this respect, it still has a long way to go 'before they can be said to have forged a partnership that makes them an effective intervention force' (Williams 1998: 17). In other words, while recognised as being of great importance, throughout the 1990s Civil-Military Cooperation, or CIMIC in current NATO terminology, has remained problematic (Zandee 1998). Since the mid-1990s there have been a number of attempts to improve the civil–military interface to better allow aid agencies to proceed with their work of conflict resolu-tion and social reconstruction (*ibid*.: 59–63). The UN reform programme and its formation of OCHA in 1997, for example, has attempted to address this issue. In 1995, UNHCR, the UN agency with the most expe-rience of working alongside the military, published a manual to facili-tate coordination between itself and the military in humanitarian oper-ations. Among other things, this sets out the need to establish Civil-Military Operations Centres (CMOCs) within military headquarters to provide easy access for aid agencies. UNHCR has also frequently sponsored military–aid agency conferences and similar joint events to discuss coordination issues and foster better understanding. While resisting joint operations, the ICRC has improved its contacts and cooperation with military establishments. In some countries the national Red Cross committees and the military have also established cooperation programmes. In the Nordic countries a number of NGOs have participated in peace-building exercises involving the military. In Italy a special school was started in 1995 for training civilians. The US Institute for Peace also trains civilian and military personnel, including NGOs, in conflict management. Similar arrangements also exist in other countries.

Within the literature, the difficulty of improving military–civilian cooperation is often put down to the very different cultures that the military and aid agencies represent (Zandee 1998: 48–50). Aid workers, for example, often regard the military as out of touch, bureaucratic and, in many cases, inappropriate. For their part, military actors see aid workers as undisciplined, disorganised and resistant to military co-ordination. While such views are often encountered, the issue is not one of attitude alone; it reflects a fundamental difference in the organisation, structure and purpose of the institutions concerned. Colonel Bob Stewart, commander of the first British deployment in Bosnia in 1992, has perceptively commented that

> The military are hierarchical, authoritarian, centralised, large and robust, while UNHCR is flat, consensus based with highly decentralised field offices which rely on a centralised logistics base. Hence while UNHCR could move their own point of main effort with speed and ease, the military on less light scales found once they were bedded down that it was less easy if not impossible to match such change. (quoted by Williams 1998: 36)

In many respects, the contrast between the flexibility of aid agencies and the rigidity of military establishments is fundamental. Travelling in Bosnia in the mid-1990s, one could not but marvel at the equipment, supplies and support networks needed to field even a modest number of troops. As with the multi-donor Rwanda evaluation of 1996, the recent military involvement in Kosovo has again raised the question of how efficient the army is in a humanitarian role. As one commentator has remarked, for every soldier that digs a latrine 'the number of other personnel to uphold the chain of command and provide security is considerable' (Grunewald and de Geoffrey 1999). The hierarchical and centralised structure of military forces derives from the demands of traditional interstate war. This structure, based on robust and self-contained forms of deployment and supported by secure supply chains, is geared, essentially, to fighting conventional wars. In adjusting to the new wars, perhaps the issue is not simply one of deepening civil–military coordination but, in effect, of the military becoming more like an aid agency in its manner of organisation and deployment. Such a radical reorganisation, however, is unlikely to happen. NATO's new Strategic Concept, published in April 1999, argues, for example, that large-scale conventional warfare, while a remote possibility at the moment, cannot be ruled out in the long term. Moreover, Russia still holds a formidable nuclear arsenal and the dangers of arms proliferation remain ever-present. It is in relation to conflicting needs – to maintain a conventional military capacity at the same time as developing a more flexible response to the new wars – that the increasing use of private security companies is likely to develop in the coming years.

Given that a radical debureaucratisation and decentralisation of military establishments is unlikely, the future for civil–military cooperation has been couched in terms of improved coordination and, in particular, better regulation of aid agency activities. Following the approach of the UNHCR, the future is seen to lie in agreeing areas of responsibility and establishing compatible communications, the formation of specialist liaison units, and so on. At the same time, military specialists have seen the development and growing support of voluntary codes of conduct among NGOs as a positive development (Williams 1998: 41; Zandee 1998: 63), indicating that NGOs are willing to accept limits to their behaviour and offering the possibility of introducing such codes into the civil–military interface.

The commercial sector

Regarding the incorporation of private companies within the strategic complexes of liberal peace, an important issue relates to the relative legitimacy and public exposure of the actors involved. Basically, while economic liberalisation and market deregulation have proceeded apace within the global economy, laws and conventions governing the activities of private companies remain largely rooted in territorial systems of legislation. Between the legitimate activities of well-established companies and the criminal pursuits of smuggling and fraudulent enterprise, there is an extensive grey area of opaque and unregulated business activity. This situation gives the commercial sector a distinct duality in relation to the new wars. Some private companies are joining the strategic complexes that support liberal peace. Others, usually smaller and adapted to exploit the opportunities of market deregulation, are key elements in the commodity chains that supply the new wars with arms, spare parts, fuel and all manner of strategic equipment and services. The commercial sector includes businesses that are assuming a regulatory role as part of their exposure and attempts to manage public opinion. At the same time, some private companies directly profit from war and operate as members of clandestine networks (see Chapter 7). Here we are concerned with the private sector as a partner of liberal peace. In terms of legitimate and regulatory activities, there are two factors relevant to this discussion: first, an emerging trend for large multinational companies to take on more direct development and security roles within their spheres of operation; and second, reflecting the privatisation of security within countries, the growth of private security companies having an international competence.

Multinational companies and security

Finding themselves within war zones, multinational companies have responded variously by pressuring the government concerned to exert greater control over internal security; by investing in private security; by paying expensive and often unethical war taxes; by paying off rebels directly; and, failing all else, by disinvesting (Friedman 1998: 16). While this mix of responses continues to be the norm, under pressure from public opinion some multinational companies are also slowly beginning to play a governance role in their own right. For example, during the 1980s the question of social responsibility and international business became a growing issue, especially in relation to the environment. More recently, this role has expanded to include human rights issues, especially regarding such things as child labour within manufacturing industries. Working together with NGOs like Amnesty International, a number of larger companies have adopted voluntary codes of conduct and incorporated industrial human rights standards within their charters. Following the decline in official development assistance and the simultaneous significant growth in private international investment flows, a new pressure on international business has also emerged. In addition to exercising governance through social responsibility, private companies are increasingly expected to use their resources and influence to play a more direct development and security role.

While the support of conflict resolution activities by multinational companies is still limited, a few emerging trends can be discerned. The UK-based Prince of Wales Business Leaders Forum, for example, was established in 1990 as an educational charity supported by major international companies from Europe, North America, Asia and the Middle East (PWBLF 1999). Some of its members, especially those engaged in the extraction of natural resources in such areas as the Caucasus, North

Africa, West Africa, Central America and Southeast Asia, have already had to adjust to the effects of conflict and political instability. Indeed, some of these are already contributing to various forms of rehabilitation or reconstruction activities, such as helping to maintain public infrastructure and supply systems in direct support of either the public authorities or NGOs.

> Conflict imposes high and often unpredictable costs on business – not least due to the demands of security and protection for employees, subcontractors and capital investment which are exposed to risk. A combination of higher standards being adopted by international business and heightened public anxiety and scrutiny of business practices has put the response to human rights challenges on the management agenda for many international companies. (*ibid.*: 209)

A few companies have reviewed their policies and practices in relation to conflict situations in order to improve management preparedness and accountability. Moreover, since the mid-1990s, a number of companies have begun to increase their collaboration with international development organisations such as donor agencies, the World Bank, UN institutions and NGOs. Conversely, such development agencies have also become increasingly interested in opening dialogue and developing greater collaboration with the business sector:

> within the past twelve months alone, the UN secretariat, UNHCR, UNHCHR, WHO and World Bank have initiated joint working with the Forum and others to engage business far more in their objectives, recognising past deficiency in their policy and experience in this area. (*ibid.*: 210)

The UK government's *White Paper on International Development* (DFID 1997), for example, made a commitment to work with the private sector in a new way – no longer in terms of tied aid or credit supports, but through efforts to use the skills and resources of the private sector in a more comprehensive manner.

> With British business, we will move away from a narrow relationship based on individual contracts to a broader sharing of approaches to the eradication of poverty, drawing on the extensive skills of the British private sector – consultants and contractors, investors, exporters and importers, business organisations, large companies and small firms. (*ibid.*: 44–5)

While still at an emergent stage, the linkages between the policy aims of development and security and the wider business sector are growing (Friedman 1998). In relation to zones of instability, major international companies with long-term capital investments such as, oil, gas, mining, major process industries (cement, chemicals, refining, etc.) and infrastructure (power, water, large buildings, etc.) are argued to have the greatest stake in long-term stability as well as having high exposure to public pressure (CRG 1997). For example, BP, Exxon, Mobil and Royal Dutch/Shell have operations in such places as Angola, Algeria, Peru, Colombia, Nigeria, Indonesia, Sri Lanka and the Democratic Republic of Congo. It is argued that such companies can contribute to conflict prevention and reconstruction in a number of ways. In their direct operations, they can ensure adequate risk assessment to identify any social issues to be addressed: the avoidance of bribery and corruption; contributing to human resource development in terms of education and training; supporting the local economy through subcontracting and local purchase policies; active engagement with business and local partners to raise business standards; and addressing security issues in a sensitive way to strengthen the rule of law and promote human rights (PWBLF 1999: 211). Companies can also operate community schemes to build local capacity and good community relations. This involves a variety of options including sharing of skills and know-how with public officials; support for civil society organisations; supporting community development partnerships; engagement in dialogue around conflict resolution and human rights issues; support for relief operations; and sharing of information and intelligence. A number of private initiatives drawing on this type of approach already exist: examples include Shell operations in the Camesia area of Peru, the Confederation of British Industry (CBI) and its Business Initiative for Peace in Northern Ireland, and BP's more recent involvement in Colombia. This commitment is emerging as part of a wider strategic network; it has been argued that private initiatives in the field of conflict resolution

> should be developed in consultation with a wide range of experts in the non-governmental world. NGOs with experience dealing with corporate policy, human rights, the environment, conflict, sustainable development, education and training, and negotiation and mediation will be invaluable partners for the private sector in the conflict prevention field. (Friedman 1998: 61)

Given the commitment of governments and NGOs to work more closely with the private sector, strategic networks linking such partners appear destined to grow and play an increasingly influential role. It should also be mentioned that the above discussion has related to large companies with conventional business interests. Over the past several years a new development has seen smaller private companies begin to challenge NGOs in terms of the provision of basic infrastructure and other relief services (Grunewald and de Geoffrey 1999). As current attempts at social reconstruction in Kosovo suggest, future complex emergencies are likely to include a growing mix of for-profit and non-profit organisations.

Private security companies

Since the 1980s private security companies have become a growing and accepted feature of life in the North. They now play a variety of roles, from guarding premises and cash transfers between banks to running prisons. Until recently, what has received less attention is that private security agencies have also become increasingly active at the international level. Although a few such companies have earlier origins, most have emerged since the beginning of the 1990s. Despite the important and innovative role that such companies are playing, private international security did not begin to attract much research attention until the mid-1990s (Pech and Beresford 1997). Even today, however, the area is relatively underresearched. The ambiguity of the corporate sector, especially in relation to the issue of legitimacy, has already been mentioned and is clearly manifest in relation to private security. Aware that a clear separation is difficult to make, Alex Vines (1999) has suggested distinguishing between private military companies (PMCs) and private security companies (PSCs). The former represent a major challenge to the state's traditional monopoly of armed violence. Consequently, they are often portrayed by commentators as occupying the illicit end of the scale. While many, such as the celebrated but now disbanded Executive Outcomes, claim to be professional organisations only providing services for recognised Southern governments (Harding 1997), their independence and association with actual warfare has raised issues of ethics, accountability and effectiveness (Vines 1999). Companies providing military assistance are examined in Chapter 7. Given the present focus on liberal peace, PSCs are of more interest here. These companies regard themselves as wholly within the realm of legitimate business and often perform security activities subcontracted by Northern governments or military establishments as a result of privatisation programmes – such as transport, guarding, catering, logistics and training duties (Dogon and Pugh 1997). In the South, providing training, security solutions and protection for embassies, international NGOs and multinational companies are typical activities. Where such private companies work in relation to Southern governments, it is usually as an extension of Northern foreign policy: providing army or police training, for example, as part of a formal assistance programme such as security sector reform.

Private military and security companies have expanded for a variety of reasons. The changing competence of nation states, the growth of privatisation, market deregulation and the post-Cold War and post-apartheid downsizing of military establishments have all contributed. The last factor, in particular, has released a ready supply of people with the necessary skills to meet the growing demand for private protection. Outside of South Africa, the base of the erstwhile Executive Outcomes, London is an important centre for the new commercial military and security companies, including Control Risks Group, Defence Services Limited (DSL), Sandline International and Saladin Security (Bazargan 1997). As Major General Stephen Carr-Smith of DSL, one of Britain's established international private security companies, explains

> Our clients include petrochemical companies, mining or mineral-extraction companies, multinationals, banks, embassies and so on. Very often the sort of 'first-in'-type companies that are trying to get things going. We provide them with a service which allows them to operate wherever they are. (*ibid.*: 2)

DSL was founded in 1981 and has 5,000 ex-military and security personnel on its database (only 100 of which are said to have access to firearms at any one time). In 1999, it was managing 130 contracts for 115 clients in 22 countries spread across South America, Africa and Southeast Asia (Vines 1999). The core employees mainly have a British special forces background. In the context of the new wars, DSL began providing security and logistics personnel to the UN mission in the former Yugoslavia in 1992. With over 450 personnel on the ground by 1995, it had become the largest contractor of its type. In 1997, when DSL was bought out by the US company Armor Holdings, its net revenue was in the region of $31.3 million. Apart from work with multinational companies and aid agencies, current commitments include contracts with the US State Department to provide security at high-risk embassies. DSL's areas of expertise include mining and oilfield security, provision of specialist manpower, guard force management, mine clearance, security and communication routes, threat assessment, crisis management and the provision of technical security equipment. While DSL regards itself as the establishment end of the private security spectrum, its operations have not been without controversy. In Colombia in the mid-1990s, for example, through a local subsidiary, DSL was involved in coordinating the defence of BP's oil infrastructure and personnel with the Colombian army and police. This resulted in charges of complicity following cases of human rights abuse by the Colombian authorities (*ibid.*: 73–4). Both companies have subsequently attempted to redress the situation.

The largest and best-known provider of private security in the US is a company similar to DSL, the Virginia-based Military Professional Resources Incorporated (MPRI). Founded in 1990, it is headed by retired senior military personnel. At the end of 1998, it had a turnover of $48 million and a core staff of 400 with a reserve pool of 7,000 ex-security personnel on its database. This reserve spans the entire military spectrum and includes over 200 former Generals and Flag officers (Cilliers and Douglas 1999). MPRI has emerged as a direct result of American military downsizing and privatisation. Given the size of the American military establishment, most of MPRI's work is within the US as a military subcontractor, engaging in such diverse activities as doctrinal development, force management, activity-based costing, training for active and reserve troops, Army Staff support, wargaming, equipment test and evaluation, and War College support. As with many defence industries, economies of scale have compelled MPRI to look to the international market to reduce cost. In 1998, for example, MPRI was managing 20 contracts worth more than $90 million. Of these, only three were international but together they accounted for roughly half of total income (*ibid*.: 113). As a result of the enhanced profitability of international work, MPRI has embarked on an aggressive external expansion programme.

MPRI, like most private security companies, claims not to get involved directly in military operations, so attempting to distinguish itself from such companies as Executive Outcomes. Its preferred role is that of advising, training and planning. As Cilliers and Douglas (1999) have argued, however, the distinction between training someone to use a gun and actually pulling the trigger is somewhat spurious. A defining characteristic of MPRI activities is that they are subject to US law and the company is required to obtain US government licences to cover its activities. Like other American businesses, MPRI regards itself as subject to federal and state laws. In this manner, those international contracts that it has obtained have been closely associated with US foreign policy, as in the case of the Democracy Transition Assistance Programme (DTAP) in Croatia. In March 1994 the Croatian government appealed to the US to help modernise its armed forces. The US government was sympathetic but, owing to the UN arms embargo on Croatia, it could not respond officially. MPRI was notified of the opportunity and, despite competition from other private security companies, won the contract on the basis of the Croatian government's belief that MPRI was the next best thing to the US military (*ibid*.: 115). DTAP was seen as a generic security sector reform programme for emerging democracies. It involves a wide-ranging training programme for officers,

NCOs and civilians within the Ministry of Defence in such areas as leadership, management and civil–military operations. Department of State licences for this programme were granted on the basis that such work was non-lethal. In August 1996, against competition from other companies, MPRI won a contract for a military stabilisation programme (MSP) to assist the Federation of Bosnia-Herzegovia Armed Forces (FAF). The aim of this broad-based training programme was to enable the FAF to field the new military equipment that it was also obtaining. This 'train and equip' project was run on behalf of the US State Department.

Regulation and private security

On the issues surrounding private military and security companies, opinion in the literature is divided. Some have suggested that those companies providing direct military services for Southern rulers, even outside the realm of donor control, can play a conflict resolution role (Shearer 1997). Using evidence from Southern and West Africa, compared to UN operations which tend to freeze the *status quo* and lock Northern governments into long-term support programmes, private military companies have managed to tip the balance in favour of incumbent rulers and so resolve conflict. In a similar vein, Pech and Beresford (1997) cite a British intelligence report on Executive Outcomes which claimed that the company was gaining a reputation for efficiency, especially with the rulers of smaller countries. Others have argued that such gains have usually been temporary and achieved using opaque and legally dubious methods. Moreover, private military companies are tantamount to an unregulated privatisation of war (Vines 1999; Herbst 1999; Cilliers and Cornwell 1999). It is not our intention to analyse this debate further save to remark that it should not be forgotten, as William Reno (1998) has shown, that incumbent rulers within weak state structures do face real internal security threats. They will attempt to meet these threats in whatever way they can. What is important here is that the debate is illustrative of a growing call for the regulation of all forms of international private security and protection.

Regarding the issue of legitimacy, both Vines (1999) and Herbst (1999) have made the useful observation that private security is expensive. Where private military companies have been able to claim success, they have usually been working for incumbent rulers with access to valuable natural resources that can be extracted and marketed relatively easily. In Africa, alluvial diamonds have been one commodity that has met this requirement during the 1990s. Without such commodities to form part of the payment, either directly or in the form of mining concessions, providing military services to weak state incumbents is a financially risky business. Both the former Executive Outcomes and its UK-based associate company Sandline International have sustained losses as a result, one example being the former's botched 1997 operation in Papua New Guinea. Few commodities can match the practicality of alluvial diamonds, and potential clients with access to such commodities are relatively thin on the ground. Tea, cocoa or coffee, for example, are unlikely to provide the revenue stream to sustain private protection, while copper, ferrochrome, gold or asbestos require the maintenance of a considerable extractive infrastructure. In such circumstances 'private security companies which want to have a sustained corporate identity will probably find the financial problems of dealing with failed states daunting' (ibid.: 124).

Both the former Executive Outcomes and Sandline International have made efforts to move into the more legitimate areas of security. Both, for example, have maintained that they are professional organisations and are not opposed to greater regulation in the security field (Vines 1999). Indeed, the dismantling of Executive Outcomes in January 1999 may well be part of a wider process of restructuring. Given the financial difficulties of working for weak state incumbents, there is also some speculation that competition will grow for the existing legitimate security business, with attempts also being made to break into new markets. In this respect, the large social reconstruction programmes in the Balkans, for example, offer new opportunities to provide security for the aid agencies and companies involved. Regarding the growing linkages with other strategic actors,

> One pot of gold that is tremendously appealing is to work for the UN itself, or other agencies that deliver aid out in the field, such as NGOs. UN officials, especially in UNHCR and the United Nations Children's Fund (UNICEF), are now exposed to unprecedented danger because they are working in failed states and are thus personally at risk. (Herbst 1999: 125)

The effective regulation of private security companies, however, is far from straightforward. To date, most attempts have been structured around the definition of a mercenary. According to the Additional Protocol 1 to Article 47 of the Geneva Convention, 1949, a mercenary is basically a foreigner who fights for private gain and, outside of this relationship, has no formal connection with any of the warring parties. A recent attempt to establish a regulatory mechanism based on such a definition is South Africa's enactment of the Regulation of Foreign Military Assistance Act in 1998. This Act aims to outlaw mercenary activity and regulate the provision of private military services abroad in a similar manner to the system for regulating arms exports. The Act, however, is widely regarded as being hastily drawn up and difficult to implement (Cilliers and Cornwell 1999). There are several problems regarding the standard definition of a mercenary, and past attempts to enforce similar legalisation in other countries have shown how difficult it is to prove a purely mercenary motivation in court. At the same time, under modern conditions, when the main asset of many private security companies is a database of names and contacts, they can operate from more or less anywhere there is a computer terminal. Following the scandal over Sandline's involvement in the supply of arms to Sierra Leone, the British Foreign Office has drawn up new guidelines covering official relations with security companies; at the time of writing, a Green Paper outlining legislative options for the control of such companies operating from UK territory is expected soon.

In many respects, the issue of future regulation appears a foregone conclusion. Security companies wishing to maintain their hold on the legitimate market, or break into it, are not opposed to legislation. At the same time, NGOs, multinational businesses and governments wishing to make more use of such companies will no doubt welcome effective regulation, which will allow the legitimate market to expand (Vines 1999: 80). Reflecting this mutual interest, DSL, for example, building on its existing work with NGOs, has already signed the International Federation of Red Cross Societies' agency code of conduct governing impartiality and accountability in humanitarian operations. While this is a voluntary code, it reflects an urge to establish legitimacy. For Northern governments, private security and even military companies are far too useful to outlaw altogether. The example of MPRI's training programme in Croatia, which the US government was able to support despite its own hands being tied by a UN arms embargo, is instructive in this respect. Private security companies are often able to do things that governments would prefer not to undertake. Moreover, when military intervention does occur, Northern politicians are increasingly aware of the negative public opinion that can arise from combat deaths in today's less formal conflicts. Astute security companies have realised that this mood is helping garner political support for an expanding rather than a declining role for themselves (Bazargan 1997). While Executive Outcomes casualty rates are confidential, in both Angola and Sierra Leone, for example, company deaths are said to have been in double figures. In other words, private casualties are much easier to bear than public ones. Finally, unlike during the Cold War, in most cases there is no need for such operations to be covert or hidden from

70

view. Through legislation and regulation and, especially, by tying them to development aims, they can be legitimised.

Multilateral and regional organisations

The end of the Cold War has produced a number of significant changes in the organisational structure and mandates of multilateral organisations. UN specialist agencies, for example, having their own institutional histories, organisational cultures and modes of funding, tended to operate independently in the past. The advent of complex emergencies and, especially, the demand for system-wide operations, has brought UN specialist organisations together in new ways and created pressures for better coordination. This requirement emerged clearly in the aftermath of the Gulf War and led to the creation at the end of 1991 of the UN's Department of Humanitarian Affairs (DHA – now OCHA) to better coordinate aid agencies in emergency situations. While improved inter-UN coordination has been the aim, in most complex emergencies this has remained problematic (Lautze, Jones and Duffield 1998). Some UN agencies have also seen their responsibilities grow and their mandates change during the 1990s. The UNHCR, for example, previously had responsibility for refugees, people forced to cross international boundaries for fear of harm or persecution in their home countries. It has now become the UN's principal humanitarian agency and, as we have seen, it has developed extensive operational links with the military. In some countries, it has also taken on responsibility for internally displaced people.

Regional organisations also became more significant during the 1990s. Reflecting similar pressures within the UN to improve coordination of humanitarian assistance, the EU, for example, established ECHO in 1993. ECHO has since become one of the main donors in the humanitarian field. Another multilateral organisation that has undergone significant change is the Organisation for Security and Cooperation in Europe (OSCE). In the early 1990s, a 'human dimension' was added to the 'economic dimension' of structural reform, leading the OSCE to emphasise the reform of internal relations, including support for human rights, civil society and democratisation. These were formally accepted as an essential complement to the economic modalities of the transitional agenda (OSCE 1995). The OSCE has since developed a much greater coordination and oversight responsibility in the Balkans. All of these organisations have been developing new linkages and ways of working with NGOs, military establishments and governments.

Donor governments

In this short review of the strategic actors and forms of governance networks that are emerging in pursuit of liberal peace, the position of governments has been left until last. While the political effect of globalisation has been to qualify and attenuate nation-state competence, it would be wrong overhastily to equate that attenuation with a growing weakness of states themselves. What is more certain is that the nature of state authority has changed and become more networked. New international and local actors have drawn out state authority and created numerous multi-levelled and cross-cutting decision-making processes. In relation to the strategic actors discussed above (NGOs, military establishments, commercial companies and multilateral organisations), governments have been closely involved in the organisational changes and networking that have been taking place. Rather than weakening *per se*, attenuation has been associated with the emergence of new linking institutions, modes of representation, contractual regimes, and so on. In this way, governments are acquiring the ability to project authority through non-territorial and non-state systems. Analysing this ability forms an important part of the following chapter.

With regard to development, for example, during the course of the 1990s government aid bureaucracies grew and changed their function in order to be able to participate more effectively within the emerging strategic complexes of state and non-state actors. With regard to the British aid department, DFID, for example, the number of professional advisers employed rose from 109 in 1990 to 237 by 1997, an overall increase of 117 per cent (DAG 1998: 12). Within this general rise, certain categories of professional adviser have grown significantly more than others. For example, social development advisers increased from 6 to 32 (433 per cent) and health and population advisers from 8 to 40 (400 per cent) over the same period. While this reflects the changing focus of Britain's development programme, it is also the case that extra people are required to support and service the emerging governance networks within which states, aid agencies and companies are now enmeshed. Among other things, the increased numbers of social and health advisers play a central implementing role in relation to the new contractual regimes governing NGOs that began to emerge during the early 1990s. In relation to the strategic networks of which they are now part, governments play a unique role. Among other things, their involvement is able to confer legitimacy on non-state actors and provide forms of access that might otherwise be denied. At the same time, governments control armed forces, the deployment of which is now increasingly related to the activities and fortunes of aid agencies and private companies alike. While overall development spending is falling, governments still control sizeable aid budgets, the spending of which is able to support many strategic actors and networks. From this perspective, it is not so much that the power of states has declined as a result of globalisation, but that governments are attempting to use their formal position and the resources they control to assert their authority in new ways. In relation to the new wars, Northern governments are pivotal players in the strategic complexes that constitute liberal peace.

Consensus and governance networks

The above review of the networks and linkages that are emerging between the strategic actors of liberal peace conveys some of the institutional depth and complexity that are involved in the move from government to governance. Given the numbers of actors, their conflicting motivations and histories, it is understandable that the key phrase of the past decade has been 'coordination'. Coordination is the modern-day philosopher's stone and, like its predecessor, it has proved elusive, despite the large amounts of money that donors have spent trying to find it. In the attempt to better coordinate strategic actors, voluntary codes of conduct and similar regulatory tools are playing an increasingly important role. Such codes can be seen as attempts to legitimise the new networks and relations that are emerging. In terms of motivating and drawing the strategic actors of liberal peace together, however, aid policy plays a key role. Within governance networks, shared policy assumptions are an important way in which different actors can communicate and coordinate their various activities. Without some degree of shared understanding as to what the nature of the problem is and how it should be tackled, governance networks would find it difficult, if not impossible, to operate. As a means of mobilising strategic complexes, policy now plays the role of politics within global governance.

The role of policy in allowing different networks to communicate is illustrated in the liberal consensus that now exists in relation to the causes of conflict and the methods of social reconstruction. While the actual implementation of such shared understanding is a different matter, at least the existence of common policy allows dialogue. The existence of such networks and the need for shared policy can be seen in what could be called the Scandinavian effect. During the 1960s and 1970s, Scandinavian aid policy was different from that of the rest of Western Europe. Scandinavian countries not only tended to give more aid, reflecting the strength of the social-democratic movements within them, they were also more likely to support progressive or radical policies – providing assistance, for example, to the national liberation struggles in Southern Africa and the Horn. At the time, this was facilitated by the absence of extensive aid bureaucracies, allowing the church and social democratic institutions a much more direct say in how aid was spent (Duffield and Prendergast 1994). This situation has now changed. Government development bureaucracies have grown. At the same time, on strategic matters, states have increasingly found that it is more effective to act together. Since state and non-state actors from a number of different territorial settings need to be able to communicate, one result has been that the aid policy of the Scandinavian countries in relation to conflict and social reconstruction is now little different from that favoured by their European neighbours. Indeed, the consensus-building activities of intergovernmental organisations such as the EU and OECD have constructed a broadly convergent and coherent policy position.

NOTES

1 For example, the 1992 Global Environment Conference in Rio de Janeiro; the 1993 Vienna Conference on Human Rights; and the 1995 Conference on Women in Beijing, at which 1,750 NGOs were accredited.
2 CARE International (Belgium), Caritas Internationalis (Vatican), International Federation for Red Cross and Red Crescent Societies [IFRC] (Switzerland), International Save the Children Alliance (UK), Lutheran World Federation [LWF] (Switzerland), Médecins sans frontières (MSF) International (Belgium), OXFAM International (UK) and the World Council of Churches [WCC], (Switzerland).
3 Examples are the Implementation Force (IFOR) and the Stabilisation Force (SFOR) in Bosnia. As with IFOR, SFOR continues to operate under Chapter VII (4) of the UN Charter and is structured and equipped to enforce compliance with the Dayton peace accords.

4

The New Humanitarianism

During the course of the 1990s, criticism of humanitarian action in conflict situations has sharpened. In particular, the charge that it often has unintended consequences – indeed, can actually fuel or facilitate war – has struck a popular chord. Towards the end of the 1990s, a new or political humanitarianism emerged, claiming to correct the wrongs of the past. Rather than humanitarian assistance as a universal right and a good thing in itself, the new humanitarianism is based on a consequentialist ethical framework. Assistance is conditional on assumptions regarding future outcomes: especially, it should do no harm, nor should it entrench violence while attempting to ameliorate its effects. In this respect, the new humanitarianism reinforces earlier policy commitments to linking relief and development, conflict resolution and societal reconstruction. The new humanitarianism reflects a willingness to include the actions and presence of aid agencies within an analytical framework of causal and consequential relations. At first glance, it appears to break with the established tradition of apolitical development discourse, a discursive structure in which the presence and power of the technocrat is hidden, so to speak, by the conceit of defining all problems as technical in origin. This appearance is reinforced by the ready adoption of the term 'political' to define humanitarian action and by the argument that neutrality is impossible in the new wars, since any assistance necessarily has political effects. This chapter examines this position and finds the appearance of a break with established discourse illusory. The apparent willingness to embrace politics actually involves a reduction and constraining of its meaning. For the new humanitarianism, politics is confined to the policy choices of aid agencies. In other words, politics has been conflated with policy. The argument that humanitarian aid fuels conflict, whether right or wrong, has the important effect of confirming the technical power of aid in relation to receiving systems still perceived as reactive mechanical objects. If aid has the ability to entrench wars, it follows that in the right hands it can also end them. Rather than being a way of addressing complex and mutating systems, political humanitarianism represents a restatement of technocratic authority in a mechanical universe.

Requiem for the prophets

In 1984 the harrowing TV pictures of famine in Ethiopia unleashed an unprecedented surge of humanitarian concern and popular mobilisation throughout Europe. In Britain, through the efforts of media celebrities such as Bob Geldof, the Band Aid trust was formed. By raising public awareness through popular songs and international music events, Band Aid eventually raised £174 million for famine relief in Africa before its closure in 1987. With the rigidities of the Cold War beginning to wane, it represented a populist form of anti-establishment politics. The public mood that it caught was that politicians, bureaucrats and official aid programmes were a major part of the problem. Reflecting this feeling, Geldof made the 'Sayings of the Week' spot in the *Observer* when he railed against delays: 'I'm not interested in the bloody system! Why has he no food? Why is he starving to death?' (Geldof 1985). In a world of plenty, public opinion in Europe was morally affronted by the images of death and want coming out of Ethiopia and Sudan. Moreover, many ordinary people were mobilised to do something about it. Besides making unprecedented donations to famine relief organisations, EU food mountains and milk lakes were picketed; public vigils were held; newspaper columns vented their outrage; politicians were bombarded with protest letters; and radio and TV programmes echoed with expressions of concern. Famine not only highlighted gross inequalities in global wealth and affluence, it also demonstrated the seeming indifference of governments and UN agencies. Using its publicly donated funds, when red tape threatened to hold up famine relief, Band Aid rented its own trucks and chartered its own aircraft. Such actions not only shamed donor governments but also gave substance to the view that humanitarian assistance was a universal and unconditional right.

In discussing humanitarian action, Hugo Slim (Slim 1998), using the analogy of religion, makes the useful distinction between prophecy and priesthood; the difference between the two lies in the tension between faith and organisation. The prophet 'confronts society with a truth and

76

is concerned with personal, social and political transformation' (*ibid.*: 29). The priesthood, however, is more concerned with maintaining the truth through enshrined ritual, standards of purity, membership and worship. In terms of humanitarian action, the priesthood is embodied in the International Committee of the Red Cross. As for the prophets, the public reaction in Europe to the famines in Ethiopia and Sudan during the mid-1980s gave a great moral and financial boost to aid agencies delivering emergency relief. A period of rapid growth and increasing influence of NGOs engaged in emergency operations began. During the latter part of the 1980s, such NGOs found themselves at the forefront of a movement that put the saving of lives above any political consideration or bureaucratic constraint. Not only was humanitarian aid a universal right, its neutrality placed it beyond politics. Indeed, politics both caused wars and famines and, at the same time, created delays and bureaucratic difficulties that hampered the relief of suffering. In retrospect, this mood was very much in tune with the rapidly approaching end of the Cold War. In the war-torn Horn of Africa, for example, international respect for Ethiopian and Sudanese sovereignty had been sufficient to dissuade the UN and most international NGOs from working in rebel areas where human suffering also existed (Duffield and Prendergast 1994). Placing humanitarianism above politics, as a right in itself, became a compelling critique of the inhumanity of the rigidities of the Cold War and of its suffocating political etiquette. For this reason, apart from saving lives, a neutral humanitarianism appeared radical and progressive; at the same time, it had widespread public support.

The growing pressure by increasingly influential NGOs for cross-line relief interventions helped shape developments immediately following the end of the Cold War. As early as April 1989, with the formation of the UN-led Operational Lifeline Sudan (OLS), a new phase of neutral, negotiated-access relief programmes working across the lines in ongoing conflicts emerged. These system-wide programmes not only brought UN organisations and NGOs together in new ways, they were based on the UN securing the agreement of warring parties to allow impartial aid agencies to provide humanitarian assistance to war-affected populations, irrespective of their location. This represented a major opportunity for the expansion of relief agencies. Taking a lead from OLS, in 1990 similar UN-led negotiated-access programmes were established in Ethiopia and Angola. Following the Gulf War in 1991, these neutral humanitarian operations were increasingly seen as a graphic expression of the changing priority accorded sovereignty within the new international system. Not only were military establishments joining the strategic complexes of an emerging global governance, a New World Order that included a right to humanitarian assistance for a while appeared to be in the realm of the possible. International intervention under UN auspices in Bosnia and Somalia in 1992 and the creation of the UN's Department of Humanitarian Affairs (DHA) strengthened such convictions.

As the mid-1990s approached, however, following the setbacks in Somalia and the increasing difficulties in Bosnia, a different view began to take shape. The insistence that humanitarian intervention was good in itself and required little, if any, justification began to be questioned. In many respects, while attempting to hold itself above politics, the prophetic movement to save lives at all costs had become a victim of its own political success. It started as a radical opposition that gathered its strength in relation to the political rigidities of the Cold War. In this respect, initially the UN system was seen as the epitome of all that was unacceptable and corrupt. This did not prevent the same system quickly incorporating the principles of a neutral humanitarianism as soon as the international climate was conducive. Although powerless to end wars, during the early part of the 1990s, through negotiated access and establishing new strategic relations with aid agencies and military establishments, the UN attempted to develop new ways of providing humanitarian assistance to all war-affected populations (Duffield 1997). The ill-fated 'safe area' policies of the time were part of this attempt. At the same time, whereas politicians had been placed on the defensive by the populism of the mid-1980s, by the early 1990s they had learnt how to harness the humanitarian juggernaut together with the media exposure and influence that it brought. When President Mitterrand travelled to Saravejo in June 1992 and publicly declared the lifting of the Serb siege with the opening of the airport for UN relief flights, it was a piece of political theatre that well reflected the prevailing accommodation. Many European politicians, such as Bernard Kouchner (France), Jan Pronk (Netherlands) and David Owen (UK), together with international figures like ex-US President Jimmy Carter, placed their names and careers in the service of humanitarian intervention. At the same time, a number of European aid departments, including Britain's Overseas Development Administration (ODA), for a while at least, would become more directly involved in humanitarian operations (ODA 1991). When the European Commission Humanitarian Office (ECHO) was established in 1993, its brief was not only to coordinate EU emergency assistance better, but also to develop an operational capacity of its own.

The incorporation of a neutral humanitarianism within a UN-led international relief system during the early 1990s gave it an institutional framework for its realisation. Simultaneously, however, its prophetic values were undermined and compromised. The new post-Cold War UN-led humanitarian operations were very different from those of the past. During the Cold War, the UN rarely intervened in ongoing conflicts. Its preferred mode of operation was to police ceasefires already agreed between warring parties (Goulding 1993). UN-led negotiated-access programmes represented a radical and profound break with tradition. They were radical in that earlier restrictions against working in non-government areas were either overcome or greatly reduced. At the same time, however, and more worryingly, work in unresolved and unstructured wars could also be seen as reflecting a new international system that was now either unable or unwilling to end conflict. Indeed, such a commitment appeared to suggest that Northern governments were now prepared to accept insta-bility and violence as part of a generic Southern predicament (Kaplan 1994). Humanitarian assistance, while still regarded as necessary, was increasingly seen a substitute for the concerted political action that was the real requirement (Higgins 1993). From being a radical aim, human-itarian assistance began to assume the form of a lowest international common denominator in the context of operations that, through experi-ence, were being redefined as long-term and politically complex. In the absence of a clear political resolve to end conflict, humanitarian assis-tance could even be seen as counter-productive. For example, in pro-viding transport and shelter, aid agencies in Bosnia were often accused of facilitating the very ethnic cleansing they abhorred.

In the absence of clear and unequivocal international structures working effectively for peace, the idea of a neutral humanitarianism able to stand above politics became increasingly strained in the seemingly intractable conflicts of the 1990s. In this respect, the strategic complexes of liberal governance do not provide such a system. Liberal peace is a contested and regionally differentiated reality that, through its fluid and changing networks, is capable of marked hierarchies of concern. At the same time, through an exposure to ongoing conflict, aid agencies began to deepen their understanding of the interaction between aid and war and the complexities involved. While external assistance is capable of playing many roles (one should not overestimate the effec-tiveness of aid in this respect), it was increasingly understood as being far from neutral. Humanitarian assistance, while it could help keep people alive, like any other resource inevitably became part of the local political economy (Duffield 1991; Keen 1991) – especially when the new wars have effectively dissolved conventional distinctions between people, army and government. In other words, in today's network wars the traditional distinctions – 'military/civilian', 'combatant/non-combatant', etc. – that a neutral humanitarianism ideally would base itself on, no longer properly exist. While wishing to stand above politics, prophetic humanitarianism inevitably has been drawn in – network war does not countenance neutrality – and been compromised through its encounter. It has fallen victim to a world in which the competence and authority of nation states have changed radically.

Faced with the prospect of long-term relief operations, which many saw as a contradiction in terms, by the mid-1990s certain strategic actors had developed a direct criticism of humanitarian assistance. This criticism tended to avoid the fact that the international community had crossed the Rubicon of undertaking work in ongoing conflicts while, at the same time, failing to develop an effective means of resolving the wars in which it was now enmeshed. Instead, the critical message was that humanitarian assistance itself was part of the problem. Despite its good intentions, it had many unforeseen consequences, some of which entrenched conflict and made it more difficult to resolve. For example, among rural communities, free food aid could lower agricultural prices and so deter farmers from planting. Far from helping them, this would reinforce their dependence on aid agencies. At the same time, through diversion, looting and informal taxing by warring parties, relief supplies themselves could become part of a self-sustaining war economy. In other words, humanitarian assistance was capable of entrenching the modalities of underdevelopment and conflict (UNDP 1994). As well as doing good, humanitarian aid is also capable of doing harm (Anderson 1996). Such criticisms have been very influential in shaping aid policy since the mid-1990s. Rather than having the saving of life as its overriding and prophetic concern, a new humanitarianism has emerged that bases actions (or inaction) on the assumed good or bad consequences of a given intervention in relation to wider developmental aims (Slim 1997). This new or principled humanitarianism complements the radicalisation of development which now sees the role of aid as altering the balance of power between social groups in the interests of peace and stability. From saving lives, the shift in humanitarian policy has been towards analysing consequences and supporting social processes.

The new humanitarianism is a genuine, if particular, response to the complexity of the new wars. A concern with consequences and processes has to be part of any reappraisal. What is important in understanding its particularity, however, is not so much the practical veracity of the new development-oriented humanitarianism – whether it will be any more successful than the regime it has replaced – as its implications for liberal governance. A concern with limiting harmful consequences while encouraging beneficial processes demands new forms of surveillance, appraisal and monitoring if desired outcomes are to be achieved. If politicians had come to terms with humanitarian assistance in the early 1990s, then very soon the official aid departments they controlled would have begun the task of creating new forms of management and regulation with which to enmesh their subcontracting and implementing partners. While sidestepping the issue that Northern governments have yet to create an international structure that can enforce peace, the view that humanitarian aid entrenches underdevelopment and conflict has motivated a thickening of the governance relations linking donors and aid agencies. Gathering momentum with the debate on relief and development, more detailed and demanding contractual agreements have emerged highlighting the need to avoid harmful consequences; the number of social advisers within official aid departments has increased, allowing donors to be more closely involved with NGOs in project design and policy implementation; more rigorous forms of project monitoring and appraisal have emerged; the number of consultative mechanisms and joint policy fora has increased; finally, since the consequences of assistance are important, new forms of surveillance and aid impact assessment are being created (Pankhurst 1999). Through the deepening of such governance relations, Northern donors have regained the policy initiative that was lacking during the latter part of the 1980s and early 1990s. In other words, compared to the prophetic years of humanitarian action, they have learnt how to consolidate and project their authority through the non-territorial and differentiated networks of global liberal governance.

The aftermath of the 1994 genocide in Rwanda and, especially, the controversy surrounding the Hutu refugee camps in what is now Eastern Congo and their eventual fate, are seen by many aid agencies as the nadir of a neutral and universal humanitarianism (Fox 1999). If the sentiments that lay behind the formation of Band Aid coalesced in the arid highlands of Ethiopia, in little over a decade they unravelled in the rainforests of the Congo. Paying little heed to what UNHCR and NGOs had been saying and trying to do, many strategic actors concluded that the aid agencies' response to the plight of the Hutu refugees crystallised everything that was wrong with humanitarian assistance. By helping to feed and shelter the refugees, NGOs and the UN were also supporting the vicious killers that lived among them and, at the same time, allowing their destabilisation of Rwanda to continue. Whereas over 150 NGOs had flocked to the sprawling and unsanitary refugee camp at

Goma in 1994, a year later their number had dropped to five following a barrage of international criticism and the collapse of donor confidence. When an alliance of regional forces exacted its own violent retribution on the Hutu refugees in 1997, despite the evidence of serious human rights abuse and appeals by aid agencies, the international community was in no mood to intervene. These events set the tone for the present period of humanitarian conditionality and regionally differentiated patterns of intervention. They also mark the great distance that has been travelled since the mid-1980s.

Where once relatively independent aid agencies were able to mobilise public concern through the media and put politicians on the spot, we now have a situation in which Northern governments have regained initiative and control of the humanitarian agenda. Through a complex transition involving the professionalisation of aid and the emergence of new forms of regulation, politicians are able to argue that the excesses of the past are no longer acceptable or necessary. At the same time, public opinion, while never to be underestimated, appears more disengaged. Not only has an interest in things international declined in the media, but politicians have shown themselves increasingly adept at managing the news from disaster zones (Hilsum 1997). Indeed, since Bosnia, rather than simply having to react to the next emergency, they have shown that, if necessary, they can sit it out (Hurd 1993). This is the political environment of the new humanitarianism. While prophetic humanitarianism may have been naïve and the agencies involved made many mistakes, one cannot help feeling uneasy about the new accommodation and its willingness to sacrifice lives today on the promise of development tomorrow.

From cosmic machines to living systems

Since the mid-1990s, the acceptance by donor governments, IGOs, UN agencies and NGOs of the necessity of conflict resolution and post-war reconstruction embodies, at least in policy terms, a commitment to transform societies as a whole. This represents a break with the past when development was something that was seen as following of its own accord from economic growth and investment. Given the related reproblematisation of security in term of underdevelopment becoming dangerous, development is now something that cannot be left to chance. In its encounter with the new wars, development discourse is regarded by many as having been politicised. This politicisation, however, is not exhausted by a commitment to radical social change. It relates to what appears to be a major change in the nature of development discourse

82

itself. Where relations of power and privilege were hidden in the past, to some extent (and under a new framework of conditions) they have now been revealed.

Arturo Escobar (1995) has analysed the depoliticised and technicised nature of development discourse. The apolitical structure of this discourse has remained essentially unchanged since its outline was first sketched during the late 1940s and early 1950s (*ibid.*: 42). Its technicist form was analogous to the framing of the South as if it were a picture. For the viewing subject (the development professional) it involved experiencing life as if he or she was set apart and unconnected with the framed object. The observing professional was absent from the encounter with the picture, as if the viewing took place from a position that was set aside and hidden. This ideological illusion made it possible to satisfy the double demand of participant observation: that is, for the viewing subject both to be detached and objective and, at the same time, to interact with the object. The framing of the South in this way also involved a medicalisation of the gaze. The popular classes were no longer seen in racial terms, as in the colonial period, but through the more modern categories of want and scarcity in relation to health, education, nutrition, capacity, and so on. Rather than a benign indifference, such characteristics now warranted unprecedented social action. In initiating this action, development discourse presented itself as a detached centre of rationality and intelligence; it was a matter of analysis and judgement for the development professional. Questions regarding the relations of power and inequality that underpinned the encounter, that is, the politics of development, were absent since they were not seen as relevant (*ibid.*: 47–52). Development discourse was a way of conceptually transforming social life into a series of discrete technical problems open to professional solutions.

This apolitical discourse has come under pressure from a number of directions, not least from those NGOs that have sought to make the views of the framed object heard above those of the viewing professional (Chambers 1983) and the growing influence of gendered analysis. At the same time, while change has occurred at some levels, development discourse is not a single or unified structure. It is embedded in many different networks and discrete systems. While there has been some adaptation along the border with the new wars, in more tranquil or abstract areas of development, for example within economic orthodoxy, the technicised discourse outlined above is still clearly recognisable. It is not only conflict, however, that has challenged the apolitical nature of development discourse. For some time, from what are known as the complexity sciences, a different view of the world to which development subscribes has slowly been emerging (Dillon 2000). The work of Fritjof Capra (1982) remains a useful introduction to this body of knowledge. Since the mid-twentieth century, the complexity sciences such as quantum theory, non-linear mathematics, biotechnology, micro-biology and cybernetics have been challenging and replacing the Newtonian world view that has held sway for several hundred years. The scientific revolution completed by Isaac Newton bequeathed to us a view of the cosmos as a vast and perfect clockwork machine governed by exact mathematical laws. Within this giant cosmic machine everything can be determined and reduced to a scientific cause and effect. The material particles that make it up, and the laws of motion and force that hold or repel them, are fixed and immutable. Set in motion at the birth of the cosmos, this huge mechanical machine has been running ever since (*ibid.*: 52). Newtonian physics has had great success and produced many discoveries that have since been absorbed into everyday life. By the mid-twentieth century, however, the Newtonian world view had been superseded. From quantum theory, for example, what Capra calls a new physics has emerged. Rather than mechanical precepts, this is based on organic, holistic and ecological principles. What is in question is not a mechanism made up of many different basic parts, but a unified whole made up from the many relations between its parts. Quantum theory, for example, does not deal with 'things' but 'interconnections'. 'As we penetrate into matter, nature does not show us any isolated basic building blocks, but rather appears as a complicated web of relations between the various parts of a unified whole' (*ibid.*: 70). The new physics is based on a shift from objects to relations as the object of study. Within this world view, the whole determines the parts, including the perceptions and actions of the observing scientist. In this respect, nothing is value-free, not even science (*ibid.*: 76–7; Rabinow 1996). This has led to a social and political divergence within both theoretical and applied science. Writing at a time when nuclear annihilation was a real possibility, Capra described this divergence as that between the Buddha and the Bomb. Updating this position to the dawn of the twenty-first century, it could be described as being between Gaia and Monsanto.

The new physics has reconceptualised matter as not inert but vibrant and dancing. It studies relationships and interconnections because there are no static structures; relations themselves are forms of exchange. Based on this changed world view, Capra has defined himself as a systems theorist: 'Systems are integrated wholes whose properties cannot be reduced to those of smaller units. Instead of concentrating on basic building blocks or basic substances, the systems approach emphasises basic principles of organisation' (Capra 1982: 286). From this per-spective, a number of useful distinctions can be made between 'machines' and 'systems'. Machines are controlled and determined by their structure and characterised by linear chains of cause and effect. They are constructed from well-defined parts that have specific functions and tasks. Systems, on the other hand, are analogous to organisms. They grow and are process-oriented. Their structures are shaped by this orientation and, since processes change, they can exhibit a high degree of internal flexibility. Systems are characterised by cyclical patterns of information flow, feedback loops, non-linear inter-connections and self-organisation within defined limits of autonomy. Moreover, using the analogy of an organism, a system is concerned with self-renewal. This is important, since while a machine carries out specific and predictable tasks, a system is primarily engaged in a process of renewal and, if necessary, self-transformation (*ibid.*: 293). Reflecting on this difference, the following chapter on how strategic actors understand the new wars argues that the dominant perspective is essentially Newtonian and machine-like in conception. In this respect, it is interesting that the approach by aid agencies to conflict resolution and societal reconstruction is precisely that of attempting to close down one machine so that another can be 'kick-started' into life (World Bank 1997b). In distinction, chapters 6 and 7 on transborder shadow economies and the political relations of network war attempt to provide a systems analysis of the complexity involved.

The politicisation of development discourse

Living systems are multi-levelled structures and each level can differ in its complexity. Each level represents an integrated whole and has a degree of relative autonomy from the others. This is the pervasive mode of organisation in nature and is a feature of self-organisation. It also reflects the organisational characteristics of network war. While origi-nating in the complexity sciences, since the 1970s systems analysis has entered the public realm through such applications as environmental science and the ecology movement. Within social studies, a systems approach, that is, attempting to look at the interconnections within a given structure in a holistic fashion, can also be seen in the growing interest in ethical studies over the past couple of decades. In relation to development studies, however, reflecting the apolitical nature of the discourse involved, until very recently a concern with ethics and the role of the development expert has been absent. One of the leading figures in this field, Des Gasper, has argued that even the major works on development assistance produced during the 1980s were 'philo-sophically innocent' in this respect (Gasper 1999: 27).

The view of the causes of conflict and refugee flows that emerged during the early 1980s adopted an apolitical multi-causal approach. That is, it represented population displacement as arising from the interplay of poverty, resource competition and weak and unrepresentative institutions. The initial formulations of what constituted a complex emergency followed this basically technicist template. When the UN's Department of Humanitarian Affairs was set up at the end of 1991, one radical recommendation had been for the creation of a Department of Humanitarian Affairs and Human Rights. The argument for this was that large-scale population displacement and human rights abuse were linked organically (Cutts 1998). However, in what now seems perverse given the recent incorporation of the language of rights within development thinking, the General Assembly resolution setting up DHA drew back from making the link with human rights. Instead, the brief of DHA was mainly administrative and included disaster prevention and preparedness, the organisation of consolidated appeals, providing coordination in emergencies and ensuring a timely move from relief to development work. Reflecting this technical mandate, complex emergencies were understood in terms of large-scale social breakdown and population displacement (caused by conflict arising for multi-causal reasons) and demanding a coordinated system-wide response. Indeed, it is only since the mid-1990s that it has been accepted within the international community at large to refer to complex emergencies as complex *political* emergencies. Pointing out this obvious connection at the time was seen as radical (Duffield 1994b).

The main reason for the politicisation of development discourse has been its encounter with the new wars. As Gasper has argued,

> the deep causes and catastrophic consequences of 'complex emergencies' have demanded attention in development studies, including development ethics. Enormously difficult emergency situations have raised exceptional moral demands and confusion. Aid agencies, unwilling or unable to respond politically to political emergencies, appear to have become integrated as resource providers into processes of violence and oppression. (Gasper 1999: 27)

It is a testimony to the insular and hidebound nature of the development profession that, as system analyses have been developing in other disciplines, it has taken an encounter with widespread and systemic violence to challenge its apolitical narrative. Even then, however, the politicisation of development discourse is far from unequivocal and, as will be argued below, has been achieved at the expense not of killers with guns but of the humanitarian ideal itself. It is against humanitarian agencies, and through them the victims of violence, that donor governments have flexed their political muscle.

In relation to the new wars, one could describe complexity in terms of their dissolving the conventional distinctions between people, army and government. In this respect, they exhibit a similar complexity to the strategic complexes of liberal peace with which they conjoin and articulate. It was in relation to conventional distinctions, and the state-based legal and international system that upheld them, that classic humanitarianism emerged. While these distinctions had substance, even if in reality they were continually compromised, the ICRC could reasonably ground its views on neutrality and restraint in war. However, in the encounter with the new complexity of contemporary conflict, the question of neutrality has come under increasing attack. Indeed, its very *possibility* and *usefulness* have been strongly questioned in relation to the new wars. When people, army and governments are interconnected rather than divided, it is difficult to be neutral within such a system. This is reinforced when, as a result of these interconnections, people themselves are often deliberate targets. At the same time, again because of the interconnections involved, even if people themselves are not being targeted, humanitarian actions can have unwanted and unanticipated consequences. They could make things worse rather than better (Anderson 1996). Closely related to this view is the insistence that humanitarian action by its very essence is political (Weiss 1999b; Cutts 1998). This is shown in the way that assistance is mobilised, the decisions surrounding who gets what, the compromises that obtaining access may entail and, not least, the consequences beyond intention that may result. Making choices in this context is regarded as necessarily a political act.

As Mark Cutts (1998) has pointed out, we need not accept the implied dichotomy, in much of the debate on humanitarian action, between politics as bad (or at least ambiguous) and humanitarianism as good (if problematic). Politics also has a legitimate concern with the relief of suffering, the restoration of peace and securing justice. At the same time, some humanitarian actions undoubtedly can do harm. From this perspective, that is, the blurring of humanitarian action and politics, it is possible to argue that while some critics have objected that humanitarian intervention is a substitute for political action (Higgins 1993), it is in fact *that very action* (Cutts 1998). Another way of looking at this is to regard the contested, regionally differentiated and pronounced hierarchies of concern that humanitarian operations currently exhibit as being *as good as it gets* in term of the politics of intervention. As Thomas Weiss has argued, it will not do 'to long for another era or pretend the bases for decisions are unchanged' (Weiss 1999b: 9). The blurring of humanitarian action and politics is a reflection of the general merger of development and security. Moreover, within the new humanitarianism, with its emphasis on using humanitarian action to help resolve conflicts and reconstruct war-torn societies, the politicisation of aid is made complete. In attempting to use the aid regime in this manner, one could well argue, donor governments are expecting a child to do the job of an adult. This is especially the case in regions where, while stability is desired, no significant strategic or economic goals are being pursued. However, aid is no *substitute* for political action because it *is* the political action. It is now a tool of international regulation and is embedded in the networks and strategic complexes that make up liberal peace.

The demise of operational neutrality

The prophetic tradition of humanitarian action gained strength in the mid-1980s and helped shape the initial post-Cold War accommodation. The difficulties of securing neutrality and maintaining impartiality, however, are very real. Not only does the complexity of the new wars work against these principles, but donor governments have also shifted policy in the direction of more distinctly political if regionally differentiated forms of engagement. The humanitarian ideal is clearly confronting a very different system to that of the past (Slim 1999). In understanding the initial response of humanitarian agencies to the complexities of operating in war zones, Cutts makes the useful distinction between the contested neutrality of the actual encounter and the 'operational neutrality' that agencies attempt to construct to enhance the perception of neutrality (Cutts 1998: 7). Even today, for example, UNHCR officially insists that its actions are neutral and impartial. While there is plenty of evidence to the contrary, it would be hard to deny that such a view is both politically and diplomatically useful for the organisation. Reflecting this position, the first system response to complexity was for aid agencies to attempt to entrench the principles of operational neutrality. By 1994, for example, three sets of voluntary guidelines, two American and one European, for relief agencies operating in conflict zones had emerged. The first was the Providence Principles (1993) from the Humanitarianism and War Project at Brown University. These were followed by the Mohonk Criteria for Humanitarian Assistance in Complex Emergencies (1994), produced by the World Conference on

Religion and Peace and, in Europe, the Code of Conduct (1994) produced by the International Red Cross and Red Crescent Movement (Slim 1997: 4). By 1999, over 150 agencies and 150 countries had signed up to the Code of Conduct, committing themselves to high standards of independence and effectiveness. Such voluntary principles and codes do not contradict the argument that neutrality is contested and aid is political. In fact, their emergence is best explained against the background of this reality. They are an attempt by aid agencies, through agreeing common standards and positions, to create a humanitarian space within a complex and often hostile environment.

During the first half of the 1990s, while actual neutrality may have been a fiction, operational neutrality did have some practical success. Even the apolitical narrative of the multi-causal complex emergency had its uses. Describing conflict as resulting from multiple causes, while analytically of limited use, was nevertheless a useful tool of practical diplomacy. In negotiating humanitarian access with warring parties, for example, it provided a neutral language through which one could talk about war and the need to address its effects without apportioning blame (Duffield 1994b). While constituting a huge ethical and political minefield, when it worked and access was secured it could at least be accepted as a lesser of evils. In this respect, while always fragile, it supported practical access in much of Africa and the Balkans during this period. An interesting reflection of both its success as a diplomatic device and the ethical issue raised is its adoption by the Sudanese government, which several times has deflected criticism of its human rights record on the grounds that it too is a victim of a multi-causal 'complex emergency' (Karim et al. 1996). At the same time, however, what success could be attributed to operational neutrality was, in the last analysis, dependent on the will of donor governments to maintain the political space on which it depended – an overarching political framework within which warring parties could be encouraged to consent. While contested and fraught with contradictions, the necessary international will existed to a greater extent during the first half of the 1990s than since this period. Its clearest expression was the international support for the UN-led system-wide humanitarian operations that, for a while, existed in Africa and the Balkans.

In general, in relation to global governance the political repercussions of these system-wide operations have been negative. As a result there has been a growing reluctance within the international community to provide a collective political umbrella for such operations. In some areas like Africa, the national interests of different Northern governments have also come to the fore, making consensus building difficult (Adelman, Suhrke and Jones 1996; Brusset 2000). At the same time, as already described, the general mood in relation to humanitarian action has become more sceptical. In this changing international climate, maintaining operational neutrality is increasingly difficult. However, this has not prevented agencies continuing to develop such structures. In 1996, for example, the Sphere Project was launched following a critical multi-donor evaluation of the international response to the genocide in Rwanda. In this case, the concern related to the variable professional standards among NGOs. The Sphere Project, which brings together a number of large NGO networks, aims to produce a global set of minimum standards for humanitarian response services (Gostelow 1999). In order to improve accountability, in 1997 a project to establish an Ombudsman for Humanitarian Assistance (HAO) was also established (Mitchell and Doane 1999). In a number of countries, such as Liberia (Leader 1999), Sudan (Levine 1997) and Somalia (Duffield 2000), as the international appetite for system-wide operations began to decline, aid agencies have tried to develop their own local agreements with warring parties in an unconvincing attempt to maintain a humanitarian space. In Africa's Great Lakes region, in the absence of sustained or coherent international backing, the effective coordination of humanitarian operations has largely passed to the warring parties in many places (Lautze, Jones and Duffield 1998). It is they who decide when and where humanitarian agencies operate and, consequently, who receives assistance.

The rise of consequentialist ethics

Within the *de facto* post-UN international regime that emerged in the latter half of the 1990s, not only have new forms of international governance come to the fore (Weiss 1998), but NGOs and humanitarian organisations have been forced beyond operational neutrality in their encounter with complexity. Agencies have had to address more directly the contested neutrality and political nature of their actions. At the same time, despite the growing fashion for rights-based approaches at the level of policy, in many operating environments agencies have had to adjust to what is in effect a legal vacuum (Slim 1997). Much of the criticism of humanitarian action has come from an ethical perspective – questioning, for example, the ethics of striving to be neutral in places like Bosnia, Sudan and Rwanda when civilians are being deliberately targeted (Donini 1995; de Waal 1997). This situation, moreover, is compounded when humanitarian action itself can be construed as deepening the problem, as in the example cited earlier of providing transport and shelter for ethnically cleansed populations and thereby, arguably, facilitating the process. While the ethics of neutral humanitarian action have become a basis of criticism, developing a counter-ethic has formed the basis of the present accommodation. The new humanitarianism is variously described as 'ethical', 'principled', 'rights-based' or 'political'. It arises from the 'bankruptcy of neutrality' and, consequently, accepts all the moral dilemmas, quandaries and hard choices that follow from this (Weiss 1999b). The intention is not to be immobilised or to become fatalistic in the face of the difficult choices involved. On the contrary, the aim is to develop systematic methods of prioritising problems, judging one's responsibility and analysing outcomes in order to make the best decision; even if the resulting actions may involve hard choices between greater or lesser evils (Slim 1997). In some humanitarian situations, moreover, doing nothing can be one of the hard choices on offer. The ethical core of the new humanitarianism lies in the ability to demonstrate good faith in how difficult decisions are reached. It requires transparency in relation to the assumptions and expectations that guide the decision-making process. While outcomes may not always be what one would have hoped, as Weiss has put it, humanitarians 'who cannot stand the heat generated by situational ethics should stay out of the post-Cold War humanitarian kitchen' (Weiss 1999b: 9).

Britain's Department for International Development (DFID) has led the way in promoting the new humanitarianism. It was the first donor agency, for example, to publish the ethical principles that would guide its humanitarian actions (Short 1998). It is interesting, however, that, apart from a commitment to impartiality and a respect for international law, these principles are largely couched in terms of DFID seeking new methods of management and regulation in relation to achieving its desired outcomes. For example, the principles include seeking better systems and mechanisms to deliver humanitarian assistance; establishing rules and procedures to prevent the misuse of aid; developing more effective needs assessments, standards and systems of accountability among implementing agencies; and encouraging local participation in order to ensure that humanitarian assistance addresses the underlying causes of conflict and rebuilds social capacities. In this respect, it is recognised that 'humanitarian intervention in conflict situations often poses moral dilemmas. We will base our decisions on explicit analyses of the choices open to us and the ethnical considerations involved and communicate our conclusions openly to our partners' (*ibid*.: 2). Since there is often no clear right or wrong in humanitarian crises, the emphasis is on transparent analysis and, after weighing up the harms and benefits and on whom they fall, making decisions in

GLOBAL GOVERNANCE AND THE NEW WARS

good faith. These principles are seen as deriving from the 'hard lessons' of the past. They reflect a rights-based humanitarianism that 'goes well beyond private charity or government largesse' and entail a shift from seeing beneficiaries 'as "victims" to be pitied, to survivors of adversity' (*ibid.*).

Slim has argued that the new humanitarianism represents a move from duty-based ethics, where actions are regarded as being right in themselves (deontological ethics), to a goal-based ethics, where good must be seen to come out of actions (teleological ethics). The attempts by prophetic humanitarianism to construct systems of operational neutrality are informed by deontological ethics. In other words, while often having consequences beyond intentions, it nonetheless works in relation to a clear ethical framework. The new humanitarianism, however, is based upon a teleological ethics that is concerned with future consequences and outcomes. 'Ethics for consequentialists becomes the complicated and uncertain processes of anticipating wider outcomes and holding oneself responsible for events well beyond the present time' (Slim 1997: 8). The present concern with consequences and the attempts to develop an ethical and transparent framework of decision making is, undoubtedly, a response to complexity. It can provide guidance in relation to many pressing issues that are not encompassed by operational neutrality, such as the physical protection of populations deliberately targeted by violent actors; the provision of humanitarian assistance to those that are being purposely denied relief; guidance on civil–military relations; and the combination of humanitarian action with advocacy (Cutts 1998). At the very least, it brings such issues into the policy arena. The emphasis on contextualisation, the analysis of consequences and the multiplicity of possible choices also stands in distinction to a tradition of universal good-practice manuals that continue to characterise the development profession (OECD 1998). However, while making a number of concessions to complexity, the new humanitarianism fails to make a radical break with the technicist and (despite the adoption of the term political) apolitical nature of development discourse. Such a break with the discursive structure as analysed by Escobar (1995) would demand that the relationship between the hidden and watching technocrat and the framed picture of the South be significantly changed. At the very least, the concealing curtain would need to be pulled away to expose the silent viewer. However, in the crisis of the encounter with the new wars, the development profession has acted to maintain its own anonymity by thrusting humanitarian action into the picture in its stead. While the development technocracy is still concealed, the encounter has been made more complex. Humanitarian aid is now seen as connected to its object through a raft of causal and consequential relationships. However, humanitarian assistance is only one small component of the wider encounter between the strategic complexes of global governance and the political complexes of the new wars. Indeed, given the manner of its sacrificial exposure, humanitarian action would appear to be dispensable and a price worth paying to maintain the concealment and responsibility of the development profession. In order to understand how development discourse has retained its structure despite the traumatic encounter with the new wars, one must examine how the new humanitarianism understands politics.

Ethics and humanitarian conditionality

In reviewing the main agency positions in relation to politics and humanitarian action, Weiss (1999b) has distinguished four: classicists, minimalists, maximalists and solidarists. On issues such as neutrality, engagement with political parties, impartiality, and so on, this spectrum of engagement opposes the traditional position of the Red Cross at one extreme with political solidarity and partisan support at the other. If one looks at these ideal types, however, as representing different historical regimes of accommodation, then the two extremes can be regarded as having earlier antecedents than the others. Classical humanitarianism associated with the ICRC, for example, emerged with the Geneva Convention of 1864 and was further elaborated in the aftermath of the Second World War with the IV Geneva Convention (1949) and the Additional Protocols (1977). Regarding the solidarity position, the rules of war that emerged during the eighteenth and nineteenth centuries outlawed the encouragement of insurrection within a sovereign state (van Creveld 1991). The Spanish Civil War (1936–9) represented an important break with this tradition. During the Second World War, the encouragement of insurrection and partisan activity within occupied territories became a *de facto* part of total war. Such activity continued into the Cold War in the form of external support for the numerous freedom struggles and wars of national liberation that emerged with decolonisation and superpower rivalry. In relation to the new wars, while a solidarity position exists, it is mainly associated with the debatable view that liberal peace represents a new imperialism.[1] It is concerned with controlling processes and markets rather than territory. In many respects, what is essentially new in the present accommodation – indeed, what characterises the present mode of engagement – is contained in the related minimalist and maximalist positions.

Weiss (1999b: 4) defines minimalist humanitarian action as 'worthwhile if efforts to relieve suffering do not make matters worse and can be sustained locally'. It is a position that is widely associated with the *Do No Harm* thesis of Mary Anderson (1996). The maximalist position, while also subscribing to 'do no harm' principles, holds that humanitarian action is defensible when coupled with efforts to address the root causes of violence through a comprehensive political strategy. In this respect, humanitarian action is subordinate to the need to return society to an equilibrium. This position goes beyond compassion and charity and argues that 'the relief of life-threatening suffering can no longer be the sole justification of outside assistance' (Weiss 1999b: 16). It is concerned with tackling the causes of conflict through the reform of humanitarian action by placing it in the service of preventing, mitigating and resolving conflicts. The maximalist position embodies the merger of development and security and complements the current policy consensus relating to conflict resolution and societal reconstruction.

> Properly conceived politically motivated assistance would use carrots and sticks, with conditionalities to reward or punish behaviour. The notion is that such maximalist projects can reduce violence – effectively turning on its head the argument that aid can be manipulated by belligerents and exacerbate armed conflict. The calculation would be that the greatest good for the greatest number over the longer term would be better served by successful conflict management than by successful relief. (*Ibid.*: 17)

Apart from a willingness to accept the hard choice of humanitarian conditionality, what is notable about the politicisation of aid represented by the maximalist position is that its main sponsors are donor governments (Fox 1999). The Dutch, Canadian, Swedish and British governments have all reorganised their aid departments to foster better links between humanitarian action and conflict resolution. It has already been mentioned that Britain's DFID has issued a consequentialist ethical framework to guide its humanitarian policy. Not only has the current Secretary of State Clare Short been outspoken in her criticism of humanitarian agencies, but DFID policy has been connected, in the latter part of the 1990s, with growing evidence of humanitarian conditionality and aid politicisation in such places as the former Zaïre, Sierra Leone, Sudan, Afghanistan and Kosovo (*ibid.*; Leader 1999; Atkinson 1998). In relation to the present fear of negative consequences and the corresponding climate of conditionality, the views of the British MP Tess Kingham, a member of the government's International Development Committee, are representative: 'Surely taking the view of the wider good – for the long-term interests of people – to actually achieve stability and development ... it may be better to withdraw aid now – to ensure that in the longer term, it is in the better interests of the people' (quoted by Fox 1999: 9).

The new humanitarianism involves a shift in the centre of gravity of policy away from saving lives to supporting social processes and political outcomes. It represents a move from people to principles and, providing decisions are taken in good faith and in a transparent manner, it can be supported by a consequentialist ethics. If it should fail, however, since the success of this policy change is far from assured, it could end up making a bad situation a whole lot worse. Indeed, evidence has begun to emerge that the move towards humanitarian conditionality has yet to produce the desired outcomes (Leader 1999; Fox 1999; Duffield *et al*. 1999). In chapters 8 and 9 this concern is examined in more detail in relation to displaced Southerners in Sudan.

Politics as policy

It is now widely accepted among many politicians, aid agencies and academics that humanitarian action is political and should be recognised as such. A consequentialist ethics has emerged to justify this position and even give support to the hard choice of humanitarian conditionality. It is worth considering, however, what exactly is meant by 'political' in this context. If we are told that humanitarian action is political, to be able to assess this position properly we need to know what politics means. Here we must ask what the proponents of political humanitarianism see as constituting the political (Weiss 1999b; Cutts 1998). Humanitarian actors are seen as political because they compete with other agencies for funds and operating space. They negotiate with local authorities for visas, transport and humanitarian access, all of which may involve compromises. They feel the pain and anguish of thinking they are helping ethnic cleansing, contributing to war economies, feeding war criminals, deciding whether or not to publicise human rights abuse, and so on.

> [T]hey also deal with and accommodate host governments and a variety of opposition or insurgent political authorities. Local economic, political and power dynamics are altered whenever outsiders enter a resource-scarce environment. To pretend that pragmatic political calculations are not taken into account as part of legitimate compromises in choosing among several unpalatable options obfuscates the actual nature of humanitarian decision making in complex emergencies. At a minimum,

the vast majority of humanitarians now acknowledge the need to minimize their impact on the relative power of warring parties or to affect them as equally as possible. (Weiss 1999b: 20)

Politics, in the sense that humanitarian action is 'political', would appear to hinge on two factors. First, it circumscribes all the decisions, actions, compromises, and so on, that humanitarian actors make during the course of their work. Second, these decisions and actions are political in that they are seen as making a difference and capable of altering outcomes. Regarding the first aspect, to define politics in this way and incorporate it within a consequentialist ethical framework reduces its meaning to that of 'policy'. While one can agree that humanitarian action is political, it is something else to confine its meaning to the ethical policy decisions taken by aid agencies. While prefixes such as 'ethical' or 'principled' are often used to describe the new humanitarianism, in many respects it is perhaps more accurately defined as 'politics as policy'. Politics has become the policy decisions that aid agencies make when faced with hard ethical choices. This is both a truism and simultaneously a reduction and confinement. It is as if the political nature of aid has been proclaimed boldly only to limit instantly the implications of what has been said. Reducing and circumscribing the meaning of politics in this manner have a number of serious implications. For example, it suggests that the apparent radicalisation of development discourse through the explicit linking of the actions of a Northern humanitarian subject with those of its Southern humanitarian object is much less comprehensive than one may have imagined. Considering the effects of one's actions in relation to a system conceived as a unified and organisational whole is a valid approach to complexity and a consequentialist ethics complements this. However, to confine the meaning of politics to the policy decisions linking humanitarian agencies and their beneficiaries represents a major limitation of the system and the borders within which politics holds sway. Despite the fervour of its converts, indeed, the impression one gets is that accepting humanitarian aid as political is now a *rite de passage* to adulthood; politics as policy does not, in fact, get us very far.

The failure of 'humanitarian aid as politics' to alter development discourse radically is most clearly seen in relation to the second component of the argument, in which policy decisions are regarded as political in that aid is seen as making a difference and being able to alter outcomes. Politics in this sense has been transformed into a type of donor-approved soul-searching among enmeshed NGOs that either supply or withhold relatively small amounts of aid. As Weiss points out above, 'the vast majority of humanitarians now acknowledge the need to minimize their impact on the relative power of warring parties or to affect them as equally as possible'. In other words, the political complexes with which aid agencies interact are, once again, perceived as a separate other – a self-contained structure that acts mechanically and predictably to outside resource flows. Rather than a promised world of living systems, we find ourselves back in a Newtonian universe of clockwork machines. Politics are the decisions that agencies take based on their assumptions surrounding the consequences of their actions on this closed and mechanical system. Like the relationship between the balls on a snooker table, in the hands of an expert, measured inputs have predicable outcomes. Moreover, if you miss the shot, at least you acted in good faith. Because the emerging political complexes are understood as if they were a machine made up of parts, the consequences of aid are typically stereotyped. The critics of human-itarian aid frequently cite its creation of dependency, the fuelling of conflict and its weakening of social and political contracts. Such negative consequences, however, are put forward as a basis for the assumption that aid can also reverse the situation. As Weiss mentions above, the maximalist position involves 'effectively turning on its head the argument that aid can be manipulated by belligerents and exacer-bate armed conflict'. In other words, the argument that humanitarian aid is political does not represent a radical break with developmen-talism; it is, in fact, its restatement. It is not so much that humanitarian agencies are bad; it is that for too long they have been pulling the wrong levers and pressing inappropriate buttons. In this respect, the time has come for politically and ethically aware development professionals once again to take charge. While the crisis of the new wars for a while appeared to promise something new, this position is a retreat from complexity. Returning to the analogy of the cosmic clock, after a minor glitch and a quick visit to the jeweller's, its mechanism is once again in perfect working order.

Humanitarian agencies and NGOs are perceived, not as part of wider strategic complexes articulating and defining themselves in relation to the political complexes of the new wars, but as a resource conduit and a mechanism for providing aid. Despite the rhetoric about politics, aid agencies are understood as if they were instruments. They have political effects because they provide a material interface with a bounded machine understood as resource-poor. The politics and ethics of the encounter are concerned with handling this situation correctly and getting the most from it. To a large extent, this explains why the critics of humanitarian action have placed the burden of moral responsibility for its alleged negative consequences on the humanitarian agencies themselves (Slim 1997: 4; Fox 1999). If one assumes that the political complexes of the South represent a closed, mechanical and reactive universe, then it is clear that the most important thing is how and under what conditions agencies prod this machine into action. Focusing on aid workers armed with sticks and carrots rather than killers with guns makes sense. After all, once in sober hands, the latter can always be controlled by adjusting the dials. At a time when development spending is declining and has all but disappeared in many war-torn societies, one is struck by the magical nature of such sentiments. There is a certain narcissism of aid at work in which relatively small inputs are credited with powers and effects beyond reasonable expectation. In terms of the organisational development of global liberal governance, it is as if the encounter with the new wars has involved the subordination of the priests and prophets of humanitarianism to the magicians and sorcerers of development.

Linking relief and development as a governance relation

The idea of 'policy as politics' is a useful way of analysing the organisational conflicts and contradictions within liberal governance relations. The adoption by many aid agencies of the new humanitarianism's sceptical ethos has been described by Hugo Slim as a 'Darwinian' organisational adaptation to a change in 'climate' resulting from the shift in donor government policy (Slim 1999). Adoption has taken place through an amoral and non-teleological process of the survival of the fittest. In terms of how disasters are now perceived, that is, as offering opportunities for development rather than relief assistance, this survivalist response has had a widespread impact on the ground (Bradbury 1998; Macrae and Bradbury 1998; Karim et al. 1996). Explaining how this adaptation has occurred through conflict and competition between different agencies and networks, Joanna Macrae has broken down the criticism of humanitarian action into a number of distinct and embedded social networks and nodes of authority (Macrae 1998). These are defined as the 'anti-imperialists, the realpolitikers, the developmentalists and the neo-peaceniks'. In uniting against the humanitarian agenda, these networks have sometimes come together to form the 'most bizarre alliances'. While all of these networks have contributed to the emergence of the new humanitarian agenda, the most important, at least in terms of giving an overall coherence to the project, have been those of developmentalism – to be more precise, the strategic networks that came together in the mid-1990s in support of the idea of a 'relief to development continuum', or the 'linking of relief and development' in conflict situations.

The continuum or linking debate among aid agencies and donor governments developed into something of a cottage industry during the 1990s. There have been innumerable workshops, conferences, reports and consultancies on the issue. While questions of timing and sequencing have given rise to points of difference, the overwhelming weight of opinion has been that relief activities should be short-term, and should support or complement rehabilitation measures. Indeed, they should be part of a comprehensive strategy that encourages the resumption of development programming at the earliest opportunity, even while conflict continues (Buchanan-Smith and Maxwell 1994). The linking debate is a good example of the general merger of development and security. It embodies the radicalisation of development and the policy shift towards conflict resolution and societal reconstruction. It also embodies the reproblematisation of security in terms of underdevelopment becoming dangerous. Strategic actors usually locate the causes of conflict within the modalities and malaise of underdevelopment. Reflecting the consequentialist ethics of the new humanitarianism, the linking debate seeks to break this spiral and help societies back onto the path of rehabilitation and development, and hence peace and stability. The linking debate has largely focused on how to operationalise such sentiments (Masefield and Harvey 1997). Given the preoccupation with prescription, even those critical of the linking position have found it necessary to concentrate on the appropriateness of attempting to promote development in ongoing conflict (Macrae *et al.* 1997; Duffield 1994c). The intention here is to examine the organisational effects of the debate. The main outcome of the linking debate and its complementary ethical humanitarianism has been to encourage the emergence of new and more comprehensive modes of regulation and strategic control within global liberal governance. Compared to the 1980s, tighter controls – the development of more stringent contractual mechanisms, more comprehensive and inclusive project design, monitoring and reporting techniques, more detailed normative guidelines, new collective fora, and so on – link donor governments, IGOs and implementing agencies. Justified by past mistakes and excesses, in particular those of humanitarian agencies, a deepening of such governance relations has been the main effect of the linking debate.

The idea of linking relief and development has its origins in the international response to the African famines of the 1970s and 1980s (Anderson and Woodrow 1989). Such famines were generally seen as the result of a so-called natural disaster. Appropriate relief responses were perceived as those that helped build up local capacities to prevent and manage future emergencies. Relief should therefore be part of a wider developmental response. Such sentiments were the common coinage of aid policy discussions in Sudan, for example, during the latter part of the 1980s (Cutler and Keen 1989). When the UN's Department of Humanitarian Affairs was established at the end of 1991, it was charged with oversight of the relief-to-development continuum. The debate among donor governments (Pronk and Kooijmans 1993) and the UN system on the relationship between conflict, humanitarian action and development began to gather momentum during the early 1990s. Within the UN system, for example, concern grew in its Development Programme (UNDP) that the rapidly increasing expenditure on humanitarian assistance at this time was beginning to threaten its position as the leading UN developmental organisation – a concern that directly encouraged official endorsement of a relief-to-development continuum and hence the primacy of development agencies in conflict situations (UNDP 1994). The critics of this UN debate have focused mainly on the appropriateness of the framework being used and its method of application. They have questioned the wisdom of extending a model developed in relation to natural disasters, one that assumes conventional distinctions and benign interactions between people, army and government, to the new wars where these qualities are blurred or have disappeared completely (Macrae *et al*. 1997). In other words, in such complex situations, *whose* local capacities are being strengthened and for what purposes?

In understanding the governance implications of the debate it is first necessary to understand what is generally meant by 'development'. To what, exactly, does relief or humanitarian action have to link, with what does it form a continuum? The linking debate has involved almost all the strategic actors and networks that constitute liberal peace. Using the example of the European Union, one of the largest donors of humanitarian assistance, it is noticeable that in the otherwise exhaustive document *Linking Relief, Rehabilitation and Development* (EC 1996b), there is no clear description of what development is. While top-down, dependency-creating humanitarian aid is given short shrift, the depiction of the development process that more responsible and effective relief operations should be helping to re-establish is found in partial and fragmented descriptions. Indeed, some of the important aspects that define the developmental goal of the *Linking* document have to be inferred or guessed at. The nearest one gets to a substantive definition of development is in the section on food security. Food security is seen as a dynamic condition resulting from the interplay of supply and demand factors. It provides a starting point or threshold that distinguishes a state of development from that of impoverishment and dependency.

> Above this threshold, people are embarked on a development pattern, which well-designed aid (which does not include food aid in kind) can help to speed up. (*Ibid*.: 13)

> [Food security provides] a starting point from which urban and rural households can begin to build up reserves (stocks, cattle, savings), develop more reliable means of production or ways of increasing their income and organise a more reliable social safety net. The upshot of all these steps is to reduce people's vulnerability to food crises. (*Ibid*.: 12)

Below this threshold, however,

> a process of impoverishment takes place which can lead to economic and social degradation, extreme dependency and increased mortality which becomes more difficult to reverse the longer it is allowed to continue .... The lack of success in reversing the tide of growing dependence caused by increasing social breakdown, partly explains why a number of cases have remained bogged down at the humanitarian stage. (*Ibid*.: 13)

It is clear from the above that 'development' is regarded as a sustainable process of self-management that has economic self-sufficiency at its core. That this view has moved a long way from earlier ideas of state intervention and the promotion of economic growth through investment and technology transfer need not detain us. Development today is a dynamic condition that involves households having control of sufficient productive resources and assets to provide for their food security and immediate social and welfare needs. Implicit in the above quotations is that self-sufficiency (being the right side of the threshold) is also associated with the ability to maintain social solidarity by resourcing informal, family-based welfare safety nets. What can also be inferred is that such a development process demands a functioning market economy to which households have easy access. In this respect, development of this type is helped or complemented by the process of liberal economic reform being managed by the international financial institutions (IFIs) and supported by donor governments. In other words, development is synonymous with economic self-sufficiency secured through self-management within a liberal market environment. In policy terms, households tend to appear as free and self-contained economic agents. With proper access to functioning markets and sufficient human and material resources, households are assumed to be capable of reproducing themselves and securing the social well-being of their members. It is the aim of development policy, including the linking of relief and development, to help secure such liberal self-management.

Deepening the relations of liberal governance

In relation to the self-management model of development, vulnerability, whether of households or individuals, refers to those various factors that either block market access, undermine productive capacity or otherwise reduce or destroy assets. In other words, households and individuals are vulnerable to the extent that they are exposed to conditions or risks that undermine their self-sufficiency. The gender issue, for example, is often approached from this direction: the subordinate position of women in relation to household structures, customary rights or local market mechanisms leaves them particularly disadvantaged. As discussed in the following chapter, conflict is usually seen in a Hobbesian light as having a destructive and negative impact in relation to the liberal policy goal of legitimate, that is, market-dependent, self-management. It is something that in different ways degrades the development assets of households – land, labour, employment, education, and so on. Conflict is a ruinous activity that mechanically thrusts people below the food security threshold into a cycle of destitution and impoverishment. The vulnerability of a population increases the further it is pushed below the development threshold, and in extreme circumstances relief assistance may be required.

The representation of development as an economic process of self-management, at the same time as acknowledging that disasters can necessitate relief assistance, creates a tension within liberal governance. As a free good, that is, something that is given rather than earned, for many strategic actors humanitarian assistance conjures up a number of free-market concerns and economic fears. Indeed, the idea of relief, especially the prospect of a long-term commitment in relation to the new wars, has created something of a moral panic in liberal circles. A particular phobia is that badly managed or unnecessary relief assistance will encourage 'dependency' among recipients – since the distribution of free goods creates economic disincentives that are antithetical to self-sufficiency and the workings of a market economy. It is argued, usually without much in the way of supporting evidence, that free goods can discourage household production, undermine markets and sap individual industry and enterprise (IDC 1999). To the extent that this takes place, humanitarian action can actually deepen the cycle of destitution and impoverishment: it can strengthen dependency. Within

102

EU policy, consequently, a tension is evident in the requirement that while a commitment to humanitarian action must remain, relief assistance should not undermine 'the way back to a long-term development process' (EC 1996b: 2).

The EU's humanitarian policy, its attempt to link relief and development, follows directly from the above concerns. The tension within this policy is clear within the statement of basic principles that emerged in 1997. On the one hand, there is an assertion that 'the sole aim of humanitarian aid is to prevent or relieve human suffering and that it is accorded to victims without discrimination'. This imperative, however, is immediately qualified by the requirement that 'humanitarian aid will seek where possible to ... remain compatible with longer-term developmental objectives, and ... that every possible step must be taken to eliminate dependency amongst populations in receipt of humanitarian aid, with a view to achieving self-sustainability' (ECHO 1997a: 1–2). While this pairing gives a rather ambiguous definition of humanitarian aid – that is, of saving lives and, where possible, supporting livelihoods – it clearly accommodates the new humanitarian ethos. This position is based on several policy statements dating from the end of 1995 and the early part of 1996. These include the *Council Conclusions on Preventive Diplomacy, Conflict and Peacekeeping in Africa* (4 December 1995), the *Commission Communications on the European Union and the Issue of Conflict in Africa: Conflict Prevention and Beyond* (ECHO 1996) and *Linking Relief, Rehabilitation and Development* (EC 1996b). There is a strong intellectual coherence linking the policy architecture within these documents and the tools for its implementation: the mechanisms for testing and canvassing policy within the donor and NGO communities; its translation into Council regulations; the creation of coordinating bodies; and the formalisation of contractual relations with implementing agencies.

In terms of theory, EU humanitarian policy endorses proactive attempts by aid agencies to protect basic resources and support livelihoods as a means of complementing rehabilitation efforts. There is also, however, a much more radical commitment to use aid to help change the balance of power and authority between groups and to restructure societies in such a way as to prevent future conflicts. Such measures support the EU's attempts to create 'structural stability' within a conflict situation (EC 1996a: 3–4). It will require a global policy framework, however, to operationalise such measures, creating forward and backward coordination linkages between the whole range of political, relief, rehabilitation and development measures and agencies (EC 1996b). Such a comprehensive framework would bring together the basic

survival inputs of humanitarian agencies with, for example, the structural development tools of the EU's Lomé Convention as well as the
macroeconomic policies of the Ifis. A global policy framework also
involves a commitment to in-depth country and regional analysis to
inform aid policy, including suggestions that the political analysis
undertaken by member states' embassy staff should also be used to
assist this endeavour. In this manner, and reflecting the current accommodation of politics and humanitarian action discussed above, it is
acknowledged that achieving structural stability through such a comprehensive policy framework is as much a political aim as a development goal.

In order to translate this policy into a governance relation linking it
to NGOs and other implementing agencies, the EU has done a number
of things. The *Council Regulation (EC) No 1257/96 Concerning Humanitarian Relief* (EC 1996c), for example, besides confirming humanitarian
assistance as a right, also codifies much of the policy outlined above –
the requirement to link relief to rehabilitation and development, the
need for a comprehensive strategy, effective coordination and in-depth
country analysis, and so on. In this respect, the *Regulation* reflects the
philosophy that has informed the development of the EU's European
Commission Humanitarian Office since its inception in 1993 (ECHO
1997a: 1). The *Regulation* has also played an important role in deepening
the relations of governance between ECHO and its implementing
partners. At the time of writing, this regulation is formulated in the
Framework Partnership Contract (EC 1998a) which is signed by ECHO
and an implementing NGO. Much of the policy architecture discussed
above and codified in the *Regulation* is reflected in the *Partnership
Contract*. Besides establishing the technical criteria for selecting NGO
partners and arrangements for project monitoring, humanitarian assistance as a right is flagged, especially in a country where 'their own
government prove[s] unable to help or there is a vacuum of power'
(*ibid.*: 1). It goes on to establish the basis of partnership on the linking of
relief, rehabilitation and development in the context of working with
local structures, the formulation of coherent and effective policies, the
involvement of beneficiaries in project design and management, and so
on. NGOs are also encouraged to share information with ECHO 'to take
advantage of the privileged information of the humanitarian organisations through their proximity to the beneficiaries' (*ibid.*: 4). In exchange,
ECHO undertakes to initiate coordination and information-sharing
meetings, and to support other forums for debate. In the case of Sudan,
for example, since 1997 policy guidelines and requirements for NGOs
receiving ECHO funding (as eventually reflected in the *Partnership*

Contract) have been part of ECHO's regular Global Plans. A Humanitarian Aid Committee (HAC) and other bodies have also been established to improve coordination and linkages between ECHO and member states.

The way in which the EU has used the linking debate, and its associated fears of dependency and the negative consequences of humanitarian aid, in order to justify increasing its regulation of implementing partners is replicated by many donor governments. Since the mid-1990s, Britain's Department for International Development, for example, has been much more closely involved with its implementing partners in terms of project design, monitoring, management and evaluation. It has already been mentioned that the principles underlying its ethical humanitarianism are largely concerned with developing new forms of regulation and control in relation to its partner agencies. Much of the justification for increased powers of regulation has rested on fears and claims regarding the past effects of aid that are, at best, equivocal and inconclusive (Stockton 1998). Claims of dependency, even during the 1980s when food aid was relatively more available than today, have been difficult to substantiate (Silkin and Hughes 1992). In other words, the move towards more effective means of regulation is not an empirical response to conditions in the South but a process whereby donor governments and IGOs have regained the political initiative.

The primacy of deepening governance relations can also be seen in relation to the effectiveness of EU policy. Its linking policy makes great play of creating coherent global policy frameworks. When it was formulated in the mid-1990s, however, even before the ink was dry, this policy was already incoherent and obsolete. Sudan, for example, has probably been among the most consistent and long-term recipients of EU emergency aid in Africa since the 1980s. In 1990, concerns about Sudan's support for international terrorism led the EU to suspend development aid under the Lomé Convention. For similar reasons, Western donor governments and the IFIs have also suspended formal development assistance. In other words, even before it was written, EU linking policy was inoperable in Sudan because there are no formal or comprehensive development tools to which relief can be linked. Moreover, on closer examination, rather than proving an exception to the rule, Sudan reflects the condition of many war-affected societies: a growing regional differentiation in aid policy means that many are unlikely to attract the range of formal development tools and the corresponding donor and IFI commitment that is envisaged in the comprehensive ambitions of linking policy. At the same time, total EU humanitarian funding has tumbled from a peak of over 700 million ecu in 1994 to 200 million in 1998. Since the beginning of the 1990s, overseas development assistance *per capita* has also been declining. This further underlines the incoherence of linking policy. It is only as a means of projecting donor authority through an enhanced ability to regulate non-state actors that it makes perfect sense. Moreover, the new forms of supervision and management introduced through linking policy have been reinforced subsequently by the consequentialist concerns associated with the new humanitarianism.

Concluding remarks

By the end of the 1990s, while formal EU humanitarian policy had yet to change, there were a number of indications that linking policy, and especially its dependence on comprehensive policy frameworks, was being abandoned. Events in Central Africa – the emergence of a region-wide conflict centred on the Democratic Republic of Congo, signifi-cantly increased concern over the effects of conflict, and perceptions of the role of development assistance have altered. The EU, in particular, has become preoccupied by the implications of continuing to support countries engaged in a region-wide conflict with development aid through the Lomé partnership (EC 1998c). The concern is that the fungi-bility of development assistance allows some countries to use it to help them wage war both internally and against neighbouring countries. In such cases, development assistance would be undermining the princi-ples of solidarity and peaceful cooperation enshrined in the Lomé Convention. In this context, the mood is shifting away from linking relief and development, reflecting the consequentialist ethics of the new humanitarianism, and towards the conditionality of all assistance to countries engaged in conflict.

In many respects, the new humanitarianism, grounded in what Weiss has called 'situational ethics' (Weiss 1999b), while being shaped by (and gathering much of its rhetoric from) the linking of relief to development, has moved away from comprehensive coordinating frameworks. As will be discussed in Chapter 8 in relation to the emergence of Minimal Operational Standard (MinOps) agreements in Sudan, the new humanitarianism prefers a relative and locally based system of reference. It relates, essentially, to the type of immediate arrangements, relations and compromises that aid agencies themselves are able to establish on the ground. It minimises the need for donor governments to provide overarching political frameworks as during the period of UN-led, system-wide operations. Nor does it require the type of comprehensive global plans envisaged by the EU. The new humanitarianism is geared to the present era of humanitarian conditionality and its accompanying hierarchy of concern. It is able to adjust to a range of possible engagements, from the more robust examples of liberal peace in the Balkans to the local activities of a few UN organisations and NGOs in parts of Africa. While the duty-based ethics of humanitarian action as right may have tended to ignore consequences, it did not normalise violence but was affronted by it. The consequentialist ethics of the new humanitarianism, however, in holding out the possibility of a better tomorrow as a price worth paying for suffering today, has been a major source of the normalisation of violence and complicity with its perpetrators. How strategic actors understand conflict is an important part of this process.

NOTE

1 For a discussion of the new imperialism position see Chapter 2, pp. 31–4.

5

Global Governance
and the Causes of Conflict

Liberal peace requires a political rationale. Strategic actors need forms of interpretation and analysis that simultaneously provide understanding and, importantly, justification for coordination and intervention. The way in which conflict is understood is an important aspect of this rationale, which is neither wholly independent nor value-free. While its intention may be to inform, its primary effect is to deepen governance networks. Modes of representation are an essential aspect of how global liberal governance transforms knowledge into power. Within governance systems, forms of representation are closely associated with the politics of policy. In relation to conflict and humanitarian assistance, for example, debates over the merits of relief versus development, or neutrality as opposed to wider forms of engagement, as well as impacting on the ground, also have an important and necessary institutional analogue. Indeed, policy debates and shifts tell us a good deal about changing patterns of rivalry and alliance between different strategic actors and organisational agendas within governance networks. They relate to the changing fortunes of different interest groups in their struggle for influence and resources. Such struggles occur both between major institutions and, importantly, among the various internal stakeholders that compose them.

Rather than a positivist trial and error process of empirical testing on the ground, policies primarily rise and fall according to the changing power and influence of the institutional and political constituencies that support them. Within governance networks, 'policy' occupies the space of 'politics'. How otherwise would one explain, for example, the imposition of structural adjustment on the South? Moreover, what is good for neoliberal economic reform is good for policy in general. Thus, in order to examine how mainstream aid policy understands the causes

108

of conflict, in this chapter the texts have not been read, as their authors' intended they should be, as if they explained or told us something about the nature of conflict. Instead, they have been interpreted as a form of discourse that helps define points of intervention and new forms of coordination and power projection. Explaining the causes of conflict is both a way of knowing and, simultaneously, a means by which global liberal governance mobilises the strategic networks of state and non-state actors that police its borders.

This is not to say that the causes described are somehow incorrect; all discourse contains truths. It is in the nature of discourse, however, to select some truths and neglect others, and to rework those that have been adopted into a coherent and functional world view. In this form, policy has a distinct duality. It not only shapes outward-looking modes of coordination and intervention, but also keeps a weather eye cast inwards toward organisational requirements and strategic agendas. Aid agencies rarely define problems in a way that automatically disqualifies their involvement. This characteristic gives aid policy a functional duality. The way problems are understood and modes of intervention are established are continually refracted through the need to maintain and defend organisational influence. As a result, strategic complexes are usually unstable and characterised by shifting patterns of alliance and competition between the actors that compose them.

New barbarism and biocultural determination

There are a number of problems in analysing the causes of conflict. One of these it that within received wisdom there are several distinct narratives reflecting the positions and agendas of different networks and actors. One of the main distinctions lies between what has been called 'new barbarism' (Richards 1996) and the more developmental and multicultural approach currently associated with aid institutions and Northern governments. New barbarism has links with the biocultural racial discourse that emerged in the West during the 1960s, a discourse that is no longer based on the earlier, colonial ranking of races and civilisations according to hierarchical criteria. What Barker (1982) has called the 'new racism' accepts the reality of cultural pluralism. Like the multiculturalism that emerged coterminously, the new racism agrees that no single culture is intrinsically better than another. There is no hierarchy of attributes; the main point and shared understanding is that cultures are *different*. Whereas multiculturalism sees such differences as a source of vitality and renewal, however, for new racism they are the origin of antagonism and conflict. Cultural differences, such as those that arise due to immigration to countries that were previously ethnically homo-geneous, are portrayed in new racist discourse as naturally and inevitably leading to social disruption and violence. Cultural difference relates to identity and identities are deeply rooted and strongly held. In Europe, such arguments, often uniting a wide cross-section of the political spectrum, have been used to mobilise support for immigration controls and the increasing restrictions placed on asylum seekers. New barbarism is, in many respects, the external or international version of new racism. In relation to conflict on the borders of liberal governance, new barbarism tends to emphasise one aspect of this racial discourse: the notion of a primordial, innate and irrational cultural and ethnic identity (Duffield 1996a). For new barbarism, the anarchic and destruc-tive power of traditional feelings and antagonisms is usually unleashed in times of change when overarching political or economic systems are either weakened or collapse.

It is interesting to note that in Russia the interpretation of ethnicity in social science and anthropology is dominated by primordialism. Archaic attachments through blood, speech, custom, and so on, are seen as having an organic cohesion of their own. A distinct ethnic population – the *ethnos* – is formed through the fusion of the social and the biological spheres. For many Russian academics and politicians, history is not only about the formation of states, but also concerns the culturally deter-mined *ethnoses* that make them up and, in the light of today's concerns, also pull them apart.

> With the emergence of ethnic politics in the former Soviet Union, ethno-graphic primordialism ceased to be merely a marginal and empirical approach and suddenly revealed its potential for being enthusiastically applied in the quest of new identities, as well as in nationalist political discourse. (Tishkov 1997: 7)

The Chechen wars of the 1990s have been popularly understood within Russia in terms of the primordial characteristics of the Chechen *ethnos*. The enduring characteristics of the 'Chechen bandit', for example, have been used to mobilise public opinion in support of conquest (Lieven 1998). Indeed, the popularity of primordialist expla-nations in both these wars has allowed the Russian authorities to wage 'an unprecedented racist propaganda campaign against Chechens as a people' (Maltsev 1999: 2). The second war, for example, saw large numbers of Chechens and other 'blacks' from the Caucasus region expelled from Moscow (Jacoby 1999).

In the West, rationales of the new barbarism type, while falling short of forming the consensus within liberal governance, have also been extremely influential. They have been effective, for example, in shaping popular understanding of the collapse of former Yugoslavia and deep-seated instability in Africa. With regard to Europe and the Transcaucasus region, the demise of communist rule is often claimed to have fomented deep-seated ethnic unrest. This reasoning forms what critical theorists have disdainfully termed the 'pressure cooker' interpretation of Soviet political history (Schierup 1992). From this perspective, the main accomplishment of communist rule was that of holding a lid on pent-up ethnic animosities. Once this grip was relaxed, hatreds stretching back centuries sprang forth unchanged and as hungry as the day they were imprisoned. In the former Yugoslavia, for example, the demise of communist rule is said to have allowed the 'Balkan mentality' a free rein (Kennan 1993). This type of explanation was favoured, for example, within Britain's Foreign and Commonwealth Office during the Bosnia conflict. Robert Kaplan's tellingly titled book, *Balkan Ghosts: a Journey Through History* (1993), painting a picture of innate and inbred hatreds, has also been credited with dissuading the Clinton administration from its initial predilection towards an interventionist line on Bosnia.

In Africa, new barbarism rationales have also been influential. Regarding the Rwanda genocide in 1994, for example, while there were exceptions, the media generally portrayed the violence as representing 'ancient tribal feuds' (Adelman, Suhrke and Jones 1996: 46), a view already well-rehearsed in relation to other African conflicts. In the case of Rwanda, however, its effects were particularly marked. Initial reporting in the *Times* and *New York Times* has been described by the multi-donor Rwanda evaluation as 'appallingly misleading' (*ibid.*: 47). Rather than organised and systematic slaughter, images of anarchic and spontaneous blood frenzy born of old ethnic hatreds dominated the reporting. Such coverage by established newspapers acted to support the widespread calls for international disengagement existing at the time. Not only was the situation beyond rational comprehension and effective control, but, since the Rwandese had brought it on them-selves, they should be left to sort things out on their own. These views were echoed in the UN Secretariat and Security Council and fed into the decision to withdraw the small UN presence in April 1994. As the multi-donor evaluation team has argued, the media representation of the situation contributed to the international indifference and inaction in the opening phase of the genocide 'and hence the crime itself' (*ibid.*: 48).

New barbarism is not confined to the media; it also has political, military and academic exponents. Echoes of new barbarism, for example, can be found in Huntington's controversial thesis on *The Clash of Civilisations and the Remaking of World Order* (1997). Here, culture and

111

cultural identities are regarded as broadly synonymous with civilisa-tional identities. Such identities, it is argued, are increasingly shaping emerging patterns of cohesion, disintegration and conflict in the post-Cold War era. In relation to the latter, civilisations 'are the ultimate human tribes, and the clash of civilisations is tribal conflict on a global scale' (*ibid*.: 207). In the emerging world order, collaboration and cohesion will be closer among civilisations that are similar or share cer-tain characteristics or values. Relations between groups from different civilisations, however, 'will be almost never close' (*ibid*.). Where such contrary civilisations touch or intermix, there is a potential for what Huntington calls 'fault line wars'. Such civilisational wars based on clans, tribes, ethnic groups, religious communities, and so on, have a long historical pedigree,

> because they are rooted in the identities of people. These conflicts tend to be particularistic, in that they do not involve broader ideological or political issues of direct interest to nonparticipants, although they may arouse humanitarian concerns in outside groups. They also tend to be vicious and bloody, since fundamental issues of identity are at stake. In addition, they tend to be lengthy; they may be interrupted by truces or agreements but these tend to break down and the conflict is resumed. Decisive military victory by one side in an identity civil war, on the other hand, increases the likelihood of genocide. (*Ibid*.: 252)

Kaplan's work has been influential in shaping attitudes to Africa as well as the Balkans. Rather than the breakdown of communist rule, however, here his focus is on the consequences of alleged Malthusian resource pressures exacerbated by environmental and economic col-lapse. In his article 'The Coming Anarchy: How Scarcity, Crime, Over-population, and Disease Are Rapidly Destroying the Social Fabric of Our Planet' – again, the title is eye-catching, while the argument draws on a range of vivid and sharply drawn images – Kaplan interprets the violence and political turmoil in West Africa as an unfocused and instinctive response, rooted in nature, to mounting external pressures. Further, this response is taken as a harbinger of trends in other marginal areas of the globe. Environmental and economic collapse, rising birth rates and soaring crime have created an explosive situation. In many West African cities the young men that Kaplan encountered were allegedly 'like loose molecules in a very unstable fluid, a fluid that was clearly on the verge of igniting' (Kaplan 1994: 46). For Kaplan, incipient anarchy in West Africa has done more than erode governments; it has released a much greater threat: by undermining and destroying public health structures it has raised the spectre of resurgent and border-hopping diseases.

Now the threat is more elemental: *nature unchecked*. Africa's immediate future could be very bad. The coming upheaval, in which foreign embassies are shut down, states collapse, and contact with the outside world will take place through dangerous, disease-ridden coastal trading posts, will loom large in the century we are entering. (*Ibid*.: 54, emphasis in original)

Goldberg has echoed Kaplan's concern that conflict and the resulting anarchic social breakdown in many parts of Africa have given rise to a new set of 'biological national-security issues' (Goldberg 1997: 35). Environmental collapse, rapid population growth and conflict have encouraged the spread of disease and the emergence of new ones. Given that disease does not respect borders or cultures, with the expansion of air travel and the increasing interconnection of people and goods, the spread of disease is taken to be as great a security threat to the United States as terrorism or arms proliferation.

New barbarism articulates with racial discourse and xenophobic tendencies in the West. Its simple messages produce a powerful narrative that occupies an important place in the popular media and in public anxieties. It also has a strong base among those political actors and social groups that favour international isolationism, tough border controls, stringent rules on migration and asylum, and a major reduction, if not the elimination, of development aid. In this respect, Goldberg is instructive. Tackling the threat of transborder epidemics, for example, has little to do with development, in this view. Aid has not only failed to solve the problem, but has encouraged the widespread corruption of government officials and deepened institutional dependency (*ibid*.: 36). Pointing to examples like Uganda, where it is thought a liberal free market ethos is taking root, he concludes that a new generation of African leaders is emerging who can exploit the market opportunities that are opening up.[1] The essence of Goldberg's argument is that the anarchy and breakdown perceived as 'new barbarism', including its emerging public health dimension, can be addressed, not by the state or development assistance, but by the disciplines and opportunities of the free market. This will provide the new overarching framework of rewards and punishments that astute leaders can use to keep the deep-seated social animosities associated with culture and identity in check.

Underdevelopment as dangerous

While the new barbarism rationale is extremely influential, it does not reflect the dominant position within global liberal governance. Its influence is usually contested and to a large extent it is held at bay – for the moment, at least. When it comes to understanding international instability, a more widely accepted viewpoint than biocultural determinism is constructed around a developmental position that sees the causes of conflict in the modalities of underdevelopment and its associated pathologies of crime and terrorism. This is the liberal alternative to the primordialism of new barbarism. Rather than being destined for violence and prompting isolation, underdevelopment, while dangerous, is open to remedy and demands engagement. The institutional basis of this rationale lies in the new strategic complexes that bring together aid agencies, donor governments, regional bodies, private companies, and so on. In short, the developmental position on conflict represents the consensual view among the strategic actors and networks that have emerged in response to it.

Developmentalism and new barbarism exist in an uneasy relation. While the former is currently dominant, its hegemony is far from secure and it is periodically under political attack by the conservative forces of isolationism and aid parsimony. There is also a deeper unease, however. While politicians and aid workers often seek to distinguish their views from the racial undertones of new barbarism, its images and representations intersect with those of development discourse in a number of places. In fact, there is a good deal of shared terrain linking the two positions. Both, for example, accept that cultural difference is an important factor in structuring social life. Since culture and identity serve distinct and often crucial social functions, it is only to be expected that cultural differences sustain and reproduce themselves. In this respect, both positions hold that individuals and groups should be free to express and retain such differences. Moreover, as already stated, for new barbarism and the multiculturalism that shapes development discourse, no one culture or society is superior to another – they are just different. In fact, in relation to the many shared assumptions linking the two, there are only two main distinctions. First, whereas new barbarism is based on fixed biocultural differences, developmentalism is structured around changeable economic categories. Because the emergence of new wars has frequently been associated with ethnic conflict, however, the distinction between the two has often been ambiguous. A final point of difference concerns the place of breakdown and violence (Duffield 1996). For the new racist discourse that shapes new barbarism, cultural intermixing inevitably carries a high risk of violence. Cultural pluralism without some external political or economic agent firmly holding a lid on the inevitable inter-group tensions is dangerous and potentially explosive. For liberal developmentalism, however, difference is not necessarily a source of conflict. It can be the site of vibrancy, invigoration and new opportunities for an envisioned social harmony – providing education plays its role, and transparent and equitable economic, constitutional and civil society mechanisms exist to resolve any emerging antagonisms.

Sharing the same cultural-relativist terrain but separated by differing interpretations of the inevitability of violence, new barbarism and developmentalism have a number of uncomfortable overlaps. For example, much of the discussion of failed states and, especially, of anarchic and post-ideological contemporary armed movements often has strong overtones of new barbarism. They also agree that development tends to reduce violent conflict. In the case of Kaplan, however, this is stated within a distinct racial–cultural framework: only 'when people have attained a certain economic, educational and cultural standard is this trait tranquillized' (Kaplan 1994: 72–3). To the sensitive ear, liberal development discourse is saying something very similar. Its language, however, rather than relying on biocultural categories, is directed toward economic and process-oriented structures. Within the strategic complexes that compose liberal governance, underdevelopment represents the greatest risk in terms of the outbreak of conflict. Underdevelopment is usually represented in terms of a social malaise resulting from the combination of various forms of scarcity (deep-seated poverty, environmental decline, uncontrolled population growth) with unrepresentative public institutions and weak civic culture (endemic social exclusion, widespread abuse of government office, economic mismanagement). The association of underdevelopment with a high risk of conflict is now a core assumption within development discourse. This assumption, however, is not entirely objective or value-free. It gained prominence in the early 1980s as the result of a successful political struggle with competing Third World and socialist interpretations (see Chapter 2). Rather than focusing on societal deviance, alternative views argued that the main problem lay outside the South. That is, conflict was related to the legacy of colonialism, declining terms of trade and an inequitable international trading system. Indeed, the radical edge of this alternative argued that underdevelopment itself was a consequence of the manner in which the developed countries had accumulated their wealth and now maintained their position. In their own way, such alternatives were probably no more balanced or objective than current development discourse. The point being made here is that, after nearly two decades, this contested history has long dropped from view. Consequently, the idea that conflict is the result of a developmental malaise now appears self-evident and unremarkable.

In analysing how the causes of conflict are depicted in mainstream aid policy, one is immediately struck by the brevity with which such issues are usually treated. In most policy documents, for example, the developmental causes of instability are rehearsed in a few sentences or paragraphs at the beginning. For example, in a major OECD policy guideline publication, *Conflict, Peace and Development Cooperation on the Threshold of the Twenty-first Century,* less than two pages out of over a hundred address the causes of conflict (OECD 1998). Such a balance is by no means untypical. This is not to say that depicting the causes of conflict is unimportant for liberal peace. Rather, what is said, however briefly, is richly layered in meaning; a few sentences are made to do a lot of work. In terms of indicating liberal governance's basic representation of conflict, the non-governmental organisation Saferworld provides a useful summary of the liberal consensus.

> In general, wars are more likely to be fought in countries which are poor or experiencing extremely uneven and inequitable economic development; which lack effective political, legal and administrative institutions able to manage social tensions; where human rights violations are widespread; and where there is easy access to arms. (Saferworld 1999: 68)

The effects of such brief descriptions of 'underdevelopment as dangerous' are not primarily explanatory. Since such views became dominant from the beginning of the 1980s, their main effect has been to encourage interconnections and patterns of coordination within the emerging strategic complexes of global liberal governance. With the end of the Cold War, and especially since the mid-1990s, the depth and complexity of such governance relations have grown. The association of conflict with underdevelopment has become the main site of consensus and cohesion among the different development and security networks that liberal peace brings together. In providing a bugle call for collective mobilisation it plays a symbolic rather than an informational role. In this respect, brief or superficial views on the causes of conflict do not reflect a policy failure. They *have* to be brief, general in application and easy to understand and communicate.

The way in which governance relations are mobilised gives important clues to the nature of the response. If conflict is associated with underdevelopment, then the promotion of development is not only right in itself, but has the added utility of encouraging stability as well. Reflecting the merger of development and security, after receiving evidence from a wide range of aid agencies, academics and private companies, a recent enquiry by the British government's International Development Committee (IDC 1999) into *Conflict Prevention and Post-Conflict Reconstruction* endorsed the distinction made by the NGO Saferworld between 'structural prevention' and 'operational prevention'. The latter involves those actions that can be undertaken in relation to open and ongoing conflict. The former, however, relates to that broad range of measures that can be employed to prevent conflict breaking out. Consequently, 'To discuss prevention at the "structural level" is in one sense simply to discuss development itself. If conflict and poverty are profoundly related then it is clear that an anti-poverty development strategy will reduce the risks of conflict' (IDC 1999: para. 25).

As a means of reducing such risks Saferworld and Oxfam, in evidence to the committee, recommended the pursuit of pro-poor economic growth, investment in education, health care, and so on; furthermore, they suggested that aid should be targeted to reduce inequalities and spread the ownership of assets – for example, by promoting land reform, increasing the availability of micro-finance, and helping develop small-scale and labour-intensive forms of agriculture. It should be noted that these NGO activities are the same as those also pursued in countries or regions that are not thought to be at risk of conflict. They are part of the armoury of conventional development work. Addressing the possibility of conflict, therefore, does not require aid agencies to do anything fundamentally new; it is better described as a redoubling of effort in order to provide more of the same. Apart from helping achieve self-sufficiency, the idea that development assistance can also prevent conflict adds an extra urgency to this task. The association of conflict with underdevelopment, and the resulting notion that prevention can be addressed through developmental activities, is a major area of consensus within liberal peace. One indication of this is contained in the comments of the IDC to the effect that much of the evidence it had received 'advocated similar policies to those contained in the Government's Development White Paper' (*ibid*.).[2] The consensus on the causes of conflict, moreover, is also an important site of reinvention.

Conflict and the reinvention of development

If one stands back from much of the conflict-related literature and agency reports that have emerged during the course of the 1990s, one gets the distinct impression that conflict has somehow been rediscovered. The incorporation of conflict resolution measures into mainstream aid policy helps reinforce this view. It is now commonplace to describe how conflict today is different from the past. As the former UN Secretary-General, Boutrous-Ghali, wrote in *An Agenda for Peace*, regional associations are deepening in the North through the decisions of states to yield a number of sovereign prerogatives to larger collective political associations. At the same time, however,

> fierce new assertions of nationalism and sovereignty spring up, and the cohesion of States is threatened by brutal ethnic, religious, social, cultural or linguistic strife. Social peace is challenged on the one hand by new assertions of discrimination and exclusion and, on the other, by acts of terrorism seeking to undermine evolution and change through democratic means. (Boutros-Ghali 1995: 41–2. Original 1992)

Wars today, rather than the state-based conflicts of the past, more commonly assume an internal or regionalised form. Moreover, unlike those associated with traditional national liberation struggles, warring parties are often regarded as pursuing sectarian economic or ethnic interests rather than universalistic political motives. A further distinguishing feature of these new conflicts, moreover, is their effect on civilian populations. Civilians are now usually the deliberate targets of organised violence. Widespread human rights abuse is therefore a feature of many of today's new wars (Kaldor 1999).

That the nature of conflict has changed is undoubtedly the case. Indeed, it is a central theme of this book. These changes and the institutional adaptations involved are playing a formative role in the emergence of global liberal governance. What is under discussion now is not the issue of change *per se*, but how liberal peace has chosen to interpret the nature of this transition. War has been appropriated in such a way as both to reproblematise security in terms of underdevelopment becoming dangerous and, through its radicalisation, to reinvent the role of development as well. In the process of rediscovering conflict and responding to its many new challenges, despite a half-century of failure (Escobar 1995; Visvanathan 1997), development has emerged reinvigorated. It has been given a new sense of purpose and international role. The manner of this rejuvenation is complex and involves the intersection and blending of several narratives. It has involved the use of arguments invoking the new wars in formulating a defence of development. In particular, this has required the representation of the new wars in such a way that they appear responsive to properly managed development assistance. In this way, development actors can attempt to head off isolationist tendencies, new barbarism anxieties and budgetary cutbacks. It also assuages development's unenviable record.

Reflecting on development failures, Northern governments and international financial institutions have tended to reinterpret the past as a mixture of unavoidable political constraints and, with hindsight, avoidable policy mistakes. On the establishment of the British government's

118

Department for International Development (DFID) in 1997, it was observed that the hopes of the 1960s and 1970s had proved illusory. Development could not be secured in a decade, and the 1970s and 1980s were marked by a number of major setbacks. Internally, many developing countries were pursuing inappropriate economic policies. Rising oil prices and the growing burden of debt meant that, for many countries, the 1980s were 'a lost decade' (DFID 1997: 8). Moreover, all of these difficulties were compounded by the Cold War.

> The end of the Cold War has transformed international politics. Until 1989, the ideological divide distorted development efforts. Both sides used aid to tie developing countries to their interests, leading to the diversion of effort from sustainable development. The new era provides a fresh opportunity to focus development efforts on poverty elimination. (*Ibid.*: 9)

The passing of the Cold War has drawn an important symbolic line between the past and the present. Development policy need not attempt anything significantly new; the fact that former constraints are said to have disappeared is sufficient to cast existing efforts in a new light. At the same time, the past, since conditions were so different, has no real connection with today's more responsive and informed practice. Current development policy therefore cannot be blamed for past failure. However, while the ending of superpower rivalry has allowed a much more open and flexible international political framework to emerge, much of the promise and optimism initially associated with the passing of the Cold War has not been vindicated. In particular, although nuclear annihilation has been avoided, as already indicated in this book, this escape has given way to a resurgence of pent-up internal conflicts and, indeed, to new types of war. As Brian Atwood, a former USAID administrator, has pointed out, since the fall of the Berlin Wall over four million people, mostly civilians, have been killed in internal and regionalised forms of conflict ranging from Africa, through to the Middle East and the Balkans (Atwood 1998). In response, the cost to the US government of peacekeeping, reconstruction programmes, refugee relief and emergency food aid has risen considerably. Moreover, since the Gulf War in 1991, the US has mounted 27 military operations, most of them related to ethnic conflict or the collapse of nation states. While the question of cost is important, USAID is concerned that such conflict is also having a much wider impact on development prospects.

> All of this is destabilising the world around us, destroying opportunities for economic growth and the continuing evolution towards democratic governance and open market systems. I would not suggest that this level

of conflict is a principal cause of the global financial crisis, but it has contributed to the crisis just as the financial collapse of nations will add to the violence. (*Ibid*.: 2)

While the end of the Cold War may have drawn a line under the past and established a new freedom to operate, the resurgence of new types of conflict, mostly beyond the control of states, is threatening to squander that freedom and erode further the potential for development that does exist. A deepening spiral of conflict and poverty can result, each twist making it more difficult for the international community to respond and stretching to the limit that political and economic capital that still exists. With each crisis there is a risk that the forces of isolationism will prevail, thereby allowing the problem to become entrenched. For Atwood, the case is overwhelming: 'this chaos is threatening our national self-interest. It is undermining global stability and it is making a mockery of our efforts to promote democracy and open-market systems' (*ibid*.: 2).

While such views are widely held within liberal governance, Atwood was also signalling USAID's insecure position within the American system of government. Compared to Europe, the forces of isolationism and budgetary conservatism are more pronounced in the USA. On more than one occasion, for example, USAID has come under strong attack by the right wing of the Republican party. These attacks include accusations that it is irrelevant to American foreign policy and that it should either be closed or absorbed by the State Department (Tanner and Fawcett 1999: 2). Even under the Clinton administration, from the mid-1990s, staff numbers were cut by a third and many overseas posts were closed. USAID has needed to demonstrate its utility and, in particular, to show the relevance of development to resolving the pressing issues of the day. Important here has been the repackaging of development assistance as structural conflict prevention (Atwood 1998: 4) – demonstrating its important contribution to national security and as insurance against the types of chaos and transborder threats expounded by the new barbarism school. While the need for such justification is relatively easy to identify in relation to the beleaguered USAID, similar requirements underpin the incorporation of war within development discourse more generally. To put it crudely, the new wars have become a lifeline for the aid and development industry.

Conflict has been accepted into mainstream development policy for a number of interconnected reasons. That new types of conflict exist is only one of these; there are also important governance and organisational interests to consider. The emergence of new forms of instability has reinforced the symbolic line that aid policy has drawn between the pre- and post-Cold War periods. Not only has conflict been rediscovered, but development assistance has simultaneously been granted a new lease of life as a structural form of conflict prevention. Hence, despite a history of failure, it has been repackaged as a valuable, indeed, as an essential weapon in the armoury of liberal peace.

Poverty and conflict

Since the inception of development discourse at the end of the Second World War, underdevelopment and poverty have been closely associated. Indeed, in international terms, they have usually served as proxies of each other and effectively have been interchangeable. The reinvention of development as a form of conflict prevention is an important part of the radicalisation of developmental politics. Indeed, it denotes a new commitment to those strategies and forms of intervention that are geared to the direct attempt to transform whole societies, including the beliefs and attitudes of their members. Consequently, although poverty has always been part of development discourse, the radicalisation of the latter has required that poverty be reincorporated in a new way. In short, because of the manner in which conflict is understood, the poor have been empowered as the natural partners of the strategic actors of liberal peace in their mission of social transformation.

Deepening poverty
Development discourse understands conflict and poverty as interconnecting in different but often reinforcing ways. Most commentators, for example, do not claim that there is a direct causal relationship between poverty and conflict. There are many poor countries that are relatively stable. At the same time, middle-income regions, such as the Balkans, have succumbed to violence and widespread dislocation. The association is usually presented in terms of poor countries representing a higher risk of conflict. A recent study by the OECD of 34 of the world's poorest countries, for example, describes how nearly two-thirds of them are either embroiled in or have only just emerged from ongoing conflict. In other words, poverty and the wider modalities of underdevelopment, while not leading to conflict automatically, nevertheless carry within them a high risk that violence may break out. Poverty is associated with conflict as a relation of probability. At the same time, violence itself is portrayed as complicating and deepening poverty. As reflected in the comments of USAID above, today's conflicts are understood as destroying development assets and social capital, making it

difficult for affected countries to regain the path of development. For example,

> the 15-year civil war in Mozambique destroyed 70 per cent of the country's schools and cost the country an estimated US$15 billion. Today, Mozambique is officially designated the world's poorest country. Violent conflict destroys economic and social infrastructure, reduces people's access to basic services and often leads to large-scale population displacement. And it can leave a legacy of bitter social and ethnic division which can last for generations. (Short 1999: 1)

While assertions that conflict deepens poverty are now common-place, such depictions are seldom backed up by reliable evidence. For example, to prove that Mozambique is the world's poorest country as a result of conflict would be very difficult, not least because reliable and comparative statistical information is notoriously hard to come by in such countries. Moreover, as Nordstrom (2000) points out, the claim that Mozambique is the world's poorest country was first made by the UN *during* the war, not following it. How the Mozambique authorities were able to pay for the war was not explained. What is lost in such statements are the 'vast networks of exchange, corruption and political power that moved [strategic supplies] from urban centres in peacetime countries to the remote outback of Mozambique' (Nordstrom 2001: 5). This position is made even more complex by the realisation that neigh-bouring countries such as Zambia and Malawi, which have not suffered a major conflict, have poverty levels not dissimilar to that of Mozam-bique. While the empirical evidence on this issue is uncertain, what is clearer is that the *idea* that conflict destroys development and deepens poverty plays an important role in mobilising the strategic complexes of liberal peace. Not only does it underpin the reinvention of develop-ment as conflict prevention, it also lends a certain urgency to the need to intervene. Morally justified in itself, intervention is also in the interests of international security since the spiral of impoverishment leading to further conflict *must* be broken.

The destruction of culture

The former chief economist of the World Bank has argued that in the quest for a new development paradigm that seeks to transform whole societies, the persistence of traditional forms of custom and practice is a clear symptom of development's past failure (Stiglitz 1998). Moreover, in future, development should not shrink away from replacing such practices with modern institutions as and when necessary. At the same time, the influential narrative of new barbarism is based on exploring the dangers and violent future that cultural difference and ethnic identity hold. Because of such concerns, liberal peace is ambivalent, if not hostile, to so-called traditional society. Consequently, while the destructiveness of conflict is deplored, its wider effects are not always regarded as wholly negative. Although violence can destroy development, a common strand within liberal governance is that it also erodes the cohesion of a society's culture, customs and traditions. Given that a radicalised development now seeks to transform societies as a whole, including the beliefs and attitudes of the people concerned, this Hobbesian outcome of violence has a certain utility. In ideological terms, it makes the process of transition easier. While the rolling back of development and the deepening of poverty provide the *urgency* to intervene, the destruction of culture furnishes the *opportunity* for aid agencies to establish new and replacement forms of collective identity and social organisation.

Returning to Mozambique, besides deepening poverty, aid agencies and Northern governments have commonly depicted the effects of the long-running civil war that ended in 1992 as those of weakening social cohesion and destroying culture. In relation to post-war reconstruction and the transition to development, many NGOs have framed their projects in terms of contributing to the re-establishment of social cohesion. In the mid-1990s, a Mozambique Participatory Poverty Assessment exercise supported by the World Bank put this view particularly well and is worth quoting at length.

> At the level of the household, mutual support networks work so as to reduce vulnerability to shocks such as food scarcity, seasonal stress periods, drought, or the illness of a family member. In many instances, these community-based mechanisms have been placed under considerable strain from household impoverishment. Conflict between traditional social structures and post-independence structures ... has weakened community level networks and the effects of the civil war dealt a further severe blow to safety nets based on social and institutional relations which were already in a state of readjustment. The capacity to make claims of kin and community members is as much dependent on the holding of assets of supporting households and informal safety nets begin to break down when these households are forced to roll back their charity. (MPPA 1996: 9)

A more sharply drawn variant of the above view relates to the claim that conflict and population displacement have greatly weakened traditional social structures and that, through a mixing and dilution of cultural practices, a form of *ersatz* peasantry has emerged. The following quote is from a development consultant studying the position of widow-headed households in Zambezia Province:

> the intense destabilisation of society through the war, the movement of people away from their ancestral villages through internal displacement, urbanisation and modernisation, ethnic inter-marriage, the introduction of a cash crop economy in traditional communities, has resulted in much less homogeneity within one ethnic group.... The social organisation of the countryside has changed enormously because of the war years and it is not possible therefore to state precisely what is the custom and practice of either a matrilineal group or a non-matrilineal group. (Owen 1996: 5–6)

The impression given here is that the cultural basis of rural society has been eroded and mixed up to such an extent that it is almost beyond knowing. In the same vein, the British government's DFID noted, in support of an agricultural extension project in Zambezia managed by World Vision, that years of civil war

> effectively destroyed most of the previous community structures through out-migration to avoid the conflict and removal of traditional social hierarchies and relationships. Following the Peace Accord of 1992 many people returned to their home areas to find almost complete destruction of housing, physical infrastructure and services and there-fore in many areas communities started to emerge afresh from family units to help meet basic needs. (DFID 1998: Annex 1,1)

This is an interesting statement on two accounts. First, it claims a degree of social and cultural destruction that would be difficult to substantiate. Second, in attempting to represent the weakening of social cohesion, the last sentence comes close to suggesting that, with resettlement following the war, an autochthonous rebirth of rural society has taken place. With culture destroyed by war, rural society has somehow returned to a natural state of family-based simplicity.

While these examples are specific to Mozambique, the idea that war has a Hobbesian effect on cultural and social relations is common within the mainstream understanding of conflict. Further examples are given in Chapter 8 regarding the representation of displaced Southerners in Sudan. Agency literature abounds with sharply drawn images of social collapse and anomie. For the NGO International Alert, for example,

> the effects of these new conflicts are even more devastating than in the case of traditional cross-border wars. *They strike at the very heart of a nation's social fabric* not only threatening its political and economic development but more importantly laying the foundations for years of hatred and mistrust between peoples. In such conflicts, violence against civilians is

now the norm not the exception and the threat of widespread killing, rape and child exploitation is leading to massive population displacements, regional instability and *disruption to long established patterns of economic, social and political relations*. The consequences of such *complete societal breakdown* for overall development objectives are enormous. (International Alert 1999: 74, emphasis added)

As with the depiction of conflict destroying development, the idea that it erodes and disrupts culture and tradition is also open to contention. Indeed, one could argue that in many cases conflict has an *opposite* effect. In making social groups more dependent on their own resources, coping strategies and social networks, conflict and displacement, while introducing elements of change and adaptation, often act to reconfirm or even strengthen social and cultural ties (Gellner 1998). In relation to Mozambique, for example, in analysing the social effects of war and displacement in Manica Province, the political economist Mark Chingono (1998) has argued just this. In times of adversity, such networks become more rather than less important. They are often fiercely defended rather than surrendering the support they provide to an uncertain *ersatz* or autochthonous existence. If one takes an historical perspective, if violent conflict did have the effect that many aid agencies ascribe to it, after centuries of turmoil in Europe, everyone should be a cultural blank. Examining conflict in more innovative terms demands that we address the possibility that violence can be, and often is, a means whereby cultural forms are maintained, changed and expanded. This alternative is explored in detail in Chapter 7 in relation to the emergence of new political complexes in the South.

It should be understood that whether or not conflict weakens culture is not a purely academic question. More consultancy or research will not necessarily resolve this issue. The representation of cultural breakdown is an important aspect of liberal peace as a *relation of governance*. For NGOs and government funding agencies it provides the justification and opportunity to establish *new forms of identity and social cohesion*. In other words, it lends itself to the radical demand that development is now about direct social transformation. Whether, for example, NGOs are embarked upon encouraging pro-poor forms of production, establishing egalitarian credit schemes or supporting gender-aware community projects, the emphasis is upon creating new forms of collective organisation and identity that change what people think and what they do. This radical agenda is made easier to initiate (but not necessarily to implement or achieve success) if the moral universe within which one operates has already either problematised indigenous ways of doing things or represented them as eroded or collapsed.

The poor as allies of liberal peace

The destructive effects of conflict, in relation to both development and culture, tend to act on the poor as *victims*. This representation establishes both the urgency and the opportunity for liberal peace to act. Liberal global governance, however, is not an imperial form of power. It is not based upon coercion but on the liberal principles of cooperation and partnership. While the manner in which conflict is understood may furnish forms of justification, it is nonetheless important that the poor themselves willingly share global governance's vision of the future. In this respect, besides justifying intervention, how conflict is understood must also empower the poor as the allies of liberal peace. The poor must be more than victims, they must be capable of volition and action as well. The manner of this empowerment is an enduring feature of liberal reformism: the portrayal of the poor as belonging to the dangerous classes that, if ignored, are prone to revolt against the conditions of their subjugation. In other words, they are not just passive victims but appear as self-acting *agents* as well.

Depicting the poor as capable of reacting violently against the modalities of underdevelopment has long been a part of development discourse. This was as true during the Cold War as it is today. In the 1992 *Agenda for Peace*, for example, Boutros-Ghali argued that conflict prevention measures to be successful in the long term must address the deepest cause of conflict, that is, 'economic despair, social injustice and political oppression' (1995: 43). During the course of the 1990s, this sentiment was repeated and refashioned in contemporary language. In the evidence supplied to Britain's International Development Committee on the causes of conflict, for example, it was noted that the main emphasis was not simply on poverty 'but on inequality and sudden economic shocks as risk factors for violent conflict' (IDC 1999: para. 18). Reflecting the views of a number of NGO contributors, Saferworld summed up the situation in the following way:

> The common theme here – which increases a society's vulnerability to civil war – is the belief among millions of people within that society that they have 'no stake in the system' – the system denies them the capacity to provide for themselves and their families, and cannot even protect them against violence and human rights abuses. (Saferworld 1999: 69)

Poverty does not cause conflict, it only increases its probability. At the same time, however, when it does occur, it is typically portrayed by liberal governance as a form of general social revolt by the poor against the oppressive modalities of underdevelopment: social exclusion, lack

126

of protection from economic shocks, human rights abuse, corruption, and so on. In the last analysis, the root cause of conflict – or, at least, the root cause that liberal governance is willing to countenance – is portrayed as the poor venting their frustration and anger at a system in which they have no stake, and from which they derive no protection or benefit. While ethnicity may often be the vehicle through which social exclusion is expressed, conflict originating from poverty and an angry despair with underdevelopment has little to do with the bioculturalism of new barbarism. Indeed, liberal peace clearly feels that such a revolt, apart from its destructive consequences, is ultimately legitimate. The point of its representation, however, is not for the North's strategic actors to cheer the poor on from the side while they get on with the job themselves. It is to provide a rationale for liberal peace to form an alliance with them; to give a listening ear to the poor, understanding their real frustrations and facilitating the necessary guidance, support and articulation to ensure that their just grievances can be righted in a peaceful way. If this were not the case, why would aid agencies and NGOs exist? Since development also strives for social inclusion and the strengthening of protection, development discourse has empowered the poor as the natural allies of global liberal governance in its pursuit of stability.

In terms of forming alliances with the poor in order to help them transform their understandable grievances into peaceful social change, liberal governance confronts a major problem: the poor cannot always be trusted to make the right decisions. Moreover, it cannot be assumed that they will see the benefits of alliance. This problem expresses itself clearly in terms of how liberal peace has problematised the issue of leadership in the social revolt of the poor. In their rejection of a system in which they have no stake, the poor are prone to pick up leaders they do not deserve and global liberal governance does not want. The *Carnegie Commission on Preventing Deadly Conflict*, in a report that well reflects the international consensus, describes the situation as follows.

> The contemporary world transformation, with all its intense pressures and unforeseen consequences, tends to pull people toward strongly supporting groups. These groups, in turn, particularly with charismatic, inflammatory leadership, may easily become harsh, separatist, and depreciatory toward others. A deadly combination of severe social stress and distinctly hateful, fanatical leadership can produce mass killing, even genocide…. Such intergroup tensions may readily be exacerbated by deteriorating economic conditions, erosion of social norms, or mass migration. Hateful attitudes may be directed either toward outsiders or minorities in one's own country – or both. (Carnegie Commission 1997: ix)

In arguing that poverty alone is not an automatic cause of violence, Saferworld has argued that this

> requires a trigger factor, most frequently the baleful actions of individual leaders.... And the more acute the sense of grievance, the more likely it is that a large number of people will be susceptible to the siren voices of extremists, and believe that they have more to gain from war than peace. (Saferworld 1999: 69)

Mary Anderson, in her extremely influential work *Do No Harm*, has expressed the liberal consensus in the following manner. The end of the Cold War

> left a power vacuum where individuals and groups vied for pre-eminence [and where often] would-be leaders have focused on divisions in their societies and have excited and manipulated sub-group identities as a means of defining their 'causes' and gaining constituencies. (Anderson 1996: 8)

The view that the poor are prone to revolt against underdevelopment yet, at the same time, tend to attract criminally violent and vengeful leaders is extremely important for liberal peace. If the revolt is legitimate and invites strategic alliance, the need to separate the deserving poor from their undeserving leaders underscores the urgency of intervention. As Brian Atwood has remarked in this context, Americans need to stop celebrating the end of history 'and start doing what Americans do best – take history by the neck, wrestle it to the ground and begin to shape the future' (Atwood 1998: 2). The problematisation of leadership underscores the urgency of intervention, but the separation of bad leaders from the poor and their civil institutions is also a central concern of conflict resolution and post-conflict reconstruction. Such a separation, for example, forms the basis of sanctions policy, as well as local-level attempts to unite the poor against their putative leaders (Anderson 1996).

The delegitimation of leadership

In seeking to ally itself with the poor in their just struggle against underdevelopment, liberal governance has encountered the problem that the poor very often already have their own non-liberal leaders. In an attempt to justify its own authority, the general approach of liberal governance has been to delegitimise indigenous leadership in violent conflict. Although the causes of conflict are usually only briefly rehearsed in mainstream aid policy, what is said is richly layered with

128

meaning. For example, almost every quotation in the preceding pages either directly or indirectly problematises, delegitimises or criminalises indigenous leadership. Organic to the common description of the new wars – their destruction of development assets, erosion of the social fabric, predilection toward widespread human rights abuse, and so on – is the reflexive action to place their leaders well beyond the pale. This is not to say that much of this narrative does not have a basis in real events – many leaders of local wars are extremely violent, woefully corrupt and beyond political redemption. However, it is important to maintain a wider awareness of the direction in which development discourse, under the momentum of its own inner logic and particular governance requirements, is leading us.

For global liberal governance *all* violent conflicts are dangerous. A common refrain regarding conflict resolution is that aid agencies are not attempting to eradicate every form of social contrariety and political antagonism. Confrontation and dispute are the stuff of change and development in normal societies. Rather, 'it is *violent conflict, harsh repression and coercive force*, rather than conflict *per se*, that are unhealthy and unacceptable factors of political life' (Rummel 1996: 16, emphasis added). The condemnation of all violent conflict by liberal peace means that the leaders of violent conflicts are automatically problematised. By their own actions, they risk placing themselves beyond the limits of cooperation and partnership. This is regardless of whether they are guilty of war crimes, which many are, or defending themselves from dispossession or exploitation, which some may be. One should not forget that, a generation ago, in the different moral universe that accompanied superpower rivalry, many people regarded violent insurgency in the South as defensible. Indeed, a whole genre of solidarity politics emerged in the West. In some cases, such as the Vietnam Solidarity Campaign, such movements achieved a good deal of acceptance and influence. In relation to violent conflict today, however, liberal governance has all but abolished the idea of a just cause. Many NGOs, the erstwhile representatives of social movements, also now agree.

Where attempts are made to explain and justify this change, it has usually been in terms of how the new wars no longer serve the same ends as the old. For Anderson, past wars are regarded as an inevitable result of both human nature and people's understandable desire for social improvement. Although people hate wars, historically conflict has been a vehicle to overcome oppression and secure the democratic rights and freedoms that many of us now take for granted. Regarding today's new wars, however, given that democratic values now shape the normative order, together with the associated growth and influence of international legal and political instruments and fora, the situation is not the same. There are 'notable shifts in the locations and type of wars that raise serious questions about war's inevitability and about its appropriateness as an instrument for achieving justice' (Anderson 1996: 8).

Liberal peace has questioned violent conflict as a legitimate vehicle for social change. We live in a world that, potentially, already has the best possible mix of social relations, economic structures and political institutions. The task is not to challenge this order but to make it work better. Regardless of their actions, the leaders of the new wars have been universally problematised and delegitimised. If aid agencies are to clear a way for themselves and form partnerships with the poor to facilitate non-violent social reform, this is a necessary denouncement. On the other hand, it also establishes the rules of the game. It denotes the type of commitment and behaviour that liberal governance requires if leaders and their followers are to gain admittance to its formal networks. It should also be noted, however, that the delegitimation of leadership accords with other, longer-established aspects of development discourse – the increasing willingness of NGOs and others, since the 1970s, to bypass state structures, as well as all forms of national and local elite groups, in an endeavour to work directly with the poor. The blanket criminalisation of the leadership of violent conflict is part of this process. In its endeavour to transform whole societies, it is an important part of the attempt by global governance to reach right down to the grassroots and this time to leave nothing to chance.

The criminalisation of conflict

In examining the means by which indigenous leadership has been delegitimised, development discourse has used two main approaches. The first, occurring in the early part of the 1990s, has been to borrow heavily from the narrative of new barbarism. Depictions of violent and anarchic groups lacking clear political programmes were prominent during the first half of the 1990s. During this period, it was common to encounter descriptions of post-ideological leaders and the movements they established as being little more than 'militias and armed civilians with little discipline and with ill-defined chains of command' (Boutros-Ghali 1995: 8–9). The second, and more recent, trend has been to incorporate certain aspects of the growing literature on war economies to make a case for the emergence of systems of criminally maintained violence. Following the experiences of Bosnia and Rwanda, a new trend has emerged involving a recognition that leadership may not be as anarchic as often depicted: instead, it is theorised as criminal.

During the course of the 1990s, a growing literature addressing the political economy of the new wars has emerged.[3] While there are differences regarding interpretation and emphasis within this literature, a common feature has been to regard current patterns of conflict as symptomatic of the creation of new social and political relations, indeed, the emergence of new political complexes in the South. While aid policy has tended to portray irrationality, breakdown and collapse, much of the political economy literature, while not condoning violence or human rights abuse, has sought to emphasise its association with society-wide transformations and the creation of new local–global networks and forms of legitimacy. Many writers within the political economy canon have long viewed with scepticism the frequent portrayals of anarchy and collapse within mainstream aid policy. Even the most war-affected countries and regions necessarily maintain structured forms of political authority and social practice, even if they are not of an expected or conventional aspect (Bradbury 1997). In relation to this type of analysis, liberal governance has tended to take a rather narrower and more self-serving view of the changes associated with conflict.

In moving from the depiction of anarchy to the criminalisation of leadership, liberal peace has tended to abstract and reify those aspects of political economy that address the profits that can be made from organised violence. These opportunities are then represented as the central motive for extreme and manipulative leaders to engage in conflict; indeed, to perpetuate it. The issue, again, is not whether such activity takes place. If only because of the ending of superpower patronage, warring parties today have to be far more independent, innovative and, yes, ruthless in terms of their own self-provisioning. Under such conditions, the emergence of what are now often called war economies is inevitable (van Creveld 1991: 216). What is in question is the attempt to draw a line around such activity, to label it and parcel it up as 'criminal'. While seemingly addressing the extremities of human behaviour, such a process is profoundly normalising. In labelling the economic dimensions of conflict as criminal a number of things follow. The idea is implanted that such activity is mainly the prerogative of a corrupt few. That is, it does not relate to wider societal changes and globalised practices. On the contrary, rather like current approaches to the (expanding) drugs trade, it is an illicit aberration that can be circumscribed and policed. This not only reinforces the need for global governance to intervene and separate the deserving poor from their undeserving leaders; perhaps more significantly, the idea that criminality is circumscribed and specific is vital if the possibility of

131

development itself is to be maintained. Once violent, corrupt and criminal leaders are neutralised or removed, liberal peace, in alliance with the poor, can once again resume normal development. The idea that the new wars may be symptomatic of much wider societal and international transformations is not seriously considered. They remain a temporary aberration on the inevitable road to development and security.

It is becoming increasingly accepted within aid policy that there is a connection between conflict and criminality. When conflict is triggered by violent and extreme leaders, it easily leads to a self-perpetuating quest for loot. 'There is a continuum now in the developing world between political conflict and violent crime, the ready flows of small arms fuelling both forms of violence and both forms of violence having a harmful effect on prospects for development' (IDC 1999: para. 9). This continuum has recently been given an institutional analogue with the formation in February 1999 of a new World Bank research programme on 'The Economics of Civil War, Crime and Violence'. In a couple of start-up papers, the programme leader, Paul Collier has established a number of directions that the criminalisation thesis is taking (Collier 1999; Collier and Hoeffler 1999). The rationale for the World Bank research programme is that in the past the study of conflict and crime has been developed within the social sciences. In particular, there has been a concern with the social and political dimensions of these problems. There is a space, therefore, for the use of economic tools to analyse systematically the existing data on crime and violence. Collier's approach has been to distinguish between 'greed' and 'grievance'. His main finding is that greed far outweighs grievance as a trigger of violent conflict. In this respect, his work represents an important attempt to expand the theme of the delegitimation of leadership. Even though warring parties usually base themselves on narratives of grievance, it is greed that is the primary driving force.

> I should emphasize that I do not mean to be cynical. I am not arguing that rebels necessarily deceive either others or themselves in explaining their motivation in terms of grievance. Rather, I am simply arguing that since both greed-motivated rebel organisations will embed their behaviour in a narrative of grievance, the observation of that narrative provides no informational content to the researcher as to the true motivation for rebellion. (Collier 1999: 1)

Despite this rider, the argument and the evidence used to support it are a powerful means of delegitimation and a good excuse for the World Bank and others to pay little attention to critical voices from the

South. In order to defend this position, a number of economic and grievance proxies are established from a large database of different countries (former Zaïre, Liberia, Sudan, Chad, for example) that one would not automatically equate with reliable, extensive and comparative statistical information. Economic proxies are the degree to which a country is reliant on the export of primary (i.e., lootable) products; the proportion of young men in the population; and the educational endowment of the society. In many respects, such proxies are a good example of the manner in which underdevelopment has been reproblematised as dangerous. For grievance, the proxies are the degree of ethnic or religious fractionalisation; the level of economic inequality; the lack of political rights; and the effectiveness of economic management reflected in the rate of economic growth over the preceding five years. Quantitative analysis of these proxies is cited to demonstrate that economic agendas rather than grievances are the overwhelming cause of most conflict. 'A country with large natural resources, many young men and little education is very much more at risk of conflict than one with opposite characteristics' (*ibid*.: 5).

Usefully for the World Bank, the only grievance that appears relevant is that relating to rapid economic decline; in other words, poor economic management. Economic inequality or political repression were not significant. Neither were high levels of social fractionalisation within a society. The reason put forward for the weak relationship between grievance and conflict is the difficulty of mobilising collective action – as demonstrated by the 'free rider' phenomenon (an individual may not like the government, but whether or not it is overthrown is not seen as dependent on the 'free rider's' personal involvement). Problems of scaling up and coordination also emerge. Where cooperation is made easier it is in relation to social capital – the trust that emerges through participation in social networks, clubs and societies. For Collier, the reason why highly fractionalised societies do not appear to have a high risk of conflict is that such social capital does not usually transcend ethnic and religious divisions. In many respects, what Collier is arguing is that although the poor may well wish to revolt, in most cases they will not do so without cross-cutting social networks or, importantly, the forcing effect of violent entrepreneurial leaders. Moreover, there is nothing like greed to forge the social networks needed to overcome problems of scale and coordination. In other words, the 'true cause of much civil war is not the loud discourse of grievance, but the silent force of greed' (*ibid*.: 7).

It should be noted that Collier assumes that the new wars still replicate the orthodox and somewhat traditional assumption that conflict pushes a society from a 'normal' state of economic equilibrium to an 'abnormal' state of disequilibrium. It is in relation to the abnormal state of disequilibrium that Collier is able to describe some of the illicit opportunities created by war. For example, conflict creates a climate of business opportunism between firms; there is a growth in criminality as the risk of apprehension declines; traders resort to illegal practices; competition breaks down and extra-legal monopolies emerge; rent seeking and predation in trade relations develop; and so on. The assumption that society moves from a pre-existing state of normality to one of abnormality is common in economistic forms of analysis. It is well represented, for example, in the UN/WIDER programme on the economics of civil war (Nafziger and Auvinen 1997). What is new in Collier's interpretation, however, is the argument that in moving into disequilibrium, and thereby illicitly profiting from conflict, leaders will mobilise to maintain this state:

> sufficiently decentralized greed-motivated rebellions tend to kill off the economic goose and so die out. If there is no trade there is no loot. To prevent this, a rebel movement will try to create a monopoly of predation and for this it must generate a monopoly of rebel violence. (*Ibid.*: 9)

Leaders, for example, will attempt to restart the export of primary products and develop other activities that maintain their position. In other words, a war economy emerges and, since it has a number of powerful winners, becomes entrenched.

> The rebels will do well through predation on primary commodity exports, traders will do well through widened margins on the goods they sell to consumers, criminals will do well through theft, and opportunistic businessmen will do well at the expense of those businesses which are constrained to honest conduct. (*Ibid.*: 9)

It is the greed of such groups rather than a grievance that drives today's new wars. It is interesting to note that Anderson, without the aid of powerful economic tools of analysis, has come to a similar conclusion. Everywhere, it is argued, ordinary people have distanced themselves from the conflicts that surround them. They do not accept any ownership of them. 'In country after country, people are saying that the wars in which they are engaged are not serving justice or solving the real problems they face. They say that their leaders have "manipulated" them into purposeless fighting' (Anderson 1996: 10). In her own way, Anderson also argues that greed rather than grievance drives the new wars. While people abhor their leaders' quest for power, they are powerless to do much about it. The criminalisation of leadership provides liberal peace with a sense of both justification and urgency in the attempt to separate the poor from their leaders. In the case of Collier, this separation is made all the more necessary by a representation of leadership as not only criminal but purposely engaged in holding a society in a state of abnormal disequilibrium. The policy recommendations following from this analysis are a mixture of inducements and policing measures. Leaders, for example, could either be bought off or isolated by increasing the economic return that derives from peace. Peace settlements should be designed with an eye to benefiting as many groups as possible. If the groups favouring conflict cannot be bought off, they have to be overcome. Such interventions should aim to reduce the profits that leaders can derive from conflict. In separating the poor from its leadership, Anderson's idea of local capacities for peace complements the approach of Collier: in this case, aid is used to strengthen the linkages between the majority of people who oppose violence, and to create spaces for peace. In many respects, such ideas encompass the reinvention of development within global liberal governance as conflict resolution and societal reconstruction.

NOTES

1 Goldberg's article coincided with attempts by the US to revive an Africa policy based on the emergence of a new, market-friendly generation of African leaders. Following the escalation of region-wide conflict centred on the Democratic Republic of Congo and the re-emergence of war between Ethiopia and Eritrea, the rationale of this policy has suffered a major setback.

2 DFID, *Eliminating World Poverty: a Challenge for the Twenty-first Century* (London: Department for International Development, 1997).

3 See, for example, Keen 1994; Keen 1998; Duffield 1994a; Duffield 1999; Atkinson 1997; Ellis 1996; Richards 1996; Reno 1998; Kaldor 1999; Chingono 1996; Griffiths 1998; Goodhand 1999; Le Billon 1999; Bayart, Ellis and Hibou 1999; Schierup 1992; Tishkov 1997.

6
The Growth of
Transborder Shadow Economies

Social regression or social transformation?

For global governance, violent conflict is synonymous with various forms of deviant or criminalised activity that result in social breakdown and collapse. Motivated by the greed or power craving of a few, it deepens and complicates poverty, erodes cultural cohesion and traumatises the majority of those caught up in it. We need not doubt that the victims of violence experience such effects; lives are blighted, futures squandered and livelihoods wrecked. War leaves an indelible mark on those that it directly touches. In viewing conflict in terms of aberration and breakdown, however, liberal peace is being rather disingenuous with the victims of violence. Ideas of deviance and collapse provide the governance networks of liberal peace with a powerful means of mobilising resources, giving urgency to its tasks, discerning opportunities and justifying actions. Highlighting the plight of victims gives liberal peace its political rationale. This is something that exists independently of specific conflicts or outbreaks of violence. At the same time, the effects of war are much wider than those experienced by its victims. It is also an important means of social reordering and transformation (van Creveld 1991: 220). In distinction to breakdown and chaos, it is also possible to see war as a given, an axis around which social, economic and political relations are measured and reshaped to establish new forms of agency and legitimacy. Just as this was true in the past, it is also the case in relation to today's new wars. Indeed, in so far as these conflicts dissolve conventional distinctions between 'people', 'army' and 'government', the implications of the social transformation involved are especially radical and far-reaching. The victims of this transformation, moreover, are well aware of its depth.

The study of the new wars as a form of social transformation has largely been pursued from the perspective of political economy and anthropology. By the beginning of the 1980s, the view that war was the result of a developmental malaise had already gained wide acceptance. At the same time, however, it was still common to regard internal wars as an extension of superpower rivalry. Contrary to many people's expectations, however, the end of the Cold War did not result in a decline in such conflicts. Indeed, despite a major reduction in super-power patronage and support, old conflicts continued and new ones broke out. This development did two things. First, it reinforced the existing trend for conflict analysis to devote greater attention to internal relations. Second, and importantly, the very fact of their survival and continued emergence suggested that warring parties had found ways of improving their self-sufficiency, even if they had not become inde-pendent of outside support (Duffield 1991). The economic basis of internal war, especially how warring parties mobilise resources and establish legitimacy in this new international environment, has become a growing area of study.

The UNITA rebel movement in Angola, since it spans both Cold War and post-Cold War periods, is a good example of the complexity of the transformation under discussion. During the 1980s, it had established a base area in southern Angola adjoining the Namibian border. In its conflict with the Cuban-assisted MPLA government, it received cross-border military assistance and support from South Africa and the USA. By the end of the 1980s, however, reflecting the thaw in Cold War relations, a number of agreements had been reached which paved the way for Cuban and South African withdrawal, together with Namibia's independence and the closure of its border with UNITA. Under UN auspices an electoral process was also established to bring UNITA and the MPLA together. As a result of international pressure, this culmi-nated in a ceasefire in 1991 and elections the following year. During the early 1990s, however, to make good its loss of superpower patronage, UNITA consolidated its presence in the diamond fields of central and northern Angola (Vines 1993). When it did badly in the 1992 elections, UNITA was able to use such resources to resume the conflict. Realising this wealth, however, has been dependent on several new and interre-lated developments. These included the strengthening of transregional smuggling routes and the forging of local connections with unregu-lated global diamond and arms networks (Global Witness 1998). UNITA has become far more internationalised through such networks than it was during the Cold War. One result of this transformation can be judged from the effects of what was called the 'war of the cities' that followed the breakdown of the 1992 elections. In less than twelve months it is estimated that 100,000 people were killed (*Africa Confidential* 1993). This can be compared to the 120,000 thought to have died during the 16 years of conflict prior to 1991 (Sogge 1992). While the accuracy of such figures can be questioned, the difference between them is sufficiently great to suggest that independent self-provisioning is not only possible, but can be made to work with deadly effect – a point underscored by UNITA's continuing ability to operate despite UN sanctions on trade in Angolan diamonds.

The self-development of UNITA, from a reliance on superpower support to having an independent and globalised existence, represents a complex process of social transformation and adaptation. The sketch given above does not reflect the full extent of that process. Not only are spatial and geographical shifts involved, but UNITA's control of resources and populations, its mode of legitimation and organisation, and its relations with outside actors, international agencies and global networks have all undergone a wide-ranging process of change and development. Today, both UNITA and Angola have outgrown the relations and structures existing during the 1960s when the war began. Regarding war as a form of aberration and breakdown, however, fails to grasp the extent and significance of this adaptive process and the complex organisational changes involved. Moreover, should peace come to Angola, these adaptations and the local–global linkages formed during conflict will be an organic part of that regime.

Within the analysis of the political economy of internal war, since the beginning of the 1990s, the point has been made that conflicts have winners as well as losers (Keen 1991). There are groups and parties that in some way – socially, politically or economically – gain from conflict. Because dominant groups are able to derive something through non-conventional forms of warfare, where only anarchy and chaos are perceived by conventional wisdom, violence has a certain rational calculus. To say this, however, is not to reduce conflict to the pursuit of advantage, profit or greed. This can result in what Richards (Richards 2000) has called 'warlord fundamentalism'. In avoiding such reductionism, it is crucial to observe that social actors, in securing their self-preservation or seeking advantage, are forced to create the social and political conditions in which new forms of wealth, redistribution and legitimacy can be realised. We may not particularly like all the structures that emerge, and some will no doubt offend our liberal views of equity and gender; but emerge they will. In other words, the political economy of internal war is founded on a double argument: the pursuit of political or economic advantage through conflict by social groups simultaneously drives a complex process of social transformation and actual development. This independent emergence of new forms of protection, authority and rights to wealth is a complex process in the sense that it is greater than the individual acts of gain and redistribution that drive it along. In attempting to move beyond seeing conflict in terms of aberration and collapse, David Keen has argued that war 'is not simply a breakdown in a particular system, but a way of creating an alternative system of profit, power and even protection' (Keen 1998: 11).

A similar position is echoed in the work of Reno (Reno 1995a) on West Africa. Concerning the economic and political strategies pursued by the Liberian warlord Charles Taylor during the first part of the 1990s, we are asked not to prejudge these in a dismissive light as local predation characteristic of weak or failed states. If one temporarily sets aside the brutal and coercive methods involved, on the contrary, they can be presented as new and innovative ways of projecting political power. While this may be an alarming supposition, given Charles Taylor's victory in Liberia's 1995 elections his methods can nevertheless be judged as successful. In relation to Taylor's earlier warlord activities, Reno asks, 'Does this transformed patrimonialism represent a new kind of state, an alternative institutionalisation of sovereign authority capable of defending itself and doing things without significant bureaucracies?' (*ibid.*: 109).

Political economy has provided many insights into the nature of the new wars. At the same time, however, some of its findings have been incorporated within development discourse. This incorporation has been achieved by separating the double argument on which it is based: the idea of conflict as private gain has been accepted while its association with social transformation has been ignored. Individual acts of appropriation or seizure can, if abstracted from their context, be presented as a series of criminalised, short-term and self-reproducing gains. Such interpretations, for example, have been used to support the concept of a self-perpetuating war economy (see IDC 1999; Collier 1999). In this sense, one can see an important difference between the political economy argument and the position of mainstream aid policy. In reducing war to sectarian economic gain, not only has the dimension of social transformation been minimised or lost, but the opposite tends to emerge. Collier (1999), for example, regards greedy and violent leaders as somehow locking in the characteristics of deviancy and breakdown. Criminalised leaders organise to maintain private profit and so perpetuate conflict's aberrant social conditions. This is not social transformation but rather a form of social regression. Moreover, the representation of destruction perpetuated by greed provides liberal peace with a means of delegitimising leadership and justifying intervention. Social transformation and actual development, however, suggest the possibility of a different set of outcomes. War as social transformation suggests the emergence of new forms of rights to wealth, political legitimacy and modes of accumulation and redistribution. Violent conflict is one part of a much wider area of actual development that lies beyond the narrow foundation of conventional economic and political models. Its independence from the strategic complexes of liberal peace defines both its fascination and its threat.

The limits of the formal economy

There is currently a tension between viewing war in terms of aberration and breakdown or, alternatively, as a form of social transformation. While all conflicts contain elements of both, development discourse has tended to criminalise the new wars, seeing them as retrograde, archaic and reactionary in relation to its particular vision of modernisation. From this perspective, the contribution of conflict to social transformation has been marginalised. There are many indications of this. Rather surprisingly, for example, the actors and warring parties involved in the new wars remain underresearched. While war has been incorporated into development discourse, few studies exist on actual rebel movements and so-called weak or rogue states that might show how such entities function politically and economically, how they are resourced, their redistributive mechanisms, how they establish legitimacy and authority, the forms of protection they provide, how they link local and global networks, and so on.[1] To mention just a few, one would be hard pressed to find such work relating to the Sudanese People's Liberation Army (SPLA) in Sudan, the Democratic Republic of Congo, the Serbian state or Saddam Hussein's Iraq. In the main, aid policy is content with brief pathologies of deviancy and breakdown. Moreover, since the implication is that such entities are temporary or transitional in nature, the type of research suggested above becomes unnecessary. The only legitimate question for liberal governance is how agencies should respond and how can aid be used to produce stability.

The marginalisation of independent social transformation is reflected in problems of conceptualisation. When images of aberration and collapse predominate, it is difficult to reconcile this condition with ideas relating to social change and adaptation. Within development discourse, seeing war as a form of transformation appears subversive and even morally offensive. Within the world of development, aid agencies are responsible for initiating and managing social change. At the same time, it is difficult to reconcile violence with the emergence of new and, indeed, innovative political and economic relations. Within the moral universe of development and conflict resolution, they contradict each other and defy connection. In seeing the new wars as agents of social transformation one is forced to enter a world of oxymorons, metaphors and strained meaning where the search for new concepts and accurate modes of expression is as urgent as the need for objective research itself.

The lack of an adequate language for describing the social and organisational effects of the new wars stems from the radical nature of the processes involved. Not only are they often violent but, in blurring the conventional distinctions between people, army and government, they have established a political dynamic that goes beyond any bounded notion of the nation state. However, much of what currently passes for post-war reconstruction in the South involves attempting to create familiar liberal forms of civil society and pluralistic state structures. This conservatism is all the more noticeable given that the strategic complexes of liberal peace have forged non-state and non-territorial networks similar to those of the new wars. The transition, however, goes beyond conventional economic as well as political models. While the extent of non-formal economic activity in the South is often commented upon, this knowledge has yet to produce an alternative paradigm. For example, in places like Angola, as little as 10 per cent of the country's estimated GNP is thought to be produced through conventional – legally established and publicly regulated – economic practices. In Mozambique the conventional economy is thought to account for only half of the country's GNP, while in Kenya and Russia it is about 40 per cent (Nordstrom 2000).[2] Indeed, over much of the South, estimates of the size of the conventional economy are often a half or less (in a few cases appreciably so) of total economic activity. Somalia, for example, strictly speaking has no official economy at all. In other words, in many places, the conventional economy of formally regulated investment, production and trade amounts to what could be called a part-time activity. Yet, despite the narrowness of this foundation it is the site on which the edifice of development economics now rests. From this small purchase, the universe of structural adjustment and market liberalisation rises in all its teleological confidence. It is through the associated and problematic government institutions of this narrow conduit, moreover, that the majority of all aid flows and activities continue to be directed.

Since it is unrecorded and unregulated, accurate figures for the size of the global shadow economy do not exist. Where estimates have been made, it is usually in relation to the criminal areas of the non-formal economy. In the mid-1990s, for example, the UN estimated that the global trade in drugs, at $500 billion a year or around 8 per cent of world trade, was larger than the oil business (Castells 1998: 169). Low compared to some estimates, the overall profit from all criminal activities was put at $750 billion. The magnitude of the shadow economy is further indicated if one examines the significance for an individual drug-producing country. During the late 1980s, for example, coca cultivators in Bolivia were estimated to have earned some $316 million from their crops. This was more than the value of all the rest of Bolivia's agricultural production (George 1992: 41–2). At this time, Bolivia was also producing about 1 million kilos of cocaine paste. Leaf cultivation and paste production were the main sources of foreign currency, exceeding the performance of all legal exports. Estimates for the total amount monetised range from $0.5 to $1.5 billion per year or, at the higher range, about a third of Bolivia's official GNP. In themselves, such magnitudes are not that remarkable. They could be matched by other cocaine producers as well as by parallel economies in Africa and the European East. Albania, for example, is estimated to realise a fifth of its national income through smuggling (Borger 1997). Moreover, as mentioned above, most estimates have been made in relation to the criminal components of transborder trade. When one considers that the shadow trade in all types of legal goods, commodities and services is now a lifeline for millions in the South, the parallel or non-formal economy must now register as a major component of all global trade. It is this economy that has expanded and reintegrated the South within the liberal world system following its exclusion from the formal networks of the informational economy.

While working in Mozambique and Angola during the late 1990s, the anthropologist Carolyn Nordstrom formulated a research question regarding non-formal economic activity. This involved asking aid agencies where the power and resources for post-war reconstruction would come from, if the conventional economy was so small? The question was posed to practitioners from more than two dozen organisations involving a range of UN specialist agencies, international financial institutions, embassies and major international NGOs. It is worth quoting at length the results of this enquiry.

> From Angola to Mozambique, most responded that non-formal economics are central to development processes. But answers were vague as to exactly what comprises non-formal economic and political powers, who is involved, how it works, and what relationships hold between

non-formal and formal economies both nationally and internationally. In the discussion of non-formal and extra-state activities, there is a general tendency to postulate that the non-formal markets, whether in Africa or of eastern Europe and Asia, are the result of a combination of changing political regimes, social transitions, and economic opportunism. The belief is that as these countries settle down in the course of normal state development, their economies will become increasingly defined by state-regulated institutions. In this way, while illegal goods (i.e., drugs and weapons) and service rings (i.e., mercenaries and prostitution) will always exist in the countries of the world, they comprise a marginal part of the world's real economy. (Nordstrom 2000: 14)

During this enquiry into the significance of the non-conventional economy, a senior World Bank economist responded that we 'simply don't deal with those things, they are not issues we are concerned with' (*ibid*.: footnote 40). Moreover, while a senior UNDP economist expressed more interest in the question, he responded that 'like most formal agencies, we are bound by mandate to dealing with formal economic arenas *only*. To compound matters, classical and contemporary economic theory simply does not have the capacity to deal with such questions' (*ibid*.).

This gap between dominant economic models and local realities predates the 1990s. It has emerged, for example, in relation to the narcotics industry in several Latin American countries during the 1980s. Despite its size and importance in relation to official GNP, Susan George has noted that the IMF, in making its economic calculations and prescriptions, proceeded as if the drugs industry did not exist (1992: 46). Since the 1980s, most aid agencies have tended to discount the specific significance of non-conventional economic activity. Where it has been recognised, it has been interpreted in terms of validating mainstream development: as something that either anticipates the aims of development (for example, local self-sufficiency) or as something that can be formalised through appropriate licensing or encouragement. The need to rethink this situation is overdue. It could be that the huge area of economic pursuit that now lies beyond the realm of conventional calculation – indeed, dwarfs the formal economy in some places – may be here to stay. As Nordstrom points out, however, if one argues that non-conventional economic and political relations require more research, the response from most aid agencies is to point out the dangers involved – that, since they are by definition extra-legal and can be prone to violence, it is difficult and risky to collect accurate information. In trying to establish the importance of international criminal networks, if the term criminal is still meaningful in the context he is discussing, Manuel Castells has encountered a similar problem. While a wealth of evidence exists regarding the importance and innovative nature of such networks,

> the phenomenon is largely ignored by social scientists, when it comes to understanding economies and societies, with the arguments that the data are not truly reliable, and that sensationalism taints interpretation. I take exception to these views. If a phenomenon is acknowledged as a fundamental dimension of our societies, indeed of the new, globalised system, we must use whatever evidence is available to explore the connection between these criminal activities and societies and economies at large. (Castells 1998: 167–8)

It may be, however, that the heart of the problem is not the safety or practicality of gathering information, or the sensationalism that marks some of the data. These problems are clear enough (Meagher 1998: 10). The real danger is the lurking possibility that the non-conventional practices and networks under discussion now rival the authority of states. In other words, the emerging political complexes in the South, in breaking with economic and political orthodoxy and forging a networked existence beyond these relations, represent a fundamental challenge to the very possibility of global liberal governance itself. 'The danger might thus be to our very conceptions of power and economy; to our theories about the nature of the relationships between state, individual, and authority' (Nordstrom 2001: 15).

For many, this challenge, with its attendant possibility of the collapse of an entire conceptual and moral universe, is an unsettling prospect. It is better, therefore, to remain within the realm of the known and the conventional. Even if the remit of such a world is increasingly narrow and constrained, in many ways this is still a lot easier than trying to think something different.

Non-formal economies

The frontiers of economic and political power are changing. In particular, globalisation has destabilised territorial notions of the state. Ideas of a 'national' economy, for example, bounded within the given territory of a particular government, have now fallen into disuse in the North. Indeed, concepts of new regionalism and new public policy have replaced them, and the triumphalist view of globalisation is a celebration of this development. Given the widespread acknowledgement of change in the North, it is curious that development discourse continues to have difficulty in formally accepting that something similar has occurred in the South by developing appropriate tools of description, analysis and, importantly, legitimation. In many respects, spreading non-formal transnational trade networks originating in the South are the equivalent of the regional economic systems that have consolidated in the North. Like the strategic complexes of liberal peace and the political complexes of the new wars, they interact with each other through relations of similarity, accommodation and competition. Whereas Northern regionalised economic systems are accepted, the global shadow economy has attracted an ambivalence ranging from a sceptical interest to outright criminalisation. In part, this problem relates to the fact that for development discourse the main problem continues to be one of defining an appropriate role for the state in relation to the formal market (Moore 1999). Given this preoccupation, one can understand that the question of non-territorial and extra-legal activity remains at best an interesting but second-order consideration. This attitude has shaped the Cinderella status that such activity has endured.

Non-territorial economic systems in the South are essentially extra-legal and evasive in their mode of operation. While often outside formal or state-regulated systems, they operate through complex relations of collusion, complicity and competition with these systems. The non-formal status of the shadow economy and the range of organisational possibilities involved has led to conceptual difficulties and produced a variety of overlapping terms (Meagher 1998). Ideas of non-formal trade and economy, for example, have been qualified by a range of terms including 'informal', 'parallel', 'second', 'black', 'shadow', 'transborder', and so on. These descriptions have attempted to capture economic activity that is non-conventional, extra-legal, unrecorded, unregulated and cross-border in character. Such activity can relate to trade in both legal and illegal goods and services. While not always easy to distinguish, the former can involve, for example, agricultural produce or raw materials produced or purchased through conventional channels but traded using extra-legal means and avoiding formal regulatory mechanisms. The latter, on the other hand, would relate to goods obtained through illegal means ranging from smuggling and commercial fraud through to direct seizure. Within shadow economies, however, both legally and illegally obtained goods are usually traded using similar evasive and extra-legal means. Historically, terms like 'informal' or 'parallel' economy have been used to denote the trading of legal goods through illegal channels. In this manner such activities have been loosely distinguished from more criminal or extensive transnational trading networks.

For the purposes of this book, the distinction between legal and illegal goods has been dropped. Given the complexity and multi-levelled nature of some of the networks involved, the distinction is not particularly useful. Many local–global commodity chains transcend the spectrum of legal/illegal activity (Le Billon 2000). Moreover, it is not the intention here to add yet another term to those already existing. Rather, the various designations that commonly denote extra-legal and non-territorial economic activity are taken as suggesting trade that can include both legal and illegal goods and, apart from local manifestations, can also be part of more extensive transnational networks, including networks that have varying shades of criminality and violence attached to them. In this respect, however, it should be stressed that it is assumed that most non-formal economic activity involves different types of extra-legal trading in goods that are legally obtained. While evading state regulations, this trade is not particularly associated with organised violence or hardened criminal activity. Indeed, many of the social groups involved may be opposed to such tendencies for moral, cultural or religious reasons. The extensive and well-established transnational Hausa–Fulani trade networks based in northern Nigeria, for example, are said to have eschewed trading in narcotics (Meagher 1998). This has been pioneered largely by Ibo networks (Bayart, Ellis and Hibou 1999 : 10). Moreover, over much of the South the informal economy represents an essential lifeline for millions of ordinary people. In many parts of the European East, for example, the collapse of the social wage inherent within the planned economy has, of necessity, been replaced with informal trade (Schierup 1992; Verdery 1996). However, the social and political relations involved in the predominant and non-violent forms of the shadow economy, especially their non-liberal character, give important clues to the nature of the new wars.

Manuel Castells has argued that networks constitute the new social morphology of the societies we live in. Their operation modifies processes of power, production, experience and culture. 'A network is a set of interconnected nodes. A node is the point at which a curve intersects itself. What a node is, concretely speaking, depends on the kind of concrete networks of which we speak' (Castells 1996: 470). Nodes can include anything from stock exchanges, private companies and governmental forums through to socially controlled coca and poppy fields, secret landing strips and money-laundering organisations. At the same time, cultural institutions such as TV systems, entertainment studios, the popular media and academic establishments are also included. The donor governments, NGOs, military bodies and private companies that are brought together in the strategic complexes of liberal peace likewise, to use Castells terminology, occupy the place of nodes within the flow of networks. The networks of transborder trade are multi-levelled systems intersected by nodes of producers, traders, fixers, carriers, suppliers, and so on. Moreover, depending on the trade involved, such networks are capable of linking some of the most remote areas of the world with the advanced technological heartlands of metropolitan society. The non-formal economy embodies the systems of actual development that keep people alive and in so doing have forged new relations of protection and legitimacy. At the same time, however, through creating flexible and adaptive networks linking local and international actors, while not usurping the role of the state, transborder economies have proved effective in challenging its regulatory authority (Roitman 2001). The international networks of which transborder trade is part, while residing in the shadows, reflect economic and political power that 'can match, even exceed, that of some states' (Nordstrom 2001: 1). Indeed, the transborder shadow economy has compelled many to adopt its logic and mode of operation (Reno 1998).

Changing interpretations of non-formal economies

The global shadow economy constitutes a significant power bloc lying outside formal regulatory structures. In many respects, this situation is indirectly reflected in the Cinderella status that the parallel economy has enjoyed within development discourse. While not being formally addressed, its existence has nonetheless been interpreted in different ways to support a number of developmental positions. Since the 1970s attitudes towards the informal economy have undergone a number of noticeable changes, from hostility through to acceptance as a positive form of proto-development, until today when, with increasing concern about 'war economies', a more negative view has returned.

Kate Meagher (1997; 1998) has given a useful and insightful account of this changing perception. The IFIs, for example, saw transborder trade in Africa at the end of the 1970s as a threat to liberal economic reform. Price distortions following independence were argued to have encouraged the haemorrhaging of foreign exchange to neighbouring countries. Such activity provided a justification for robust reform and economic adjustment measures to rectify imbalances and eliminate parallel trade. During the course of the 1980s, however, criticism of the social effects of structural adjustment began to grow (Cornia 1987). In response to increasing poverty levels, the UN's International Labour Organisation (ILO) rehabilitated the local 'informal economy' as an essential survival mechanism for the poor. At the same time, popular resistance in the South to structural adjustment continued to erupt.

Following cuts in public spending and nutritional subsidies, food riots, for example, were common during the 1980s (Walton and Seddon 1994). Faced with criticism and resistance, by the end of the 1980s the World Bank had changed its position on the parallel economy. Anxious to create allies for structural adjustment, it redefined the groups involved in non-formal activity as a surrogate constituency that was supportive of economic liberalism. From being a threat, the parallel economy was reinterpreted as a popular form of resistance to arbitrary colonial borders, patrimonial corruption and state inefficiency (World Bank 1989). In other words, the informal economy was reinvented as a reassertion of social solidarity and popular economic initiative in the face of restrictive state practices. It was part of the revolt of the poor against the modalities of underdevelopment, as discussed in the previous chapter. The informal trader became a living expression of liberalism's ubiquitous *economic man* and hence a genuine force for modernisation. In this form the shadow economy has been variously claimed by aid agencies as complementing their developmental efforts. In relation to economic policy, for example, since informal practices fall outside regulatory frameworks, policy recommendations have usually focused on how to 'graduate' them to the level of the conventional economy (de Vletter 1996: 2).

While this populist view of parallel trade still dominates the literature and is periodically rediscovered, since the mid-1990s the mood has begun to shift once again towards interpreting non-formal economic activity in negative terms.

> There is increasing frustration with the tendency of transborder operators to exploit differential patterns of implementation of structural adjustment reforms between countries. Furthermore, the manic effects of the deregulation of trade and financial markets, combined with the intensifying pressures of globalization on the sovereignty and institutional capacity of African states has triggered increased concern with the rising tide in many African states of corruption, violent conflict, the plunder of natural resources and involvement in drug trafficking. (Meagher 1998: 2–3)

This revision is not only reflected in World Bank views (1997a); it also relates more generally to the reproblematisation of security in terms of underdevelopment becoming dangerous. In particular, as has already been argued, the appearance of non-formal transborder trade networks has been used to criminalise war economies and their socially regressive leaders (Collier 1999).

The expansion of non-formal economies

Gathering momentum at the end of the 1970s, liberal economic reform has had a profound effect on the dynamics and trajectory of non-formal economies. The changes induced by reform have affected all levels and social groups within the South. During the 1980s, even within the liberal camp, criticism grew that structural adjustment was magnifying the effects of a hostile external environment rather than ameliorating it. Encouraged by adjustment policies, public expenditure was cut, government bureaucracies were downsized, food subsidies abolished, markets deregulated, and so on. In many respects, the adjustment programmes reflected the orthodoxy then emerging in the North regarding globalisation and the new public policy: the grounding of economic policy on domestic budgetary restraint, coupled with the promotion of trade liberalisation. In the South, however, such policies were introduced in a much more aggressive and mechanical fashion and with few of the mediating and compensatory mechanisms existing in the North. The UNICEF-supported study on *Adjustment with a Human Face* represents an influential example of the criticism of the time (Cornia 1987). Using comparable social welfare data from Africa, Latin America, the Middle East, and South and East Asia, the authors argued that during the first half of the 1980s three decades of modest progress drew to a halt in many developing countries. While much of this related to deteriorating global conditions, the economic stabilisation and adjustment programmes introduced by the IFIs tended to amplify the stagnation and decline of social welfare indicators. Domestic budgetary restraint exacerbated rising unemployment, growing poverty levels, declining food intakes, decreasing educational and health coverage, growing infant mortality rates, growing malnutrition, and so on. By 1985, over much of the South,

> After six consecutive years of decline and stagnation, the capacity of many individuals, households and governments to resist crisis has significantly weakened, while the effect of years of poor nutrition, less accessible health care, and declining educational opportunities has accumulated to the point at which permanent damage has already been done to the physical and mental capacity of much of the future labour force. (Cornia 1987: 35)

Like conflict a decade later, the effects of structural adjustment were presented by its liberal critics in terms of a deepening of poverty and a breakdown of social cohesion. For many, the 1980s became a 'lost decade'. Reflecting its governance role, this view was instrumental in pushing the reform process to adopt a more active social dimension than had existed previously. By 1990, the World Bank had fully accepted that adjustment needed to be actively focused on poverty. It was no longer acceptable to leave poverty reduction simply to the trickle-down effects of market reform. In setting the tone for the increasing radicalisation of development policy during the 1990s, the Bank now argued that supporting programmes have to be established to help the poor change the way they do things to make the most of liberalisation (World Bank 1990).

In many respects, however, the 1980s was not a lost decade. It was a period of profound social transformation in the South. This process affected all groups in society as the disappearance of old forms of patronage and wealth creation associated with the developmental state impelled the emergence of new ones. Social groups, networks and institutions were dissolved, reconstituted and redeployed in the expanding spaces of the non-formal economy and the emerging liberal world system. New methods of wealth creation have emerged out of the global process of privatisation and deregulation. The growth of non-territorial shadow economies has involved the incorporation and novel use of resources derived from international markets. The marginalisation from the emerging informational economy and the decline of commercial investment 'has resulted in a drive for new forms of economic integration' (Roitman 2001: 3). The South is not an economic void but the site of non-liberal forms of reinvention and reintegration.

In Africa, in relation to the state, the impact of structural adjustment served to accelerate the dismantling of non-viable state patronage networks based on public bureaucracies. As an alternative, the process of privatisation encouraged by the IFIs has seen many Southern rulers develop transborder networks as a new basis for political power (Reno 1998). At the same time, while the downsizing of the public sector and standing armies has increased the ranks of the unemployed, it has also provided the necessary personnel for the expanding shadow economy. In Chad, for example, the demobilisation of the army began in 1992. Rather than giving up arms, however, many former soldiers have either recycled themselves through various regional rebel movements, entered the illicit small-arms trade or joined one of the numerous organised gangs of highwaymen (Roitman 2001). Demobilisation following the end of the Cold War, similarly, can be seen to have provided the trained manpower to staff Russia's growing mafia networks (Varese 1994). The same can also be said about the downsizing of the West's armed forces and the growth of private security companies during the 1990s (Duffield 1998).

In the Chad Basin, where numerous subregional and transregional regimes of accumulation now dominate the borders of Nigeria, Cameroon, Niger, Chad and the Central African Republic, the transformation has also affected the urban-based merchant class. Until the end of the 1980s, this class was able to produce its rents through debt financing. Following the contraction of bilateral and multilateral aid, it was forced to reconfigure its wealth-creating activities. 'Their past engagements as transporters and suppliers for public works projects have been reformulated in terms of the remaining or evolving possibilities for enrichment: their convoys have taken up paths running through Nigeria, Cameroon, Centrafique, Chad, Libya and Sudan (e.g., smuggling petrol)' (Roitman 2001: 4). As for the unemployed, 'Those who once found employment in local agro-industry, the health and educational sectors, and development and public works projects now work as transporters, guards, and carriers along the Nigerian, Cameroonian, and Chadian borders' (*ibid.*).

In northern Uganda during the course of the 1980s, structural adjustment propelled many small traders into the transborder parallel economy (Meagher 1990). This was the result of attempts to shift income from traders to farmers by raising producer prices and taxing merchants. Given that farmers are dependent on small traders for market access, this has increased the instability of rural production. Under the impact of economic reform, this largely unrecorded social redeployment during the 1980s has fuelled a massive expansion of all forms of extra-legal parallel and transborder activity. The irony is that structural adjustment, initially introduced to curb parallel activity, has encouraged its continued growth. In relation to West Africa, where research on parallel activity is relatively extensive, structural adjustment has encouraged the shadow economy in a number of ways. Meagher (1998: 6–11) has argued that one factor has been the uneven and partial application of adjustment programmes across the region. Within different countries, moreover, distinct development requirements and objectives existed. Exploiting such differences is an important source of profit within the shadow economy. At the same time, the existence of the franc zone had left many West African countries immune from devaluation until 1994. This had created large pockets of regionally integrated, relatively stable and semi-convertible currencies existing side by side with currencies that had opposite characteristics. Structural adjustment also instigated a great upheaval in national economies and accelerated the decline in living standards. These changes encouraged all types of cost cutting by traders and customers alike through the development of evasive parallel networks. Privatisation also played a role in that the state credits arising from this process were diverted into transborder trade. The evidence suggests that not only have shadow networks grown, but their regional penetration and transcontinental character have also deepened. Illicit Nigerian petrol, for example, is now traded in Mali, Burkino Faso and Ghana. At the same time, cheap Asian textiles, clothes and manufactured goods are widely traded throughout Africa using parallel networks.

In 1988, Meagher (1990) described the organisation and activities of the parallel market in Arua, northern Uganda. This market was closely linked to the transborder hub located at Ariwara, some 30 km distant in northern Zaïre. These markets were local linkages in a coast-to-coast transborder network that, at its extremities, linked parallel activity in Senegal and Guinea Bissau with Kenya and Somalia. The central dynamic of the Arua and Ariwara markets, however, was based on the transregional linkage of Zaïre, Sudan and Uganda. A central demand underpinning the markets was for convertible currency – in this case, US dollars, gold and coffee. At the same time, however, there was a strong cross-border demand for foodstuffs. Cassava and dried fish originating up to 800 km away were being traded. Transactions were based on hard currency using complex exchange rates. There was no barter. Zaïrois were bringing gold and coffee for manufactured goods, foodstuffs and petrol. Sudanese were supplying US dollars for foodstuffs, clothing and coffee. Ugandans were bringing imported manufactured goods and foodstuffs for gold and US dollars to support the parallel market in Kampala. Not only were exchange rates complex, but market demand was specific. For example, Lois jeans were imported by Zaïre but not by Uganda, where Lee jeans were preferred.

Under the impact of structural adjustment, some parallel activities have declined, such as trade in local agricultural commodities between different ecological zones and the activities of small-scale operators. In particular, transborder networks have been put under pressure by the impact of liberalisation on profit margins and the tendency for demand to weaken with declining living standards. In West Africa, however, rather than a contraction the evidence suggests

> a massive shift to cheap low-quality consumer manufactures from Asia and Nigeria. The down-market shift in transborder commodities, combined with the greater national, regional and inter-continental penetration of trading networks, appears to have been sufficient to support an increase in transborder flows even in the context of squeezed profits and declining consumer purchasing power. (Meagher 1998: 10)

Rather than the 1980s being a lost decade of deepening poverty and collapse, the expansion of the shadow economy has been a form of actual development, with the creation of new and independent forms of authority through reintegration with the liberal world system on the basis of innovative local–global shadow networks. Not only has this involved social redeployment on a major scale, but it has also seen a reversal of earlier patterns of development. Among the transborder economies of the Chad Basin, for example, what Roitman (2000) has called the 'economy of the bush' has been stimulated greatly by the expansion of the shadow economy. Border areas in particular – dotted with depots, hideouts, bulking and redistribution points – have become zones of economic resurgence:

> the stimulation of economic activity in the bush is partly a result of the combined efforts of the economic refugees of structural adjustment programs and decreasing foreign aid, on the one hand, and the military refugees of downsized and underfinanced armies, on the other. (*Ibid.*: 5)

With the resurgence of the bush economy, the urban networks that have predominated over the countryside for decades are themselves 'now subservient to the "economy of the bush"' (*ibid.*). In the franc zone of the Chad Basin there has been an exodus of bills from urban areas to support the informal economy based on the borders. Even within urban areas, a similar process of reordering has been under way. In Mozambique, for example, the more dynamic aspects of the burgeoning informal sector in Maputo are dominated by younger and more educated entrepreneurs (de Vletter, 1996). The older and less educated victims of development retrenchment and the downsizing of public institutions dominate the new poor.

A complex transborder shadow economy: the coffee trade across Sudan's war zone

Transborder shadow economies are complex and mutable. Like organisms, with time they grow, change their shape, develop new functions, age and decline, only to reappear once more and develop afresh. The example given below describes a transborder network that existed at the end of the 1980s: the trade in coffee from the former Zaïre across Sudan and to countries beyond. The complexity of this network lies in its local–global linkages, in the interaction of state and non-state actors and, importantly, in its ability to transcend zones of war and peace.

The parallel currency market

In Sudan during the 1980s, the emergence of a parallel foreign exchange market was a crucial aspect of the shadow economy. It has been estimated that during 1978–87 capital flight from Sudan amounted to $11 billion dollars, a sum roughly equivalent to Sudan's foreign debt (Brown 1992). At the same time, Sudanese expatriates working in the Middle East were making significant extra-legal US dollar remittances back to Sudan. Some of this hard currency was being transported across the war zone of South Sudan, and traded on the coast-to-coast trans-border networks of northern Uganda and Zaïre. Competition over control of the parallel currency market was an important factor shaping political relations in North Sudan at this time (Jamal 1991). Tradition-ally the illegal dollar trade has been in the hands of a few powerful Khatmiyya merchants. The Khatmiyya was an Islamic sect linked to the Democratic Unionist Party (DUP) which, towards the end of the 1980s, was in a fractious coalition with the Umma Party and the fundamen-talist National Islamic Front. Following the fundamentalist-backed coup of June 1989, the internal struggle to control the parallel currency market became increasingly bitter, resulting in the government's disso-lution of the Khatmiyya sect in September 1992 and the execution of several prominent black-marketeers.

Shadow trade across the war zone

The involvement of Sudanese army officers in trade within the war zone has been widespread since the beginning of the war in 1983 (Africa Watch 1990). Most of this trade exploits the shortage of food and basic commodities among war-affected populations by using the army's ability to prevent population movement and its monopoly of transport. It is a form of unequal exchange heavily stacked in favour of the merchant-officer. During the latter part of the 1980s, one point of entry into the transborder economy for dollar remittances exploited the DUP/Khatmiyya links with the army. The dollar trade went through Juba, the capital of South Sudan. For several years, however, the Sudanese People's Liberation Army had cut all overland routes and deterred civilian airlines from landing. During this blockade, the only way in or out of Juba from the North was by military transport aircraft or periodic donor/NGO relief flights. The Ugandan border, roughly a hundred miles to the South, was linked to Juba by irregular army convoys.

The coffee trade in northern Uganda

Northern merchants and hard currency were flown into Juba through military connections and conveyed to the Ugandan border by armed convoy. That the amounts of hard currency conveyed were significant can be judged from the fact that the exchange rate on the Ugandan parallel currency market fluctuated according to the timing of the Juba convoy. Within northern Uganda, Sudanese merchants traded these dollars on the Uganda/Zaïre parallel market. Meagher's detailed description (1990) of the working of this market and the transborder networks involved has been mentioned above. In the late 1980s Sudanese merchants were especially interested in trading dollars for coffee from Zaïre. The Zaïrian government, like the Ugandan, had imposed a fixed price on coffee growers. In Sudan, however, there was a free market. At 13 cents a kilo, Zaïrian coffee was among the cheapest in the world and, despite the transhipment across a war zone, Northern Sudanese merchants claimed a profit margin of a thousand per cent (Ryle 1989).

The priority of merchant over humanitarian supplies

From Uganda, coffee and other merchant goods were transported, again by army convoy, back to Juba. From Juba, the coffee was flown by military transport to Khartoum where it was traded on the national and international markets. It should be noted that the public reason for army convoys from the Ugandan border was to bring international food aid to the war-displaced population in and around Juba. The convoy system proved extremely unreliable in this respect. Not only was the route becoming increasingly insecure by the end of the 1980s, but, as with other military convoys in Sudan, merchant supplies would invariably be substituted for relief food (Africa Watch 1990). In Juba, this substitution had several effects. During the growing SPLA blockade the price of foodstuffs had climbed steeply, leaving many of the town's residents in a similar position to the displaced population that was eligible for relief (Graham and Borton 1992). Merchant goods imported under army auspices could therefore be traded at a premium. From the point of view of humanitarian assistance, however, the unreliability of the convoy system and the insecurity of the overland routes forced donors and NGOs to rely increasingly on expensive, stop-gap airlifts of emergency supplies.

This short example gives an idea of the complexity and multi-levelled nature of transborder shadow economies and their ability to transcend war and peace. This particular network would eventually decline when the overland route to the Uganda border was closed by insecurity a couple of years later. It can only be expected, however, that the organisational systems involved would adapt and open other areas of shadow activity.

Non-liberal characteristics of non-formal economies

So far, the discussion of the non-formal economy has attempted to focus on the extra-legal trade in legal goods. It is not always easy to distinguish legally obtained goods from illegal ones in such networks. Indeed, as seen in the above case study, they can incorporate both. At the same time, discussing the non-formal economy in terms of corruption or criminality is not particularly helpful. In this respect, it should again be stressed that the expansion of the shadow economy has been based largely on the growth of multiple forms of extra-legal trade in legal goods. Moreover, the resurgence of this type of parallel activity constitutes the major part of the economy over much of the South. In this form it is an essential means of survival for large sections of the population and is not necessarily associated with criminality or organised violence. It represents what one could call the normal way of life for many people. As such, it often adapts and draws on resources and networks based in some way on locality, kinship or ethnicity. These social networks, moreover, inscribe their own forms of legitimacy and regulatory codes on the shadow economy.

Although the growing policy significance of the new wars has once again brought parallel trade into a negative light, populist views of the informal economy such as the following remain important: that parallel trade represents a reassertion of local solidarity; that it is redistributive in nature; that it is independent of the official economy and the state; and, not least, that it is gender positive. One can define these views as populist in the sense that they complement the development aims of those agencies that claim their existence. Kate Meagher, a leading writer on parallel trade, has directly challenged this interpretation (Meagher 1997). While the transborder economy is an essential means of support for many people and, in its predominant form, is not particularly associated with violence or crime, it nonetheless has few of the characteristics described by the populist view. It has promoted new forms of privilege, authority and rights to wealth. Moreover, rather than being independent of the state, the shadow economy intersects the state at many levels. State actors have developed complex relations of dependence, complicity and control in relation to the non-formal economy. These are examined in more detail in the next chapter. Finally, those nodes within parallel networks that command real influence remain under patriarchal control. The main point of Meagher's critique, however, is the important argument that while the non-formal economy is expanding, *it is essentially non-liberal in its structure and aims*. In other words, rather than representing economic man awaiting a magic policy formula to bring him from the shadows into the light of the conventional economy, parallel trade, even in its predominant form, is antagonistic and subversive in relation to free-market institutions and liberal political values. Transborder shadow economies tend to oppose formal attempts to promote economic regionalisation and, rather than a free market ethos, are more likely to pursue informal protectionism. This is not to say that shadow economies do not embody their own forms of protection, legitimacy and values, which they do, but that the systems involved are antithetic to the norms and expectations of global liberal governance.[3]

The shadow economy is not just an unofficial mechanism for uniting disjointed official economies. It is not value-free, nor does it arise spontaneously in the spaces created by the deficiencies and shortcoming of conventional institutions and an overbearing state. Neither is it simply a survival strategy or a coping mechanism. On the contrary, parallel trade is part of a set of relations that reflect a 'struggle for advantage in which the official development strategies of countries within the same region are pitted against each other, and vested interests are intrinsically opposed to economic rationalization' (Meagher 1997: 182).

In relation to Southern Africa, Nordstrom (2001) has argued something very similar. Informal markets shape economic possibilities, execute political power and establish cultures, rules of exchange, codes of conduct and so on. Shadow networks are cultural and political instruments governed by social principles. The literature on Africa and the European East contains many examples of such non-liberal tendencies. In West Africa, while Gambia's liberal import policy is highly profitable for its commercial elite, owing to extensive import smuggling, it is markedly less so for Senegal. This Gambian advantage led to its foot-dragging in negotiations concerning confederation and economic integration with Senegal. Ultimately, the confederation project collapsed in 1989 (Meagher 1997: 182). By the end of the 1980s, several years before the outbreak of fighting in the former Yugoslavia, the increasing dominance of parallel trade within the republics, and their attempts to link directly to the global market, had propelled their sub-economies to adopt increasingly autarkic behaviour, even to the extent of unofficial and economically irrational customs and border controls preventing inter-republic trade (Schierup 1992). In reviewing the so-called transition in Romania, Verdery (1996) mocks the conventional vision of a liberal-democratic future and argues that the evidence is far more compelling for a return to feudalism.

Since they are extra-legal, the nodes that animate the networks of the non-formal economy lend themselves to different forms of social

157

control. While it can be meritocratic in its own terms, the shadow economy is not a transparent system. Sectarian criteria based on local, kinship, ethnic, religious or political considerations frequently shape its organisational modalities. In other words, socially bounded or politically closed communities usually control networks. Unlike the trend towards economic integration in the North, the social groups managing transborder trade tend to oppose formal integrationist structures. While strategic collaboration is an important and necessary feature of shadow networks, profitability depends on maintaining differences and discrete forms of control. In this respect, rather than emulating liberalism's support of deregulation and free-market economics, the parallel economy is based on various forms of protectionism. Another aspect of the non-liberal character of parallel activity is its mercantilist pedigree. The networks that are producing patterns of regional integration in the North are primarily based on production rather than trade. Intra-firm trade in components and services between parent companies and regional affiliates now accounts for 30–40 per cent of global trade. Value is added not by trade alone, but also by the ability to integrate the production of regionally interlinked companies through the application of information technology (Meagher 1998: 14). The parallel economy, however, is essentially trade-based. While it is capable of sustaining local forms of production, value is realised primarily in the transborder trade networks through which such commodities flow. Where the shadow economy is a predominant activity, this aspect of its structure tends to reproduce the dependent position of the South in the global economy. That is, it continues to rely on the (parallel) export of primary products at the same time as the (parallel) import of manufactured goods and specialist services.

Another important characteristic of the shadow economy that Meagher (1998) has highlighted relates to the issue of financial speculation. Market deregulation has led to a tremendous increase in Northern speculative financial transactions. Of the trillions of dollars that daily flow around the global marketplace, less than 10 per cent are connected with the real economy. The remainder are largely concerned with gambling on the future performance of stocks and markets. While its magnitude is unknown, it has been argued that money laundering by criminal networks has become part of such huge speculative flows. Indeed, given its willingness to take risks, it has probably amplified the turbulence and volatility of such movements (Castells 1998: 201). In this respect, however, much of the South is effectively disconnected from the financial flows that interconnect the regionalised economic systems of the North. Moreover, regarding the predominant form of the shadow economy in the South, that is, the extra-legal trading in legal goods, a different situation holds. Evidence suggests that parallel economies remain almost wholly concerned with the real economy. Contrary to trends in the North, the deregulation of global financial markets 'does not appear to have led to a significant detachment of parallel financial activities from real economic activities' (Meagher 1998: 13). In other words, the capital tied up in the nodes and networks of the shadow economy is largely involved in real exchanges involving the movement and realisation of actual commodities, people and services.

Revisiting underdevelopment as dangerous

Official statistics paint a picture of a 'lost decade' during the 1980s when many countries became 'economy-less' – yet a real economy of shadow and networked trade has expanded to fill the implicit vacuum in such data. While the virtual economy in the North is learning how to work on thin air, the real economy in the South has learnt how to provide employment, supply foodstuffs, source clothing and manufac- tured goods, and maintain flows of all types of domestic consumables, medical supplies and equipment. Moreover, the extensive local–global networks that have emerged have the flexibility and liquidity to maintain such flows. This process of actual development is the outcome of a complex process of dissolution, redeployment and reintegration. Besides provisioning, this transformation has established new types of legitimacy and rights to wealth. In this respect, it is worth revisiting the liberal reproblematisation of security in terms of underdevelopment as dangerous. For global governance the danger is the threat posed by the probability that the poor will revolt against the modalities of underde- velopment and, in the process, attract violent and extreme leaders. From the perspective of actual development, the danger for liberal peace it that the poor have helped forge new and independent forms of wealth creation, rights and political legitimacy that are essentially non- liberal in character. Rather like economic growth in East Asia, which was facilitated by ignoring orthodox development paradigms (Stiglitz 1998), actual development has come about not because of structural adjustment, market liberalisation and the activities of aid agencies, but as an indirect, subversive and antagonistic response to these develop- ments.

The non-liberal characteristics of the shadow economy are not nec- essarily associated with open violence. However, these structures of everyday life do provide a model of economic formation that has been adopted and developed further by the political complexes associated with the new wars. In this respect, rather than being absolute and distinct states, 'war' and 'peace' in the South share many of the same relations and structures. They represent a speeding up or slowing down of similar conditions. Where networked war economies have emerged, however, it is not usually the case that those social groups controlling predominant forms of extra-legal trade have decided to become violent (Meagher 1998). This outcome relates to the emergence of new groups and nodes of authority that have the necessary power to mobilise the networks of the shadow economy in support of their claims. While this chapter has analysed the process of social transformation relating to the new wars in terms of the general economic relations necessary for its understanding, we must now examine its associated political relations.

NOTES

1 For studies that have attempted to address such issues see Richards (1996) for Sierra Leone; Reno (1998) for West Africa; Roitman (2001) for the Chad Basin: Nordstrom (2001) for Southern Africa; Verdery (1996) for Romania; Schierup (1992) for the former Yugoslavia; and Lieven (1998) for Russia.
2 Also see Castells (1998: 166–205) and George (1992: 41–2).
3 For a discerning description of Chechen society in these terms, that is, as a 'liberal nightmare', see Lieven 1998: 352–4.

7

Non-Liberal Political Complexes and the New Wars

Complex political emergencies or emerging political complexes?

Development discourse implicitly adopts a social evolutionist approach regarding the problems of the South. While Africa is usually regarded as facing the challenge of development, the European East is viewed in terms of the problem of transition. In practice, however, both are seen as progressing, albeit often haltingly, toward a liberal-democratic future. Encouraging market reform, promoting privatisation and helping create representative and effective public institutions are essential parts in this process of becoming. However, such teleological assumptions – regarding progress as a series of intermediate stages leading to a higher form – have a number of limitations. Developmentalism is mechanistic in that it tends to imply that societies and social groups have no volition or will of their own. In the normal course of events, certain conditions will lead to other predictable stages. Badly managed humanitarian aid, for example, can create dependency and fuel wars. Conversely, if properly handled, it can have the opposite effects. At the same time, however, the paradox of development is that actual outcomes and existing behaviour continually contradict the expected scheme of things and are always threatening to upset the causal chain.

Rather than a fundamental change of paradigm, the main consequence of policy failure has been to focus development studies on prescriptive analysis and problem-solving engagement. Developmentalism appears as a body of knowledge that grows incrementally on past failure. It is as if, for fifty years, successive generations of development experts have been trying to work out what went wrong so that they can get it better next time. Apart from this general orientation, however, the rationalisation of failure takes two main forms. First, challenging behaviour is circumscribed, labelled as deviant and excluded; the criminalisation of conflict is an example of this. Second, where this is not practical or, indeed, self-defeating in relation to the development project, deviant behaviour is redefined as an unfortunate but necessary price to pay for eventual progress. Chapter Four examined the new humanitarianism and the trend toward humanitarian conditionality from this perspective. Election irregularities in the European East, for example, become signs of the immaturity of the democracies concerned (Guerra 1996), something which will disappear as the habits of socialism die out. At the same time, the wholesale looting by politico-mafia networks of Russia's state assets during the 1990s was legitimised by free-market economists as an inevitable stage in the transition process (Lieven 1998: 1–11; Castells 1998: 180–90). The recent revelation that $20 billion in IMF aid to Russia has flown out of the country and been laundered in Europe and the USA appears to have done little to dent this extraordinarily resilient optimism (Vulliamy 1999) – a resilience perhaps born of the fact that beyond such faith the policy toolbox is rather empty.

Instead of analysing actual relations and treating systems as if they were fully formed and completely grown, development discourse interposes an image of the teleological stage that the societies it engages with *are thought to be at*. It then proceeds to interpret events and actions in relation to what *it is assumed they will become*. Essentially, what is minimised or ignored is the possibility that we are witnessing the emergence of new and singular political dynamics in international affairs, something that lies outside the accepted teleological scheme of things. Development discourse downplays the prospect that 'the shadow sovereigns of today may foreshadow new power formulations barely emergent on the horizons of political and economic possibility' (Nordstrom 2001: 16). Indeed, as William Reno has argued, it may be that the old balance of power is now so radically altered as to disclose a 'profound revolutionary change' (Reno 1998: 226). The idea of a 'complex political emergency' reflects the dominant and conservative view. Complex emergencies arise on the borders of liberal peace where it encounters political systems whose norms differ violently from its own (Dillon and Reid 2001). These events encapsulate behaviour that violently upsets the developmental schema of things. For liberal peace, the violence involved deepens poverty, destroys social capital and undoes years of development. Rather than a means of analysing actual relations, however, the idea of a complex political emergency expresses a relation of governance. Such events are represented as a multi-causal phenomenon requiring a system-wide response by the strategic complexes of liberal governance.

The concept of a complex political emergency carries with it the ideological means of justifying, mobilising and coordinating the state and non-state actors of liberal peace. It would make more sense, however, to rephrase the encounter so that liberal peace is seen to confront not complex political emergencies but emerging political complexes on its borders.[1] Rather than remaining a pure projection, the object of governance is endowed with the possibility of a will and volition of its own. This implies elites able to choose between a range of options rather than just following blueprints. In turn, this focuses attention on the need to analyse, unencumbered by social evolutionary schema, the actual social and political dynamics involved. It is in this sense, and in distinction to the concept of a complex political emergency, that the term emerging political complex is used here. Emerging political complexes exploit the power and flexibility of non-formal economies. They provide the nodes of legitimacy, redistribution and rights to wealth in such economies. In relation to the new wars, it is these political complexes that have the authority and ability to mobilise the resources linked by the networks of the shadow economy. In this respect, while usually intersecting the institutions of recognised states, the emerging complexes imply political projects that now go beyond conventional forms of territorial, bureaucratic or juridical authority. Their legitimacy no longer derives from creating and maintaining nation-state competence within defined borders. Indeed, many so-called weak states are able to dispense altogether with the bureaucracies of conventional nation states and abandon the realm of public welfare to external agencies. In this respect, they have dissolved the conventional distinctions between people, army and government (van Creveld 1991). Such political projects, however, are neither deviant nor irrational. In their response to globalisation and the opportunities it has created, they have integrated themselves within the liberal world system by amplifying and extending the everyday relations and structures of actual development.

From nation states to multiple authorities

Nation-state competence can be defined as the ability of states to independently govern and maintain economic, social and welfare standards in their own territories. Under the impact of globalisation, such competence has been qualified and attenuated in both the North and the South. In the latter, however, this has been a more radical and unmediated process. In many regions, especially in Africa, the strategic complexes of liberal governance have occupied the space previously controlled by national economic and welfare actors (de Waal 1997). The formal state and economic structures with which liberal peace connects and through which it operates, however, represent only a narrow foundation in the societies concerned. As nation-state competence has declined, the welfare vacuum created has mainly been filled by the expansion of the transborder networks of the shadow economy. Globalisation has effected a complex process involving the deconstruct-ion and decentralisation of the power and authority of nation states. The growing influence of external actors is one aspect of this process. At the same time, decentralisation has also been internal. Through an enhanced ability to forge local–global linkages, market liberalisation has increased the ease with which new centres of authority have been able to emerge.

In attempting to describe this process of decentralisation and draw out some of its implications, one view that has been put forward is that of neo-medievalism (Cerny 1998; Deibert 1997; Verdery 1996). The idea of neo-medievalism is, of course, a metaphor. In no sense is the world going backwards. The feudal period existed in a localised rather than a globalised environment and, one need hardly add, it was very different from today. Neo-medievalism should also be distinguished from the new barbarism approach as reflected, for example, in the work of Kaplan (1994). This understands conflict in terms of an alleged re-surfacing of innate or age-old cultural and ethnic hostilities. In contrast, neo-medievalism is a metaphor for describing certain characteristics of contemporary social and political systems, a tool that provides a number of insights that development discourse's social evolutionism tends to miss. Yet it also reflects the conceptual difficulty and absence of agreed terminology encountered once one attempts to step outside the implicit teleology of state-centred development discourse.

Rather than concentrating sovereignty, feudal political authority was defined by its 'parcelling out' (Verdery 1996: 208). This shaped a political order characterised by multiple zones of authority with over-lapping and often competing boundaries existing in relation to a weak central sovereignty. The impact of globalisation and market liberalisa-tion are seen to be producing a similar effect, especially in relation to the growing importance of non-state actors operating at international and subnational levels. From this perspective, Cerny (1998) has attempted to describe certain aspects of the current international system: the trend toward competing institutions and overlapping jurisdictions of state and non-state interest groups; a greater fluidity of territorial boundaries both within and across states; the growing importance of identity and single-issue politics; increasingly contested legal statutes, property rights and conventions; the spread of geographical and social 'no go areas' where the rule of law no longer extends, and so on. The disparate and differentiated elements of this system are said to combine to create long-term patterns of 'durable disorder', situations in which governments can neither address root causes nor allow important systems to collapse completely.

The process of decentralisation and the emergence of overlapping and competing centres of authority tends to question conventional teleological assumptions and expectations. In Chapter 6 we noted Verdery's mocking suggestion that the European East's trajectory, far from demonstrating evolutionary progression towards liberal democracy, promised instead a 'transition to feudalism' (1996: 204–28). A similar imagery informs the work of Schierup (1992; 1999) on the break-up of Yugoslavia. Here, we are asked to consider the crisis as a form of 're-traditionalisation' of contemporary social and political relations. Concerning Africa, Reno (1998) and Ellis (1995) have argued that warlord structures, in their relations with both foreign companies and dependent civilians, have established patterns of political authority reminiscent of the precolonial chieftaincy system. These authors have evoked such postmodern back-to-the-future images as a counter to the social evolutionary and triumphalist trends within development discourse. Rather than conventional forms of liberal democracy, these alternative views redefine contemporary political projects in terms of the emergence of multiple and overlapping centres of authority in the context of weak, complicit or otherwise ambiguous forms of central sovereignty. At the same time, they suggest the possibility of emerging political complexes that are creating new forms of legitimacy through their ability to forge local–global networks. Such innovations suggest that the spread of conventional forms of liberal democracy cannot be taken for granted.

The transformation of the developmental state

Both the African development state and the socialist party state based a large part of their political legitimacy on the establishment and manipulation of patron–client relations. Regarding the development state, interaction with the outside world shaped the possibility of using development resources to establish political networks. Relative economic scarcity created for development assistance an important role in incorporating existing authorities within the international system and, at the same time, holding together internal networks of allies and inter- mediaries (Reno 1998). Colonial rule had tended to limit the emergence of local elites that could challenge the legitimacy of the colonising power. Commercial activity in Africa, for example, was frequently entrusted to the diaspora of Greek and Lebanese traders that criss- crossed the continent. At the same time, forms of native administration composed of traditional leaders were also created. As well as answer- ing administrative necessity in many cases, such authorities served to limit the modernising influence of emerging urban elites. In such cir- cumstances, independence during the 1950s and 1960s was synony- mous with the transfer of sovereignty to state systems that were often neither fully unified nor possessed of the range of competencies usually associated with nation states. Moreover, early tensions in this process were often unresolved and threats to elite security remained.

During the Cold War, development assistance and financial loans provided the basis for expanding the bureaucracies of the develop- mental state. Such bureaucracies were the means by which rulers built alliances and forged new clientage networks in the face of internal opposition. They provided an opportunity for nepotism and favouritism on the part of rulers and rent seeking by office holders. Moreover, through the principle of sovereignty and superpower concern to main- tain internationally recognised territorial alliances, the bureaucracies of the developmental state were the main conduit for external assistance. Besides a means of largesse and rent seeking, however, state office could also become the base for political opposition. Rulers were often forced to choose between satisfying popular demands for welfare spend- ing, and so building legitimacy, or using resources to manage political threats within state bureaucracies or from outside strongman opposi- tion. In many areas, rather than building wider legitimacy, the trend was to downsize bureaucracies and so limit the organisational base for internal opposition (Reno 1996: 4). At the same time, the resources released could be channelled into other uses, for example the creation of a parallel military budget and shadow security structures. Debureau- cratisation, that is, the conscious reduction of the social and public welfare activities of the state, may appear irrational in terms of address- ing internal opposition. However, by limiting and concentrating the amount of state patronage in fewer hands, it reinforces the dependence of those remaining client networks. At the same time, unlike the unifying logic of the nation state, the process of debureaucratisation denotes the emergence of systems of authority that have divested them- selves of effective responsibility for whole swathes of society. The humanitarian operations of the 1990s have underscored this point.

While the process is uneven, structural adjustment and the end of the Cold War have increased the trend toward debureaucratisation. Demands by donor governments, the World Bank and the IMF to cut state bureaucracy have complemented the moves of many rulers to protect themselves from internal state-based opposition through public sector downsizing. At the same time, cuts in development spending have further eroded the attractiveness of the developmental state as a viable resource base for political alliances. The process of privatisation and market deregulation, however, has a double-edged character. While it has allowed rulers access to new resources and the possibility of establishing privatised client networks, it has also encouraged the expansion of the transborder shadow economy. Warlord and strongman entities that previously would have had to accommodate themselves to the developmental state now have the possibility of establishing an independent and parallel existence outside formal state structures. Reflecting this condition, Ellis has described the situation in Liberia during the early 1990s in terms of

> a mosaic of militia zones of control, where civilians have some degree of protection but must pay tribute in kind to the local warlord, constantly shifting frontier zones in which civilians are liable to raiding from all sides. The aim is control of people and acquisition of booty more than to control territory in the conventional military manner. (Ellis 1995: 185)

Similar views of decentralisation and the emergence of multiple authorities have been expressed for Sierra Leone (Reno 1995a) and for Southern Sudan during the latter part of the 1980s (Duffield 1994a). The process of political decentralisation under the impact of globalisation has both changed and increased the internal security threats faced by juridical rulers. As Reno (1998) has argued, one way that so-called weak state incumbents have dealt with this is to deepen the process of debureaucratisation. While offering the appearance of conformity with donor demands for privatisation and public sector downsizing, being unencumbered with demanding office-based clients and extensive public responsibilities is an attractive option in terms of the new opportunities offered by market deregulation. Reflecting van Creveld's (1991) view of the imitable quality of war, many incumbents of so-called weak states have come to mimic the strategies and tactics of the warlord and strongman oppositions that they often face.

The transformation of the socialist party state

Unlike the developmental state, the socialist party state was largely autarkic. The resources for patronage and clientage systems came from its internal organisation. Contrary to the popular conception of the strength of totalitarian rule, such states now appear as comparatively weak. Like Africa, they also suffered from continual crises of legitimacy. The nature of socialist production contained a number of inherent tensions and contradictions. Instead of capitalism's inner logic of maximising profit and promoting consumerism, central planning encouraged different and contrasting trends, such as the hoarding of materials by the managers of enterprises in order to increase their bargaining power with other state functionaries. In consequence, most people endured erratic supplies and endemic shortages. Relations of clientage between managers and consumers, together with hoarding to increasing bargaining power, were factors that continually undercut central party control and legitimacy (Verdery 1996: 22–3). Similar weaknesses affected vertical power relations. Socialist production with its pervasive shortages bred an oppositional consciousness among workers. The typical response of the party was twofold: first, the development of an extensive machinery of surveillance; and second and more positively, an attempt to actualise the paternalistic socialist state through social spending and redistribution. Whereas capitalism aims to sell goods, the socialist party state attempted to secure legitimacy by giving goods and services away. Endemic shortages, however, continually undermined this legitimacy. Moreover, they prompted the emergence of the so-called second economy. Since the planned economy could not guarantee supply, people developed a range of informal activities to obtain the goods and services they needed. This could include workmen moonlighting with materials obtained from their factory, shopworkers keeping scarce goods for special customers, or collective farmers cultivating private plots. However, the second economy was not a substitute for the planned economy, as is the case with contemporary parallel trade (*ibid.*: 27). Rather, it was parasitic upon the resources and deficiencies of the socialist party state.

In relation to the neo-medieval metaphor, Verdery (*ibid.*: 208) notes that the Soviet work organisation had an affinity with feudalism. Unlike Western capitalism, where the firm is essentially an economic institution, the Soviet enterprise was an important social unit providing access to goods, services and patronage: a base of political power in its own right. As the competence of the socialist party state began to erode slowly from the 1970s onwards, the directions of the transformation that occurred were shaped by the existing contradictions and tensions within the system. In particular, as the centre weakened, there was a growing autonomy of regions, together with their enterprises and related client networks. By 1990, the regions in the Soviet Union were already exerting a visible autonomy from the central government (Humphrey 1991). A situation had developed in which it was increasingly uncertain were government and the law resided. Productive enterprises and firms were being run in an increasingly personalised way as separate suzerainties, with managers and local political bosses attempting to use their control of resources as leverage to protect their workers and clients. In many ways, eroding nation-state competence was leading to a greater dependence on locality and the erection of local barriers to exclude outsiders and migrants. 'The collapse of the party-state reinforced the tendencies to personalism and patronage inherent in such arrangements, making many people dependent on their locality, their workplace, or their boss for access to food, housing and loans' (Verdery 1996: 206).

Scheirup's (1992; 1997) analysis of the break-up of Yugoslavia reflects and amplifies this approach. The effects of Yugoslavia's 'self-management' reform, rather than modernising the socialist system, led to a growing autonomy of the republics and a weakening of the Yugoslav Federation. By the 1980s, the republics where already beginning to look and act like small nation states. Local party bosses and managers attempted to maintain legitimacy by continuing to provide employment and social services despite worsening economic conditions. In competition with the others, each republic, often at the level of the individual enterprise, tried to forge links with international companies. Technology transfer was uncoordinated and irrational. The deepening crisis tended to reinforce local relations and kinship ties. In a reversal of the international trend toward urbanisation, this included a strengthening of urban–rural links. Maintaining family land or helping relatives on their farms was an increasingly important dietary supplement, a trend that would develop further during the Bosnian war (Duffield 1994b). Republican structures were

> to blend organically with the most authoritarian features of the social and political relations of real socialism. The local party elites and the increasingly 'national' working classes of the single republic's autonomous provinces were to be bound together by innumerable ties of an increasingly traditionalistic character. These were displayed in idioms such as kinship, friendship, locality and ethnicity, taking the form of a complex network of reciprocal favours, pervading the entire society. (Schierup 1999: 47)

Based on the bureaucracies that self-management had created at the republican and provincial levels, ethnic particularisms developed politically into distinct nationalist ideologies. Such movements supported the emergence of separatist economic tendencies. Republics attempted to protect their interests and those of their clients, including forming linkages with foreign companies, by blocking and undermining similar attempts by others. As a prelude to war, closed sub-economies emerged and the level of intra-republic investment dwindled. The term 'ethnic cleansing' entered the public domain following the brutal activities of Serbian paramilitary units in Croatia and Bosnia in 1991–2. This process, however, has a history in the region and was used by all parties prior to the outbreak of open war (Schierup 1993). From 1990, for example, following the first multi-party elections in Croatia, Serbs were purged from the government bureaucracies. A similar process of administrative cleansing took place in Bosnia–Herzegovina following the election of ethnically oriented parties in 1991.

While the Balkan war may have coined the term 'ethnic cleansing', it is clear that the process of social exclusion and inclusion involved has a much wider application. It is typical of the reworking of political authority in a period of declining nation-state competence under the impact of globalisation and the opportunities that it creates. Rather than a new barbarism contained in the alleged reappearance of age-old and suppressed ethnic hatreds (Kaplan 1994; Kennedy 1993), these processes are the important ones. Africa and the European East provide many examples. Regarding the latter, the effects of the demise of central sovereignty have been greatest where pre-existing federal systems collapsed as republics declared their autonomy: in Yugoslavia and parts of the former Soviet Union. While less violent, similar processes have been taking place in other areas including Hungary and the Czech Republic.

The privatisation of protection

Historically, the nation state's monopoly of violence was one of its crowning achievements and a central plank of its modernist achievements (Derlugian 1996). Indeed, this monopoly was central to establishing the conventional distinctions between people, army and government. As the competence of the nation state has been attenuated with the emergence of new centres of authority, what the law is and who represents and upholds it have become blurred and ambiguous. In many areas of the South, existing legal statutes, property rights and customary practices have been undermined. At the same time, many post-adjustment states have not improved their legal competence to redress this situation (Verdery 1996). This development has affected all strata and groups within society. In some regions, the new rich of privatisation, for example, are no longer able to call on the bureaucracies of the state to protect their wealth. At the same time, where customary law safeguards the access of subaltern groups to land, for example, it could be argued that re-establishing legal competence is not in the interests of ruling elites wishing to attract foreign companies to exploit that land. Such blurring and tensions have seen a growing demand for and consequent expansion of all types of private protection.

Protection and legitimacy among non-state actors

The inability or unwillingness of the state to uphold the rule of law has had powerful repercussions throughout Africa and the European East. Concerning subaltern groups, a useful distinction is that between the proliferation of weapons systems and the diffusion of small arms. In the former category are large, sophisticated weapons such as tanks and aircraft, usually delivered to juridical states. In overall terms, trade in such items has declined significantly with the ending of the Cold War. While total figures are uncertain, this is not the case with the diffusion of small arms (ICRC 1999) – a wide range of cheap and durable weapons like assault rifles and rocket launchers that can be carried by a single person but are, nonetheless, extremely effective. New supplies from the downsizing of post-Cold War arsenals and the expansion of new sites of production, especially in the European East, have kept the largely unregulated trade in small arms at high levels. Helped by the growth of shadow economies, small arms have become widely diffused throughout many parts of the South. Some African subsistence groups, for example, are now armed with automatic weapons in order to protect their rights and livelihoods (Turton 1989; Keen 1994). A recent study in Somalia, for example, estimated that small arms of some description could be found in most households (Forberg and Terlinden 1999). During the spring of 1997, insurgents in Albania seized around 750,000 weapons, or 80 per cent of the national arsenal, from military stores. Some of these weapons found their way into the regional systems of transborder trade. Others are in the households of ordinary Albanians, an insurance against the uncertainty around them.

Abundant supplies of small arms currently exist within the networks of the shadow economy. Through such networks, weapons are regularly recycled from one major conflict to another. Transborder trade within the Chad Basin, for example, helps provision the ongoing conflicts in Niger, Chad, Central African Republic and Sudan. Apart from small arms, this includes petrol, hardware, electronic equipment, foodstuffs, cement and stolen 4x4 motor vehicles (Roitman 2001: 3). The prices of small arms vary according to supply. Where they are readily available, some reports claim assault rifles can sell for below their cost of production. In Mozambique and Angola, for example, in 1996, assault rifles were reportedly fetching as little as $15 or the equivalent of a bag of maize (ICRC 1999: 18). A major irony is that part of the supply of small arms to the South is the product in the North of 'successful arms controls agreements that have required members of NATO and the former Warsaw Pact to eliminate hundreds of thousands of weapons from their inventories' (ibid.). At the same time, the nature of small-arms production has changed. Formerly, small-arms production was concentrated within the industrialised world and among a few of its allies. Between 1985 and 1995, however, the number of manufacturers of small arms is estimated to have increased by 25 per cent to involve some 300 companies in over 70 countries, many of them in the South.

A paradox of the present situation is that while the end of the Cold War has prompted a general downsizing of military establishments and arsenals in the North, through increased availability, the growth of parallel trade and, especially, the demand for protection, large areas of the South have been rearming with all types of light weaponry. Moreover, the intersection of the arms trade with the resources of the shadow economy has created new nodes of authority and legitimacy. Arms and parallel trade interconnect to constitute an emerging frontier of wealth creation in a world in which structural adjustment and the debureaucratisation of the state have limited traditional opportunities. In the Chad Basin, the same networks that provision the regional conflicts are also engaged in the illegal trading of ivory from the Lake Chad area and the Central African Republic. At the same time, they organise the transshipment of narcotics from Nigeria and Afghanistan into Western Europe (Roitman 2001: 3). Within Afghanistan, the shipment of poppy resin to the border with Tajikistan can see its value rise from $25 to $3,000 per kg (Goodhand 1999: 5). The journey is dangerous and, as in Africa, carrying and guard duty are monopolised by young men. In order to protect themselves, and the investment of the cultivators, they need arms. Businessmen also need protection and are able to draw on the ranks of the unemployed refugees of the developmental state. In Somalia, for example, at the beginning of 1997, a local company, Barakaat, opened one of the first banks in Mogadishu for several years. Of the company's 300 employees, a third were armed guards (Bellos 1997). That NGOs have also been forced increasingly to avail themselves of private protection in many parts of Africa and the European East since the early 1990s, is symptomatic of this general trend.

Non-state forms of regulatory authority

Within the Chad Basin, Roitman (2001) has described how many of the young men and demobilised soldiers drafted into the shadow economy as guides, carriers and guards, also engage in organised highway robbery. To dismiss this as criminality, however, is to miss the interesting point that those involved 'are making claims to rights to wealth' (*ibid.*: 5). Many of the young men concerned have some education, yet they have to scavenge and traffic for money. They often talk of their situation as one of 'war' where forceful seizure is the norm. Other contenders – customs officials, police, state functionaries and assorted bandits – also practise forceful seizure. At the same time, those who benefit from seizure also complain about exclusion and lack of compensation or redress: soldiers and officials who do not get paid, for example, or lack basic amenities and equipment; or ex-soldiers who have received inadequate indemnities. Lack of training and alternative opportunities compels them to enter the shadow economy. While the bush economy may appear insurgent, however, it is also a realm of well-known strategies of accumulation and legitimated patterns of obtaining rights over wealth. Within the transborder economy, regional elites, especially merchants and military officers, exercise a regulatory authority in relation to controlling access to shadow networks. Such regulatory authority operates at all levels. At its higher reaches, trade commission on deals, right of entry taxes, royalty payments for maintaining network connections, protection fees, and payment for safe delivery of goods secured through customs fraud are levied. At the local level, similar taxes are imposed on local merchants; protection and entitlement dues are obtained from guards, guides and runners; and road tolls and entry taxes at unregulated border markets are collected. In return, such payments for access cement relationships, secure protection and legitimate the nature of shadow activities. They even give rise to forms of redistribution in terms of members of the merchant–military complex financing local schools, mosques or other public infrastructure.

> Those who find themselves outside the bounds of national welfare and security come to judge prestations associated with unofficial regulators as legitimate since they grant access to possibilities for accumulation, protection, and services which are not secured through the state or public infrastructures. In this sense, the relationships the local populations establish with those controlling regional networks of accumulation respond to their claims to rights to wealth. (*Ibid.*: 8)

For local populations, the extractive power of non-state regulators is consistent with social order, redistribution and retribution. Rights to

173

wealth through seizure are legitimated through processes of normative regulation and redistribution: 'social hierarchies generated [among local people] endure to the extent that they are deemed to rectify or subvert either long-standing or recently created conditions of exclusion' (*ibid.*: 9).

The Chechen mafia, for example, repatriated a lot of money to Chechnya after the first (1994–6) of the recent wars. For some commentators, this was the only realistic hope for post-war reconstruction. Before the present war, such wealth had been visible in mosques and palatial residences. Conversations with ordinary Chechens brought out that 'a large part of the population was being helped, even if only at a second or third hand, by rich relatives somewhere in their extended families' (Lieven 1998: 352). As with transborder trade generally, however, while an ordering and legitimating force, such relations are usually non-liberal in nature. They are based on separatist and protectionist tendencies that, in extremes, can produce schism and conflict. While often deriving justification on the basis of exclusion from state systems of regulation and distribution, the emergent forms of social order can themselves accentuate or produce new types of social exclusion. It should not be forgotten, however, that ethnic cleansing simultaneously implies the reaffirmation of the identity and legitimacy of the group on whose behalf the cleansing is being carried out. In its enactment, it also reinforces the lines of patronage and protection that the socially included group must now rely on. In the Balkans, for example, public opinion surveys provide little evidence that the general population has rejected its ethno-nationalist leaders (Magnusson, Bular and Strelov 1996). Indeed, successive elections, to the dismay of aid officials, appear to have confirmed their legitimacy. In the transition zone between North and South Sudan (see Chapter 9), locally based commercial–military complexes derive part of their regulatory authority from the ethnic subjugation and harsh exploitation of Dinka agro-pastoralists displaced by the civil war. Many local groups, privileged within this regulatory authority, benefit from this exploitation. In other words, emerging non-liberal forms of rights to wealth and social legitimacy can also involve processes of delegitimation and oppression. Actual development does not necessarily or easily translate into liberal development. At the same time, given that new forms of social order can emerge, even involving rights through seizure, one cannot assume, as development discourse does, that separating the poor from their undeserving leaders is either feasible or, indeed, justified. In the end, it may be better to address the actual situation rather than the imagined or preferred version.

Warlord and strongman entities

In terms of the emergence of new non-state forms of regulation and legitimacy, an extreme form relates to what can be called warlord or strongman entities. The term 'warlord' first came into popular usage as a way of describing the decentralisation of power in China during the 1920s: the appearance of local strongmen able to control an area and exploit its resources while at the same time keeping a weak central authority at bay. By the early 1980s, this concept had reappeared in Africa to describe, for example, the situation in Chad (May 1985). A factor which one should emphasise about modern warlords, however, is the linkages that they forge with the international economy. Today's successful warlords may act locally but they think globally. A difficulty in studying warlord or strongman entities is that they are extra-legal. This problem, however, extends to the whole question of parallel and shadow economies. Reno (1995b) has argued that warlord entities should not be seen negatively as an indication of a sovereign void. Rather, they should be regarded in a more singular and historic light as representing viable and innovative non-state forms of political authority. Globalisation has given local actors the chance to rework the nature of political authority and experiment within the opportunities created by globalisation. '"Warlordism" and incumbent rulers' intentional destruction of institutions are examples of debureaucratisation and shifts in political forms, rather than "state of decay" in the sense of abjuring any institutionalisation of political authority' (*ibid.*: 9).

Modern warlords have pioneered the forging of links with the global marketplace and the use of foreign companies as a means of establishing local authority. Charles Taylor's National Patriotic Front of Liberia (NPFL) is an example of this variant (*ibid.*: 11–18; Reno 1995a). Starting out as a small-scale invasion force in 1989, the NPFL reached its zenith in 1992–3. By this time, Taylor exercised control over much of Liberia and part of Sierra Leone, a fluid area the NPFL called 'Greater Liberia' or 'Taylorland'. While dispensing with juridical state structures, Greater Liberia had its own currency, banking system and TV station. Complementing local coercion, in order to cement his control Taylor established a vigorous external trade in timber, agricultural produce and diamonds. This trade was conducted through a number of foreign firms and commercial networks. For militia support, Taylor relied on the marginalised youth, those elements particularly alienated from the decaying patrimonial network of the developmental state (Reno 1995b: 28). In Sierra Leone, as elsewhere, disaffected youth, often with an education but lacking conventional means of exercising their ambitions, have also been attracted to warlord figures (Richards 1996).

175

Foreign firms were essential in consolidating Taylor's social position. Firestone Tyre and Rubber Corporation and French commercial interests were involved. During the early 1990s, Taylor was France's third-largest supplier of tropical hardwoods. In this respect, NPFL activity is a good example of the blurring of legitimate and extra-legal parallel activity in the present period. It is indicative of a grey zone of international commercial activity which has become increasingly important as global markets have expanded into unstable areas (Pech and Beresford 1997). Taylor also formed alliances with other global networks following similar survival strategies. For example, a privatised Ukrainian weapons manufacturer, COLA, provided small arms. Regarding internal commercial relations, several prominent Monrovian families headed companies in Taylor's area. These included Logging International Timber Inc. and Bong Bank. He also incorporated Lebanese companies active on the coast. With their cross-border links into Côte d'Ivoire, they opened up another route for arms supplies.

During the early 1990s, Taylor was a pioneer in the use of foreign companies as a source of hard currency and, importantly, as a means of controlling territory physically and thereby denying resources to opponents. As a non-state system, Taylorland was also free from creditor demands and public bureaucracy; constrained only by immediate concerns and necessary alliances, it was institutionally more flexible than its state-based rivals. During the course of the decade, many weak-state incumbents would adopt similar methods. Compared to the patrimonial dependence on bureaucracies of the developmental state, the growing reliance on foreign firms and intermediaries is an innovative development and signals a new mode of integration into the world economy.

The articulation of state and non-state regulatory systems
The networks of the shadow economy work through and around states. While parallel networks and state institutions are distinct, they interact through complex relations of competition, complementarity and complicity. Warlord and strongman entities, while they may exist outside of the state, and can be in open conflict with it, are usually not attempting to live apart from it or, indeed, to replace the state altogether. While Somalia is a possible exception, the history of the warlord Charles Taylor, for example, is instructive in this respect. Having forged an independent existence, he became Liberia's head of state in 1995. As discussed below, juridical sovereignty continues to attract the support of the international community. Not only do Northern governments not wish to see sovereign voids, but juridical states confer legitimacy in

relation to the integration of their economies into the global market place. Juridical leaders can sign international contracts and broker recognised deals. While state and non-state networks of regulatory authority are often in competition or even warfare, they are also frequently complicit as each attempts to use the resources and networks of the other for either direct or mutual advantage. In relation to the Chad Basin,

> while antagonisms are noted when it comes to the state's official regulatory authority over these regional economies, complicity is evident insofar as the state is dependent upon these regional economies for rents and the means of redistribution. Likewise, while these networks can be described as trans or subnational, they make important, or even essential, contributions to the national political economy. (Roitman 2001: 2)

The shadow economy can make extra resources available to state incumbents; at the same time, shadow operators often need the legitimacy that state institutions can confer. Within the Chad Basin, one aspect of the complicity between the two systems is the prevalence of commercial-military trade networks that often bring states and non-state systems of regulatory authority together. The example in the previous chapter concerning the trade in coffee across Sudan's war zone is a case in point. For many military officers, the profits from illicit trade and fraudulent activity are an attractive proposition when set against low official salaries. In exchange for access to the commercial networks of merchants, military officers are able to supply protection and, by their involvement, to legitimate seizure. Apart from direct involvement, state actors are able to derive resources from the shadow economy in terms of the informal taxation of unregulated bush markets, the extraction of protection money, and so on. In terms of what the parallel system requires of the state, the single most prevalent demand is for legal paperwork that falsifies the origins and status of goods, people, modes of transport, ports of entry, and so on (*ibid*.: 11). From Angolan diamonds to ivory from the Central African Republic and Nigerian petrol, border officials, customs officers and government functionaries across the continent are engaged in a huge process of reclassification and falsification without which the shadow economy would not be possible (Bayart, Ellis and Hibou 1999).

Relations of complicity between state and non-state systems of regulatory authority also appear in situations where one would expect to find direct competition and opposition. What Keen (1998: 17–20) has called 'cooperative conflict' involves a frequently reported characteristic of the new wars in terms of rebel and government forces frequently avoiding pitched battles (Liberia), coordinating their movements in and out of villages (Sierra Leone), trading between warring parties (former Yugoslavia), paying ransoms for captured fighters (Chechnya and Peru), and selling arms and ammunition to the other side (Cambodia, Chechnya, Sierra Leone and Sri Lanka). Despite the innovative quality of non-state systems of regulatory authority based on shadow trade, they are unlikely to replace so-called failed state structures. One reason for this is that although the formal economy may represent a part-time activity and states themselves have debureaucratised, the international community continues to channel its development efforts through state institutions. Moreover, in the aftermath of war, it is formal state institutions that aid agencies usually attempt to 'reform' or 'reconstruct'. While development assistance has decreased, the international legitimacy that sovereignty continues to confer, and the networks that are opened through it, mean that we will continue to see examples of warlords like Charles Taylor becoming state incumbents, even if this means that states themselves begin to act more and more like strongman entities. At the extreme lies Somalia, which appears to be surviving and adapting to its stateless existence.

Protection and authority among state incumbents

The Russian mafia

While there are some broad similarities in terms of the trend toward the decentralisation of political authority in Africa and the European East, there are also many differences. For example, the predominant pattern of privatisation and the types of post-adjustment states being constructed contrast markedly. Regarding privatisation, in the European East this process has largely been fuelled by the emergence of new and indigenous classes of property and asset holders, as in the acquisition of enterprises by their former managers or political *nomenklatura* (Verdery 1996: 209). In Africa, while this has also occurred, the involvement of foreign companies, especially in relation to the extraction of natural wealth or the provision of specialist services, is much more pronounced (Reno 1998). Such differences have influenced the appearance of divergent strategies of state incumbent protection.

In relation to Russia, Varese (1994) has argued that the rise of the Russian mafia, after the fashion of Sicily, can be understood in terms of the transition from a condition of monopoly ownership to one of private property in the context of the inability of the state to legally define and, especially, protect that property. In Russia, mafia groups have arisen in the wake of the post-1986 economic reforms (*ibid.*: 231). As further rounds of reform and privatisation have increased the numbers of property owners, the state has been noticeably ineffective in producing clear legislation regarding that property or in protecting property rights. Consequently, the demand for private protection among the new property owners has grown. So too, have the opportunities for extortion and racketeering. Estimates for the number of mafia-style groups operating in Russia in the mid-1990s, for example, range from 2,600 to 5,000 (*ibid.*: 232). By that time, some sources suggest, virtually all small businesses and between 70 and 80 per cent of larger firms and commercial banks were paying protection money to such groups (Castells 1998: 180–1). This accounted for between 10 and 20 per cent of capital turnover, or about half of total profits. Faced with an unresponsive state and a reasonably effective protection racket, people and firms have come to rely on the latter. They represent an emerging form of social order and legitimacy. Although his example is the Russian mafia, Varese makes an important general point: that a demand for protection alone is insufficient to explain the spread of mafia organisations. It also requires a ready supply of people willing and able to carry out violent and protective duties (1994: 246–7). In Russia, an important part of this supply has come from the post-Cold War downsizing of the security and police services. During the early 1990s, for example, the discharge rate in the armed services alone was some 40,000–50,000 per year. In other words, conditions have allowed supply and demand to meet.

Russia's mafia networks underwent a major period of expansion and consolidation between 1986 and 1993 (Castells 1998: 181). Helped by the establishment of transborder networks, this process has seen the emergence of a politico-commercial-mafia complex within Russia. This does not mean

> that crime controls politics, or that most businesses are criminal. It does mean, none the less, that business operates in an environment deeply penetrated by crime; that business needs the protection of political power; and that many politicians, in the 1990s, have amassed considerable fortunes through their business contacts. (*Ibid.*: 187)

Castells has argued that enough evidence exists to make the case that the initial motivation in the formation of the politico-commercial-mafia complex was 'the pillage of Russia' and that the linkages between the nodes of this complex have continued to develop during the course of the 1990s (*ibid.*: 183). The initial tool of this pillage was privatisation. The rapid process of liberalisation and privatisation in the 1991–2

179

period was intended to create an economic and political climate that would make reform irreversible. It also created the conditions for the wholesale seizure of state property. In a manner similar to developments in the Chad Basin, new rights to wealth through seizure have emerged. With the rapid demise of the institutions of the planned economy, few things remained 'but the prevailing notion that it was perfectly appropriate to cheat the state' (Marshall Goldman quoted by Castells 1998: 184). Following the collapse of the Soviet Union in 1991, huge financial empires and giant energy and utility companies led by former communist *nomenklatura* quickly emerged. Given their origins, these commercial ventures had intimate ties with the political world. The pillage of state property, however, was facilitated by the growing linkages between the politico-commercial nexus and the Russian mafia. In particular, it was dependent on the mafia extending the networks of the shadow economy beyond Russia into the West and, at the same time, linking up with other criminal networks involved in the fields of illicit trade and money laundering.

Through the internationalisation of the politico-commercial-mafia complex, the pillage of Russia has taken a number of forms including the illicit trade in oil, weapons, raw materials, and rare and precious metals. Some estimates put the illicit smuggling of capital in 1992 at $20 billion and the parallel outflow of oil and other materials at about $17 billion, or several times the amount of foreign direct investment during the 1991–6 period (*ibid*.: 189). Castells claims that a well-placed informant told him that when the Yeltsin cabinet came to power in 1992 the gold and hard currency reserves of the former Soviet state had almost entirely gone (*ibid*.: 186). At the same time, the complex also increased its control of Russia's privatised industries as well as investing in real estate, hotels and restaurants through the recycling of laundered money. Other activity which has come to light involves a massive diversion of Western aid assistance provided through the IMF. The CIA is alleged to have first alerted the Clinton administration to the embezzlement of aid funds in 1995 (Vulliamy 1999). Liberal optimism that this was just a transitional problem, however, meant that nothing was done – until a recent scandal involving allegations that the Bank of New York was part of a huge money-laundering operation involving some $20 billion in IMF assistance. Investigations surrounding these allegations have uncovered some of the links between sections of Russia's political establishment and the commercial–mafia nexus (Farrelly 1999). So far, the response has been limited to setting in train moves to strengthen American money-laundering legislation (Martinson 1999). The Bank of New York investigation has revealed that some of Russia's giant natural resource and energy utilities, for example Gozprom, the world's largest gas company, appear linked to illicit trade, tax evasion and money-laundering networks (Farrelly 1999).

Money laundering is essential if the profits from shadow trade, tax evasion and racketeering are to be fully realised (Castells 1998: 178–9). The first stage involves the placement of dirty money into the financial system. This is usually through offshore banks and similar financial institutions located in countries with few controls. Leonid Dyachenko, Yeltsin's son-in-law, for example, is said to have accounts in the Cayman Islands (Atkinson 1999). Using a number of techniques to avert suspicion, money from such locations is fed into the mainstream banking system. The second stage involves the separation of the funds from their source. This is achieved through currency swops, invest-ments in stocks, using dirty money as loans fronting for legitimate funds, and so on. The speed with which such transactions can now be completed adds to the difficulty of detection. The investigation into the Bank of New York scandal has uncovered a network of shell companies in Eastern and Western Europe linked to the Russian politico-commer-cial-mafia complex. Through a series of measures – multi-country reg-istration, using relatives or accomplices to act as board members, exploiting loopholes in the commercial and privacy laws of the country concerned, and so on – the linkages in the network are concealed. The final stage involves the integration of laundered money into the legiti-mate economy. In the past, this has often involved the purchase of property and stocks, usually in countries with the least controls. Western Europe, for example, is reckoned to have some of the weakest money-laundering regulations among the developed economies (Atkinson 1999). Since money laundering is a good example of a networked activity, the techniques that are used and the means by which dirty money is integrated into the legitimate economy will continue to adapt and mutate. Analysts at Britain's National Criminal Intelligence Service, itself a misnomer given the non-territoriality of much of its business, argue that information technology and biotech-nology are opening up as areas of future criminal investment (Thompson 1999).

Private military protection

In Russia, the mafia has emerged in response to the protection needs of the new political and, especially, commercial elites. In assisting the elites to realise their wealth, it has also played an essential but covert role in linking the politico-commercial nexus to the wider flows of the global economy. In Africa, liberal economic reform has similarly placed new demands for protection and international integration on state incumbents. Unlike Russia, however, in the absence of local resources this protection has not usually emerged from within the countries concerned, with the exception of irregular militia forces such as those in Rwanda (African Rights 1995) or Sudan (Africa Watch 1990). Instead, protection has been associated with the growing involvement of a variety of external private companies and corporate groups offering protection in exchange for cash and favourable commercial contracts (Mills and Stremlau 1999). Chapter 3 has already examined a number of the political and organisational aspects of the international private security business, including the issue of regulation. While there is a growing interest in the privatisation of international security, currently there is little research in this area. Moreover, during the 1990s most of the work, with William Reno among the exceptions, has focused on the nature and legitimacy of the mercenary role (Cilliers and Cornwell 1999). What has been neglected is the part played by private security in relation to the real internal security needs of African elites.

In terms of the global economy, Africa has ceased to be a generalised supplier of raw materials and primary products. The resulting overall decline in commercial investment has established the widespread view that the continent is largely disconnected from the global economy (Castells 1996: 133–6). Like nature, however, social life abhors a vacuum. Although Africa's total investment and share of formal global markets have declined significantly, in certain key areas they have been maintained and even increased. For example, investment in Africa's extractive industries has kept up a pattern of steady growth since the 1980s (ODI 1997), despite the fact that many of the countries concerned have been sites of long-running conflicts and, like Angola, have dismal records of economic reform. Remaining investment has tended to concentrate on the selective extraction of valuable minerals such as bauxite, gold, diamonds and oil, together with forest products like tropical hardwoods and supermarket niche commodities such as exotic fruits and vegetables. At the same time, the transnational shadow economy has undergone a huge expansion. Together, these developments suggest that Africa has not been disconnected from the global economy; rather, *it has been reintegrated in a new way*. Market deregulation, selective investment and the increase in parallel trade are indicative of the emergence of a new type of political economy.

Most of the African commodities extracted within the formal economy lack a local market. Indeed, they are sold and traded directly within the global economy for hard currency. Lacking a local market, mineral and hardwood extraction, for example, does not require the public infrastructure that one associates with a conventional market economy – an educated and disciplined workforce; effective distribution and sales networks; and buoyant and predictable consumer demand. On the contrary, extractive and niche export industries are relatively self-contained and insulated in relation to the rest of the society. That they are able to exist even in environments that are insecure also attests to their adaptability and resilience. Their main concern is to be able to extract commodities and realise them in the global marketplace with as few local commitments and difficulties as possible. In many respects, such industries complement the logic of liberal economic reform and its preference for privatised and debureaucratised facilitator states. At the same time, however, debureaucratisation and cuts in aid spending have meant that state actors are no longer able to maintain the patronage networks associated with the bureaucracies of the developmental state. Moreover, with the expansion of the shadow economy, new and challenging forms of regulatory authority have emerged outside of the state, such as the various forms of local authority and legitimacy based on strongman or warlord figures. Given this tension, an important feature of the reintegration of Africa within the global economy lies in the mutual advantage and accommodation that have emerged between external commercial interests and juridical state actors in the face of such internal security threats. William Reno (1998) has analysed this relation in depth.

An essential part of the accommodation has been the growing use of private military companies (PMCs) during the 1990s, to protect valuable natural wealth against the threat of seizure from internal strongman entities based in the shadow economy. At the same time, usually through associated companies, such deals have often furnished the minimum necessary infrastructure to extract and market that wealth. In Africa, small and adaptable South African companies have been important in pioneering this new form of politico-commercial protection and global integration. Moreover, this development is symptomatic of a radical change in the nature of international relations with the passing of the Cold War. In the past, the nature of international order was based on the political control of territory. Today, it is more concerned with the control of markets and processes (*ibid.*: 71). The actions of private companies in helping protect and market natural wealth have tended to commercialise politics. The field of commercial protection can roughly be divided between those (usually larger and better-established) companies that seek a legitimate status and smaller, more opportunistic enterprises. The former, for example, associate with juridical states and their protection needs. They include, for example,

Defence Services Limited (DSL), London; Military Professional Resources Incorporated (MPRI), Virginia; and even the celebrated, but now defunct, South Africa-based Executive Outcomes (EO). Other companies, however, have forged links with warlord entities and have helped them enter the global marketplace.

At the other end of the spectrum, PMCs need the legitimacy provided by association with recognised states. Indeed, the recognition of the sovereignty of weak states by the international community, even if by common consent it is largely a façade, plays an important role in legitimating the external exploitation of the resources that such entities often only nominally control. The formal recognition of sovereignty is an important way in which global markets control and exploit national resources. The privatisation of protection and security is well suited to this new environment. While still in a process of formation and subject to an uncertain outcome (Vines 1999; Cilliers and Cornwell 1999), it would seem certain to expand its role, especially since the current trend appears to be one of legitimation through regulation. Private protection addresses actual tensions and needs that formal states are no longer able to encompass. In relation to weak states, for example, it has already been mentioned that private security is one way in which incumbent rulers can protect national assets against internal threats from shadow strongmen or warlords. At the same time, the commercial sector itself also requires such protection. Moreover, the involvement of foreign companies in this way helps meet the strong insistence of the international community on privatisation, state debureaucratisation, economic efficiency and market access. Private security provides one solution for these differing requirements and needs. Whether it represents a lasting solution, however, is a different question.

In terms of elite protection in a weak state, the example of Sierra Leone has wider application. As a means of political survival based on mineral extraction, Sierra Leone's rulers have relied upon foreign companies to protect and exploit the country's diamond reserves. Valentine Strasser, for example, who came to power in 1992, like the warlord Charles Taylor in Liberia (Atkinson 1997), used foreign companies in this manner. During the first half of the 1990s, several of these companies attempted, with partial success, to use their own security forces to police their concessions. In 1994 Sierra Rutile (a subsidiary of the American-owned Nord Resources) explored the possibility of using the British firm Gurkha Security Guards (GSG) to provide protection for its mining activities (Reno 1996: 14). The effective use of private protection in Sierra Leone, however, is associated with the involvement of the South African PMC Executive Outcomes. The corporate structure of which Executive Outcomes (EO) was part has already been described (see Chapter 3). EO itself disbanded in January 1999. Between April 1995 and February 1997, however, when it was operational in Sierra Leone, it was part of a network of companies that brought together security, mining, civil engineering and financial interests. Compared to the limited success of other PMCs, EO had a very considerable impact. Its initial role was to support the military government of Valentine Strasser until elections in February 1996. The new civilian government then continued to use EO's services until the company left in February 1997. During this period, it was able to clear the Revolutionary United Front (RUF) first from the outskirts of Freetown and then from around the mineral fields, tipping the balance of power in favour of the government, allowing elections to be held and ultimately pushing the RUF into a peace agreement. In May 1997, however, only a couple of months after EO had left Sierra Leone, the military again ousted the elected government and invited the RUF to join them – a reverse which illustrates both the protracted nature of such instability and the unproven long-term utility, despite their growing number of supporters, of PMCs as a means of conflict resolution (Vines 1999).

What is interesting about Executive Outcomes, and has wider significance in relation to other private security companies, it that it usually exchanged its services for a stake in the mineral wealth of the country concerned. Before disbanding, it was operational in about twenty countries, mostly in Africa, Angola and Sierra Leone being its two best-known engagements. Ranger and Heritage Oil, members of the same corporate group, helped finance EO's operation in Angola (1993–5) in exchange for government oil concessions. In its two-year operation, it is also alleged that the Angolan government handed EO $80 million for its services. It is interesting to note that, during the same period, it is estimated that the illicit diamond fields controlled by the warlord Savimbi (the head of UNITA), with whom EO was in conflict, grossed nearly ten times this amount (van Niekerk 1995). In Sierra Leone, Branch Energy obtained a diamond concession as part of EO's involvement. For the 22 months it spent in this country, it is claimed that the government also paid $35 million in cash (Shearer 1997: 205). Exactly how much EO earned in these various operations is disguised by different concessions and cash payments being made to various members of the corporate network.

In terms of its military operations, EO used a modern variant of the approach developed during the wars of colonial conquest: a relatively small core of trained and disciplined troops supported by local army units or militia forces. In Sierra Leone, for example, EO's own personnel averaged around 150, only touching 300 for a few months at the height of the fighting (*ibid.*). The company's ground forces were predominantly Angolan, mainly officered by white South Africans. For a private company, this core was supported by an impressive range of equipment. For example, Ibis Air, an associate company, had two MI-17 helicopters, two Hind M24 gunships, two jet fighters, several Boeing 727 transports and a number of other small aircraft. For many rebel groups, EO represented a potent force. More generally, it was widely acknowledged as the first corporate army that Africa has seen since the nineteenth century (Harding 1997).

Executive Outcomes formally closed in January 1999. At the time of writing, there is some speculation as to the reasons for closure and what, exactly, has become of the network that it created. One thing seems certain, however: closure was not due to lack of work or opportunity. During 1998, EO had already begun to change its corporate structure. Closure was part of this wider restructuring in response to South African legislation attempting to restrict foreign military activities, new developments in the mining and private security sector and, one may suspect, the disapproval felt by its corporate members of the exposure that EO was beginning to attract. Senior personnel have been dispersed to other companies and the network has been dissected in a manner that keeps its most powerful nodes hidden (Pech 1999: 96–7). Because EO was registered in the UK and offshore, it is possible that it will remain active through one of its former subsidiaries, such as Sandline. Moreover, prior to closure, the trend had been to secure contracts with clients through individual consultants rather than the group of directors linked to specific companies as was the case in the mid-1990s. This ensures that the corporate interest remains hidden.

> The EO group's present activity in Africa is therefore hidden by a brokerage system and new fronts in a complex web of affiliated corporations. Today, it is harder to identify where and what is still active, who their clients are, how they are organised and which corporate entities are involved than ever before. While EO may no longer formally exist in South Africa, the industry continues to expand and, as it grows in complexity and sophistication, is increasingly hard to monitor. (*Ibid.*: 96)

In mid-1997, EO was the first PMC to establish a website. As a means of recruitment, this has given EO an ability to put together anything from a small group of specialists to a large counter-insurgency force. Some of the critics of mercenary activity have read the closure of EO as a victory for South Africa's 1998 *Regulation of Foreign Military Assistance Act*. But as Cilliers and Cornwall argue, 'the ability of a company whose major asset is a well-managed database of former military personnel and the right connections to relocate to a different country, to mutate and change or conceal its identity, must serve to sober too enthusiastic an analysis' (1999: 239). As soon as private protection began to attract attention, the flexibility afforded to networked organisations allowed EO to mutate and assume a different shape.

Mafia and private protection compared
It has already been noted that an important distinction between Russian mafia organisations and private protection in Africa is that between internal and external agency respectively. This difference relates to major divergences in the local availability of the necessary skills and resources. Another distinction relates to the legality with which such ventures are viewed. While mafia operations are generally regarded as criminal, the status of private protection is more ambiguous. The better-established companies would argue, with some justification, that they are playing a legitimate role. At the same time, however, there are many structural similarities between mafia organisations and private protection agencies, arising both from the qualification of nation-state competence and, especially, from its declining ability to enforce the rule of law. They both answer the growing needs of elites to protect themselves from internal rivals and, at the same time, to forge new linkages with the global economy. In relation to the politico-commercial nexus, the Russian mafia plays a similar role, for example, to private security companies concerning weak state rulers in Africa. Both couple the use of violence with extensive parallel and grey international networks of intermediaries and contacts. In this respect, there is an affinity between the networked, mutable and covert organisation of money laundering and the opaque and flexible corporate structure of international private protection. Mafia groups and private protection are symptomatic of the blurring of legality and illegality in the new international order. At the same time, they are powerful expressions of a defining feature of global liberal governance: the need to control processes and markets rather than territories. Thus they demonstrate the general trend toward the commercialisation of politics and the ambiguous world of legitimacy that this has created.

The new wars as network war

The merging of war and peace
Just as legality and illegality have blurred, in relation to the new wars, so the conditions of 'war' and 'peace' are relative rather than absolute

and opposed conditions. Indeed, there are many similarities between these states (Bojicic, Kaldor and Vejvoda 1995). In many parts of the South, both war and peace are characterised by high levels of unemployment and underemployment. Both conditions exhibit debureaucratised and fragmented systems of public administration, and high degrees of autonomy among political actors. War and peace are also dependent on extensive transborder shadow trade and non-territorial networking. In this respect, they are similarly reliant on a wide range of external support ranging from finance to manufactured goods, energy and food aid. Through the widespread diffusion of small arms, societies at war and peace can also be armed to comparable levels. In many parts of the South, countries at war, recovering from war or, indeed, with no experience of war can all appear remarkably similar. While the degree of organised violence and the social displacement associated with war can distinguish it from peace, even here one has to be careful not to overstate the matter.

Levels of violence, death and displacement during peacetime can be worryingly similar to those of wartime. The ICRC, for example, has examined the frequency of weapons injuries during and after a period of conflict in the Kandahar region of Afghanistan (ICRC 1999: 40–1). A formal peace returned to the district in 1995 when it came under the undisputed control of one faction. The study showed that weapons injuries decreased by only a third between the periods of war and peace. Moreover, most of these injuries were not related to uncleared landmines but to the wilful use of small arms. In other words, 'peace' in Kandahar is a relative condition in which armed violence runs at two-thirds of the 'war' levels. This condition is not confined to Afghanistan but can be found in many parts of the South. The number of murders in peacetime El Salvador reached 8,500 in 1995 as against a yearly average of 6,250 during the conflict there. In South Africa, 27,000 people were murdered in 1997 compared to 12,000 in 1989. While many peacetime killings are unrelated to clear political agendas, they reflect the persistence of a violent political economy despite the absence of war. This condition is often manifest in terms of high crime rates, zones of insecurity and travel restrictions. Uganda, for example, although seen as a success by the international community in terms of economic reform, would qualify here. Northern parts of the country have been in a state of insurgency since the 1980s. In Angola, Nordstrom (2001) has remarked that it is difficult to distinguish war from peace. During 1998, the UN attempted officially to implement the peace accords that had been agreed between the government and UNITA. Despite this understanding, the conflict and violence continued.

The aid agencies, however, proceeded to act as if a state of peace did indeed exist.

A number of implications flow from the merging of war and peace. Development discourse and the activities of most NGOs and aid agencies tend to reify open violence and turn it into an abstract and distinct thing-in-itself. This misses the important point that, today, the relations of contested and violent peace are very similar to those of war. However, this mistaken view is not due to an inadequate understanding or lack of analysis, but serves an important governance function within liberal peace. Chapter 9 examines this process in some detail with regard to Sudan. The reification of conflict means that it can be blamed for the failure of development. In this manner, it becomes a means whereby aid agencies can reinvent themselves in times of official peace. When a formal peace eventually returns to Sudan, for example, one can almost predict what will happen. NGOs will enthusiastically transform themselves into post-conflict reconstruction agencies and optimistically canvass for funding in terms of the new development opportunities they will claim have emerged. However, the underlying and fundamental antagonisms that characterise the political economy of Sudan and that have instigated violence in the past will persist.

In many respects, the new wars of the 1990s appear, if anything, as a quickening or amplification of the internal relations and contradictions that have shaped formal peace. The resulting conflicts, in many cases, can be regarded as successful in that they have allowed the logic of violent peace to be worked through. Consider the separatist tendencies that characterise ethno-nationalism. The war in the Balkans has resulted in Croatia, Serbia, Bosnia Herzegovina (divided into three ethnic enclaves) and Macedonia establishing ethnocentric political systems. In the Caucasus region, Armenia, Azerbaijan and Georgia (practically divided into three or four enclaves) are similar. Kosovo, Moldovia and Slovakia could also develop in this manner (Iveković 1999). While not established by overt violence, the secession of the Baltic states of Latvia, Estonia and Lithuania from Russian control has also added to the growing list of ethno-nationalist states which implicitly or explicitly define citizenship in ethnic terms and, moreover, use both *de facto* and *de jure* measures to oppress and exclude minorities. For such states, maintaining internal social boundaries is important for realising the sectarian political legitimacy on which they depend and, on this basis, defining the boundaries of official peace.

Network war

Where the new wars differ from violent peace is in terms of degree rather than absolute or opposed conditions. Where open conflict exists it suggests nodes of authority with sufficient power to mobilise transborder networks to the extent necessary to sustain such violence – for example, by controlling natural wealth or advantage such as gems, gold or hardwoods, as already discussed in relation to private protection. Network war is an extreme form of the competition that exists between non-state and state systems of regulatory authority and is often connected with the manner in which markets are controlled and integrated into the global economy. Thus warlord and strongman entities involved in conflicts in Southern and West Africa, for example, have been able to create new forms of legitimacy and rights to wealth through seizure and, at the same time, to forge new linkages with the global economy in order to realise that wealth and to provision the conflict that gives rise to it. The networks being mobilised, however, those of shadow trade, simultaneously form the basis of everyday life: they lie alongside, intertwine with and, in some cases, duplicate the networks that form the numerous post-adjustment survival strategies keeping millions of people alive. Conflict does, however, place special demands on parallel networks, such as the need to control and export high-value commodities and to link with the grey and criminal networks of the small-arms trade and commodity and money laundering. Yet the networks involved are often the same as those that bring in the clothes, foodstuffs, medical supplies and manufactured goods for general consumption (Nordstrom 2001), as illustrated in the earlier case study of shadow trade in coffee across the war zone in South Sudan. The networks that support war cannot easily be separated out and criminalised in relation to the networks that characterise peace; they are both part of a complex process of actual development.

The new wars reflect forms of authority that can mobilise the full potential of transborder trade. The exercise of this authority also amplifies the non-liberal characteristics of the shadow economy in general. This relates to more than protectionism and various forms of regional competition. It is also reflected in the development of modes of making war that, like the economy itself, fall outside the regulatory framework traditionally associated with nation states. Network war has dissolved the conventional distinctions between people, army and government (van Creveld 1991). The new wars, as well as requiring the mobilisation of networks to realise wealth and provision violence, are similarly concerned with restricting the effectiveness of other networks, taking them over or eliminating them altogether. It is in this sense that one can describe the new wars as *network war*. It has already been pointed out that the networks of the shadow economy are not value-free linkages connecting disparate activities but normative, cultural and political relations capable of agency in their own right. Network war pitches such normative systems, commodity chains and forms of regulatory authority against each other. Rather than states or armies, the new wars variously ally or oppose the political, economic and social networks that support all forms of diaspora, ethnic community, regimes of social order, discrete politico-commercial linkages, market hegemonies and so on.

Network war, since it is concerned with social, cultural and political relations, does not recognise the existence of civilians in a traditional sense. How can one be a 'civilian', for example, in a religious, ethnic or racially defined conflict, especially when opposing forces are responsible for ascription? Within the new wars, *people are social beings rather than juridical subjects*. Everyone is part of an economic, cultural, political or ethnic network. The advertising profession in the North has long recognised this and, as a matter of routine, regularly divides populations into network identities and marketing clusters. When the insights of modern consumerism are applied to conflict, a range of possibilities opens up. At its extreme margins are attempts to eliminate entire social networks, that is, genocide; the wilful starvation of specific groups; public campaigns of exemplary terror, mass rape, mutilation and selective dehumanisation; the withholding of humanitarian assistance; the wholesale displacement of social groups; and the destruction of cultural icons and art treasures. In terms of more mundane actions one will find everyday racial discrimination, the barring of employment and political rights to certain social groups, acts of physical abuse, random murder, intimidation, and so on. That the new wars, in pitching social and political networks against each other, are a site for the widespread violation of human rights can be taken as a given. Part of the problem, however, is that we continue to view network war in terms of a framework of conventions and international law that was developed in relation to the territorial power and regulatory authority of nation states. As that authority has declined, concerns over human rights violations have understandably grown. It is a sobering thought, however, that the rights industry has expanded at a time when the concept of human rights as a universalistic and effective regulatory tool in the actual world appears to be on the wane.

While the new wars dissolve conventional distinctions between people, army and government and, in the process, violate human rights, it should not be forgotten that there is a wide variation in the nature and severity of network war. While genocide is possible, it is an exception rather than a rule. At the same time, although it is common to argue that the new wars deliberately target civilians, and figures of 80–90 per cent casualty rates are often quoted, there is little real evidence to back up such oft-repeated claims. While social and cultural conflicts no doubt take a heavy toll on the lives of ordinary people, since they are the repository of such modalities, the new wars usually occur in circumstances that make accurate statistical analysis, let alone comment on the status of the casualties, difficult to make. One of the few adequate sources is the ICRC surgical database, begun in 1991. An analysis of the first 17,086 people admitted for weapons injuries suggested that 35 per cent were female, males under 16, or males 50 and over. This is, of course, only a rough proxy for people who may not have been combatants. A study in Croatia using death certificates and employment records to assess the civilian proportion of conflict fatalities estimated 64 per cent non-combatants among the 4,339 cases studied (ICRC 1999: 16). This type of variation leads one to assume that network war, like the shadow economy, contains its own conventions, norms and codes of conduct. Moreover, these can vary from place to place. It is an area, however, about which we know very little (Richards 1996). At the same time, as Nordstrom (2001) has argued, we must also assume that just as the emerging political complexes are able to wage war, in many places they are also the only force realistically capable of reinstating a peace. In this respect, in terms of post-Cold War networks being a force for renewal, the Zapatista insurgency in Mexico is interesting in its attempt to win rights for indigenous peoples and tackle the one-sided logic of economic globalisation (Castells 1997: 72–84). At the same time, however, the Zapatista movement also reinforces another dimension of the new wars and one that has already been discussed in relation to the shadow economy and private protection: such conflicts are not purely internal events, and

> war today, by definition, is constructed internationally. We may well speak of internal wars, but they are set in vast global arenas. We may speak of contests within or between states, but a considerable part of war and post-conflict development take place along extra-state lines. War, and peace, unfold as much according to these extra-state realities as they do state-based ones. (Nordstrom 2001: 2)

In relation to private protection, foreign commercial companies have been able to provide one solution to the security needs of weak states and, indeed, strongman entities in Africa. At the same time, however, the success or not of such protection has an important bearing on the commercial control of markets and on how resources and populations are integrated into the global economy. The internationalization of conflict in this manner has an important bearing on how the relative states of war and peace unfold and interact.

The commercialisation of politics

In the North since the 1970s, the worlds of business and politics have drawn closer together. The new public policy of budgetary restraint, privatisation and internationalisation has provided the framework for this association. Reflecting the prominence of markets, and the need for political actors to adapt to their needs, politics in the North, like the everyday life that it reflects, has increasingly been commercialised. To put this another way, the business sector in the North is playing a growing social and political role as a result of the process of privatisation, marketisation and the influence of public–private welfare and service initiatives. Under the impact of globalisation, a similar process has occurred in the South. In this case, an extreme form of the commercialisation of politics manifests itself in the new wars. Commercialisation in this case, however, is wider than the rather narrow interpretation that this phenomenon usually receives, as when conflict is blamed on greedy leaders who create self-sustaining war economies (Collier 1999). While network war has to be self-provisioning and locally regulated patterns of violence offer many opportunities for significant profit and gain (Keen 1998), commercialisation also extends to the international control of markets and their integration within the global economy. In particular, it relates to how economic reform, privatisation and market deregulation have been transformed and manipulated by a wide range of local and international actors to achieve political ends.

An important feature of the strategic complexes that form liberal peace is the development and security role that has been allotted to the business sector. While policy makers want to increase the engagement of commercial companies in such matters, in terms of actual response, the ascribed role is still very much under construction. Where the business sector has been drawn into agreement with the aims of liberal peace, usually it has been the larger multinational companies, especially the extractive industries, and employers' organisations that are well established in the public domain. Such companies and organisations have realised that signing up to the codes of conduct and aspirations of liberal peace can bring benefits such as improved public perception, a better market position and the hope of a more secure business environment. In relation to private protection, the same is true of those companies operating at the legitimate end of the market or wanting to progress toward it: they benefit from contracts issued by Northern military establishments, multinational companies, embassies, aid agencies, and accepted and recognised Southern states. Beneath this thin and emergent layer of respectability, however, the role of the private sector in relation to the aims of liberal peace has generally been ambiguous and often antagonistic. Since the mid-1990s, it has become increasingly common to problematise the role of humanitarian assistance as capable of playing a negative role in relation to conflict (Anderson 1996). In this respect, however, the contribution of economic reform and market liberalisation in terms of facilitating the parallel marketing of resources and the provisioning of the new wars is far in excess of any effects that may be ascribed to humanitarian assistance.

Structural adjustment has encouraged the expansion and internationalisation of the shadow economy. At the same time, market deregulation has allowed multi-layered and intersecting networks of legitimate, grey and criminal enterprise to establish the marketing and supply chains of the new wars. The commercialisation of politics in relation to conflict is not simply about the growing roles of commercial calculation in relation to violence or foreign firms in shaping local agendas. It is more complex and goes to the heart of the *paradox of globalisation*. Roitman (2001) has questioned whether Reno's analysis of the private security companies helping weak states to manage and control internal adversaries is in fact a new relation. The developmental state was also a conduit for externally provided aid that was often used for similar purposes; in both cases, external actors help to shape internal outcomes. What is new in the present relationship, however, is that during the Cold War Northern states or their intermediaries supplied the external resources used to manage or reward internal clients and adversaries. This aid relationship gave the North influence over politics in the South. What is new is the ability of emerging political complexes to forge their own links with international markets and private companies in order to realise wealth, create new forms of legitimacy and provision conflict. In many respects, the North, short of direct intervention with (even then) an uncertain outcome (Von Hippel 1999), has lost a good deal of influence in terms of being able to affect the course of political competition. As a result of deregulation, Northern governments have little control over the global marketplace. This has given network war a distinct *independent* character. This autonomy, moreover, has fed into the insecurity of liberal peace and the consequent reproblematisation of underdevelopment as dangerous. In many respects, it is not underdevelopment that is dangerous but the ability that the South now has of independently exploiting the opportunities of globalisation.

While structural adjustment has given a major boost to the shadow economy, privatisation and market deregulation have enabled foreign companies of varying shades of legitimacy to establish themselves in the nodes of the marketing and supply networks that support the new wars. From this perspective, a fundamental contradiction within global liberal governance is that its development and security aims are premised upon market openness. Indeed, deregulation constitutes the most basic and sacred canon of the liberal order (Stiglitz 1998: 25). Difficulties, setbacks, even conflict itself, are usually interpreted as restrictions or impediments that stand in the way of market openness. The knee-jerk solution is to call for more openness, fewer restrictions and greater deregulation. The whole rationale for inviting the business sector to play a development and security role is founded on the belief that free markets promote development and security. The UN Secretary-General Kofi Annan, in a recent report commissioned by the Security Council on *The Causes of Conflict and the Promotion of Durable Peace and Sustainable Development in Africa*, argued that greater market openness and adjusting to a globally competitive trade environment were vital for peace and development. Moreover, 'Many African economies need not only greater access to the international market but also to remove domestic constraints which limit their capacity to take advantage of existing opportunities offered through the Uruguay Round [international free-trade] agreements' (Annan 1998: para. 99).

The problem for global governance is that to the extent that deregulation and market liberalisation have promoted wealth creation and a liberal social order, they have, in equal measure, fostered the informalisation of the economy, the spread of shadow trade, the criminalisation of many international transactions and the spread of network war (Gray 1998; Castells 1998). The two are not unconnected but organically linked. The paradox of globalisation is that the more the new wars disrupt international relations, the louder the call for more openness and less restrictions (Reno 1998). The measure of real wealth within this complex is the ability, seemingly, to extricate and insulate oneself from the inherent contradictions of the liberal world system. In the North this ranges from private health care and education through to gated residential areas and private leisure complexes. The majority, on the other hand, inherit a system that appears primed for self-destruction. Concern about openness remains confined to the issue of volatile and unregulated flows of financial capital, especially with the recognition that these flows are capable of destabilising economies and increasing poverty in countries strategic to the North. Network war, however, and the flows of commodities, manufactured goods and services that sustain it, belong to a different level of the global economy. The countries concerned are largely outside the flows of conventional financial investment and trading. Moreover, the networks in which they are enmeshed belong to the world of actual exchanges, movements and commodity chains.

Commercial complicity and network war

Rebels, warlords, mafia groups and weak state rulers are rarely self-reliant. They usually need all kinds of goods and services that have to be procured internationally. In such circumstances assets and natural wealth – gems, hardwood, drugs, oil, gold, ivory, seafood, art treasures, rare metals, spare parts, and so on – become hard currency. With such resources, there are plenty of companies and private enterprises willing to do business. Moreover, within the unregulated global arena, ideas of legality and illegality easily blur and become virtually meaningless. International law, for example, does not cover rebel areas. Moreover, transborder marketing and supply networks are usually multi-levelled and can slide in and out of legality at each intersection. Even when international sanctions and restrictions apply, shadow networks are sufficiently flexible and mutable to adjust quickly to alternative routes and methods. The continuing growth and mutation of the global drug economy, for example, despite extensive international policing, is a good example of the adaptability of parallel and grey trade. Even the world's 'poorest countries' have managed to find the extensive resources required to pursue network war. In Angola and Mozambique, for example, such war payments have produced

> coastlines fished out by foreign trawlers for millions of dollars worth of seafood shipped internationally; gem mines hosting a brisk, lucrative and illegal international trade; war-orphans sold into international pros-titution and labor rings; looted goods being carried across borders to purchase everything from luxury items to war-supplies; future resource (oil, timber, land-lease, industrial) rights sold off to (super)power and multinational corporation interests ... [w]hile 'armies' ... of local profi-teers risked their lives smuggling, poaching, slaving, money changing, etc. (Nordstrom 2001: 7)

In the early 1990s, the Liberian warlord Charles Taylor was able to market the rubber and timber he controlled through his connections with a number of American and French companies, including the Firestone Tyre and Rubber Corporation. At the time, Taylor was supply-ing a third of France's hardwood imports (Reno 1995b). Arms were being supplied through COLA, a recently privatised Ukrainian arms manufacturer. During the 1990s, UNITA's ability to wage war has been underwritten by its control of 60–70 per cent of Angola's diamond fields and its ability to develop flexible transborder marketing and supply networks. Between 1992 and 1998, it is estimated that UNITA generated $3.7 billion through illicit diamond sales (Global Witness 1998). Aware of this problem, in June 1998 the UN applied sanctions on the sale of rough diamonds of Angolan origin lacking an official government certificate of origin. In July 1998, the EU applied similar measures. A year later, however, these sanctions had made no real impact on UNITA's resource base (Brittain 1999). What change had occurred had been in relation to the logistics of the trade. Operatives and intermediaries 'have simply altered the routes and obtained deceptive paperwork from obliging countries' (Global Witness 1998: 9). In the past, Angolan's parallel diamond networks had run through Zaïre and South Africa. Moreover, using countries friendly to UNITA in Central, West and North Africa, including Côte d'Ivoire, Morocco and the Central African Republic, diamonds had been flown to Europe and Israel. While some networks still go through what is now the Democratic Republic of Congo, political change in Central Africa and the UN/EU embargo have tended to concentrate network activity on South Africa, with other African countries still used to access global markets. Transborder routes are also switched more regularly to avoid detection (*ibid.*: 13).

The shadow trade in Angolan diamonds has been maintained by two factors. The first is the relative ease with which network operators can obtain certificates of origin from other African countries, thus falsifying the source of the rough diamonds. It has already been mentioned that the provision of bogus paperwork is a mainstay of the shadow economy and an important means whereby state and non-state regulatory systems intersect and articulate. The second factor is the complicity and lack of transparency within the international diamond market. The South Africa-based company De Beers, through its Central Selling Organisation, values and sells 80 per cent of the world's diamonds. In its attempts to maintain a controlling influence on the world diamond trade, De Beers has developed a complex corporate structure composed of many foreign-registered subsidiaries. Through these, or third-party companies, falsely certificated rough Angolan diamonds find their way onto the legitimate market through Antwerp and Israel. In this respect, both the Belgian and Israeli governments have been slow to register their compliance with UN sanctions. As Global Witness has argued, 'the lack of transparency and corporate responsibility in the diamond industry has been central to the continued financing of UNITA, and hence the fuelling of civil war in Angola' (*ibid.*: 7).

This problem, however, is not confined to the diamond industry but is more generalised. Moreover, the ability of companies in a deregulated market to work around sanctions regimes is also illustrated in the fate of the US trade sanctions applied to Iran, Libya and Sudan in 1996. Because of the inability to enforce these sanctions, they were repealed in April 1999. Regarding Iran, US sanctions were undermined by small European and Asian oil companies anxious to secure lucrative contracts to pump Turkmenistan oil and gas across Iran (Meek 1998). The eventual repeal of trade sanctions was based on the realisation that the only losers in this arrangement were American companies (Reuters 1999). In relation to Sudan, the role of foreign oil companies is a useful example of the changing international environment. Large companies such as Chevron and Total Oil began oil exploration in South Sudan in the late 1970s. Both of these enterprises eventually pulled out in 1984 following a renewal of open conflict in the region and rebel attacks on their installations. During the rest of the 1980s and early 1990s, no further oil activity took place. In September 1999, however, to great acclaim in the Khartoum press, the first 600 barrels of Sudanese oil were shipped from Port Sudan. This was the first tangible result of the Greater Nile Oil Project which was initiated in the early 1990s (Field 1999). This initiative brings together four companies that together control 12.2 million acres of concession land in South Sudan. The principal partner is the China National Petroleum Company (CNPL) with a 40 per cent stake, together with Malaysia's Petronas Carigali (30 per cent), the Canada-based Talisman Energy (25 per cent) and Sudan's National Oil Company (5 per cent).

This largely foreign consortium has been operating despite US trade sanctions and, since 1996, a UN diplomatic embargo on Sudan. Talisman Oil, exploiting weaknesses in registration and company law, has been able to circumvent Canadian government opinion that had been supportive of the US line. Talisman has also been a useful member of the initiative because of its familiarity with advanced technology and the financial networks that it can access. China, wishing to diversify its oil supply, has been responsible for the building of the pipeline from South Sudan to the Red Sea outlet at Port Sudan. It is claimed that 2,000 of the 7,000 Chinese labourers involved are prisoners working in exchange for remission of sentence (ibid.: 10). China is also one of the region's main weapons suppliers (HRW 1998). Together with Malaysia, it played an important role in limiting UN sanctions on Sudan to a diplomatic embargo following Khartoum's alleged involvement in the attempt to assassinate President Mubarak of Egypt in Addis Ababa in 1996. Security for the pipeline has been privatised – in this case, however, the troops used are irregular ethnic militia forces armed by the government and known officially as the Sudan Defence Force.

The global marketplace is a complex, multi-layered and constantly mutating system through which the marketing and supply of all types of goods and services essential for the new wars takes place. Opaque corporate structures, foreign subsidiaries, third-party transactions, shell companies, and so on are the methods as much of money laundering as of the marketing of diamonds, the provision of private protection or the supply of arms. Tens of thousands of companies and subsidiaries of varying sizes occupy various nodes within the spectrum of shadow, grey and legitimate networked activity that constitutes actual international business. Networks intersect, adapt and mutate according to circumstance in a vast and dynamic arena that can be used for many purposes: developing new businesses, mainstreaming advanced technology or fighting non-formal wars. Despite commercial complicity with network war, reflecting the free-market ethos, the International Chamber of Commerce, WTO and OECD have all refused, so far, to accept the need for legally binding codes of conduct for multinational companies (Global Witness 1998: 7). Where such codes are developing, they are voluntary in nature and limited to the larger and more established multinational companies. The one area where some action has been taken concerns the illicit trade in small arms. Even here, however, initiatives have been either voluntary or limited to the actions of companies or governments working within conventional territorial jurisdictions.

In 1992, after decades of inaction on the subject, the UN established a voluntary *Register of Conventional Arms Transfers*. Several studies of the problem have also been undertaken (e.g., Sköns and Ström 1994), together with the monitoring of arms embargoes to conflict areas such as Central Africa, which have led to calls for restriction. Since 1994, the G8 group of leading countries has also issued periodic statements in support of the UN position. Under the auspices of Norway and Canada, in July 1998 the Group of 21 like-minded states drew up an agenda of common understanding of the problems of the unregulated traffic in small arms. In 1997, the EU also began a programme to prevent and combat illicit arms transfers. This has resulted in a legally binding *Code of Conduct* issued in December 1998. Under this code member states are committed to refusing arms export licences to companies where the trade involves countries that have a poor human rights record. There have also been a number of similar initiatives by other international and regional organisations. While these moves have been welcomed by aid agencies as better than nothing, they have a limited impact. Concerning the EU *Code of Conduct*, for example, while allowing the governments of member states to follow an ethical foreign policy, it gives the same governments little control over national companies that purchase and transport arms outside the EU. This, moreover, is the normal manner in which the small-arms trade is conducted by EU-based companies. The companies involved in supplying warring parties do not usually do business with British or French arms firms, for example. Partly because the advanced weapons systems that such companies produce are often inappropriate, the trade is more likely to involve networking with East European or Russian arms suppliers using aircraft registered in Africa or elsewhere. While the profit will flow back into Western Europe, such transactions do not come under EU territorial jurisdiction. 'Often arms will be delivered by a shipping firm based in one country, whose plane is registered in a second, which flies out from a third, and which picks up arms in a fourth' (Honisbaum and Barnett 1999).

NGOs such as Oxfam have called for it to be a criminal offence for companies to violate an official arms embargo. Given the lack of transparency within the global marketplace, however, and the ease with which involvement can be hidden, even this would be difficult to enforce. Despite the problem of the small-arms trade being well-known and widely acknowledged,

> relatively few practical measures have been adopted to effectively control international transfers of small arms and light weapons. In contrast to the controls in place for nuclear and chemical weapons and major weapons systems, which took decades to develop, efforts to control small arms and light weapons remain tentative and modest. (ICRC 1999: 60)

The overriding commitment of the international community to market openness and deregulation has forced attempts to control war economies – already reliant on voluntary forms of compliance – into relatively narrow country- or commodity-specific forms of policing activity. This is the only way in which the different demands and tensions within the liberal world system can be reconciled. The current attempts to enforce UN sanctions against the illicit trade in Angolan diamonds are a good example. At the time of writing, the UN sanctions committee for Angola has been given funds to investigate how UNITA supports its war aims and procures armaments. Depending on results, the UN is now said to be ready to name and shame the countries and companies involved (Brittain 1999). While this is useful, indeed, refreshing in its boldness, having to resort to such a strategy indicts the limited nature of international regulation. Moreover, rather than seeing it as a problem of expanding and generalised shadow trade under conditions of market deregulation, the UN appears to be approaching the issue as a type of discrete criminal activity requiring a policing action. Current plans, for example, include the tracking and interdiction of illegal flights and the installation of customs monitors in surrounding African countries. While theoretically it may be possible to draw a line around Angolan diamonds, the regional networks involved are part of much wider politico-commercial systems. They are part of the transnational networks that support the regional political economy as a whole. Moreover, these connections give this trade and the groups involved great powers of social and political mutation. The UN approach to Angola, although commanding far fewer resources, appears similar to the less than successful US 'war on drugs' in Latin America. If history tells us anything, it is to be sceptical of the effectiveness of global policing.

NOTE

1 This rectification was first suggested by Mick Dillon in a conference on 'The Politics of Emergency' in the Department of Politics, University of Manchester, May 1997.

8

Internal Displacement and the New Humanitarianism

Displacement and Complicity in Sudan (Part 1)

The focus of this case study is the long-running conflict in Sudan. In particular, it examines the role of aid in relation to internally displaced Southerners living in government areas of the North. The case study is an example of the relations of accommodation and complicity with violence that exist within liberal peace. It also examines how the concerns of the new humanitarianism, especially the need to link relief to development in conflict situations, is part of this accommodation. Unlike refugees, the internally displaced have not crossed an international border. Consequently, despite being a growing category of aid recipient globally, in terms of international responsibilities and UN mandates, the position of the internally displaced remains ambiguous. Since the beginning of the war in 1983, the UN estimates that some 4 million Southerners have been internally displaced from the war zone (UNHCU 1998e: 4). Although these people make up the largest population of its type in the world, UNHCR exercises no special responsibility towards them. About 1.8 million displaced people are thought to be located in and around Khartoum while the remaining 2.2 million are in the so-called transition zone, the border regions between Northern and Southern Sudan.

The transition zone lacks a precise definition or geographical location. It loosely denotes those areas where Arab and African ethnic groups meet and overlap. While relatively secure compared to some areas further South, it is characterised by inter-group tension and periodic outbreaks of violence. The case study considers the displaced in the transition zone in western Sudan. In particular, it focuses on South Darfur which borders Northern Bahr al Ghazal to the South. This border represents part of the formal division between North and South Sudan. In South Darfur, it is estimated that there are 100,000 displaced

Southerners (UNHCU 1998a: 2). Most of these are Dinka from the Mulwal clan and originate from the Gogrial area of Northern Bahr al Ghazal. In South Darfur, they are settled among Baggara Arabs, including Rizegat and Mahliyya. Both the Dinka and Rizegat are cattle-herding groups and there is a history of conflict between them regarding grazing rights. Since the mid-1980s the state has used this tension to encourage Baggara militia to raid the Dinka in Northern Bahr al Ghazal and loot their property. Such raiding has been responsible for a large part of the internal displacement from the areas. Exactly how much, however, is unknown. Despite over a decade of involvement, the aid community has yet to produce a systematic history or ethnographic account of displacement and how it has affected different ethnic groups. In this respect, the exploratory work of John Ryle and Kwaja Yai Kwol (1989) has yet to be superseded.

Providing aid in Sudan has been greatly affected by the agreements reached between the UN and the Sudanese state in relation to Operation Lifeline Sudan (OLS). Formed from UN agencies and NGOs, this is the main institution for providing humanitarian assistance to areas controlled by both sides of the conflict. The manner in which OLS was established in 1989 effectively led to *de facto* partition in Sudan (Karim *et al.* 1996). Under the OLS arrangement, in exchange for UN management in non-government areas (OLS Southern Sector), the state retained its full control in the remainder (OLS Northern Sector). As a result, there are very different operating conditions in UN and government areas. While the war has always been a limiting factor, for most of OLS's existence aid agencies have enjoyed greater access and freedom of movement in OLS Southern Sector. In government areas, however, both the UN and NGOs have been subject to far greater restrictions and control. The first major wave of Dinka displacement into the North, for example, occurred in 1988. In response, a number of international NGOs were able to establish a restricted presence in the transition zone. In 1990, following the change in government the previous year and increasing controls on international agencies, this presence was curtailed. Following the second major wave of displacement in 1992, the government invited international NGOs to re-establish a presence in the transition zone. This involvement, however, is different from that of the late 1980s. Under pressure to indigenise their organisations, the government demanded the exclusion of expatriates from all but senior management positions located in Khartoum. Moreover, travel restrictions have made it difficult for expatriates to move outside the capital. Permission can take weeks, if not months to obtain, and may then involve further restrictions regarding place and time. Consequently, project monitoring has become dependent on the information supplied by the NGOs' locally based Sudanese staff, who are not affected by such direct restrictions. At the same time, international NGOs have been expected to work more closely with Islamic NGOs, many of which have direct links to the Sudanese state (African Rights 1997).

The material for this case study comes from a variety of sources. In 1988, at the time of the first wave of Dinka displacement, I was Oxfam's Country Representative for Sudan. Oxfam, together with Save the Children Fund (SCF) (UK) and Médecins sans frontières (MSF) (Belgium) initiated the first relocation project in the transition zone. In this case, it involved helping move Dinka trapped in Rizegat areas of South Darfur to more secure areas. During 1996, I was technical coordinator for an in-depth evaluation of OLS. This was the first time both sectors of this operation had been examined in this manner (Karim *et al*. 1996). More recently, I acted as team leader in the Northern Sudan component of an evaluation for ECHO of the impact of humanitarian assistance in Sudan (Duffield *et al*. 1999). The fieldwork for this study was completed in March 1999 and has been particularly influential in shaping this case study. It should be stated, however, that the conclusions of the case study are my own and do not necessarily reflect the views of the organisations associated with the above work. In many respects, the case study represents an inversion of conventional thinking regarding humanitarian assistance and conflict – particularly of the conventional belief that assistance can create dependency among beneficiaries and even fuel war itself. The case of the Dinka in government areas of Sudan provides a different picture. For most of the past decade, where the Dinka have been assisted, they have not received humanitarian assistance in a minimalist meaning of the term. They have mainly received the forms of help advocated by the proponents of developmental or goal-oriented relief and the new humanitarianism: targeted rather than general food aid, coupled with projects to improve food security and economic self-management through the provision of seeds and tools, loans, micro-credit schemes, and so on.[1] At the same time, in recent years a consequentialist ethical framework, in this case associated with the emergence of rights-based programming and protection, has come into vogue. Since the condition of the Dinka has not improved during the 1990s – either in terms of general health, economic well-being or political security – these initiatives have yet to show any success.

In attempting to address the reasons for this apparent failure, the case study has been divided into two chapters. This chapter examines the conceptual representation of 'internally displaced people' or IDPs as they are known among aid agencies. The following chapter analyses how aid supplied on the basis of this ideological construct has rein-forced the oppression of the Dinka in government areas. Regarding the IDP identity, apart from being a de-ethnicised concept, it confirms the predominant view that 'displacement' is a special but temporary con-dition. Displacement denotes a combination of transitional problems that emerge when a group of people is uprooted from one location and has to adjust to living in a new and different area. Consequently, over time one can expect the problems associated with displacement to lessen and eventually disappear. In distinction to this view, this study sees Dinka displacement as resulting primarily *from their being Dinka*. At the same time, the problems and difficulties that they face in the transition zone are not so much due to their being assetless strangers in a new area, but arise *again because they are Dinka*. Within the political economy of Sudan, the Dinka occupy a special and subordinate place. It is a condition that overrides ideas of displacement as a temporary problem of adjustment. Neither is it significantly affected by states of 'war' or 'peace'. In this respect, if humanitarian assistance is supposed to fuel 'war', although in Sudan the mechanisms by which this is sup-posed to happen have yet to be clearly established (Duffield *et al.* 1999; Karim *et al.* 1996), then goal-oriented humanitarianism in the transition zone can be argued to have reinforced those everyday relations that denote 'peace'. In other words, aid agencies have strengthened and tacitly supported those economic and political relations of desocialisa-tion, subordination and exploitation that constitute normal life. In the transition zone, since the Dinka are enmeshed in such relations, aid policy has been complicit in their oppression.

A note on the political economy of Northern Sudan

Since the nineteenth century, Sudan's commercial economy has been concentrated in the Niles region of the North. An important and long-term characteristic of this largely agrarian economy is that profitability has been dependent upon the existence of cheap, desocialised labour: a workforce that lacks social status, position, and any associated political or citizenship rights. During Turco-Egyptian rule (1821–81) and then the Mahdist regime (1881–98), for example, commercial agriculture in the Niles region came to depend on state-sponsored slave raiding in the South (Johnson 2000). During the nineteenth century, Southern slaves and captives were essential features of the political economy of Northern Sudan. At the beginning of the colonial period (1899–1956), slavery was abolished and the South was effectively closed by the colonial administration to Northern interests.

205

During the colonial period, commercial agriculture in the North entered a new period of expansion based on Westerner migrant labour (mainly of Nigerian and Chadian origin). Such people are commonly known as *Fellata* in Northern Sudan and formed the backbone of the labour force on the Gezira cotton scheme and in the opening of the fertile but underpopulated agricultural lands of eastern Sudan. Because of their industriousness, the *Fellata* were generally looked on with favour by the colonial regime and encouraged to settle (Duffield 1981). In contrast, the Arab pastoralist groups who made up the bulk of the population in the North proved reluctant to join the wage economy. Although non-Sudanese, some *Fellata* achieved positions of rank within the system of local administration.

While the *Fellata* were a sizeable minority in Northern Sudan, their association with the colonial administration acted against their participation in the independence movement. This was dominated by Arab groups from the Niles region. When Sudan achieved a negotiated independence in 1956, the *Fellata* were largely denied Sudanese citizenship as a result of the manner in which the independent state framed and manipulated the nationality laws; they were marginalised within the post-independence political structure. The exploitation of *Fellata* labour was facilitated by their low political status and the widespread and virulent racial prejudice to which they are subject. In the Niles region of Sudan, the term *Fellata* is used by Arab groups as a derogatory term associated with ignorance, disease and shiftiness.

Westerners (including groups from Darfur as well as those further west) remained the mainstay of the commercial agricultural labour force until the 1970s. From this period, Southerners have become increasingly important. In a process that mirrors the erosion of the *Fellata*'s political status, Sudan's postcolonial governments have progressively undermined the political position that Southerners had achieved in the colonial system of native administration (Keen 1994). This process has been taking place since the 1960s, and has been significantly deepened during the current war. While Southerners are by law Sudanese citizens, their incorporation into the Northern economy coincided with the Islamisation of state politics and the decline of secularism. Southern labour in the North lacks political status not for being non-Sudanese (for example, the *Fellata*), but for being non-Islamic. As with the *Fellata*, however, the exploitation of this labour is also facilitated by widespread and virulent racial prejudice. Indeed, the Arab–African racial hierarchy that exists in Northern Sudan is in many respects comparable with that of apartheid South Africa. To a very significant extent, Southerners – together with the Nuba of the Nuba

Mountains region in Southern Kordofan – lack political or legal redress against land appropriation, highly exploitative labour relations, violence, theft and other abuses. Since this was true in peacetime (1972–83), it helps to explain why many Southerners joined the 1983 rebellion that started the present war and led to the formation of the Sudan People's Liberation Army (SPLA). War has deepened this political marginalisation, not least because Southerners and the Nuba have been readily stigmatised as rebel sympathisers and therefore undeserving of the protection of the Sudanese state.

In the past, apart from the exercise of unaccountable force, various legal, political and commercial measures have been used to reproduce the cheap and desocialised labour on which the commercial agrarian economy (mechanised rainland farming, irrigated schemes, riverain agriculture, etc.) of Northern Sudan depends. As the long history of violence and conflict in Sudan suggests, such an economy is inherently unstable. Displaced Southerners currently in the North occupy a marginal and subordinate position in Sudan's political economy. Moreover, since the SPLA draws much of its support from among the Dinka, the vulnerability of displaced Dinka has been increased by association. The displaced are subject to a wide range of unequal and highly exploitative relationships including child abduction, household slavery, non-remunerative sharecropping arrangements, casualised agricultural and urban labour, menial domestic service and so on. Indeed, to speak of 'market forces' in such a context would appear to be highly misleading; economic transactions take place in 'forced markets' – that is, markets profoundly shaped by the use of various kinds of force (Keen 1994). The distortion of markets has been simultaneously a cause and an effect of famine. Indeed, famine in the South has served important economic as well as military functions in reducing labour and livestock prices, boosting grain prices, and evacuating famine victims from coveted grazing land and oil-rich regions of the South (like the Bentiu and Abyei areas). The relations of patronage and oppression that shape Sudan's exploitative political economy are largely ethnically structured. At the same time, Dinka subgroups themselves have evolved distinct strategies for economic and cultural survival. Displacement due to conflict and famine has both speeded up and radically changed a process of economic migration to the North that was already under way by the 1970s. By making it difficult to maintain connections with home and kin (and the associated protection and resources that such networks provide), forced migration due to war has tended to reinforce the exploitative and desocialising relations inherent within Sudan's political economy.

Development discourse and internal displacement

During the course of the 1990s war-displaced Southerners in Northern Sudan only received humanitarian assistance, in the sense of basic survival goods, for a couple of years toward the beginning of the decade. While they were the object of numerous projects over the entire period, in examining the impact of aid on the social and political dynamics in government-controlled areas of Sudan, it is not humanitarian assistance *per se* that is under discussion but the effects of the goal-oriented or developmental relief that predominated during this period. For the sake of brevity, this mix of initiatives, which continues to contain some relief assistance, will be referred to simply as 'aid' or 'aid policy'. Given the nature of Sudan's political economy, the question as to what effect external aid has had on the relations and systems involved can now be phrased more concretely: *what have the consequences of aid policy been for the dependence of Northern Sudan's political economy on cheap and desocialised labour?* In answering such a question, directly at least, aid policy is ambiguous. In many respects, such dependence or attempts to subordinate and exploit specific social groups are not the main concern of donor governments and aid agencies working in Sudan. It is beyond their legitimate remit. When such questions are addressed, it is usually in terms of who controls the process and the manner and degree in which things are done. In other words, it is not the end itself that is the problem; the real issue is how objectives are achieved. In this respect, when the Sudanese government and the international community have clashed, which they have on many occasions, it has not usually been over issues of substance but over questions of management and degree. This character gives international strategic actors in Sudan a distinct ambivalence in relation to the political complex that they confront. In the case of Northern Sudan, the evidence presented here suggests that during the course of the 1990s, UN agencies, donor governments and NGOs, albeit largely unintentionally, complemented state aims and facilitated the desocialisation and subordination of displaced Southerners.

Part of the reason for this complicity is the continuing inability of aid policy to address political complexity (Karim *et al.* 1996: 205). This statement may come as a surprise given the shift to goal-oriented relief in the mid-1990s and, more recently, the incorporation into agency work of the seemingly political concerns of human rights and protection associated with the new humanitarianism. On the surface, aid policy appears to be in a constant state of change and evolution. Despite claims of non-linearity and rights-awareness, however, in practice aid policy in Sudan is still geared to an enduring liberal self-management model of development. As argued below, NGOs have reinterpreted and redefined the more conventional civil and political understanding of human rights in terms of reconfirming this model. As social and political beings, displaced Southerners remain 'invisible' (African Rights 1995). Premised on attempts to restore economic self-sufficiency and establish parity between communities, now defined as a right, aid policy continues to avoid confronting the social and political constraints created by Sudan's existing political economy. This inability to address complexity has led aid policy to latently reinforce the subordination of displaced Southerners. At the same time, the dynamics of displacement, the survival strategies of the Southerners concerned, and the ethnically structured systems of exploitation within which Southerners are enmeshed continue to be poorly understood. In this context, examining just how the displaced *are* represented by aid agencies is important in analysing the impact of international assistance.

Complicity, aid agencies and the state

Since the mid-1980s, the Sudanese state has been clear and consistent in its general policy toward displaced Southerners. This policy, moreover, has survived a change in government in 1989. Economically, the issue is one of making displaced Southerners an integral and self-supporting labour component of the agrarian and urban economy of Northern Sudan. Politically, through acculturation, education, urban planning and Islamisation, Southerners are to be resocialised as new Sudanese citizens. Taken together, this incorporation defines the place of Southerners within the historic project of political Islam (African Rights 1997). In terms of the economic incorporation of displaced Southerners, from the outset the international community has been at one with state policy. Both have supported measures to reduce alleged aid dependency, especially reductions in food aid, in order to improve the utility of displaced Southerners and promote their economic self-management (Karim *et al.* 1996: 135). Since the early 1990s, the government, like many aid agencies, has also called consistently for the move from relief to development. Enlarging the economic role of displaced Southerners within the North has been central to this shared state and agency vision. While, for political reasons associated with Sudan's alleged sponsoring of international terrorism, Western governments have suspended development assistance, there is a good deal of realist pragmatism if not sympathy for the government's position among diplomats in Khartoum.

While it has been argued that humanitarian aid weakens the social responsibilities that warring parties bear for those under their control (de Waal 1997), for state actors wishing to debureaucratise and reduce public spending, the idea that development equates with the 'self-sufficiency' of their citizens must come as welcome news. However, although there is a good deal of complementarity between the state's general economic aims and aid policy, where there are differences in Northern Sudan, it is largely in relation to the political means that the government is using. With regard to urban planning in Khartoum, for example, the international community does not object to the relocation of displaced Southerners *per se*. These have been settling around the capital since the late 1980s, often living in extremely poor conditions. The problem is that throughout the 1990s, relocation has been carried out in an overly authoritarian and ill-planned manner, by using excessive force and compulsory demolition, and withholding legal redress (UNHCU 1997).

Where there are differences between the Sudanese state and the aid community in terms of policy towards the displaced, they mainly arise over the politics of implementation, especially in regard to control and management issues. The main response of donor governments to disagreements over such issues was the staggered suspension of development assistance, beginning at the end of the 1980s. This, together with an occasional démarche when state obstruction has become particularly intransigent, largely exhausts the room for collective international manoeuvre (Brusset 2000). Reflecting this limited influence,[2] throughout the 1990s the international community has tended to downplay, ignore or accommodate tensions surrounding state strategy in government-controlled areas of Sudan. For almost fifteen years, international NGOs, for example, have accepted restricted access, limited ability to monitor projects, and high levels of government interference. Most notably, however, as argued in the *OLS Review*, donor ambivalence in the North has resulted in an inability to uphold the humanitarian principles upon which OLS was founded and, in particular, has led to a widespread failure to protect those displaced by the war. Only recently, and still with some equivocation as we shall see, have such issues been addressed in relation to rights and protection. In the meantime, where they are active, aid agencies have continued to concentrate their efforts on attempting to reduce economic vulnerability and promote self-management among Southerners in isolation from the largely hostile and unsupportive environment in which the displaced find themselves.

The IDP identity

The process of desocialisation of Southerners by the state has been under way since the 1960s. The abolition of Native Administration marked the growing subordination of Southerner representation within the structures of local government. By the mid-1980s, especially in the North–South border areas of western Sudan, the political vulnerability of the Dinka was such that their property and cattle became fair game for surrounding Arab groups, so precipitating the 1988 famine in Bahr el Ghazal (Keen 1994). During the 1990s, the process of desocialisation continued and expanded to incorporate cultural and social dimensions. Through policies of acculturation and Islamisation, especially through the system of primary education run by Islamic NGOs in some settlement areas, the state is attempting to de-ethnicise displaced Southerners (African Rights 1997). In this respect, the conflict in Sudan is different to the ethnic cleansing that one has seen, for example, in the Balkans. Ethnic cleansing depends on ethnic identification and the solidification of ethnic divisions, even if none clearly existed before. It is a process that is associated with the production of maps, the drawing of boundaries, and the labelling and reallocation of people (Campbell 1998). The process in Sudan, however, is different. Rather than ethnic cleansing, it is more aptly described as a process of cultural suppression. In this respect, the absence of any ethnic maps accompanying the war in South Sudan is most noticeable; indeed, of political or social maps of any form. In relation to cultural suppression, maps can be dangerous and threatening. Boundaries often denote identities, claims to land and forms of legitimacy that can conflict with the world views of dominant groups. It is commonly held in the North, for example, that displaced Southerners have moved into government areas for protection and of their own volition. Indeed, due to war and migration, there are relatively few Southerners actually left in the South. In March 1996, as part of an evaluation of Operation Lifeline Sudan, the Secretary-General of the Supreme Council of Peace gave a good rendition of this long-standing official position.

> In 1983 there were five million Southerners in South Sudan. After the war [sic] three million came to the North. Khartoum alone has 1.5 million of these. Of the two million left, one and a half million died in the war. We know this because the government counted 600,000 on its side and SPLA also counted 600,000. Therefore, there are about 800,000 in South Sudan. Moreover, half of these are under government control in the main towns. The remainder are under the SPLA or scattered in camps in the neighbouring countries. From this we know that there are only 300,000 people in the rebel areas. (Roll 1996)

Despite the odour of cultural genocide that such statistical exercises give off, the UN, NGOs or donor governments based in Khartoum have never challenged such questionable assertions. Moreover, many of the agencies concerned are also working in non-government areas where markedly different population statistics exist. Indeed, within SPLA areas a figure of 6.8 million Southerners presently in the South is often claimed (Karim *et al.* 1996: 225). Not only does the focus of aid agencies on economic vulnerability complement state aims, but development discourse has subjected Southerners to its own form of desocialisation. In government-controlled areas, this takes the form of representing them as 'IDPs'. The area specialist John Ryle summed up this identity in the late 1980s in the following terms.

> Lip service is often paid to the 'culture' and 'traditions' of southerners, as though their identity and their aspirations did not also have political and economic dimensions. Migrants of very diverse origins and backgrounds, speaking different languages, practising different religions and having different modes of livelihood, become collectively 'the displaced'. They are thus characterized only by their present condition, homeless, without identity, in limbo. This terminology tends to homogenize and dehumanize the inhabitants of the South. It conspires inadvertently with a strain in northern discourse about non-Muslim and non-Arab inhabitants of the Sudan which lumps all southerners together and defines them thus with negatives, as non-believers, without real religion, not fully deserving of moral respect. It cannot be stated too strongly that recognition of the distinctive social relations of particular groups of southerners, as with any other peoples, is a necessary prerequisite for effective intervention. Relief/Development discourse perceives the displaced as lumpen and destitute because they are without material indicators of who they are, as though they did not bring their language, their social institutions, their resilience with them. (Ryle and Kwol 1989: 16)

During the course of the 1990s, international NGOs and donor governments in Northern Sudan, rather than challenging this view of the displaced, have deepened and entrenched it. From the moment that NGOs first encountered Southerners in Northern Sudan, they were transformed into IDPs. At a stroke, all sense of history and cultural difference was lost. Southerners ceased to be members of distinct ethnic groups or subgroups, coming from different regions and ecosystems, following diverse survival strategies and already differentially integrated into the ethnically structured networks of Northern patronage and power. If the main donor response to political complexity has been the suspension of development assistance, then an equally important NGO and UN response has been that of simplification. The IDP identity overcomes the problem of complexity by understanding Southerners

through the pre-existing categories of developmental studies – as independent households ranked in terms of varying degrees of wealth, self-
sufficiency and economic vulnerability. Southerners have been problematised in relation to such developmental categories. Thus, reflecting
the way that liberal peace understands conflict, the war is held to have
had a Hobbesian effect on social solidarity. In this case, the conflict has
'been a traumatic experience undermining and destroying normal
Dinka community structures and traditions' (UNHCU 1999: 1).

Wealth ranking and natural economy

Reflecting development discourse, IDPs are no longer seen as members
of ethnic groups supported by reciprocating social networks and integrated within the wider society through complex relations of debt,
clientage and exploitation; they present themselves as, essentially, self-
contained free economic agents who are understood largely in terms of
the immediate wealth, resources or skills they command. While they
may be more disadvantaged in one location as opposed to another,
there is no necessary or structural connection between Southerners and
whatever environment they are in. The prime unit for this abstraction is
the household (or HH to use a common NGO acronym). In Sudan, as in
other aid-dependent countries, NGO appraisals and situation reports
differentiate households according to the resources or assets they own,
control or have access to. Concerning the Dinka in South Darfur, an SCF
(UK) report, for example, describes them in the following terms: 'The
majority of the displaced are children in addition to elderly and dis-
abled people and [include a] high incidence of female headed households' (SCF (UK) 1996). It is the uneven distribution of internal
resources between and within households that animate them and the
individuals concerned. Households can be ranked and differentiated
according to a variety of criteria – the number of members they have,
the number of dependent children in each household, the frequency of
female-headed households, the amount of livestock, the area of land
owned or rented and so on (Masefield and Harvey 1997). Ranking
households according to such productive criteria is typically used to
distinguish the rich, average, poor and very poor within a given
community.

In both government and non-government areas of Sudan, the UN's
World Food Programme (WFP) uses such criteria to target food aid to
those that are judged the most vulnerable. As Jaspars has argued,
however, aid beneficiaries do not necessarily share this economic
understanding of vulnerability (Jaspars 1999: 9–10). Among Southerners,

vulnerability can be understood in terms of the web of kinship obligations and social reciprocity that individuals and families can (or cannot)
call upon. Vulnerability is an ethnically networked phenomenon. This
often contradicts the crude wealth ranking resulting from NGO rapid
appraisal techniques. For example, wealth-poor households may be
well connected in terms of the network of social reciprocity to which
they have access. Moreover, local perceptions of disaster agents such as
drought, flooding or conflict are interpreted differently in terms of the
distinct and contrasting effects that these events have on social networks
and the support they are able to give. The result of this misconception,
as Jaspars has documented for non-government areas of Sudan, is that
WFP has consistently failed to achieve its targeting aims. This is not a
particular fault of WFP, however. The economic model of vulnerability
dominates perceptions within the aid community generally.

Where an element of complexity enters this economic representation, rather than how households interact and are integrated and subordinated within wider networks, systems and partnerships, it is
mainly internal to the model itself. For example, the local status of
households can vary over time according to the succession of generations. Young labour-rich households can eventually find themselves
labour-poor as children marry and move out. At the same time, environmental decline, drought, economic crisis, and so on, can all take
their toll. In describing the general situation in Kordofan, CARE, for
example, observes that the 'households of Kordofan can be classified as
resource poor or "fragile" due to their location on poor or marginal
land, their lack of ownership of livestock and their lack of access to
water and education. The population represents a chronically food
insecure situation' (CARE 1998: 1).

Within this model, gender is usually represented in terms of the
problems faced by women in realising their full economic or market
potential. For example, not only do they have a subordinate position
within the household, but through the succession of generations, widowhood and so on, their position is rendered especially precarious.
Moreover, this subordination is often reinforced by customary practices
that limit women's access to community goods. 'The husbandry of goats
and poultry are considered to be primarily the responsibility of women.
Therefore, women and children are most likely to suffer when
depletion of these resources occurs' (*ibid.*).

Economic vulnerability, and the process of wealth ranking on which
it rests, is a category of natural economy. This describes a mainly internally structured and self-contained mechanical system. Within natural
economy, IDPs appear as an extreme example of resource loss: as

people who have lost everything through the destruction of war. In terms of wealth and vulnerability, IDPs present themselves to most NGOs as 'the lowest rung on the ladder' in North Sudan. In many respects, IDPs are archetypal free economic actors with nothing to lose but their labour – a role that the Sudanese state has cast them in from the start.

De-ethnicisation and self-management

The IDP identity, like the process of cultural suppression being prac- tised by the state, is a form of de-ethnicisation. In this respect, it should be noted that no international NGO working in Sudan collects or analyses project or employment information in terms of ethnic identity or affiliation (IRC interview 1999). This is an interesting situation for several reasons. In many Western countries, such information is a well- known and, indeed, a *mandatory* tool of public administration. In Sudan, its absence is even more noticeable given the clear, pervasive and often violent role that ethnicity plays in political life. With the state pursuing a strategy of cultural suppression, the absence of such analysis among aid organisations, many of which have now proclaimed them- selves rights-based agencies, is another example of the complicit embrace that unites them. In some cases, it is not so much that NGOs do not analyse their work in ethnic terms; the impression is that, like the government, they wish such categories did not exist. CARE, for example, initially organised its camp for Dinka in End Nahud, Kordofan, in such a way as to 'downplay tribal affinities. Huts were distributed to the displaced and spatially categorised into four zones (A, B, C and D) irre- spective of tribal or sub-tribal origins to facilitate the Camp administra- tion' (el Amin 1998: 5). As if to illustrate the shallowness of this view- point – in which economic categories override those of identity and history – the CARE report notes further that 'movement from one zone to another through the exchange of huts [has] led to zones turning into clusters almost made up of closely related members of a sub-tribe' (*ibid.*).

Within Sudan, international NGOs are uneasy in relation to ethnicity and identity. They do not quite fit the NGOs' world view and rationale for being there. In the 1980s, this was already noticeable, as were its political implications.

> Coyness about the tribal affiliations of the oppressed inhibits recognition of the importance of ethnicity in coping with adversity: displacement divides families but it does not destroy the tribe. Language, too often, is perceived as a barrier rather than an asset – a common possession that

gives particular groups of Southerners a degree of cohesion that allows them to remain themselves, members of distinct groups that are collectively undergoing a time of tribulation. It is such differences between groups of displaced people from the south that agencies should recognise and build on. By considering these differences as obstacles, the relief/development discourse again inadvertently connives with the body of opinion in the North that puts the national integration of the country – and the obliteration of its non Arab-Islamic elements – ahead of the well-being of its citizens. (Ryle and Kwol 1989: 35)

There are several reasons why NGOs, at least in Sudan, find it difficult to work with or even acknowledge the existence of ethnic categories. First, it would run counter to state strategy of ethnic suppression and hence make life even more difficult for them. Second, and perhaps more fundamentally, it strikes at the heart of what NGOs are trying to do in Africa. Ethnic categories conflict directly with liberal views of progress and modernity. Not only have they been equated with war and breakdown, but they tend to contradict the new forms of organisation, identity and egalitarian structures, for example in relation to gender, that NGOs see themselves as facilitating. In Sudan, however, Southerners have responded to displacement by maintaining and adapting ethnic networks. As John Ryle has suggested, this would imply that if NGOs wished to be more effective they should consciously work with a particular ethnic group or clan and provide appropriate support in relation to the networks and strategies that its members have created (Duffield *et al.* 1999). For most NGOs, however, this would be seen as social regression rather than progress. Indeed, one can almost feel the cringe that such a suggestion would elicit. Hence, throughout the 1990s, they have understood IDPs through the economistic categories of development discourse. For example, while often classed as the 'poorest of the poor' in government areas, the Dinka themselves have also been ranked and differentiated according to the wealth categories of economic vulnerability. The 1998 OLS Food Economy Baseline assessment for Ed'Dien in South Darfur, for example, divides IDPs in the province into four socio-economic categories: rich (8 per cent of total 'HH' surveyed); mid (21 per cent); poor (45 per cent); and very poor (27 per cent) according to the number of goats owned (ranging from 0 to 8 in four divisions (OLS 1998). These four wealth rankings were further subdivided according to the number of households producing above or below the agricultural threshold of five sacks. Although the Dinka might be on 'the lowest rung', they can nevertheless be ranked, differentiated and classified using the same economic logic as is applied to indigenous communities.

The liberal self-management aspiration of aid agencies does not adequately address the political and ethnic complexity of Sudan. At the same time, however, it has great practical utility. For example, it does not contradict state perceptions and aims, and therefore avoids making life even more difficult. Exercises in wealth and vulnerability ranking also help aid agencies target resources. In this way, the economic vulnerability/self-sufficiency model of society provides a framework for outcome simulation. By varying resources to the different parts of the mechanical model, desired outcomes can be anticipated and reported back to donors. For example, reducing food aid to discourage dependency; providing seeds and tools to increase food security, and so on. Aid policy as simulation is well reflected in the harm–benefit analysis of the new humanitarianism which is discussed in more detail below.

For a decade, NGOs have been trying to encourage the Dinka to become self-managing through the provision of agricultural inputs and, since the mid-1990s, the reduction of food aid. With the growing realisation that these attempts have not been successful, more recently the aid community has placed growing emphasis on attempts to secure for the Dinka access to their own land. In particular, this absence has been 'effectively used as a means to ensuring their availability as a cheap source of labour' (UNHCU 1999: 2). While this position appears to make sense, it is based on the assumption that the problem for the Dinka is not the oppressive social and political relations they are subordinate to in Northern Sudan because they are Dinka. Rather, it is their lack of economic parity with surrounding communities (ibid.: 4). Moreover, it should be noted that the same agencies attempting to secure land for some Dinka are also pointing out the continuing stress that migration among communities from the Northern parts of Darfur and Kordofan would cause. This is just one indication that access to a smallholding in Sudan is by no stretch of the imagination a guarantor of self-management within the marketplace.

At present several projects are under way in the transition zone to help a number of Dinka secure access to land. In one of these, as an initial step in an ambitious NGO consortium pilot scheme involving 4,000 households, at the time of writing Oxfam was planning to resettle 100 households currently in South Darfur. These households will be selected 'from a number of camps. We will concentrate on those families with resources and a pioneering spirit' (Oxfam interview 1999). Like the CARE example above, this assumes that the Dinka have not organised themselves according to clan affiliation or other relations of social reciprocity that cut across mechanical divisions between rich and poor. By focusing on those with 'resources and a pioneering spirit' important sources of patronage and protection may well be removed from those communities. Such a position is consistent with wealth ranking, however, especially when one makes the liberal assumption that there is no organic connection between the categories involved.

As noted by the *OLS Review*, despite the dominance of economistic assumptions in depicting the IDP identity and, moreover, the overriding urge to make them self-sufficient, it is somewhat surprising to find that 'the real options available to the war displaced to achieve food security have not been investigated in the Northern Sector' (Karim *et al*. 1996: 120). This statement is as accurate today as it was several years ago. In other words, while self-sufficiency through land acquisition is a goal, there has been no analysis of the actual viability of such ownership: the realistic return that could be expected from the land, the proportion of household expenditure that this would cover, the ability of such households to buy in basic services, the commercial infrastructure of the areas of settlement, and so on. Regarding the planned relocation of Dinka in South Darfur, even some members of the NGO consortium involved are sceptical of success given the absence of any serious study of household economics, together with the surrounding social and political relations in the areas to which the Dinka are to be moved (SCF (UK) interview 1999). In the meantime, faith in the reality of liberal self-management continues to outweigh such considerations.

Internal displacement as economic migration

For most donors and NGOs, once they are in government areas, war-displaced people become similar to indigenous economic migrants – although recognised as having different origins, they are nevertheless both expressions of the common problem of economic vulnerability. Within the categories of natural economy, the displaced are simply the 'lowest rung' of the same resource deficit ladder. The corollary of this view is that the very poorest members of the host community are in a similar position to that of IDPs (CARE interview 1999). Moreover, due to the war and the critical stance that most Western donors adopt toward the government, within the aid lottery the Dinka often fare better than indigenous groups. For example, during the 1998 famine in the war zone of Bahr el Ghazal, between August and November the NGO therapeutic feeding programme at Aweil had a far better success rate than a similar government-run programme in El Fasher in Northern Darfur during the same period (SCF (UK) interview 1999). The failure of the latter was due to neglect and a lack of funding exacerbated by the embargo on development assistance.

For the aid community in government areas of Sudan, the problems faced by IDPs and host communities are essentially the same: declining food security, absent or reduced public services, the lack of productive resources, increasing environmental degradation, stress migration and so on. In an attempt to attract more development resources to Northern Sudan, the European Commission (EC) delegate launched a 'Humanitarian Plus' strategy toward the end of 1998. In order to formulate this strategy, NGOs receiving EC funding were asked to share their views of the problem. Those replying described a situation in which IDPs were just one part of a wider developmental malaise. In relation to Darfur, for example, the situation was one of a growing impoverishment following from climatic change and neglect. Due to recurrent crises, the result for many families 'is a continuing depletion of assets, growing inability to sustain the family and increasing misery' (SCF (UK) 1998: 1). A similar situation was described in neighbouring Kordofan.

> Vulnerable or impoverished groups are those that move in and out of poverty over time, as their circumstances change. In this context, the main group that can be classified as vulnerable in Northern Sudan are the farming families who depend on good climate and rainfall each year for crop production. Fluctuations in the earnings of such groups make them more likely to live under the poverty line. Furthermore, as living standards continue to deteriorate, more of the population is becoming chronically impoverished due to the sale of their productive assets in lean periods. (CARE 1998: 2)

In framing a Humanitarian Plus strategy, the EC delegate duly reflected such views.

> Despite the enormous amounts of EU money spent on humanitarian assistance, the needs of the Sudanese people have grown, making them increasingly dependent on aid. The ongoing civil war, in conjunction with climatic hardships, national and international neglect, and declining resources, has rendered the situation desperate in some regions. The point has been reached that if aid is not delivered on time, for any political, security or climatic reason, the outcome could be disastrous. In its present form, humanitarian aid does not represent the full solution to the exigencies of Sudan's population. (EC 1998b: 1)

Given such views, it is not surprising to find that NGO projects directed toward the Dinka in the transition zone and towards the food-insecure indigenous communities living in Northern areas of Darfur and Kordofan are basically the same: they attempt to target (or withhold) resource inputs in order to promote self-sufficiency. In the case of SCF (UK), for example, since the early 1990s it has been making regular emergency seed distributions to the Dinka in Ed'Dien province and poor farmers in the El Fasher and Um Kaddada provinces of Northern Darfur. The rationale and object of these interventions – to improve productive capacity of the beneficiaries concerned – is essentially the same. Incidentally, agencies such as SCF (UK) and CARE have been running similar types of projects in the same areas since the mid-1980s. On the face of it, they appear to have had little success. If one looks at the files held in the offices of such agencies, it is easy to form the impression that they have only been active since the mid- or early 1990s. In interviewing these NGOs in March 1999, it was interesting to find both SCF (UK) and CARE attempting to establish a food security early warning system in the Northern provinces of Darfur and Kordofan, respectively. Those senior staff interviewed were unaware that their organisations had made similar efforts during the mid-1980s.

The policy of linking relief and development has played an important part in bringing IDPs within a general development framework. In the case of one NGO, not only was the reduction of relief assistance seen as beneficial in terms of reducing dependency, it was also necessary to prevent accentuating differences between the displaced and host populations (IRC interview 1999). In this respect, one would not wish to argue that indigenous communities in Northern Sudan do not have problems or that food insecurity and a decline in public services do not exist. The problem is that the developmental approach of the aid industry ignores the structural characteristics of Sudan's political economy: its dependence for profitability on a source of cheap, malleable and desocialised labour. This has fashioned a special place for the Dinka who occupy a subordinate and dependent position in terms of the local systems of power and patronage. Refracted though the relations of the commercial–military nexus in the transition zone, they find themselves at the bottom of the racial hierarchy. It also ignores the reality that, since 1987, the Sudanese state has followed policies and enacted legislation that legally, politically and economically have distinguished Southerners in the North from other groups. In other words, the state has characterised them as different. This is not to argue, however, that Southerners are necessarily all worse off than poor indigenous groups, although most are. Rather, it is that they are integrated differently into Sudan's ethnically structured political economy.

Rights-based development and consequentialist ethics

The 1996 *OLS Review* (Karim *et al.* 1996) provided a sustained critique of the economic model of development described above. It argued that not only was it a form of depoliticisation, but it failed to understand the wider system within which Southerners had been incorporated; moreover, it was an important contributory factor in the lack of protection being afforded them in government areas of Sudan. But with the exception of protection – where a formal if equivocal response has been made to the recommendations of the *OLS Review* – in the main, reform has addressed organisational and managerial weaknesses. Regarding the critique of policy itself, in the three years following the *OLS Review* a largely *ad hoc* process of change has coexisted with strong elements of continuity. Not least, the basic liberal self-management model of development continues to predominate.

Despite the charge of depoliticisation contained in the *OLS Review*, many NGOs continue, as before, to see their main role as meeting social and economic needs. NGOs such as IRC, SCF (US) and GOAL, for example, persevere with their fifteen-year avoidance of human rights or advocacy issues. The reasons cited remain those of wishing to maintain a service to all beneficiaries and fears for the safety of local staff (IRC interview 1999). This is even the case when, in relation to Southerners in the Khartoum area, 'we realise that much of our work is a stop gap measure resulting from problems created by the government' (GOAL interview 1999). At the same time, however, over the past couple of years, a number of NGOs such as Oxfam and CARE, together with some donors (ECHO 1997b) and UN agencies (UNICEF 1998), have begun to address the issue of human rights. In particular, such agencies are developing a 'rights-based' approach to their work.

Given that many of these organisations have been working with Southerners in Northern Sudan for the past decade or so, it is worth asking why, after so long, the issue of human rights is being addressed now. The simple answer is that human rights are *not* being addressed – not in a traditional civil and political understanding of the term, at any rate. The growing trend among aid agencies and donor governments is to elevate the importance of economic, cultural and social rights (ODI 1999). Since September 1998, for example, CARE has been committed to a rights-based approach in Sudan. A report that it commissioned to chart how this should be done is a good illustration of the situation (O'Brien 1998). Essentially, a distinction is made between human rights interpreted in legal terms and associated with monitoring and enforcement, and human rights understood as a moral force derived from the universality of their application. The legalistic interpretation is said to be unworkable now owing to the declining significance of sovereignty and state-based forms of regulation. As legal rights, '"human rights" are founded in legal regimes that frankly, like good Swiss cheese, are complex and full of holes' (*ibid*.: 1).

Rather than the outmoded legalistic vision of human rights, it is the moral interpretation that is suggested for CARE's work. In distinction to monitoring and enforcement, this relates more to education and implementation issues concerning CARE's core social and economic work. In other words, it is not a case of reforming the NGO to address human rights but the reverse: *it is the aid agency reforming its concept of human rights to bring it in line with the work that it already does*. Like war, human rights are just one more thing that liberal development discourse has accommodated and absorbed. The *Informal Guidance to Resident Coordinators on Human Rights Communications* issued by the UN Development Group, for example, suggests that all petitions, complaints and issues relating to the politico-legal meaning of rights are primarily the responsibility of the UN's Geneva-based Office of the High Commissioner for Human Rights (OHCHR). Such matters should be flagged and forwarded to OHCHR and, if necessary, appropriate advice can be sought. In relation to the 'technical assistance' being provided by the UN mission, however, Resident Coordinators should be prepared to engage all partners frankly on human rights issues. In particular, they should help partners realise 'the full range of civil, cultural, economic, political and social rights, including the right to development' to which coordinated UN actions aspire (Speth 1999). In other words, the concrete but sensitive civil and political issues should be directed outside the country to a non-operational agency, while the more abstract and consensual view of development as a right can be fully and frankly discussed.

Consequentialist ethics (see Chapter 4) have also made their appearance in Sudan. A number of agencies have begun to develop forms of 'harm–benefit analysis'. Through this means, the rights of war-affected populations have been absorbed within development discourse. CARE, for example, has adopted a harm–benefit approach derived from Mary Anderson's influential thesis on *Do No Harm* (1996) to inform its own work (O'Brien 1998). Harm–benefit analysis is a consequentialist simulation exercise to guide action by indicating what might be the net benefit or harm to project partners of different courses of action on the part of the aid agency or other actors. For example, an aid agency providing humanitarian assistance to a certain group of people would list the beneficial effects of such aid (saving life, protecting livelihoods, etc.) against the possible negative effects (making the group a target for attack, promoting dependency, etc.). If the negative effects outweigh the positive, a case exists for withholding assistance. Escaping the taint of conditionality, such acts can be rationalised as being for the greater good and thus part of a principled or new humanitarianism.

Actual harm–benefit analysis, however, can be more complex than the brief example given above. By trawling through human rights law, conventions and principles, O'Brien has attempted to establish a rights analogue that can be applied to a wide range of humanitarian situations (December 1998). Thus whatever course of action the NGO should take, including withholding humanitarian assistance, can be interpreted from a human rights perspective. For example, if assistance is withdrawn because it is felt to be distorting local labour markets, this can be justified by citing the Universal Declaration of Human Rights, Article 23, defending the right to full and productive employment, fair pay and equal treatment irrespective of gender or ethnicity. Using this approach, it is possible for an NGO to reinvent itself as a 'human rights implementer' (ibid.: 7). Yet little if anything has changed in terms of what NGOs actually do. It is as if aid agencies have suddenly discovered that the selfsame economic self-management model of development that they have been pursuing since the 1980s is a human right as well. CARE, for example, is happy to focus the rights issue on the social and economic work it already does and its avoidance of sensitive political issues (CARE interview 1999). The same is true of Oxfam which has also transformed the self-sufficiency aims of its traditional developmental work in Sudan (income generation, micro-credit, etc.) into a human right (Oxfam interview 1999).

Rather than actually changing what aid agencies do, the rights-based approach appears linked to the need to reinvent a new identity periodically in an increasingly competitive and sceptical world. That core work changes little, however, is well summed up in the introduction to UNICEF's similar adoption of a rights-based approach: 'rights-based programming does not mean that everything we do must change. In fact, the policies and programme of cooperation supported over the last 20 to 30 years are largely consistent with [international child and women's rights conventions]' (UNICEF 1998).

The chance that the socio-economic interpretation of human rights by aid agencies is but the latest design of the Emperor's new clothes is a real possibility. Indeed, compared to the actual development within the shadow economy, aid agencies appear to be able to do very little. In order to survive in such a situation, the development process is perhaps better described as a process of virtual development: an unceasing activity of agency simulation coupled with a periodic reinvention of identity when failure threatens to reveal itself. Certainly, since the rights-based approach validates what agencies are already doing and distances them from politico-legal interpretations, it holds out little hope of any increased action against the pervasive violence, abuse and coercion that characterise Sudan. In this respect, the UN system, NGOs and donor governments operating within government areas have a poor and complicit history. The rights-based approach, while giving aid agencies a new lease of life, appears set to reconfirm that accommodation.

Protection and self-management

Regarding the protection of displaced Southerners, the Khartoum-based UN Humanitarian Coordination Unit (UNHCU) has recently made a number of changes and expanded the personnel involved (UNHCU 1998d). Since August 1997, six Sudanese IDP coordinators have been recruited under this programme. This initiative has made an attempt to address the political complexity of Sudan. Certainly, in government areas, it is the most significant development to date to improve the protection and well-being of Southerners. It should be noted, however, that, as with human rights, there has been a transformation in the meaning of protection. In this case, what is being protected is not so much the civil and political rights of the displaced themselves but the 'promotion of self-reliance' and their free access to this process (*ibid.*: 2). If the new humanitarianism involves a shift from saving lives to supporting processes, then protection likewise has become associated with the latter. This can be illustrated with reference to a recent NGO consortium (SCF (UK), Oxfam and IRC) proposal to move 4,000 Dinka households at present in Ed'Dien province to locations further west in Buram and Nyala provinces.

By common consent, the main problem for the Dinka in Ed'Dien is that they have settled among the Rizegat, their 'traditional conflict partners', and, because they lack access to their own land, have become vulnerable to exploitative sharecropping relations (Abd-el-Gadir 1999). This has meant that, despite past assistance, the condition of the Dinka in Ed'Dien province, like the situation of Southerners in other areas, has not improved much. The NGO solution is to move the Dinka to areas where there is no history of conflict with the local population and, especially, to give them access to their own land. The IDP coordinator for the region helped the NGO consortium in accessing land for the Dinka. In this process 'protection', like human rights, has been redefined as a social and economic rather than a political issue. 'The most important factors in strengthening the protection of the community will be their own self-support through meeting basic needs such as food product- ion, rebuilding livestock assets, and contributing toward health and education services' (UNHCU 1999: 4).

Following relocation to areas where there is no 'tradition' of conflict with the host community, the intention is to promote socio-economic 'parity' with that community. Once this is achieved, it is argued that the Dinka will be eligible for integration within local representational structures (*ibid*.: 4). As SCF (UK) argues, the aim is to achieve 'full citi- zenship rights' through self-sufficiency (Abd-el-Gadir 1999). The inference is clear: apart from a few locations where conflict with host communities is a deep-seated cultural and historical factor, the main problem for Dinka integration and political representation is lack of socio-economic parity with local communities. From this perspective, self-sufficiency not only becomes a right, but informs the role of protec- tion as well: 'Experience indicates that the socio-economic empower- ment of displaced communities combined with community mobilisa- tion and advocacy is the best way to ensure protection' (UNHCU 1999: 5).

The problem is that 'socio-economic empowerment' means the same mix of agricultural and community support initiatives that has achieved few, if any, of its stated objectives in North Sudan since the mid-1980s. The claim that a deepening development malaise hangs over Darfur and Kordofan is a tacit admission of this situation (SCF (UK) 1998; CARE 1998). The resilience of the liberal self-management model of development and the apparent lack of any real alternative should be noted. The fact that this model has achieved little in Sudan has been dis- guised through a process of periodic reinvention. The first major reincar- nation was the mid-1990s policy of linking relief and development. This argued the possibility of self-sufficiency even in the context of war. Following a critique of this position from a civil and political perspective (Karim *et al.* 1996), rather than changing, the aid community responded by adapting human rights and protection to suit the underlying socio- economic paradigmatic foundation. This allows the same NGOs, doing similar things, to reappear afresh as 'human rights implementors' or 'protection agencies'. The price of reinvention, however, is complicity with a system that seeks to desocialise and subordinate the Dinka.

Minimum operational standards and complexity

The incorporation of the narratives of human rights and protection, together with the adoption of harm–benefit forms of analysis, reflects the way in which development discourse is attempting to address complexity. Despite these presentational adaptations and incorporations, however, development's underlying liberal self-management paradigm remains unchanged. Explaining this paradox would require a detailed analysis of the organisational agendas, the internal agency dynamics and the web of governance relations that form the strategic complexes linking NGOs, donors, IFIs, governments and so on. Aid as a governance relation is largely independent of the needs and requirements of 'beneficiaries'. In other words, it does not exist in a value-free or positivist relation to them. However, rights, protection and harm–benefit analysis are attempts to adjust aid policy to political complexity. In this respect, the UN's development of a relational framework through which to engage state actors in government areas of Sudan deserves mention.

While elements of this relational framework preceded the 1998 famine in Bahr el Ghazal, it was in response to this that the Minimum Operational Standards (or MinOps) approach first clearly emerged. MinOps in government areas are different from the Ground Rules approach that emerged in SPLA areas in the mid-1990s (Karim *et al*. 1996). Whereas the latter are premised upon warring parties upholding humanitarian law and similar universal conventions, as the name implies MinOps denote the most basic criteria that different parties have to agree to in order to achieve a specific aim (UNHCU interview 1999). Unlike the Ground Rules, MinOps are local and relational frameworks of agreement that make no special mention of international law or conventions. Apart from the specific issue framed by the agreement, they place no wider responsibilities or commitments on warring parties. In this respect, the Ground Rules, while being more legalistic and universal in form, have proved difficult if not impossible to enforce (Levine 1997). It is rather ironic that the more legalistic Ground Rules developed first in relation to non-state actors, while the more recent and relativised MinOps approach has developed in connection with the Sudanese state.

One of the first MinOps agreements relates to the use in 1998 of El Obeid airport for relief operations into government and non-government areas of South Sudan. The agreement is based on ten points covering access to the airport, UN use of communication equipment, travel between government and non-government areas, and so on. Similar agreements have set *Minimal Operational Standards for Agencies in Wau* (UNHCU June 1998b) and *Conditions for Relocation of Displaced Communities in Wau Town* (UNHCU July 1998c). As part of the ongoing Inter-Governmental Agency for Development (IGAD) peace process, in

November 1998, a Technical Committee for Humanitarian Assistance comprised of government, SPLA and OLS representatives was convened in Rome under the chairmanship of the UN Secretary-General's Special Envoy for Humanitarian Affairs for Sudan. This Committee produced a signed *Security Protocol* (UN 18 November 1998) covering the safety of aid workers and a *Minimum Operational Standards for Rail Corridors and Cross-Line Road Corridors* (UN 18 November 1998).[3] All of these agreements are similar in stipulating minimum necessary local operating conditions, the obligations and requirements of the respective parties, shared protocols and so on.

The MinOps approach is one that requires further research and evaluation. In terms of addressing complexity, it could hold some useful pointers. Part of its attractiveness is its flexibility and linkage to defined outcomes. Agreements are location-specific and defined in relation to definite aims that are easy to monitor. This approach can incorporate the redefinition of human rights and protection in socio-economic terms as well as harm–benefit analysis. There are also problems, however. Local and task-specific agreements do not necessarily have any broader significance for warring parties or any connection with international law or conventions. In many respects, the MinOps framework is one that the Sudanese state has been demanding for some time. It has always favoured local agreements as opposed to arrangements that may have wider or long-term significance. Thus it quickly distanced itself from the first signed tripartite OLS agreement (May 1994) covering relief operations in the South. This OLS agreement was endorsed by high-level government and SPLA representation (Karim *et al.* 1996). The November 1998 security and transport corridor MinOps, however, was signed on behalf of the government by a member of the Southern States Coordinating Council, and for the SPLM by an adviser to the Chairman on Political and Economic Affairs. Thus compared to the 1994 agreement the yet-to-be ratified November 1998 MinOps framework has all the feel of a devalued exercise. Meanwhile the SPLA, for the past few years, has also being trying to force aid agencies to agree to its own charter of operation outside the established Ground Rules framework. It would seem that this development, together with the move towards MinOps in government areas, is a reflection of the weakening and relativisation of the international framework of consent that sustained OLS through most of the 1990s.

Another difficulty surrounding the MinOps approach is structural. Since a legal view of human rights is no longer the basis of the agreement, consensus is achieved through a lowest-common-denominator understanding of the problem at hand. Given the complementarity between the state and the aid industry concerning the need to promote the economic self-sufficiency of the displaced, one can understand the continuing predominance of the economic self-management model of development: it provides a lowest common denominator. It is something around which both government and the aid agencies can agree and upon which MinOps agreements can be created, including those involving rights and protection issues. In this context, liberal governance's preferred partnership mode of intervention can assume three stages: first, agree a shared definition of the problem; second, according to this definition apportion roles and responsibilities to the various stakeholders; and, finally, establish a monitoring and reporting mechanism to encourage self-compliance and organisation. While this is one approach to complexity, a weakness lies in the shared definition of the problem. A good example here is the stance advocated by UNICEF on child and women abduction in Sudan's transition zone. The shared definition of the problem, which allows for the sensitivity of this issue for the state, is as follows:

> The framework is based on the understanding that the problem of abduction is linked with the civil war and the effects that this has had on the breakdown of traditional value systems that would forbid the targeting of children and women, the inability of indigenous mechanisms of conflict resolution to cope with the demands of incompatible interests, and the spread of insecurity. (UNICEF 1999: 1)

Apart from being a good example of aid policy's Hobbesian view of conflict as something that destroys culture, this statement of the problem is misleading and historically unsound. It implies that the war has corrupted an earlier state of innocence. However, inter-group abduction is an established feature of ethnic border zones. Whether UNICEF likes it or not, it has long been part of the 'traditional value systems' of the groups involved (see Howell 1951). The UNICEF stance thus illustrates the historical distortion, self-delusion and compromise that liberal partnership arrangements can require in order to function. This is not to say that they can never succeed in establishing a regulatory system. It does suggest, however, that they will seldom solve the problems that they have been created to address. In this respect, to depict war as the primary cause of abduction only appears to raise the profile of this practice, while actually diminishing its importance and the real difficulties of attempting to control it. According to the definition it will disappear with peace. Since it predates the war, this is a debatable inference.

NOTES

1   The debate on linking relief to development tends to imply that in countries like Sudan, prior to the early 1990s, all relief assistance was top-down and dependency-creating. This is a major oversimplification of the situation. Concerns with dependency were as great during the 1980s as today. In the case of Sudan, there were many attempts to work through local structures, increase capacity, develop sophisticated targeting techniques, and so on (Cutler and Keen 1989; Walker 1987).
2   As discussed in Chapter 7, the involvement of East Asian and Canadian companies in Sudan's oil industry is a good example of the inability of the international community to enforce a common position on trade sanctions.
3   At the time of visiting North Sudan (March 1999), an agreement on the Minimum Rights of Beneficiaries was in draft form. A hardening of the government position, however, was delaying further discussions in this area.

9
Aid and Social Subjugation
Displacement and Complicity in Sudan (Part 2)

The previous chapter has examined how donor governments and aid agencies have responded to the Dinka in the government areas of Sudan. In particular, it has been argued that through the agency of the IDP identity the aid community has been complicit in relation to state policies of desocialisation and exploitation. This chapter shifts focus to examine more fully the consequences of this accommodation for the Dinka in the transition zone of South Darfur.

Advantages to dominant networks

International aid in the transition zone has helped to reinforce the position of the dominant commercial and political groups and the networks they control. This was the case during the 1980s (Keen 1994) and remained so during the 1990s. In relation to these networks, the Dinka have a double utility: as cheap, malleable labour that can be exploited at minimum cost; and as a subordinate client group that can be managed and manipulated to attract outside resources. Within the transition zone, state administrators, commercial farmers, military officers, local leaders and host communities have all benefited in different ways and to greater and lesser amounts. At the same time, the poor health and economic conditions among most Dinka remained unchanged during the course of the 1990s. The redefinition of human rights and protection in terms of the promotion of self-management has meant that aid agency models and forms of simulation are effectively blind to these structures of dominance and exploitation. Indeed, despite the periodic reinvention of NGO identity and the ascription of new mandates, the aid community has fed this system since the 1980s.

Some of the opportunities and benefits that Dinka displacement represent to Northern networks can be contradictory. For example, the government in Khartoum usually emphasises that all Southerners are full Sudanese citizens. This facilitates their strategic incorporation into the labour force, legitimises cultural suppression and is useful in fending off donor criticism of human rights abuse. At the same time, however, local government authorities or commercial farmers in the transition zone of western Sudan tend to emphasise the existence of a separate IDP problem. In this way, it is hoped to attract NGO or other outside assistance into a resource-poor area. Such differences illustrate two things. First, among dominant groups and networks in Northern Sudan there is not a single mode of regulation. Indeed, differences, tensions and rivalries exist in relation to central and more outlying systems. For example, in Darfur province, the continuing Rizegat practice of abducting Dinka women and children in Northern Bahr el Ghazal is no doubt a genuine concern and embarrassment to some members of the Khartoum government. Second, the variation in the mode of regulation relating to displaced Southerners is largely dictated by the changeable nature of local commercial–military networks and interest groups.

Cheap and desocialised labour

The long-term dependence of Sudan's political economy on cheap, malleable and desocialised labour has already been outlined. At the same time, aid policy, through the propagation of the IDP identity and liberal self-management, has furnished a complementary form of desocialisation. In examining the role of the Dinka as cheap labour, the question of food aid has to be addressed since it has a direct bearing on this issue.

The effects of reducing food aid

In the government areas of Sudan, the state decides what populations are in need and, consequently, it controls which groups come under the umbrella of the UN's OLS operation and are therefore eligible for humanitarian assistance. The non-government areas of the Nuba Mountains, for example, have been barred to aid agencies since the inception of OLS. Since 1989, the state has consistently pressed for the limiting of food aid to displaced Southerners, arguing that it creates dependency, demeans both the beneficiary and the image of Sudan, and conflicts with its own plans to integrate them into the national labour force. It was not until 1992, three years after OLS began and following strong lobbying from donor governments and the UN, that Southerners settled around Khartoum were allowed to come under OLS. However, this only applied to those Southerners settled in formally recognised 'peace camps' around the capital. Those outside these designated areas received no official aid. During the course of the 1990s, the state has made several changes to the definition of the 'displaced', all of which have had entitlement implications. In mid-1999, the government was planning to abolish the distinction between the displaced and resident populations, and to redefine the camps as residential areas. This change of status would presumably again remove many Southerners in Khartoum from the OLS framework and would add pressure on donor governments to reconsider their embargo on development assistance.

While donor governments have many differences with the state regarding aid policy, they are in general agreement about the problems of food aid and the need to reduce and limit its availability. In overall terms, the big drop in OLS food aid occurred between 1994 and 1995 when it fell by around 70 per cent from 85,129 to 23,914 metric tonnes (Karim *et al.* 1996: 140). The assumption behind this reduction was that the famine conditions of the early 1990s had now passed. This led to growing donor and NGO scepticism about whether further food aid was needed. During 1994, for example, the EC, the largest contributor of food aid to Northern Sudan, significantly cut its contributions (Duffield *et al.* 1999). This reduction was part of a general pattern of declining donor support for free food distribution based on the assumption that it would encourage self-sufficiency. One of the important findings of the *OLS Review*, however, was that this cutback was taking place at a time when the poor nutritional status of most Southerners had not only showed little or no improvement since the late 1980s, but in some places appeared worse (Karim *et al.* 1996: 127). At the same time, there was no evidence of growing self-management among these groups. Regarding SCF (UK), for example, in 1995 the Dinka in Ed'Dien were still clearly unable to repay seed credit. While the host population was able to repay 90 per cent of the loan, the Dinka could only manage 20 per cent (*ibid.*: 198). The cut in food aid was also being made in the absence of any real understanding of the ongoing effects of the war, the situation of the Dinka and the manner in which they were being integrated into the North's political economy. From this position, the *OLS Review* concluded that the move to food security thinking

> has led to a shift in the role of food aid, and a reduction in food aid
> support over time, in a situation where the emergency needs of benefi-
> ciary populations have not changed. In this regard, it is difficult for the
> Review Team to avoid the conclusion that programming around food is

not linked to information about the realities faced by populations in need, but to trends and pressures in the policy arena. (*Ibid.*: 150)

The *OLS Review* was unable to establish any clear information on how OLS was arriving at food aid estimates. In government areas, this appeared to involve a largely speculative process in which 'the calculation of food aid needs is highly susceptible to unsubstantiated assumptions about the increasing level of self-reliance among OLS beneficiaries' (*ibid.*: 134).

Since 1993, NGOs in government-controlled areas have been placing increasing emphasis on supporting livelihoods and reducing dependency. What food aid is still being given has been repackaged as agricultural support, food for work incentives and other rehabilitation initiatives (*ibid.*: 203). In Ed'Dien province in South Darfur, for example, SCF (UK) has followed this approach. It began distribution of seeds and tools among the Dinka in the province in 1993, and reduced food aid in 1994, 1995 and 1996. This reduction marked a move from providing a full ration[1] for nine months towards greater targeting to cover a much shorter part of the year. This has usually involved either a full or half ration for four months, depending on assessment. This reduction was supposed both to encourage the Dinka to become more economically active and to provide continuing assistance for the lean part of the year. 'By providing relief food to the displaced during April to August, the displaced are able to devote their efforts to cultivating their farms and work as hired agricultural labour in the hosting community farms' (SCF (UK) 1996).

The *OLS Review*, however, took a more critical view of this general trend.

Rather than promoting food security ... the reduction in food aid rations appears to be forcing displaced populations to intensify other survival strategies. At the same time ... the rate at which rations have been reduced has outpaced the rate at which alternative sources of food and income generation have expanded. (Karim *et al.* 1996: 203)

With the passage of time, the concerns of the authors of the *OLS Review* would appear to have been vindicated, while the optimism of the aid agencies has been shown to be misplaced. The policy of reducing food aid to promote self-sufficiency has been a notable failure. General health and malnutrition rates, where they are still recorded,[2] have continued to show that the condition of the Dinka remains poor. When ECHO visited Ed'Dien in September 1998, for example, an 'alarming' increase in malnutrition was recorded in the one camp inspected. This had reached 27 per cent in August (Dodd and Welten 1998: 1) and was exacerbated by the absence of any medical support. As for the Dinka in Ed Nahud, West Kordofan, despite CARE's involvement since 1989, 'the displaced residents in the Camp, who are mainly composed of women and children, remain vulnerable and the general health, nutritional and sanitation conditions in the Camp are still poor' (el Amin 1998: 2). Similar descriptions of continuing and persistently poor levels of health, nutrition, education and employment among displaced Southerners in Khartoum also exist (Loveless 1999).

The failure of the aid agencies to increase self-sufficiency in the transitional zone through the reduction in food aid has been indirectly acknowledged by the NGOs concerned. It is being presented, however, as a problem relating to the Dinka not having access to their own land. Whereas the opportunity for agricultural labour among surrounding groups was seen as helping promote self-sufficiency in the mid-1990s, it is now regarded differently. It is argued that the inability to properly cultivate for themselves has made the Dinka dependent on unsustainable and exploitative labour and debt relations with local groups. Regarding Ed'Dien province, for example, SCF (UK) argues that

Despite the massive humanitarian assistance rendered [the displaced] they continue to suffer chronic household food insecurity, which is attributed to lack of access to arable land for their own (HH) cultivation, which subjects them to engage in the exploitative relations. (Abd-el-Gadir 1999: 1)

Citing the lack of land, rather than a reduction of food aid, as the reason for growing dependence on non-sustainable labour relations tends to hide the aid community's complicity in this development. Indeed, in the case of SCF (UK) we are told that this has happened despite 'massive humanitarian assistance' in the past. Given the actuality of cuts, this claim is less than accurate. The current NGO plans to relocate Dinka groups in areas where they can own their own land is, in effect, another restatement of the enduring liberal self-management model of development. Resulting from policy failure, exploitative relations between the Dinka and the host community are now acknowledged and often partly described by NGOs. This is a departure from the situation in the mid-1990s when such relations were seldom mentioned (Karim et al. 1996: 126). However, due the primacy of the self-sufficiency model, these relations are localised and treated as the outcome of traditional animosities or particularly rapacious commercial groups – in other words, as problems that land and relocation can solve.

Targeted food aid and cheap labour

It is interesting that the policy of food aid reduction in order to promote self-sufficiency has, in the space of several years, become transformed into its opposite: minimal and targeted food aid appears to maintain a labour regime that would otherwise be non-sustainable. WFP's use of the Food Economy Approach to target food aid in Sudan illustrates this point. The Food Economy Approach is a simulation method that was first developed in non-government areas of Sudan in the mid-1990s by SCF (UK). In the past few years it has been applied in the North as well. The aim of the approach is to construct a profile of the various food sources to which a household has access: cultivation, trade, wage labour, gathering wild foods, etc. Changes in the external environment may restrict one or more particular sources. Under normal conditions, it is assumed that a switch to other sources within the household food economy can make good the shortfall. Regular assessment can monitor this situation and, in times of stress, help predict the amount of deficit to be made up through food aid.

There are a number of problems with the Food Economy Approach. As pointed out in the *OLS Review*, it was developed in relation to the agro-pastoral subsistence environment in South Sudan. As applied to displaced Southerners, however, it has been extended uncritically to an essentially non-subsistence cash economy. In such an environment, while the Food Economy Approach can list the potential sources of food, it is blind to the 'strategies that people actually use to obtain food, and the constraints they face in so doing' (Karim *et al*. 1996: 128). In other words, WFP's currently methodology takes no account of the deeply unequal and exploitative relations in which the Dinka are enmeshed in government areas.

The 1998 Food Economy assessment for Ed'Dien province illustrates this point (OLS 1998). A rapid resource assessment exercise estimated that on average during the year the displaced secured 50 per cent of their food intake through own purchase, 18 per cent through own culti-vation, 6 per cent through collecting wild foods, 2 per cent through trade, and 10 per cent through relief. This left an overall deficit of 14 per cent in food needs (24 per cent if one discounts the 10 per cent relief already received). The main recommendation arising from this assess-ment was to suggest that during 1999, in addition to the provision of agricultural inputs prior to the rainy season, a full ration of relief food would be needed during the 'hunger gap' between June and September (*ibid*.). Two points arise from this assessment. First, given that a sizeable deficit would seem to be acceptable (14 per cent even after relief assistance), it is little wonder that the health and nutritional situation of the Dinka has shown little improvement over the decade. Second, the assessment indirectly indicates just how non-sustainable and deeply exploitative are the clientage and labour relations on which the Dinka have to rely. Sharecropping, farm labour, casual urban employment, domestic service, and other income- and food-earning activities fall well short of the levels of return needed for basic survival, let alone self-sufficiency. In this situation, targeted food aid, in so far as it helps the Dinka to just stay alive rather than reducing dependency, has under-pinned and reinforced a highly exploitative labour regime and made a significant contribution to the profitability of, among other things, com-mercial groundnut production in North Sudan. Moreover, the inverse relation between food aid and profitability has not been lost on local actors. The *OLS Review*, for example, cites the executive manager of an Islamic NGO (Muwafaq) complaining that it was difficult to get the Dinka to work on its commercial farm projects. He suggested that no food aid should be distributed during the periods of land preparation and harvesting (Karim *et al.* 1996: 204).

Representation, debt and clientage

Debt relations among the Dinka are contracted both individually and collectively. Arrangements relating to sharecropping or advances on food aid allocation are usually of the latter kind and are mediated through recognised Dinka representatives in the displaced camps. The reason for this is that the displaced – as individuals – lack collateral, so that once a loan is given, or resources are transferred, there is little to prevent the Dinka decamping and moving elsewhere, leaving the debt unpaid. In 1998, for example, Oxfam gave out 60 fishing nets to Dinka it had targeted as vulnerable in the Ed'Dien area. Since it was regarded as a development activity, the nets were given on credit. The intention was that the loan would be repaid from the proceeds of dry fish sales. The project partners would thereby learn the benefits of work and thrift and, indeed, that it is better to give a man a fishing net than food aid. In the event, only five people returned to Ed'Dien after the first fishing season; the rest disappeared with their nets. Moreover, all the returnees were empty-handed, complaining that what fish had been caught had been forcibly taken by Arabs. Oxfam, consequently, lost its investment (Oxfam interview 1999).[3] In comparison, managing debt and clientage relations by the commercial–military nexus is more effective since it makes use of internal systems of governance.

For purposes of local administration, the government has estab-lished a system of local Dinka sultans to act as representatives and

236

middlemen between the Dinka and the wider society. With the exception of Khartoum, where Dinka sultans are usually drawn from traditional ruling families, in the transition zone it is more common to find that Dinka representatives are state appointees. Invariably, they are men chosen on the basis of their government allegiance and mal-leability. Conversion to Islam, for example, is frequently a trait of such official representatives of the displaced. While not of traditional ruling families, such men wield a great deal of patronage and influence among the displaced Dinka and represent new forms of legitimacy. They are able, for example, to use their local connections to exert control over food aid, local employment and credit. This system not only generates rivalries between sultans, and between them and the other Dinka, but also enables sultans to develop links with the governing commercial–military network. Individual Southerners dissatisfied with their position within this system are ill-placed to do anything about it. Opposition to recognised sultans usually comes from men who are able to gather their own followings among the displaced. Recognised sultans, however, can counter internal opposition through the threat of informing state security officials that troublemakers are SPLA sympathisers (Displaced interview 1999). In some cases, opponents have been detained and beaten by the authorities (UNHCU interview 1999).

An example of the role of Dinka sultans in controlling the displaced and managing the interface between them and external agencies occurred when an aid evaluation team of which I was part arrived in Ed'Dien in March 1999.[4] The government's Humanitarian Assistance Committee (HAC) representative for the area, who was also closely linked to security, had formed the impression that the team was there to investigate human rights issues. That evening, he privately convened a meeting of local sultans to inform them of our visit and instruct them on what to say. The following day, the HAC representative escorted the team to a nearby displaced camp at Khor Omer. The resulting interview with the sultans, which the HAC representative recorded in a notebook, was guarded and non-controversial. The team was told that the main reason for displacement was hunger in the South. Moreover, the main problem in the camp was the cut in food aid that the aid agencies had instigated several years earlier.[5]

In South Darfur and West Kordofan, it is the Dinka sultans who com-municate the terms of employment in sharecropping and agricultural labour offered by the merchants and commercial farmers, and sub-sequently act as labour contractors (Abd-el-Gadir 1999: 8). Given the limited remuneration for these activities, and the need to purchase such things as salt, sugar and clothes, debt relations are a feature of employment. While individually contracted debts take place, the Dinka sultans play an important role in arranging loans and enforcing debt repayment. Typically, the sultan will negotiate a loan from a merchant or commercial farmer on behalf of his clients. As collateral for such loans, apart from bonded labour, the only ready security that the Dinka represent is food aid and agency development inputs. Loans are taken out by Dinka sultans, and frequently repaid by them, either wholly or in part from the food aid entitlement of their clients. The cooperation of the Dinka in using their entitlements in this way is often secured through intimidation, including threats that the camp will be attacked if the loan is not repaid (UNHCU interview 1999). Given the history of violence in South Darfur, this is not an idle threat.

Dinka sultans operate within a complex network of corruption, patronage and debt relations linking the displaced with government officials, commercial farmers and different factions of the host community. In terms of their management of debt relations, the sultans have a vested interest in maintaining control of the distribution of food aid. In the past this has contributed to the generation of internal tensions. Dissatisfied with the brokerage role of particular sultans, competitors usually try to attract their own followings in order to threaten the authority of the recognised sultan (Displaced interview 1999). Occasions when targeted food aid is delivered to the displaced camps (usually monthly during the hunger gap) can be particularly tense. This is when sultans repay collective loans to merchants and commercial farmers. NGOs have been aware of these problems, although they rarely record them in writing. Since the mid-1990s, for example, there have been several attempts in Ed'Dien to introduce individual ration cards. Until 1998, when individual registration was finally introduced, the sultans resisted this. In the displaced camp at El Goura, the changeover in April 1998 led to a major clash. On the first food aid delivery of the 'hungry season', expectant beneficiaries crowded the lorry in an attempt to seize their allocation before the already assembled merchants could claim their sultan-mediated repayment (UNHCU interview 1999). The resulting altercation, involving police action, resulted in an opposition faction and its leader departing and moving to the camp at Adilla (Displaced interview 1999).

In the mid-1990s the *OLS Review* cited local estimates that 25 per cent of food aid destined for the Dinka at Ed'Dien was being diverted. At the same time, under an agreement with the local relief committee, 20 per cent of the allocation for the Dinka was claimed by the host community. In effect, and in addition to the dependency-reducing cuts in food aid already in place, the Dinka were only receiving about half their allocation (Karim *et al.* 1996: 204). The introduction of individual registration cards will no doubt allow NGOs and WFP to get a better idea of the numbers of Dinka living at each camp. It will also make it more difficult for sultans to expropriate camp food aid allocations. However, camp registration strengthens the ties linking particular Dinka to particular camp networks, thus allowing the sultans and commercial farmers to develop new forms of clientage and control. In adaptive systems, old problems mutate into new ones. A possible indication that this may have already happened comes from the ECHO visit to Ed'Dien in September 1998. Not only did the visit record alarmingly high malnutrition rates in the Khor Omer camp, but surprise was expressed at this situation given that food aid for 90,000 people had been distributed in the middle of the year. Recent attempts at registration, however, suggested a population in the target camps of 30,000 (Dodd and Welten 1998). There was some doubt whether the lower figure was accurate since it may have excluded those absent due to sharecropping. However, high levels of malnutrition in the context of such figures may indicate that new forms of regulation and diversion may have emerged.

Sharecropping and bonded labour

The commercial production of groundnuts developed in the transitional zone from the 1960s. Sharecropping is the main means of commercial production. In discussing the role of the Dinka as sharecroppers, one is talking of their involvement in a process of economic secession whereby the Dinka have replaced earlier sources of labour. Since the 1970s, Dinka seasonal migrants have been increasingly engaged in sharecropping in the transition zone. With the onset of the war and the spread of insecurity, displacement has seen the Dinka integrated as the mainstay of the agricultural labour force. In Ed'Dien province, for example, the Dinka are said to make up 85 per cent of the agricultural labour force (WFP interview 1999). Unlike pre-war seasonal migrants, however, largely cut off from the subsistence network in the South, the Dinka have to survive within a mainly commercial environment. Some merchant farmers employ over 130 Dinka sharecroppers on their groundnut farms (SCF (UK) interview 1999).

Apart from lulls in June and September, groundnut cultivation begins in April with the cleaning of the farm and finishes in December following the harvest. Weeding (July–August) and harvesting (October–December) are particularly demanding. To take advantage of more fertile soil, commercial groundnut farms usually lie at some distance from centres of habitation. For this reason, especially during the periods of peak demand, it is usual for the labourers to remain in the fields for several weeks at a time. The sharecropping arrangement involves a verbal agreement entitling the cultivators to half of the harvest in exchange for their labour and means of sustenance. Apart from the necessary agricultural inputs, the farm owner provides food and water to the labourers during the period of cultivation. Water is important since distant farms usually lack any source of drinking water. A farm owner will therefore be required to make periodic deliveries. This pattern of employment has particular significance for the Dinka. In order to maximise efficiency and, especially, cut costs on food and water, throughout the transitional zone it is common for farm owners to insist on only able-bodied men and women as labourers (Abd-el-Gadir 1999; el Amin 1998: 9–10). Women with dependent children are excluded from sharecropping. The food and water provided, therefore, is not sufficient to support an entire family. Women with dependent children have to remain in the camp, or if they are able, to rely on poorly remunerated domestic employment in the urban areas.

The subsistence gap in family income that arises from sharecropping is a main cause of debt during the course of the agricultural season. Loans taken from the farm owner are deducted with interest from the sharecropper's half of the harvest. In some cases, it is not uncommon for sharecroppers to finish the season with little or nothing to show for their endeavours. During slack periods, as a means of limiting debt the Dinka will also work as day labourers on the farmers of smaller farmers. Some younger men will also migrate to large agricultural schemes in central and eastern Sudan. If the camps are too distant from a town to offer women the chance of domestic work, they collect firewood, weave grass mats and engage in prostitution and the illicit brewing of beer. In the January to March period, when little farming activity taking place, the displaced camps in the transition zone are at their fullest. It is during this period that households are particularly dependent on the limited earnings of women and targeted food aid. As the evidence of WFP's Food Economy assessments indicate, the combined food and income returns of all the activities open to the Dinka fall significantly short of that necessary for physical survival. The Dinka are caught in a complex network of individual and collectively mediated debts in the context of a hostile and exploitative environment. As the evidence suggests, the result for many is malnutrition, ill-health and premature death.

Looting and asset realisation

Since Southerners first began arriving in significant numbers in Northern Sudan in the late 1980s, the development inputs that NGOs have often provided as a means of improving their economic self-management have frequently been seized by more powerful surrounding groups. As early as 1986, for example, when working for Oxfam in Sudan, I helped set up two projects that provided a few Dinka men in Khartoum with donkey-drawn water carts and, for women, goats. These were standard development-type projects in that resources were provided on credit with the intention of boosting income and child nutrition respectively. That Southerners were subject to intimidation in Khartoum was already well known among NGOs. The project justification, however, included the argument that because the inputs were mobile, in case of trouble the Dinka would at least have the opportunity of moving with their property. In the event, the projects were shown to be both naïve and dangerous for the Dinka involved. The donkeys, carts and goats quickly ended up in the hands of predatory neighbours. The goats, in particular, created a tense situation in which the police, acting on the claims of local groups, detained several beneficiaries on the accusation of theft. Oxfam had to intervene at the police station and be satisfied with freeing the accused, minus their goats. Given this history, it is rather surprising to learn that, since the early 1990s, NGOs, including Oxfam, have continued to mount such projects, often with similar results.

Since the mid-1990s, Oxfam has been working in a developmental fashion in three displaced camps in the Ed'Dien area: Abu Matariq, El Goura and Adilla. The provision of donkey-drawn water carts and goats on credit has been a feature of such projects. In the case of the former, the distance of sharecropping farms or available fertile land from local water sources was one of the project justifications. It would seem, however, that in all of these camps (including Adilla which is in a non-Rizegat area) some of the carts have ended up in the possession (either actual or *de facto*) of the host community. This asset transfer is part of the bonded labour and debt culture that the Dinka are caught in. Rather than being the formal owners of the donkey cart, which was the intention of the NGO, some Dinka have been transformed into day labourers receiving a meagre return 'that hardly meets the cost of a meal for an average family. Others had their carts confiscated for non-payment of loans taken from some traders' (UNHCU 1999: 2).[6] At times of inter-group tension, however, forcible seizure also takes place. In March 1998, for example, dry season grazing tensions were particularly high as Rizegat herders began their annual move into Northern Bahr al Ghazal. Resistance by the SPLA to what is regarded as an encroachment resulted in a number of Rizegat deaths and prompted violence against the Dinka living in Abu Matariq, an important Rizegat area. The camp was looted and the Dinka were forced to flee to other areas, including Nyala. In the incident, apart from other property, all fifteen of the donkey carts provided by Oxfam were seized by the Rizegat (Oxfam interview 1999). Most were taken in the fields where the Dinka are particularly vulnerable. In the event, the agency only managed to secure the return of three of them.

The direct seizure of property belonging to the Dinka is a common feature of life in government areas of Sudan. In Khartoum, a variant of this concerns the periodic destruction of squatter housing that has been occurring since the late 1980s. Because no compensation is given for the buildings and building materials destroyed, it represents a real material loss to the Dinka. It is a loss, moreover, that NGOs and donors, although protesting the issue, have been willing to live with and, to a limited extent, make good. Within the transition zone, asset seizure is an ever-present threat. In western Sudan, the dry season movement of Arab nomads into the South (February–April) is a particularly sensitive period. During the violence at Abu Matariq in March 1998, the Dinka exhibited a response that appears to be part of a more general survival strategy: the hasty sale and realisation of NGO-donated relief and development assets to finance flight in times of impending trouble. In other words, what the Rizegat did not loot, the Dinka themselves quickly sold (Oxfam interview 1999). This would seem to be a common response to tension in South Darfur, with the Dinka being in a state of readiness to realise whatever resources they have. This response is also seen in relation to political rivalry and violence among the Dinka themselves. The incident at Al Goura in April 1998 (see above), when some Dinka attempted to prevent their food aid allocations being handed over to local merchants, has already been mentioned. In this case, those households involved in opposition to the recognised sultan quickly sold their assets in order both to prevent seizure and to raise the money to move to Abu Karinka camp (Displaced interview 1999). A culture of asset seizure and destruction creates counter-trends toward asset realisation and conversion to cash. Unfortunately, both serve to reinforce the subordinate and marginalised position of the Dinka.

Why stay in the transition zone?

Given the onerous conditions they face, one wonders why the Dinka stay in the transition zone. Why not abandon sharecropping and move to an area where protection might be greater and employment a little more remunerative? The more convincing answers to this question involve issues of kinship, patronage and protection. At the same time, for most Dinka the varying conditions within government areas represent relative rather absolute differences. The Dinka in the Ed'Dien area, for example, are Mulwal from the Gogrial area of Northern Bahr al Ghazal. Despite the history of raiding and violence that they have suffered at the hands of the Rizegat, some have daughters and female relatives married into various Rizegat subsections. In the hope of the protection that this may afford, some have remained in the area. At the same time, they have kinship links with other Dinka from the same sub-clans. Moreover, while NGOs frequently portray hostility toward the Dinka in South Darfur as mainly coming from the Rizegat, while other groups are more friendly, some local informants hold contrary views. Unlike the Rizegat, the Mahliyya, for example, do not own cattle and are therefore not involved in the annual tensions over dry season cattle grazing. Day-to-day intimidation of the Dinka in Mahliyya areas, however, is described as greater than among the Rizegat (SCF (UK) interview 1999). Where the Rizegat differ is that when violence does break out, it is more organised and on a bigger scale than in other areas. This contrast does not augur well for current NGO attempts to relocate Dinka to non-Rizegat areas on the assumption that they will be safer and free from the exploitative relations described above. The Nyala region, for example, is frequently cited as more stable than Ed'Dien. It is also the case, however, that some of the Dinka who fled to Nyala following dry season disturbances in 1998 are now back in the camps in Ed'Dien (Oxfam interview 1999).

While sharecropping in Ed'Dien is onerous and unrewarding, to people who have little it does offer a few advantages. The sustenance provided and collateral represented by the future harvest can represent a small area of certainty in a precarious life. Working for a local merchant farmer also offers Dinka labourers some physical protection. They are less likely to be molested and abused if sharecropping with a local strongman. In some cases, it is also possible for sharecroppers to build up a rapport with the farmer and thus experience a more indulgent relationship – the provision of better food or cigarettes, for example, or help with medical expenses. Through local arrangements, in some areas the displaced can also gain access to their own land, either directly or through a renting arrangement. The latter usually involves giving up a tenth of the harvest to the landowner. This land, however, is invariably worked-out and infertile. Moreover, the Dinka working such land, sometimes distant from the nearest settlement, are more

open to abuse and to having their belongings and produce forcibly confiscated. Such factors tend to reinforce sharecropping as a lesser evil
among more perilous alternatives.

Institutional advantages

Aid farming through committees

The Sudanese state has frequently portrayed itself within the UN
General Assembly as the victim of a complex emergency (Karim *et al.*
1996) – that is, as suffering from multiple problems associated with
drought, environmental degradation and insecurity. Since 1992,
reflecting the aid community, it has also elevated the need for long-
term development above that of short-term relief. Through urban
planning and relocation in Khartoum, for example, displaced Southerners have been incorporated within the government's development
plans and its attempts to reassert national unity. All of this, however,
requires resources. Since 1988, following the first major wave of Southerners entering Northern Sudan, the state, often in collaboration with
the UN, has periodically launched planning documents covering the
needs of the Southerners in the transition zone and the resource
requirements of urban planning in Khartoum. A similar process has
also been happening lower down the administrative structure. A key
finding of the *OLS Review* was that the process of federalisation,
coupled with the decline in public spending, was placing a growing
pressure on humanitarian assistance at the regional level to make good
the erosion of public goods. In 1992, for example, following the second
major influx of Dinka into South Darfur, aid agencies were invited back
into the area. According to one aid worker, local government officials
presented them with 'wishing lists' of medical, educational, water and
training resources required by the authorities to cope with the
emergency (Pearson 1992).

The process of federalisation has continued with more new provinces
being created since the mid-1990s. Lacking central government funding,
provinces have been given the freedom to raise their own public finances
through local taxation, a move which has been seen, among other
things, as discouraging inter-province trade (ECHO 1999: 10). Adilla
used to come under the authority of Ed'Dien. Since September 1998,
however, Adilla has been a new provincial authority that also includes
Abu Karinka, where there is also a displaced settlement. According to
the new Deputy Commissioner, while the Dinka are happy and well
integrated, they are placing an extra burden on the scarce health, education, environment and water resources of the area (Local government

interview 1999). At the same time, there is a concern that despite the creation of new provinces, all the international NGOs have remained in Ed'Dien and none have established a presence in Adilla. This is something that the local authorities would like to encourage. Such cases of dominant groups using the predicament of a subordinate group to attract and thereby share or lay claim to scarce resources can be described as 'aid farming'. Some projects, such as the rehabilitation of water yards in the transition zone, have benefited both the Dinka and host populations. Donor governments, however, have generally been unresponsive to clear examples of aid farming. There is scepticism regarding the motives of the authorities and a belief that much of the assistance requested is the proper responsibility of government. Most NGOs have similarly avoided official wish lists as a means of project design.

Where aid farming has been more successful, it relates to the bureaucratic means of control that dominant networks have developed in relation to aid disbursement. The *OLS Review* has argued that, in setting up OLS, the UN agreed to the state retaining its ability to control and manage humanitarian aid in its own sphere of influence in exchange for UN management in non-government areas (Karim *et al.* 1996: 90–1). This has given the government and its aid and humanitarian agencies a good deal of control in relation to deciding access and assessing need. Under the federal constitution, individual states have been granted the responsibility for relief matters within their territory. Aid-related committees are organised at the state, provincial and local levels. At a federal level, the Humanitarian Assistance Committee (HAC)[7] is responsible for overall coordination and has a representative in each state capital and, in some places such as Ed'Dien, in provincial towns as well. As pointed out in the *OLS Review*, the multiplicity of committees has created a number of overlapping layers of authority between aid agencies and the Dinka (*ibid.*: 91–3). In Khartoum, for example, there are seven government committees claiming some responsibility for displaced Southerners. In South Darfur, the High Committee for the Displaced is based in Nyala. It comprises representatives from the provincial government departments (health, water, etc.), security, police, local and international NGOs, and official Dinka representatives. Besides cross-cutting ties with other government departments, there are also a number of subcommittees that, depending on specialisation, are chaired by either local government officials or NGOs. Under the authority of the High Committee, in Ed'Dien province there is a Provincial High Committee for the Displaced with a similar representational structure. The local NGO representatives include the Sudanese

Red Crescent and the Sudanese Society for Environmental Protection. The subcommittees involved cover water, food and health (SCF (UK) interview 1999). Until 1998, SCF (UK) chaired the food committee.

In many respects, the number of government committees, together with their levels and depth of representation, has expanded in an inverse relation to their actually doing anything on the ground. Despite their number and complexity, actual implementation is usually left to NGOs. Moreover, despite what might look like a comprehensive organisational structure, most local relief committees tend to operate irregularly with many functions being more or less redundant. The Provincial High Committee in Ed'Dien, for example, is supposed to meet monthly but seldom does so. The subcommittees also meet on an *ad hoc* basis. Local government officials lack motivation and interest. More generally, such committees only function when aid agencies are conducting a needs assessment, or when there are resources to be distributed. The Wau Relief Committee, for example, besides security personnel, includes porters, drivers, support staff and youth representatives. In exchange for facilitating relief distribution, in the mid-1990s it was receiving 2 metric tonnes (mt) of sorghum, 0.5 mt of pulses and 16 gallons of oil per distribution for division among its members. In many respects, the main function of local relief committees is not to implement or manage in relation to intended beneficiaries, but to control and regulate external assistance in ways that either directly or indirectly serve the interests of committee members and their client networks. The need to command and regulate access to resources has been seen as one reason for the increasing number of committees and the depth of their structures (Karim *et al.* 1996: 93). Rather than technically neutral management structures, relief committees are better understood as part of a complex system of local governance. In the transition zone they have links with the commercial–military nexus and hence the shadow economy. They are part of an ethnically structured network of social and political relations within which the Dinka are subsumed. Their different members bring together and mediate such things as debt relations, Dinka representation, commercial interests, food aid diversion, security and aid farming.

Such committees also play an important role in relation to the assessment of need among the Dinka. Assessing need has little to do with actual conditions or real requirements. As already mentioned, in the mid-1990s donor governments and the EU unilaterally reduced food aid shipments due to concerns about dependency, although little evidence to this effect was being relayed to them by their local representatives. Assessing need is a complex social and political process. In

246

relation to Sudan, the *OLS Review* has attempted to unpack some of the complex relations and mechanisms involved (Karim *et al*. 1996: 110–54). The different interest groups involved with needs assessment often have conflicting views. Regarding food aid, for example, the Khartoum government has generally favoured reduction as this fits with its strategic concern to integrate Southerners within the commercial labour force. Local merchants and military figures, however, who are capable of manipulating debt relations and benefiting from aid diversion, think differently. For their part, NGOs, since they wish to pursue development options, have often come to the negotiations with an exaggerated sense of Dinka ability to achieve self-sufficiency. In government areas, needs assessment has typically been a process of negotiation, compromise and balance between international aid agencies and local networks of governance. Negotiated assessments of this sort have typically paid little attention to the actual living conditions, life chances and survival strategies of Southerners. Moreover, when one factors into this equation problems of access, delays in delivery, population movements and so on, it should come as no surprise that estimates of need rarely correlate with actual deliveries of relief assistance (*ibid.*: 142). Despite assurances that the situation has improved over the last couple of years (WFP interview 1999), with such a complex and adaptive system, problem mutation rather than steady state improvement is the more realistic scenario.

Dependency revisited

The above analysis of the place of the Southerners in the political economy of Sudan has focused largely on the Dinka in the transitional zone, especially, the Ed'Dien area of South Darfur. While local differences exist, similar structures and relations of incorporation operate in other areas such as Khartoum. This analysis suggests that the current policy framework of attempting to encourage self-management among Southerners through modest development inputs supported by targeted food aid, is not working. Aid has tended to reinforce the structures that exploit and dominate the Dinka. The result is that there has been no appreciable improvement in the plight of the Dinka living in the North for the last decade. The Dinka in government areas represent both the crisis and limitations of liberal development policy. Moreover, the present policy attempt to address this failure by providing the Dinka with their own land makes no allowance for the nature of the wider system of which they are part. Despite this change, we can therefore expect aid policy to continue to fail.

In approaching the crisis of developmentalism, the above analysis suggests several things. Aid policy currently reinforces an ethnically structured system of exploitation. This occurs at several levels. The de-ethnicised IDP identity acts as a form of desocialisation that complements the strategy of cultural suppression pursued by the state. In terms of the actual assistance provided, complex forms of aid diversion and aid farming among dominant networks reinforce the marginalised position of Southerners. The main response to this crisis has been aid policy's linking of relief and development in the mid-1990s. The problem with this attempted rectification, however, is that aid's ability to reinforce dominant structures occurs irrespective of whether the assistance is of a relief or a development type. One reason for this is that development discourse presents the problem as essentially one of economic vulnerability. It is blind to the complex social and political system of dominance to which the Dinka are subjected. The appropriation of a human rights narrative by aid agencies, in that rights have been redefined in terms of social and economic considerations, appears destined to repeat again the same omission. Not only do development inputs and resources often end up in the hands of surrounding groups, but the structure of dominance can produce seemingly perverse results. The reduction in food aid, for example, can be interpreted as a *Do No Harm* approach to a situation where aid agencies have doubts over the effects of their actions. The reality, however, has been to reinforce the subjugation of the Dinka and increase their reliance on non-sustainable labour relations. While food aid should be increased, if only to improve the bargaining position of the Dinka, the existing debt and clientage system means that much of this would be diverted to more powerful groups. At the same time, development inputs aiming to increase economic self-sufficiency are also transferred as debt repayment, forcibly seized or, in periods of desperation, sold off by the Dinka themselves to secure their flight and immediate survival. In many respects, aid *per se* appears as an inappropriate means of addressing the problems faced by the Dinka. The whole problematic of liberal self-management, with its magical and narcissistic views of the impact of small amounts of assistance on what are experienced as a closed, mechanical and de-ethnicised communities of independent households, is under question.

It is not just that aid policy is failing, but that its rationale and approach appear inadequate and misplaced; like using a hammer where a screwdriver is required, it is the wrong tool for the job it is expected to do. Where aid policy may have had some success, this is often as an indirect consequence of its intended aims. For example, rather than being eaten, food aid can provide collateral for a bridging loan from a local merchant to secure other necessities. Rather than being used to earn a steady income, a donkey cart can be sold in order to raise money quickly so that a family can flee an area of insecurity. Perhaps aid policy could be more successful if it provided resources in ways that people actually used them – for example, as money for transport, buying up local debts or paying off middlemen. To make aid more effective, rather than being blind to ethnicity, NGOs would also have to consider working with a particular ethnic group or clan in support of their survival strategies. Instead, however, development discourse attempts to create a new moral universe of liberal self-management. In relation to this moral universe, it is worth reconsidering the notion of dependency. The Dinka in government areas of Sudan have gained little from over a decade of international assistance. In this period, however, NGOs have reinvented themselves several times, moving from relief to development and, more recently, from community to rights-based programming. At the same time, national and local relief committees have increased and created a multi-levelled and overlapping system that in many areas incorporates local commercial and military interests as well the formal representatives of the Dinka themselves. Both the aid industry and the systems of regulation that have emerged in Sudan have profited in different ways from displacement. This profit is not only material; indeed, relatively speaking, such transfers are not that big. It includes the development of new forms of legitimacy, authority and competence. If one wishes to examine dependency, one must look at this institutional level: the complex pattern of organisational, collective and private gain that can be found where local politico-commercial networks conjoin with those of the aid industry. In other words, if aid has created dependency, it is among local dominant groups and international strategic actors that form the new development–security terrain.

Redefining dependency in this manner goes some way to understanding the difficulties involved in formulating an alternative approach. The above analysis would suggest that the main failing of aid policy lies in the inability or unwillingness of aid agencies to address the wider, ethnically structured networks of dominance that reproduce Southerner subjugation. Stated another way, donor governments are unable to alter the political economy of Sudan, especially its dependence on cheap, desocialised and malleable labour. Many members of the international community might argue that such deep-seated issues are not their responsibility. These structures and relations, however, far better represent the reality of Sudan than abstract models based on independent households, wealth ranking, self-sufficiency and market deregulation. If aid policy is unable to address the reality of the situation, one may well ask what donor governments and NGOs are doing in Sudan. Aid policy is now geared to a radical agenda of social transformation. If in actuality, however, it is reinforcing an abusive and exploitative system, then perhaps aid agencies should leave? Institutional dependency provides one answer as to why they do not. Sudan is one among many 'complex emergencies' that help keep strategic actors in business. NGOs, for example, need countries like Sudan in the same way that a fish needs water. It is a business, moreover, that has expanded greatly since the 1970s. There are now a lot of jobs, careers and political reputations at stake in the field of international development. In a global context in which economic polarisation and poverty levels have significantly increased over the same period, it is also an industry that is heavily reliant on repackaging, reinvention and spin.

Institutional dependency helps one to understand why NGOs, for example, discuss the realities of Sudan in an off-the-record fashion. In private, the limitations of project work will be acknowledged, as will the hopeless plight of the Dinka and the machinations of surrounding groups and actors, but little if any of this finds its way into official reports and, especially, the public domain. In this way, the utopia of liberal self-management lives on until its next reinvention. It does not, however, give the complete story. One of the reasons that donor governments are unable or unwilling to address the realities of Sudan is that there is no collective international policy in relation to political Islam. Leaving aside the American cruise missile attack on a Khartoum suburb in 1998, among EU member states opinion is divided between the pragmatic French/German position as opposed to the more rights-oriented Dutch/British. Political Islam is another reality that aid policy is unable to address. This absence of an international consensus underpins a number of interesting contrasts and differences.

If one examines the Balkans, for example, the type of conflict analysis and framework of response that aid agencies have developed there would seem well suited to Sudan. The conflict has been understood as having an important ethnic dimension in which specific groups have lost out just because of who they are, rather than what they may have done. Sudan is similar. In the Balkans, however, donors and NGOs have articulated the political nature of the conflict much more clearly than in Sudan. At the same time, in terms of approaching social reconstruction, a more politically aware programme of legal rights education, funding free media, supporting rights centres and litigation, voter registration, awareness campaigns, confidence-building measures and so on is being pursued. While such policies have no guarantee of success, it is interesting that the same NGOs, when involved in Northern Sudan, have adopted none of these measures. This is despite the fact that many of them, especially those aiming to improve political and legal representation, would make good sense in relation to Southerners. They would go a little way to restoring what ordinary Southerners have lost since the 1970s. In Khartoum there are presently quite a few unemployed Dinka lawyers. Given the problems of urban planning, relocation and child abduction in the transition zone, it is surprising that no NGOs are employing or funding such people to defend the position of affected Southerners in the courts. This is despite the fact that some Dinka, overcoming considerable difficulty, have been able to use the court system to secure the return of abducted children (Local court interview 1999). When pressed on this issue, the common NGO response was to plead the sensitivity of such work and their lack of protection. In other words, Sudan is not the Balkans and lacks a relatively unified framework of international engagement.

Aid policy and complexity

The view that humanitarian assistance can cause more problems than it solves has served to problematise the actions of aid agencies. It is now widely accepted that aid can cause harm as well as good (Anderson 1996). In addressing this problem, it is now common for NGOs working in war zones to weigh their actions in terms of the net harms or net benefits that it is assumed will be the outcome. As a form of simulation, the consequentialist logic of harm–benefit analysis is one means of addressing complexity. Like a computer game, however, simulation is only as good as the parameters and limitations of the code that informs it. When 'harms' are couched in terms of aid promoting dependency or fuelling war, in the absence of specific evidence as to how this takes place, and 'benefits' are uncritically taken from the yet-to-be-achieved project objectives of the NGO concerned, the exercise can easily become one of reconfirming the *status quo*. For effective simulation, a more informed, inclusive and compressive model is required. Aid agencies have yet to construct such a model and, at the same time, establish organisational systems that can deal effectively with complex information. Among other things, this would involve moving away from the economistic framework of isolated households and self-managing communities that dominates development discourse. One is dealing with a complex, politically structured and networked system where strategic actors and political complexes conjoin and interact. In relation to this system, the economic self-management model of aid policy is unable to predict outcomes adequately. In fact, it continually gets them wrong. Apart from a problematised and sacrificial representation of humanitarian assistance, it excludes aid's strategic networks and the relations of accommodation and complicity contained within them. Consequently, it does not accurately reflect the system as a whole, while local political complexes continue to be understood as closed mechanical structures awaiting development.

Discussions of aid and its effects are confined to an imaginary world of self-contained and reactive household units, ignoring the reality that the strategic networks of global governance and the political complexes of the new wars conjoin and intermesh to form a new development–security terrain. The flows and networks interconnect and affect all involved: government structures, non-state actors, host community organisations, commercial–military alliances and aid agencies, as well as the beneficiaries themselves. Within a complex and integrated system structured by relations of dominance and legitimacy, the effects of aid policy flow downwards, upwards and across these networks. In unexpected and multiform ways relations and networks are simultaneously changed and reinforced. This can be seen, for example, in those instances where dominant groups have established new forms of organisation (such as committee structures) and claims to legitimacy in order to regulate external assistance. Since we are dealing with a complex and integrated system, however, change and reinforcement also occur when aid is *not* given. The expansion of the transborder shadow economy, for example, has occurred in the wake of formal economic disinvestment and the reduction in development spending. In a similar manner, the reduction of food aid in the mid-1990s, as part of the move to 'developmental' relief, served to reinforce the dependence of many Dinka in the transition zone on servile and bonded forms of sharecropping. Development agencies and their ability to intervene do not exhaust the possibilities for social transformation.

Concerning the claim that humanitarian aid creates dependency and fuels conflict, one can make several responses. First, convincing and detailed empirical evidence is lacking, certainly to support the blanket acceptance that this position has won. Second, the claim is often disingenuous since it is usually those that seek to claim the magic of aid for themselves who make it. Finally, if we wanted to examine the effects of aid properly, we would need to move away from the rather narrow model in which aid is conceived as a form of transfer (organisational, behavioural, economic, etc.) between two unconnected systems. Complex relations of similarity and difference, complicity and antagonism enmesh strategic and political complexes. Within such a terrain, the effect of aid is largely organisational and has social, cultural and political ramifications. In this respect, one could argue that *the main consequence of aid of any form (relief, developmental, financial, commercial and so on) is to change and reinforce the dominant relations and forms of discourse that it encounters and through which it flows*. This is the case for Northern strategic complexes as well as political complexes in the South. It is also true even when those relations are non-liberal in nature. Indeed, this is the basis of aid failure and its infinite ability to generate unforeseen or unwanted consequences. It also underpins the relations of complicity and accommodation that characterise liberal peace.

This formulation is different from the conventional view that singles out humanitarian assistance as detrimental while implying that other forms of aid are somehow better, more predictable or more effective. Regarding dependency, moreover, beneficiaries are usually not part of the local structures of dominance and legitimacy. Consequently, a problem for most humanitarian operations is that beneficiaries often receive less than their entitlement, in some cases, markedly so.[8] Assistance is filtered through the structures of dominance and legitimacy that surround most direct aid recipients. These structures, however, are varied and context-specific. Without proper investigation, one cannot be sure what their role is or what exactly they do. At the same time, aid can change and reinforce dominant relations in many ways. Such effects are not confined to the material or organisational sphere; they can also include social matters of legitimacy, political recognition or moral authority. Indeed it is in such social and organisational areas that the present aid regime probably has its main effects. Moreover, existing structures of dominance are not always opposed or antagonistic to popular causes or the interests of aid beneficiaries. In non-government areas of South Sudan, for example, while aid has been diverted and misused, an unintended consequence has been to allow structures of local authority to maintain the subsistence economy in the face of government attempts to destroy it (Duffield *et al*. 1995; Karim *et al*. 1996; Duffield *et al*. 1999). For the groups concerned, this is a positive outcome. Where this system has been compromised due to the war, Southerners displaced to the North have found themselves within a very different and antagonistic system of dominance and legitimacy. Here, in strengthening these relations, the role of aid has been to reinforce their subordination and exploitation.

A final point in relation to complexity is the belief that the aid encounter can produce a steady-state solution. Ideas of self-sufficiency and sustainability, together with the teleological assumptions that underpin the vision of 'development' itself, all imply that aid can produce a steady-state situation. It is implicit within common notions of development that an endpoint will eventually be reached or, alternatively, a magic formula will be found whereby communities will become self-sufficient forever. Despite fifty years of simultaneous development failure and expansion of the international aid bureaucracy, it remains a sad but indubitable fact that many aid workers retain a self-image of working themselves out of a job. Indeed, the way in which most NGOs collect money from the public demands this delusion. Steady-state conditions, however, do not exist either in nature or in the social world (Capra 1982). Rather than achieving such a state, complex systems are metamorphic and continually change and mutate. If the main effect of aid is to change and reinforce the relations of dominance and legitimacy that it encounters, *the resulting system continually mutates over time to produce new forms and structures.* Aid interventions or aid withdrawals produce counteracting reactions and adaptations. For example, when an aid agency attempts to monitor food aid delivery better to prevent diversion, which most of them do, the system usually mutates and new forms of expropriation emerge. Problems that aid agencies feel they have tackled today reappear in new guises tomorrow. Complex systems are flexible and capable of great powers of adaptation. The shadow economy, money laundering and methods of corporate concealment, for example, are innovative, mutable and endlessly adaptive. In relation to aid, donors searching for technically perfect projects or concise best-practice guidelines premised on a belief in a steady-state ending are not only deluding themselves, they are wasting money. If liberal peace is to be effective, it must first of all develop the means to address complexity: it must adjust its human resource base, change the way in which it uses information and reorder its institutional priorities in the reasonable expectation that problems will never be solved – they will simply change and mutate.

Concluding remarks: peace and the reinvention of development

The inability of aid policy to confront complexity in Sudan has a number of implications. The most important of these is the tendency to reduce all the problems in the path of aid agencies, beneficiaries, development and so on to the effects and consequences of the ongoing war. Since it is seen as a major factor in creating economic vulnerability and impoverishment, it is presented as an important cause of disparity and lack of harmony between communities. It has caused the breakdown of traditional value systems, been responsible for the spread of criminal acts, and so on. It has already been noted, for example, that UNICEF regards the abduction of women and children in the transition zone as a direct outcome of the war. On a wider front, the war can also be related to the continuing donor embargo on development assistance to Sudan, a policy that has further compounded all these problems. In September 1998, for example, several NGOs, including the rights-based CARE and Oxfam, made a direct appeal to the UN Security Council to throw its authority behind a search for peace in Sudan. That these agencies are still operating in the government areas is, perhaps, an indication that the war is not the main problem in Sudan, or at least not the determining problem as suggested by the aid agencies. It is, however, a convenient way of explaining failure.

An end to the war in Sudan is desperately needed and should be encouraged at every opportunity. Yet it must also be realised that ending the war will do little to change the violent political economy that characterises Sudan and the subordinate and exploited position that Southerners occupy within it. While the war has reconfirmed the latter, these relations predate it and will continue even when peace eventually comes. Indeed, as the short discussion of the oil industry in South Sudan illustrates (see Chapter 7), peace will probably accelerate the commercial exploitation of the South by the North. There is nothing on record that suggests this will be a particularly sustainable or equitable developmental process for the Southerners involved. Indeed, given that a whole generation has been lost to education in South Sudan, peace will probably see its incorporation as an annex of cheap labour and resources for Northern-controlled projects and enterprises. In many respects, aid agencies should now be preparing for the complexity of such a peace. Unfortunately, however, given that the failures and difficulties of the past have been lain at the door of conflict, even a violent and contested peace will provide a golden opportunity for the aid industry to reinvent itself once again. It will draw a line under history and write off past policy failure as due to the war. Old staff will be purged and new development expertise drafted in as part of the enthusiasm to carve out fresh mandates and opportunities. UN and NGO bodies will be among those groups that benefit most from peace. Hence the palpable optimism that will surround every act and pronouncement. In terms of what they actually do, however, they will no doubt yet again promote liberal self-management – this time with a sense of renewed hope and vigour, and sporting new labels. That they will fare any better is debatable.

NOTES

1 The minimum and basic food necessary to maintain life.

2 The shift toward goal-oriented or developmental relief has seen a corresponding decline in nutritional assessment exercises.

3 Due to the donor embargo on development assistance, Oxfam has decided to use its own funds for such development purposes.

4 The other member of the team, apart from two Dinka research assistants, was the area specialist John Ryle.

5 At Khor Omer camp, the HAC representative was concerned that the team's Dinka research assistants were talking to camp members out of his earshot. Consequently, the visit was cut short and we were instructed to return to the provincial headquarters. Soon after arrival, the research assistants were taken away for questioning by security people. After we protested, they were eventually returned, minus their notebooks. We were told that they must remain in our custody under house arrest until the end of the visit. Moreover, their safety was in our hands since any contrary actions would place them at serious risk. In the meantime, the HAC representative, for an appropriate financial incentive, would personally accompany us to the other displaced camps in the area for the duration of our visit. Given the situation, apart from securing the safety of the research assistants and lodging a formal complaint in Khartoum, there was little else we could do. This situation is indicative of the oppressive relations in which the displaced within South Darfur find themselves. Moreover, several international NGOs and UN agencies have Northern Sudanese representatives in the town. All knew of this detention and were sympathetic to the plight of our Dinka assistants. None, however, felt it prudent to report the incident to their offices in Khartoum.

6 Regarding remuneration, it is rather bizarre that UNHCU has depicted the very low level of earnings among the Dinka as resulting from their rural background and ignorance of market mechanisms. Sub-survival wages arise from fact that the 'IDPs do not know how to value their own labour' (UNHCU 1999). After a decade in the transitional zone and even longer as migrant labour, one would have thought that they would know by now. The implication is that the Dinka simply have to ask for more to improve their lot.

7 HAC replaced the Relief and Rehabilitation Committee (RRC) in 1996.

8 In Sudan, this has been a recurrent theme of evaluations since relief operations began in the mid-1980s. See de Waal 1988; Cutler and Keen 1989; Duffield et al. 1995; Karim et al. 1996; Buchanan-Smith et al. 1999; Duffield et al. 1989. Indeed, the return of famine conditions to South Sudan in 1998 in the midst of a relief operation says a good deal about the levels of aid being received.

10

Conclusion: Global Governance, Moral Responsibility and Complexity

Internal Displacement and the New Humanitarianism

A hundred years ago the world was poised at the beginning of a new century. Two interconnected developments shaped the years that followed. The nation state reached the apogee of its development, while the twentieth century proved to be the bloodiest and most violent period in world history (Hobsbawm 1994). Today, the nation state is no longer in its ascendancy. Among other things, its power has been reconfigured and transformed through the growing influence of the non-state and non-territorial relations of global liberal governance. Following this change, it is possible that we will not see death and destruction on such a scale again. However, the paradox of the nation state was that the same power that could mobilise societies for total war could also enforce total peace – or, at least, those stages of regulated political competition that we regard as peace. In this respect, for most countries over the past hundred years, periods of peace have outweighed times of conflict. The concern today, however, is that we have entered a new era of war. Organised violence may no longer take the earlier form of short but world-shattering outbursts. While operating at a lower destructive level, it appears to assume more systemic, intrusive and non-controllable forms. From security-conscious airline operators to armed African cattle herders, in different ways the threat or actuality of pervasive violence now affects all of us most of the time. The challenge for global liberal governance is to equal or better the relative security that existed for much of the Cold War when nation states had a greater regulatory influence. Since this ability cannot be taken for granted, it should be a primary concern for everyone.

A cosmopolitan politics?

Globalisation and the increasing depth and complexity of governance relations have given rise to speculation on what formal characteristics,

257

if any, global governance might take (Held, McGrew, Goldblatt and Perraton 1999). Ideas range from the emergence of a transnational civil society (Korten 1990) to a consolidation of a cosmopolitan politics (Kaldor 1999). Such views hold the possibility that global networks linking different local, national and international groups and institutions will come to embody and operationalise humankind's shared values and responsibilities. In the case of cosmopolitan politics, global networks are thought capable, eventually, of assuming the role of an international state, able to re-establish a monopoly of violence and uphold the rule of law to the extent that some nation states now lack this ability. Precursors of transnational or cosmopolitan politics are often seen in the growing influence of international NGOs; the lobbying activity of environmentalist and women's groups; the emergence of international human rights tribunals; or the increasing role of IGOs such as NATO or the Organisation for Security and Cooperation in Europe (OSCE). In this respect, it is argued that a possible new cosmopolitan politics 'based on goals such as peace, human rights or environmentalism, is emerging side by side with the politics of particularism' (ibid.: 139). The role of cosmopolitan politics would be to mobilise the groups and networks that support such values against the proponents of war and violence.

It is possible to interpret the differentiated regional networks of liberal peace analysed in this book as representing a cosmopolitan politics in a state of emergence. The strategic complexes of liberal peace, however, are part of an already existing system of networked global liberal governance. These flexible and mutating systems have been forged in the furnace of practical engagement with the new wars. Moreover, rather than playing a transparent or progressive juridical role, the strategic complexes of actually existing global governance have a more ambiguous function. They are capable, for example, of mobilising public opinion and significant material resources in opposition to violence and human suffering. Yet, as the analysis of network war and the Sudan case study suggest, the same strategic networks can also be implicated in a process of complicity and accommodation. In other words, while opposing the violence and dislocation of the new wars, the strategic complexes of liberal peace also embody the selective, regionalised and conditional relations of global governance that now link North and South. Moreover, unlike cosmopolitan politics that sees itself as upholding international law and common values, liberal governance has a radical mission to transform societies as a whole, including the attitudes and beliefs of the people within them. In other words, while cosmopolitan politics defines itself as an arbiter of universal

258

norms in the process of formation, liberal governance presents itself as an actually existing political project. The tensions between the two would suggest that if a formal cosmopolitan politics has a future, it will be a hard-fought and contested one.

Rediscovering research as a moral force

The merging of development and security has given global liberal governance an expansive and inclusive political logic. Not only has this convergence allowed new interactions and networks to form between a variety of state–non-state, public–private and military–civilian actors, but it has also underpinned new forms of political mobilisation. The reproblematisation of security in terms of underdevelopment becoming dangerous has added urgency and justification to development's new radical agenda of social transformation. A new security framework has emerged in which stability is now regarded as unfeasible without development, while development is non-sustainable without stability. For a number of NGOs, this fusion has led to an uncomfortable realisation. It has become increasingly difficult to separate their traditional non-governmental development and humanitarian activities from the wider aims and implications of this new security framework. At the same time, those who support such agencies or help them achieve their aims are also implicated through this strategic realignment. The merger of development and security has created an inclusive form of political mobilisation. Besides NGOs, it now includes consultants, researchers, private companies, media groups and even members of the supporting public. The political inclusiveness of liberal peace raises many ethical questions and worries. For example, how do aid agencies and concerned individuals chart independent forms of action? In this respect, the very inclusiveness of liberal governance can be interpreted in a different light.

Following the criticism of humanitarian action, Hugo Slim (1998) has argued that the humanitarian prophetic tradition needs revitalising and updating in the changed conditions of the post-Cold War era. In order to do this, Slim suggests a stakeholder analysis of violence. This includes both primary stakeholders – the leaders and followers directly responsible for war – and secondary stakeholders that in various ways maintain it. The latter are comprised of three groups: 'the suppliers, facilitators and cultural sustainers of inhumanity' (*ibid.*: 38). This useful formulation extends the remit of ethics and politics beyond the new humanitarian concerns with the policy choices of aid agencies. Indeed, it embraces the entire transborder system of network war and the various relations of international complicity and accommodation that support it. Market liberalisation, albeit unintentionally, has eased the emergence of trans-border war economies. While commodity chains pass through various levels of legality and illegality, at each stage commercial suppliers, either directly or indirectly, are complicit in the system of violence. The facilitators of violence are those strategic actors in positions of power who either tolerate war by their actions make it easier. This can include the politicians of powerful states and officials of donor organisations as well as those international interests that support the present neoliberal hegemony that has placed markets above morality. In relation to the 'cultural sustainers' of violence, Slim refers to the tendency to inter-nalise and normalise violence in both the North and the South – to accept it as normal for particular peoples or regions, to side with one against the other, and so on. Here one might include the depoliticised and desocialised discourse of aid agencies and NGOs that can actually reinforce subjugation and exploitation.

From the perspective of this analysis, one can reinterpret the relations of global liberal governance and the new wars as a connected system of moral responsibility. While in essence the idea of a shared international responsibility is not new, its restatement in this case is to build on what we know of conflict and the response of the international community to it. The transborder nature of network war, together with the strategic nodes and flows of liberal peace, combine to produce a new and complex development–security terrain. This terrain defines the contours of the shared system of moral responsibility. The role of knowledge and research is to expose the different levels, interconnections and motiva-tions that shape this system. In showing the linkages and how the whole fits together, research becomes a moral force rather than just a means to technical solutions. All too easily, the hunt for prescriptions and policy options can uncritically deepen and extend the power of liberal gover-nance, a system that is very often part of the problem that is being addressed. We must be prepared to stand back and see the system as a whole. In this respect, the aim would be not only to show its intercon-nections but, in so doing, also to make it possible to form coalitions of concerned actors that bridge the networks and systems involved.

There are three main areas where new knowledge, mainly requiring innovative forms of ethnographic study, is required. These are, first, the nature of the political complexes associated with the new wars; second, how such complexes are integrated within the liberal world system; and, finally, the mode of operation of global liberal governance itself. In relation to the political complexes of the new wars, the relationship between leaders and led is of primary importance. Research should aim to uncover the new forms of protection, legitimacy and rights to wealth that actual development has forged. While these systems may be non-liberal, they nonetheless represent real forms of power and authority, and understanding how they work is of vital importance. In this respect, how such complexes are integrated within the liberal world system is crucial to their existence. We need to understand the local–global connections and shadow commodity chains through which populations, regions and markets have been reintegrated into the global economy. Such networks and nodes are multi-layered social and political systems in their own right. Through reconnecting the flows and discursive practices at each level an important aim of such research would be to uncover more effective means of regulation. At the same time, it would seek to re-establish the links between the world's 'rich' and 'poor'. Liberal discourse has largely severed such connections and made them appear as separate acts of nature. This lessens the responsibility that knowledge of their interconnection imparts. Finally, the strategic complexes of liberal governance should, themselves, become an object of study. Such research, however, requires further explanation.

Organisational reform and complexity

As an object of research, the strategic complexes of liberal peace present a dual problem: they are means of mobilisation, justification and reward in the pursuit of stability at the same time as being forms of operational intervention geared to social transformation. This duality encompasses the fundamental contradiction and limitation of liberal power. Its embrace of conflict resolution and societal reconstruction reflects a radical agenda of social transformation. In practice, however, liberal governance must achieve this goal through partnership, agreement and participatory methods. Southern governments and peoples must themselves embrace and carry out this radical agenda. In most cases, the difficulty of achieving this aim internationally has tended to push global governance towards accommodation and complicity with systems that differ violently from itself. This limitation of liberal power in addressing complexity has two main consequences. First, it continually creates pressures to drop its partnership approach and directly impose a radical agenda of social transformation: to change from liberal peace to liberal war. However, given that states increasingly have to act together, apart from a few special cases, securing the political will for such direct action is very difficult to obtain. Consequently, the main effect of the limitations of liberal power is that Northern governments and aid agencies have had to adapt to policy failure. Indeed, they have learnt how to project this reality as success.

In many respects, in studying strategic actors from the point of view of their operational interventions, one is essentially studying organisational adaptation to policy failure. To put this another way, one is examining permanent crisis management and methods of system survival among organisations poorly adapted to complexity. Most donor governments, IGOs and aid agencies, for example, are in agreement that in addressing the new wars they need more detailed and specific forms of political analysis to shape aid policy (OECD 1998). The EU has even suggested that, in creating country strategies, the political analysis undertaken by the embassies of member states should be fed into policy making (EC 1996b). While this seems common sense – good policy can only come from a good understanding – the call for better or more detailed analysis is of limited use in the present situation. Most governments and aid agencies lack the organisational structures to allow them to use such information effectively. ECHO is a good example of this wider problem. Apart from being understaffed, its institutional culture mitigates against an effective use of knowledge and experience in a complex environment. For example, its Brussels-based HQ staff are EU functionaries while its field officers are employed on fixed-term contracts. Under EU regulations, field staff, despite having gathered valuable local experience, cannot be employed in Brussels. At the same time, EU functionaries are periodically moved from section to section. In other words, while the need for more in-depth analysis is acknowledged, ECHO is organised in such a way as to undermine the synergies that this might create.

This problem is not confined to the EU; to varying degrees it characterises most donor governments, foreign ministries, aid agencies and the UN system. It reflects a mode of bureaucratic organisation that emerged in relation to an international state-centred system. It is based on the model of the international civil servant working in a rule-based environment. Because it is a rule-based system – governed by agreements, protocols and defined expectations – international civil servants need not be fully conversant with the countries or sections in which they are working. For example, international functionaries need not know a great deal about agriculture, fisheries or relief work to play the corresponding aid role within a country to which they have only recently been assigned. Indeed, the culture tends to emphasise regular movement between countries, sections and responsibilities. Within a rule-based civil service environment, such variety is counted as valuable experience and has a recognised institutional worth.[1] In relation to complexity, however, rule-based systems depend on predictable outcomes. They are geared to the expectation of steady-state conditions such as 'development' or 'peace' in relation to which agreed measures and packages of assistance stand in a known sequential position: that is, they relate to conditions which are understood as having an end or conclusion. However, steady states exist neither in nature nor in the social world. The new wars and the political complexity associated with them have radically challenged this bureaucratic mode of organisation and its related expectations of order. Rule-based organisations have been transformed into systems of crisis management as environments have become less predictable and more chaotic. The present consensus concerning the need for more in-depth country analysis, new measures and greater policy coherence is symptomatic of this crisis.

Despite the move from statist relations of government to those of networked governance, organisational culture has yet to undergo a corresponding process of systemic reform. While falling short of radical change, donor organisations and aid agencies have nevertheless responded to the mismatch between complexity and existing institutional cultures in a number of ways. Some, for example, have employed social advisers to supply appropriate advice. More generally, there has been a huge expansion in the employment of consultant specialists as a quick means of obtaining the information that organisations no longer appear able to produce for themselves. In many respects, however, this has not proved to be a particularly satisfactory response to a changing and mutating environment. Among other things, social advisers and consultants have often been placed in the role of interpreting and, especially, summarising complex problems. Indeed, the claim is often made that unless reports are succinct and easily accessible, busy policy makers will not read them. This creates a situation where, on the one hand, a consensus exists that more in-depth analysis is needed yet, on the other, unless information is pared down to basic essentials, functionaries are unable to absorb it. Under such pressures, demands have grown for summary 'good practice' manuals and guides. While promising to show 'what works' or provide checklists of essential things to do, these guides reproduce the illusion of a replicable and predictable environment. Indeed, they usually reflect a mechanical or Newtonian understanding of the impact of aid on recipient organisations and groups.

Adapting to policy failure also involves turning organisational weaknesses into strengths in terms of allowing adjustments to take place that would not otherwise be possible. The representation of the nature and effects of war in such a way as to allow the reinvention of development as conflict resolution, together with the periodic repackaging of development's basic liberal self-management model, has already been discussed. The organisational weaknesses upon which such reinvention depends are the same failures in information flow and institutional memory discussed above. Within aid agencies, for example, the reinvention of basic development models cannot be understood apart from the high levels of staff turnover and associated limited institutional memory. This is not to suggest that an organised conspiracy exists (most institutions would not be able to orchestrate such a thing even if they wished). Reinvention occurs because it satisfies sufficient organisational needs to make it a system probability. It gives agency managers the appearance of innovation and the acceptance of new challenges. To junior staff anxious to build careers on the basis of fixed-term contracts, periodic repackaging allows the possibility of direct involvement. In such an environment, a lack of institutional memory coupled with multi-levelled information discontinuities can be a positive benefit.

In studying the strategic complexes of liberal governance from the perspective of policy failure, a key issue is how, exactly, policy is formed. One thing is sure: despite the technical presumptions of development discourse, the North does not relate to the South as if the latter were a scientific laboratory. Policy is not formed through a positivist and incremental process of learning. Rather than a laboratory, the South is better described as a mirror that reflects policy decisions and aid fashions that have been formulated elsewhere. The idea of policy as politics gives one an indication of how policy creation can be analysed – as a form of stakeholder exercise. In order to emerge, policies have to have the support of strong groups and interests within institutions: leadership figures and entrepreneurs who can initiate policy and forge the wider coalitions necessary for their chosen line to gain acceptance. Policy formation involves political rivalry and alliance not only within institutions but between them as well. Uncovering this process would require innovative forms of ethnographic analysis. It would also suggest that addressing policy failure is more complex than finding a better way of doing things. Not only are many organisations culturally maladjusted to complexity, as the recent failure to significantly reform the UN would suggest, but this maladjustment is actively maintained by powerful groups and networks. Indeed, successful careers are often built out of the innovative reworking of failure.

Rather than searching for better policy or commissioning more detailed forms of analysis, the real task is reforming the institutions and networks of global governance to address complexity. Without reform, policy failure and the associated pressure to turn liberal peace into liberal war will continue to shape the international scene. Reform would require turning rule-based bureaucracies into adaptive, learning and networked organisations. This would have major implications for human resource management, career structures and staff development. It would also attract the resistance of entrenched interests and many established policy entrepreneurs. Without a radical reform of institutional culture, however, it is difficult to see global liberal governance delivering the relative security of the past. In order to encourage this process, the rediscovery of research and knowledge as a moral and connecting force has a vital role to play.

NOTE

1   International NGOs have a similar but different problem. Home country headquarters are usually relatively small compared to the numbers employed overseas. Headquarters staff are usually permanent and, while they often stay for long periods within specific sections, their position is highlighted by the large number of staff employed abroad on fixed-term contracts, often for only one or two years. This results in a continual churning of field staff.

Bibliography

Abd-el-Gadir, Mohamed Al-Amin. Proposal for South Darfur Pilot Resettlement Scheme. Khartoum: Save the Children Fund UK; 1999 February.

ActionAid. Understanding Conflict: A Report from an ActionAid Workshop. Jinja, Uganda: ActionAid; 1994 July 17–23.

Adams, Nassau A. Worlds Apart: The North–South Divide and the International System. London: Zed Books; 1993.

Adelman, Howard, Suhrke, Astri and Jones, Bruce. The International Response to Conflict and Genocide: Lessons from the Rwanda Experience. Early Warning and Conflict Management: Study 2. Copenhagen: Steering Committee of the Joint Evaluation of Emergency Assistance to Rwanda; 1996 March.

Africa Confidential. Angola: The Worst War in the World. Africa Confidential. 1993 August 27.

Africa Watch. 'Denying the Honour of Living'…. Sudan: A Human Rights Disaster. New York: Africa Watch; 1990.

African Rights. Rwanda: Death, Despair and Defiance. London: African Rights; 1995.

——. Sudan's Invisible Citizens: The Policy of Abuse Against Displaced People in the North. London: African Rights; 1995 February.

——. Food and Power in Sudan. London: African Rights; 1997 May.

Anderson, M. B. and Woodrow, P. J. Rising From the Ashes: Disaster Response Toward Development. Bolder: Westview; 1989.

Anderson, Mary B. Do No Harm: Supporting Local Capacities for Peace through Aid. Cambridge, MA: Local Capacities for Peace Project, The Collaborative for Development Action, Inc.; 1996.

Annan, Kofi. The Causes of Conflict and the Promotion of Durable Peace and Sustainable Development in Africa. New York: United Nations; 1998.

Arrighi, G. World Income Inequalities and the Future of Socialism. New Left Review. 1991(189): 39–65.

Atkinson, Dan. Laundered in Britain. The Guardian. 1999 September 3: 18.

Atkinson, Philippa. The War Economy in Liberia: A Political Analysis. Relief and Rehabilitation Network Paper 22. London: Overseas Development Institute; 1997 May.

——. ActionAid Submission on British Government Policy in Sierra Leone. London: ActionAid; 1998 March.

Atwood, Brian, Administrator (USAID). Remarks of J. Brian Atwood. Conflict Prevention in Today's World. Washington DC: Georgetown University; 1998 October 14.

266

Bahro, Rudolf. The Alternative in Eastern Europe. London: Verso; 1978.

Barker, Martin. The New Racism. London: Junction Books; 1982.

Bayart, Jean-François, Ellis, Stephen and Hibou, Béatrice. The Criminalization of the State in Africa. Oxford and Bloomington: The International Africa Institute in Association with James Currey and Indiana University Press; 1999.

Bazargan, Darius. High-Risk Business. G2 (The Guardian Supplement). 1997 September 8: 2–3.

Bellos, Alex. Somali Business Echoes the Boom of Rival Gunfire. The Guardian. 1997 June 20: 20.

Berg, E. J. Backward Sloping Labour Supply Functions in Dual Economies: The African Case. Quarterly Journal of Economics. 1961; 75:469–92.

Blair, Tony. A New Generation Draws the Line. Newsweek. 1999 April 19; CXXXIII (16):41.

Bojicic, Vesna, Kaldor, Mary, and Vejvoda, Ivan. Post-War Reconstruction in the Balkans: A Background Report Prepared for the European Commission. Sussex European Institute Working Paper No. 14. Sussex University: European Institute; 1995.

Borger, Julian. Albania Racked by Regrets. The Guardian. 1997 April 26: 13.

Boutros-Ghali, Boutros. An Agenda for Peace. New York: United Nations; 1995 (original 1992).

Bradbury, Mark. A Review of OXFAM (UK and Ireland) Somalia Programme: 1995–7. Oxford: OXFAM; 1997 May.

—. Normalising the Crisis in Africa. Disasters. 1998; 22(4):328–38.

Brittain, Victoria. UN Gets Tough With Unita. The Guardian. 1999 July 9: 14.

Brown, R. P. C. Public Debt and Private Wealth: Debt, Capital Flight and the IMF in Sudan. London: Macmillan; 1992.

Brown, William. Prospects for Integration with Europe. New Political Economy. 1997; 2(2):333–6.

Brusset, Emery. Sudan's Foreign Policy Environment: Some Implications for Humanitarian Assistance. In: Leone, Geoff and Schümer, Tanja, eds. The Wider Impact of Humanitarian Aid: The Case of Sudan and the Implications for European Union Policy. Baden-Baden: Nomos Verlagsgesellschaft; 2000; pp. 131–60.

Buchanan-Smith, Margaret, Collins, Steve, Dammers, Christopher amd Wekesa, Fred. Evaluation of Danish Humanitarian Assistance to Sudan: 1992–1998. London: Overseas Development Institute; 1999 July.

Buchanan-Smith, Margaret and Maxwell, Simon. Linking Relief and Development: An Introduction and Overview. Institute of Development Studies Bulletin: Special Issue on Linking Relief and Development. 1994 October; 25(4):2–16.

Campbell, David. National Deconstruction: Violence, Identity, and Justice in Bosnia. Minneapolis: University of Minnesota Press; 1998.

Capra, Fritjof. The Turning Point: Science, Society and the Rising Culture. London: Wildwood House; 1982.

CARE. CARE Sudan Strategy Paper for Emergency Plus Project in Kordofan State: September 1998. Khartoum; 1998 September.

Carnegie Commission. Executive Summary of the Final Report. Preventing Deadly Conflict: Executive Summary of the Final Report. Washington DC: Carnegie Commission on Preventing Deadly Conflict; 1997.

Castells, Manuel. The Rise of the Network Society (Vol. 1 of The Information Age: Economy, Society and Culture). Massachusetts and Oxford: Blackwell; 1996.

—. The Power of Identity. Massachusetts and Oxford: Blackwell; 1997.

—. End of Millennium. Oxford: Blackwell; 1998.

Cerny, Philip G. Neomedievalism, Civil War and the New Security Dilemma: Globalisation as Durable Disorder. Civil Wars. 1998 Spring; 1(1):36–64.

Chambers, Robert. Rural Development: Putting the Last First. Essex: Longman; 1983.

Chandler, Dave. The Role of International Institutions in the Democratisation Process: The Case Study of Bosnia-Herzegovina Post-Dayton. Paper presented at 2nd Convention of the European Association for the Advancement of Social Sciences: Conflict and Cooperation. Nicosia, Cyprus: University of Cyprus; 1997 March 19–23.

Chingono, Mark. War, Economic Change and Development in Mozambique, Paper presented at Workshop on Economic and Social Consequences of Conflict. Oxford: Queen Elizabeth House; 1998 Oct. 23–24.

Chomsky, Noam. The New Military Humanism: Lessons from Kosovo. London: Pluto Press; 1999.

Cilliers, Jakkie and Cornwell, Richard. Africa – From the Privatisation of Security to the Privatisation of War? In: Cilliers, Jakkie and Mason, Peggy, eds. Peace, Profit or Plunder? The Privatisation of Security in War-Torn Africa. South Africa: The Institute for Security Studies; 1999; pp. 227–45.

Cilliers, Jakkie and Douglas, Ian. The Military as Business – Military Professional Resources, Incorporated. In: Cilliers, Jakkie and Mason, Peggy, eds. Peace, Profit or Plunder? The Privatisation of Security in War-Torn Africa. South Africa: The Institute for Security Studies; 1999; pp. 111–22.

Clark, J. Democratizing Development: The Role of Voluntary Organizations. London: Earthscan Publications; 1991.

Collier, Paul (World Bank). Doing Well Out of War. Paper presented at Conference on Economic Agendas in Civil Wars. London; 1999 April 26–27.

Collier, Paul and Hoeffler, Anke (The World Bank and CSAE, Oxford). Justice-Seeking and Loot-Seeking in Civil War. Paper presented at Conference on Civil Conflict, Crime and Violence. Washington DC: World Bank; 1999 February.

Cook, Robin. It is Fascism That We Are Fighting. The Guardian. 1999 May 5: 20.

Cornia, Giovanni Andrea. Economic Decline and Human Welfare in the First Half of the 1980s. In: Cornia, G. A.; Jolly, R., and Stewart, F., eds. Adjustment With a Human Face: Vol. 1. Oxford: Clarendon Press; 1987; pp. 11–47.

Cottey, Andrew. The Pursuit of Peace: A Framework for International Action. Bristol: Saferworld; 1994 September.

Cox, Robert W. Critical Political Economy. In: Hettne, Bjorn, ed. International Political Economy: Understanding Global Disorder. London: Zed Books; 1995; pp. 31–45.

Crawford, Barry. Holy War on Islam. Living Marxism. 1994 March; 24–26.

CRG. No Hiding Place: Business and the Politics of Pressure. London: Control Risks Group; 1997.

Cutler, Peter and Keen, David. Evaluation of the EEC Emergency, Rehabilitation and Food Aid to Sudan: 1985–88. Brighton, University of Sussex: Institute of Development Studies; 1989 January.

Cutts, Mark. Politics and Humanitarianism. Refugee Survey Quarterly. 1998; 17(1):1–15.

DAC. DAC Guidelines on Conflict, Peace and Development Cooperation. Paris: Development Assistance Committee, Organisation for Economic Cooperation and Development (OECD); 1997.

—. Policy Statement. Conflict, Peace and Development Cooperation on the Threshold of the 21st Century. Paris: Development Assistance Committee, Organisation for Economic Cooperation and Development (OECD); 1997 May.

DAG. Evaluation of DFID Support to Poverty Reduction: Draft Working Paper 2 – Development of a Poverty Perspective. Development Administration Group, University of Birmingham; Institute of Development Policy and Management, University of Manchester; Centre of Development Studies, University of Wales; Oxfam; 1998 September.

de Vletter, Fion, Study on the Informal Sector in Mozambique (Maputo and Sofala).

Maputo: Poverty Alleviation Unit, Ministry of Finance and Planning; 1996 May.

de Waal, Alex. Famine Crimes: Politics and the Disaster Relief Industry. London: African Rights and the International Africa Institute with James Currey; 1997.

de Waal, Alex. Is Famine Relief Irrelevant to Rural People? IDS Bulletin. 1998; 20 (2): 63–69.

Deacon, Bob and others. Global Social Policy: International Organisations and the Future of Welfare. London: Sage Publications; 1997.

Deibert, Ronald J. 'Exorcisms Theoriae': Pragmatism, Metaphors and the Return of the Medieval in IR Theory. European Journal of International Relations. 1997; 3(2):167–92.

Deichmann, Thomas. The Picture That Fooled the World. Living Marxism. 1997 February; 24–33.

Demirovic, Alex. NGOs: Social Movements in Global Order? Paper presented at American Sociological Association Conference. New York; 1996.

Derlugian, Georgi M. The Social Cohesion of the States. In: Hopkins, Terence K. and Wallerstein, Immanuel, eds. The Age of Transition: Trajectory of the World-System, 1945–2025. London: Zed Books ; 1996; pp. 148–77.

DFID. White Paper on International Development. Eliminating World Poverty: A Challenge for the 21st Century. London: Department for International Development; 1997 November.

——. PEC Submission 98 (6): Mozambique – Zambezia Agricultural Development Project (ZADP Phase 2). London: Department for International Development; 1998 January.

Dillon, Michael. Post-Structuralism, Complexity and Poetics. Forthcoming in Theory, Culture and Society. 2000 December.

Dillon, Michael and Reid, Julian. Global Governance, Liberal Peace and Complex Emergency. Draft. Alternatives. 2000 March.

Dodd, Tom and Welten, Johan, Sudan Desk Officer and Acting Head of Delegation (ECHO and EC Delegation). Mission Report: Ed Daien – 22 September 1998. Khartoum: EC Delegation; 1998 September.

Dogan, Rhys and Pugh, Michael. From Military to Market Imperatives: Peacekeeping and the New Public Policy. Plymouth International Papers (PIP) No. 8. University of Plymouth: International Studies Centre; 1997 July; pp. 1–32.

Donini, A. Beyond Neutrality: On the Compatibility of Military Intervention and Humanitarian Assistance. The Fletcher Forum. 1995:31–45.

Donini, Antonio. The Policies of Mercy: UN Coordination in Afghanistan, Mozambique, and Rwanda. Occasional Paper No. 2. Providence, RI: Thomas J. Watson Jr. Institute for International Studies; 1996.

Duffield, Mark. Maiurno: Capitalism and Rural Life in Sudan. London: Ithaca Press; 1981.

——. Underdevelopment and the International Movement of Labour. Annali Del Dipartimento Di Scienze Storiche E Sociali (University of Lecce, Italy). 1982(1):461–90.

——. War and Famine in Africa. Oxfam Research Paper No. 5. Oxford: Oxfam Publications; 1991.

——. The Emergence of Two-Tier Welfare in Africa: Marginalization or an Opportunity for Reform? Public Administration and Development. 1992; 12:139–54.

——. The Political Economy of Internal War. In: Macrae, Joanna and Zwi, Anthony, eds. War and Hunger: Rethinking International Responses to Complex Emergencies. London: Zed Press; 1994a; pp. 50–69.

——. Complex Political Emergencies: An Exploratory Report for UNICEF With Reference to Angola and Bosnia. Birmingham: School of Public Policy; 1994b March.

——. Complex Emergencies and the Crisis of Developmentalism. Institute of Development Studies Bulletin: Linking Relief and Development. 1994c October; 25:37–45.
——. Symphony of the Damned: Racial Discourse, Complex Political Emergencies and Humanitarian Aid. Disasters. 1996 September; 20(3):173–93.
——. NGO Relief in War Zones: Toward an Analysis of the New Aid Paradigm. Third World Quarterly. 1997; 18(3):527–42.
——. Post-Modern Conflict: Warlords, Post-Adjustment States and Private Protection. Civil Wars. 1998 Spring; 1(1):65–102.
——. Globalisation and War Economies: Promoting Order or the Return of History? Feltcher Forum of World Affairs. 1999 Fall; 23(2):21–38.
——. Humanitarian Conditionality: Origins, Consequences and Implications of the Pursuit of Development in Conflict. In Leone, Geoff and Schümer, Tanja, eds. The Wider Impacts of Humanitarian Assistance: The Case of Sudan and the Implications for European Union Policy. Baden-Baden: Nomos Verlagsgesellschaft for the Conflict Prevention Network (SWP– CPN); 2000; pp. 97–130.
Duffield, Mark; Jok, Madut Jok; O'Reilly, Fionna; Ryle, John and Winter, Philip. Sudan: The Unintended Consequences of Humanitarian Assistance – A Report of the European Commission Humanitarian Office (ECHO). Dublin: Trinity College; 1999 November.
Duffield, Mark and Prendergast, John. Without Troops or Tanks: Humanitarian Intervention in Eritrea and Ethiopia. Trenton, NJ: Africa World Press Inc/Red Sea Press Inc; 1994.
Duffield, Mark, Young, Helen, Ryle, John and Henderson, Ian. Sudan Emergency Operations Consortium (SEOC): A Review. Birmingham: School of Public Policy; 1995 February.
EC. Council Conclusion on Preventive Diplomacy, Conflict and Peacekeeping in Africa. Brussels: European Commission; 1995 December 4.
——. Communication from the Commission to the Council. The European Union and the Issue of Conflicts in Africa: Peace-Building, Conflict Prevention and Beyond. Brussels: European Commission; 1996a March 6.
——. Communication from the Commission to the Council and the European Parliament on Linking, Relief, Rehabilitation and Development (LRRD). Brussels: Commission of the European Communities; 1996b April 30.
——. Council Regulation of (EC) No. 1257/96 of 20 June 1996 Concerning Humanitarian Aid. Official Journal of the European Communities: L 163. 1996c July 2; 391–6.
——. Framework Partnership Contract. Brussels: European Community; 1998a February 11.
——. Emergency Plus Strategy. Khartoum; 1998b October.
——. Cooperation With ACP Countries Involved in Armed Conflicts. Brussels: European Commission; 1998c December 5.
ECHO. ECHO Funding Proposal for Humanitarian Operations in Sudan and Northern Uganda: June 1996–March 1997. Brussels: European Commission Humanitarian Office; 1996 April.
——. ECHO Strategy 1997: Working Paper. Brussels: European Commission Humanitarian Office; 1997a February 24.
——. ECHO Global Plan for Sudan, April 1997–March 1998. Brussels: European Commission Humanitarian Office; 1997b February 27.
——. ECHO Global Plan for Sudan, April 1999–March 2000. Brussels: European Commission Humanitarian Office; 1999 February.
Edkins, Jenny. Legality With a Vengeance: Famines and Humanitarian Relief in 'Complex Emergencies'. Millennium. 1996 Winter; 25(3):547–76.
Edwards, Michael and Hulme, David, eds. NGO Performance and Accountability:

270

Beyond the Magic Bullet. London and West Hartford: Earthscan and Kumarian Press; 1995.

el Amin, Khalid A. En Nahud Camp Southern War Displaced Residents' Future. In CARE Intervention: From Relief to Self-Reliance, Prospects and Options. Khartoum: CARE-Sudan; 1998 December.

Ellis, Stephen. Liberia 1989–1994: A Study of Ethnic and Spiritual Violence. African Affairs. 1995(94):165–97.

——. Analysing Africa's Wars. Anthropology in Action. 1996 Winter; 3(3):18–21.

Emmanuel, A. Unequal Exchange. London: New Left Books; 1972.

Escobar, Arturo. Encountering Development: The Making and Unmaking of the Third World. New Jersey: Princeton University Press; 1995.

EU. Communication on the European Union and the Issue of Conflicts in Africa: Peacebuilding, Conflict Prevention and Beyond. Brussels: European Commission; 1996 May.

Fagen, Patrica Weiss. After the Conflict: A Review of Selected Sources on Rebuilding War-Torn Societies. War-Torn Societies Project, Occasional Paper No. 1. Geneva: War-Torn Societies Project; 1995 November.

Farrelly, Paul. The Rape of Russia – Elite's Underworld Links Exposed. The Observer. 1999 September 5: 24.

Field, Shannon. The Pivotal Role of Oil in Sudan's Civil War. Sudan Democratic Gazette. 1999 November; X(114):10–11.

Forberg, Ekkehard and Terlinden, Ulf. Small Arms in Somaliland: Their Role and Diffusion. Berlin: Berlin Information Centre for Transatlantic Security (BITS); 1999 March.

Fox, Fionna. The Politicisation of Humanitarian Aid: A Discussion Paper for Caritas Europa – November 1999. London: CAFOD; 1999 November.

Frank, A. F. Sociology of Development and the Underdevelopment of Sociology. Catalyst. 1967(3):20–73.

Freedman, Lawrence. Bosnia: Does Peace Support Make Any Sense? Nato Review. 1995 November; 43(6):19–23.

Friedman, Jordana D. The Corporate Sector and Conflict Protection: A Research Study. London: International Alert, The Prince of Wales Business Leaders Forum, Council on Economic Priorities; 1998 October 27.

Furedi, Frank. The New Ideology of Imperialism. London: Junius Publications Ltd; 1994.

Gasper, Des. Ethics and the Conduct of International Development Aid: Charity and Obligation. Forum for Development Studies. 1999; (No. 1):23–58.

Geldof, Bob. Sayings of the Week. The Observer. 1985 October 27.

Gellner, Ernest. Trust, Cohesion and Social Order. In: Gambetta, D, ed. Trust: Making and Breaking Cooperative Relations. Oxford: Basil Blackwell; 1998.

George, S. The Debt Boomerang: How Third World Debt Harms Us All. London: Pluto Press; 1992.

Global Witness. A Rough Trade: The Role of Companies and Governments in the Angolan Conflict. London: Global Witness Ltd; 1998 December.

Goldberg, Jeffrey. Our Africa Problem. The New York Times Magazine. 1997 March 2; 34–9, 59–62, 75–6.

Goodhand, Jonathan. From Holy War to Opium War? A Case Study of the Opium Economy in North Eastern Afghanistan. University of Manchester: IDPM; 1999 October.

Gostelow, Lola. The Sphere Project: The Implications of Making Humanitarian Principles and Codes Work. Disasters. 1999; 23(4):316–25.

Goulding, M. The Evolution of United Nations Peacekeeping. International Affairs. 1993 July; 69(3):451–64.

Graham, R. and Borton, J. A Preliminary Review of the Combined Agencies Relief Team (CART), Juba 1986–91. London: Overseas Development Institute; 1992 March.

Gray, John. False Dawn: The Delusions of Global Capitalism. London: Granta Books; 1998.

Griffin, K. Foreign Aid after the Cold War. Development and Change. 1991; 22:645–85.

Griffiths, Hugh. The Political Economy of Ethnic Conflict: Ethno-Nationalism and Organised Crime. Unpublished manuscript. 1998.

Grunewald, Francois and de Geoffrey, Veronique. Kosovo: Drawing the Lessons from a Disaster. RRN Newsletter No. 15. London: Overseas Development Institute; 1999 November; pp. 3–4.

Guerra, Stefano. The Multi-Faceted Role of the ODIHR. OSCE ODIHR Bulletin. 1996 Spring; 4(2):10–20.

Gundel, Joakim. Humanitarian Assistance : Breaking the Waves of Complex Political Emergencies – A Literature Survey. CDR Working Paper, No. 99.5. Copenhagen: Centre for Development Research; 1999 August.

Hammock, John. When Giving Aid Means Giving Your Life. Boston Sunday Globe. 1999 July 11: D1.

Harding, Jeremy. The Mellow Mercenaries. The Guardian Weekend. 1997 March 8: 32–4, 37.

Harris, N. The End of the Third World. Harmondsworth: Penguin; 1987.

Held, David, Goldblatt, David, McGrew, Anthony and Perraton, Jonathan. The Globalization of Economic Activity. New Political Economy. 1997 July; 2 (2): 257–77.

Held, David, McGrew, Anthony, Goldblatt, David, and Perraton, Jonathan. Global Transformations: Politics, Economics and Culture. Cambridge: Polity Press; 1999.

Herbst, Jeff. The Regulation of Private Security Forces. In: Gregg Mills and John Stremlau, eds. The Privatisation of Security in Africa. Johannesburg: The South African Institute of International Affairs; 1999; pp. 107–28.

Higgins, R. The New United Nations and the Former Yugoslavia. International Affairs. 1993 July; 69(3):465–83.

Hilsum, Lindsey. In the Land of the Lion King. The Times Literary Supplement. 1997 May 23: 9.

Hirst, Paul and Thompson, Grahame. Globalisation in Question. Cambridge: Polity Press; 1996.

Hobsbawm, Eric. The Age of Extremes: The Short Twentieth Century. London. Michael Joseph; 1994.

Honisbaum, Mark and Barnett, Anthony. British Firms in African Arms Riddle. The Observer. 1999 January 31: 9.

Hoogvelt, Ankie. Globalization and the Postcolonial World. Baltimore, Maryland: Johns Hopkins University Press; 1997.

Hopkins, Terence K. and Wallerstein, Immanuel, eds. The Age of Transition: Trajectory of the World-System – 1945–2025. London: Zed Books; 1996.

Howell, P. P. Notes on the Ngrok Dinka. Sudan Notes and Records. 1951; 32(2):239–93.

HRW. Sudan: Global Trade, Local Impact – Arms Transfers to all Sides in the Civil War in Sudan. New York: Human Rights Watch; 1998 August.

Hulme, David and Edwards, Michael, eds. NGOs, States and Donors: Too Close for Comfort? Houndmills, Basingstoke and London: Macmillan Press Ltd; 1997.

Humphrey, Caroline. Icebergs, Barter and the Mafia in Provincial Russia. Anthropology Today. 1991; 7: 8–13.

Huntington, Samuel P. The Clash of Civilizations and the Remaking of World Order. New York: Simon and Schuster; 1997.

Hurd, D. Extract From Travellers Club Speech. The Guardian 2. 1993 September 17: 3.

Hutchinson, S. Imagined Administration: SPLA Civil Policy in Western Nuerland. Talk given at. Workshop on the Sudanese Civil War, Part 1: The War in the South; St Anthony's College, University of Oxford. 1992 December 5.

ICRC. Arms Availability and the Situation of Civilians in Armed Conflict. Geneva: International Committee of the Red Cross; 1999 June.

IDC. Sixth Report. Conflict Prevention and Post-Conflict Reconstruction, Vol. I, Report and Proceeding to the Committee. London, The Stationery Office: International Development Committee; 1999 July 28.

IFRCS. World Disaster Report: 1996. Oxford: Oxford University Press for International Federation of Red Cross and Red Crescent Societies; 1996.

International Alert. Memorandum from International Alert: 6 March 1998. Sixth Report of the International Development Committee. Conflict Prevention and Post-Conflict Reconstruction, Vol. II, Minutes of Evidence and Appendices. London: The Stationery Office; 1999 July 28; pp. 73–9.

Iveković, Ivan. Modern Authoritarian Ethnocracy: Balkanisation and the Political Economy of International Relations. In: Schierup, Carl-Ulrik, ed. Scramble for the Balkans: Nationalism, Globalism and the Political Economy of Reconstruction. London: Macmillan Press Ltd; 1999; pp. 62–91.

Jacoby, Jeff. Putin's Cruel War is Fuelled by US Dollars. Boston Globe. 1999 October 28.

Jamal, A. Funding Fundamentalism: The Political Economy of an Islamist State. Middle East Report. 1991 September–1991 October 31; 21(172):14–17, 38.

Jaspars, Susan, WFP Consultant. Targeting and Distribution of Food Aid in SPLM Controlled Areas of South Sudan. 1999 January 13.

Johnson, Douglas H. The Sudan Conflict: Historical and Political Background. In: Leone, Geoff and Schümer, Tanja, eds. The Wider Impact of Humanitarian Assistance. Baden-Baden: Nomos Verlagsgesellschaft; 2000; p. 4569.

Kaldor, Mary. New and Old Wars: Organised Violence in a Global Era. Cambridge: Polity Press; 1999.

Kaplan, Robert D. Balkan Ghosts: A Journey through History. London: Macmillan; 1993.

——. The Coming Anarchy: How Scarcity, Crime, Overpopulation, and Disease are Rapidly Destroying the Social Fabric of Our Planet. Atlantic Monthly. 1994 February: 44–76.

Karim, Ataul, Duffield, Mark, Jaspars, Susanne, Benini, Aldo, Macrae, Joanna, Bradbury, Mark, Johnson, Douglas and Larbi, George. Operation Lifeline Sudan (OLS): A Review. Geneva: Department of Humanitarian Affairs; 1996 July.

Keen, David. A Disaster for Whom?: Local Interests and International Donors During Famine among the Dinka of Sudan. Disasters. 1991; 15(2):58–73.

——. The Benefits of Famine: A Political Economy of Famine and Relief in Southwestern Sudan, 1983–1989. Princeton NJ: Princeton University Press; 1994.

——. The Economic Functions of Violence in Civil Wars. Adelphi Paper 320. London: International Institute of Strategic Studies; 1998 June; pp. 1–88.

Kennan, F., ed. Introduction: The Balkan Crisis 1913 to 1939. In: The Other Balkan Wars. Washington DC: Carnegie Endowment; 1993.

Kennedy, Paul. Preparing for the Twenty-First Century. New York: Random House; 1993.

Korten, David. Getting to the 21st Century: Voluntary Action and the Global Agenda. Connecticut: Kumarian Press; 1990.

Laclau, E. Feudalism and Capitalism in Latin America. New Left Review. 1971; (67):19–38.

Lautze, Sue, Jones, Bruce and Duffield, Mark. Strategic Humanitarian Co-ordination in the Great Lakes Region, 1996–1997. New York: UN Office for the Coordination of Humanitarian Assistance (OCHA); 1998 March.

Le Billon, Philippe. A Land Cursed by Its Wealth? Angola's War Economy (1975–1999). Helsinki: UNU/WIDER; 1999 November.

——. The Political Ecology of Transition in Cambodia 1989–1999: War, Peace and Forestry Exploitation. Development and Change. 2000.

Leader, Nicholas. Humanitarian Principles in Practice: A Critical Review. Relief and Rehabilitation Network (RRN) Discussion Paper. London: Overseas Development Institute; 1999 December.

Levine, Iain. Promoting Humanitarian Principles: The South Sudan Experience. Relief and Rehabilitation Network (RRN), Network Paper: 21. London: Overseas Development Institute; 1997 May; pp. 1–31.

Lieven, Anatol. Chechnya: Tombstone of Russian Power. New Haven and London: Yale University Press; 1998.

Loveless, Jeremy. Displaced Populations in Khartoum: A Study of Social and Economic Conditions. Save the Children (Denmark); 1999.

Macrae, Joanna. The Death of Humanitarianism? An Anatomy of the Attack. Disasters. 1998; 22(4):309–17.

Macrae, Joanna and Bradbury, Mark. Aid in the Twilight Zone: A Critical Analysis of UNICEF's Work in Chronically Unstable Situations. New York and London: UNICEF/Overseas Development Institute and the Humanitarianism and War Project; 1998 February.

Macrae, Joanna, Bradbury, Mark, Jaspars, Susanne, Johnson, Douglas and Duffield, Mark. Conflict, the Continuum and Chronic Emergencies: A Critical Analysis of the Scope for Linking Relief, Rehabilitation and Development Planning in Sudan. Disasters. 1997 September; 21(3):223–43.

Magnusson, Kjell, Bular, Nenad and Strelov, Damir. Attitudes and Values of Citizens in the Federation of Bosnia and Herzegovina: A Sociological Survey on the Eve of the Elections 1996. Split: Public Opinion, Market and Media Research (Split) and the Centre for Research in International Migration and Ethnic Relations, University of Stockholm; 1996 August 7.

Maltsev, Yuri N. Why Russia Is Destroying Chechnya. Moscow: The Mises Institute; 1999 October 1.

Malwal, Bonar. Regime Dissolves Khatmiya Religious Sect. Sudan Democratic Gazette. (29):6.

Martinson, Jane. US Unveils Plans for Crackdown on Global Money Laundering. The Guardian. 1999 September 24: 15.

Masefield, Abi and Harvey, Paul. Rehabilitation: An Annotated Bibliography for the CARE, Rehabilitation, and the Greater Horn Project. Brighton: Institute of Development Studies, University of Sussex; 1997 March.

May, R. Political Authority in Chad: The Relevance of the 'Warlord' Model. Presented at. African Studies Association of the United Kingdom; University of Birmingham. 1985 May 24.

Meagher, Kate. The Hidden Economy: Informal and Parallel Trade in Northwestern Uganda. Review of African Political Economy. 1990 Spring(47):64–83.

——. Informal Integration or Economic Subversion? Parallel Trade in West Africa. In: Lavergne, Real, ed. Regional Integration and Cooperation in West Africa. Trenton NJ: Africa World Press, Inc. with International Development Research Centre, Ottawa; 1997; pp. 165–87.

——. Synthesis Paper. A Back Door to Globalisation? Structural Adjustment, Globalisation and Transborder Trade in West Africa. University of Oxford: Nuffield College; 1998 December.

Meek, James. Iranian Pipelines Mock Blockade. The Guardian. 1998 February 3: 14.

MFA. Preventing Violent Conflict: A Study – Executive Summary and Recommendations. Stockholm, Sweden: Ministry for Foreign Affairs; 1997.

Mills, Gregg and Stremlau, John, eds. The Privatisation of Security in Africa. Johannesburg: The South African Institute of International Affairs; 1999.

Mitchell, John and Doane, Deborah. An Ombudsman for Humanitarian Assistance? Disasters. 1999; 23(2):115–24.

Moore, David. 'Sail on Ship of State': Neo-Liberalism, Globalisation and the Governance of Africa. Journal of Peasant Studies. 1999 October; 27(1):61–96.

Morales, R. and Quandt, C. The New Regionalism: Developing Countries and Regional Collaborative Competition. International Journal of Urban and Regional Research. 1992; 16(3):462–75.

Morss, E. R. The New Global Players: How They Compete and Collaborate. World Development. 1991; 19(1):55–64.

MPPA. Mozambique Participatory Poverty Assessment: Phase 1 Rural Summary. 1996 June 7.

Nafziger, Wayne E. and Auvinen, Juha. War, Hunger, and Displacement: An Econometric Investigation Into the Sources of Humanitarian Emergencies. Helsinki: UNU/WIDER; 1997 September.

Nordstrom, Carolyn. Out of the Shadows. In: Callaghy, Thomas, Kassimir, Ronald and Latham, Robert, eds. Authority and Intervention in Africa. Cambridge: Cambridge University Press; 2001.

O'Brien, Paul. Sudan Case Study for CARE International. Kampala: Human Rights and Humanitarian Principles; 1998 December.

ODA. News Release. Immediate Help for Disaster Victims. London: Overseas Development Administration; 1991 August 14.

—. Conflict Reduction through the Aid Programme: A Briefing for Agencies Seeking Support for Conflict Reduction Activities. London: Overseas Development Administration; 1996 October.

ODI. Aid and Political Reform. Briefing Paper: Overseas Development Institute, London; 1992 January.

—. NGOs and Official Donors. Overseas Development Institute Briefing Paper. 1995 August; (4):1–4.

—. Foreign Direct Investment Flows to Low-Income Countries: A Review of the Evidence. Briefing Paper No. 3. London: Overseas Development Institute; 1997 September.

—. What Can We Do With a Rights-Based Approach to Development? Briefing Paper. London: Overseas Development Institute; 1999 September; (3).

OECD. Development Cooperation Guideline Series. Conflict, Peace and Development Cooperation on the Threshold of the 21st Century. Paris: Organisation for Economic Cooperation and Development; 1998.

OLS. OLS 1998 Ed Daein – Food Economy Baseline Assessment. 1998 October 18.

OSCE. OSCE Handbook: 20 Years of the Helsinki Final Act. Vienna: Organisation of Security and Cooperation in Europe; 1995 April.

Owen, Margaret. Report Prepared for the British Development Division in Central Africa, Harare. Widowhood, Inheritance, Land Rights and Food Security in Zambezia. London: Empowering Women in Development; 1996 June.

Pankhurst, Dona. Report Prepared for OXFAM. Conflict Impact and Monitoring Assessment: Does It Exist? Can It Work? University of Bradford: Department of Peace Studies; 1999 April.

Pearson, Chris, Humanitarian Aid Monitor (European Commission). Mission Report, Ed Daen Conference, 24/25th October. Khartoum: European Commission; 1992 October 27.

Pech, Khareen. Executive Outcomes – A Corporate Conquest. In: Cilliers, Jakkie and

Mason, Peggy, eds. Peace, Profit or Plunder? The Privatisation of Security in War-Torn Africa. South Africa: The Institute for Security Studies; 1999; pp. 81–110.

Pech, Khareen and Beresford, David. Corporate Dogs of War Who Grow Fat Amid the Anarchy of Africa. The Observer. 1997 January 19: 19.

Pronk, J. P. and Kooijmans, P. H., Minister for Development Cooperation and Minister for Foreign Affairs (Ministry of Foreign Affairs, Netherlands Government). Humanitarian Aid: Between Conflict and Development. The Hague: Development Cooperation Information Department, Ministry of Foreign Affairs; 1993 December.

PWBLF. Memorandum from the Prince of Wales Business Leaders Forum. Sixth Report of the International Development Committee. Conflict Prevention and Post-Conflict Reconstruction, Vol. II, Minutes of Evidence and Appendices. London: The Stationery Office; 1999 July 28; pp. 209–13.

Rabinow, Paul. Making PCR: A Story of Biotechnology. Chicago: The University of Chicago Press; 1996.

Reno, William. Reinvention of an African Patrimonial State: Charles Taylor's Liberia. Third World Quarterly. 1995a; 16(1):109–20.

—. Warlords and Debureaucratising African States. Paper Presented at Annual Meeting of the Midwest Political Science Association; 1995b April.

—. Humanitarian Emergencies and Warlord Politics in Liberia and Sierra Leone. Paper presented at The Political Economy of Humanitarian Emergencies. Helsinki, Finland: UNU/WIDER; 1996 October 6–8.

—. Warlord Politics and African States. Boulder, Colorado: Lynne Rienner Pubs, Inc.; 1998.

Reuters. Iran Claims Sanctions Victory. The Guardian. 1999 April 30: 15.

Richards, Paul. Fighting for the Rain Forest: War, Youth and Resources in Sierra Leone. London: James Currey; 1996.

—. Post-Modern Warfare in Sierra Leone? Reasserting the Social in Global–Local Constructions of Violence. In Callaghy, Thomas, Kassimir, Ronald and Latham, Robert, eds. Authority and Intervention in Africa. Cambridge: Cambridge University Press; 2000.

Rodney, Walter. How Europe Underdeveloped Africa. Dar Es Salaam: Tanzania Publishing House; 1972.

Roitman, Janet. The Frontiers of Wealth Creation and Regulatory Authority in the Chad Basin. In: Callaghy, Thomas, Kassimir, Ronald and Latham, Robert, eds. Authority and Intervention in Africa. Cambridge: Cambridge University Press; 2000.

Roll, Lino, Secretary-General (Supreme Council of Peace). Interview. Khartoum; 1996 March 27.

Rummel, Reinhardt. The Common Foreign and Security Policy and Conflict Prevention. London: International Alert and Saferworld; 1996 May.

Ryle, John. How to Profit From a War. The Independent Magazine. 1989 September 25; 16.

Ryle, John and Kwol, Kwaja Yai. Displaced Southern Sudanese in Northern Sudan with Special Reference to Southern Darfur and Kordofan. London: Save the Children Fund, mimeo; 1989.

Saferworld. Memorandum from Saferworld: February 1998. Sixth Report of the International Development Committee. Conflict Prevention and Post-Conflict Reconstruction, Vol. II, Minutes of Evidence and Appendices. London: The Stationery Office; 1999 July 28; pp. 68–73.

SCF (UK). West Sudan Programme: Food Aid for Ed Daein Displaced. 1996 December.

—. An 'Emergency Plus' Strategy for Darfur. Khartoum; 1998 September 27.

Schierup, Carl-Ulrik. Quasi-Proletarians and a Patriarchal Bureaucracy: Aspects of Yugoslavia's Re-Peripheralisation. Soviet Studies. 1992; 44(1):79–99.

——. Prelude to the Inferno: Economic Disintegration and the Political Fragmentation of Yugoslavia. Balkan Forum. 1993 March; 1(8):80–120.

——. Memorandum for Modernity? Socialist Modernisers, Retraditionalisation and the Rise of Ethnic Nationalism. In: Schierup, Carl, ed. Scramble for the Balkans: Nationalism, Globalism and the Political Economy of Reconstruction. London: Macmillan Press Ltd; 1999; pp. 32–61.

Schumacher, E. F. Small is Beautiful: A Study of Economics as if People Mattered. London: Abacus; 1974.

Shearer, David. Dial an Army: Executive Outcomes in Sierra Leone. The World Today. 1997 August–1997 September 30; 53(8–9):203–5.

Short, Clare, Secretary of State for International Development (Department for International Development). Principles for a New Humanitarianism. Principled Aid in an Unprincipled World; London. Church House; 1998 April 7.

——. Secretary of State for International Development. Memorandum from the Secretary of State for International Development: 9 June 1998. International Development Committee. Conflict Prevention and Post-Conflict Reconstruction, Vol. II, Minutes of Evidence and Appendices. London: The Stationery Office; 1999 July 28; pp. 1–5.

SHRV. Dinka and Lokoro Tribes Face New Perils. Sudan Human Rights Voice. 1993 June; 2(6):6.

Silkin, T. and Hughes, S. Food Security and Food Aid: A Study From the Horn of Africa. London: CAFOD/Christian Aid; 1992 September.

Sköns, Elisabeth and Ström, Gabriele Winai. Weapon Supplies to Trouble Spots – A Background Paper for the Human Development Report 1994 of the United Nations Development Programme. Stockholm: International Peace Research Institute; 1994 November.

Slim, Hugo. Doing the Right Thing: Relief Agencies, Moral Dilemmas and Moral Responsibility in Political Emergencies and War. Studies on Emergencies and Disaster Relief, Report No. 6. Uppsala, Sweden: The Nordic Africa Institute; 1997.

——. Sharing a Universal Ethic: The Principle of Humanity in War. The International Journal of Human Rights. 1998 Winter; 2(4):28–48.

——. Fidelity and Variation: Discerning the Development and Evolution of the Humanitarian Ideal. Boston, Tufts University: Fletcher School of Law and Diplomacy; 1999 April 23.

Smith, Edwin M. and Weiss, Thomas G. UN Task-Sharing: Towards or Away from Global Governance? Weiss, Thomas G., ed. Beyond UN Subcontracting: Task-Sharing with Regional Security Arrangements and Service Providing NGOs. London: Macmillan Press Ltd; 1998; pp. 227–58.

Sogge, D. Sustainable Peace: Angola's Recovery. Harare: Southern African Research and Documentation Centre; 1992.

Speth, James Gustav. Informal Guidance to Resident Coordinators on Human Rights Communications. New York: 1999 February 23.

Stiglitz, Joseph E., Senior Vice President and Chief Economist (World Bank). Towards a New Paradigm for Development: Strategies, Policies, and Processes. Paper given at 1998 Prebisch Lecture. Geneva: UNCTAD; 1998 October 19.

Stockton, Nicholas. In Defense of Humanitarianism. Disasters. 1998; 22(4): 352–60.

Stubbs, Paul. Nationalisms, Globalisation and Civil Society in Croatia and Slovenia. Paper Presented to Second European Conference of Sociology, European Societies: Fusion or Fission? Budapest; 1995 30 August– September 2.

Suhrke, Astri. Towards a Comprehensive Refugee Policy: Conflict and Refugees in the Post-Cold War World. In: Bohning, W. R. and Schloeter-Paredes, M. L., eds.

Aid in Place of Migration? Geneva: International Labour Office; 1994; pp. 13–38.

Tanner, Victor and Fawcett, John. A Report to USAID's Office of Foreign Disaster Assistance (Part of the OFDA Former Yugoslavia Review 1991–7). ODFA after Dayton: The Emergency Shelter Repair Program: The Political Repercussions of Reconstruction Aid. Washington DC: Cheechi and Company Consulting; 1999.

Thompson, Tony. High Tech Crime of the Future Will Be All Mod Cons. The Observer. 1999 October 3: 11.

Tishkov, Valery. Ethnicity, Nationalism and Conflict in and after the Soviet Union: The Mind Aflame. London: Sage Publications; 1997.

Topçu, Yasemin. Humanitarian NGO Networks: Identifying Powerful Political Actors in an International Policy Field. Berlin: Wissenschaftszentrum Berlin für Sozialforschung; 1999 January.

Turton, D. Warfare Vulnerability and Survival: A Case From Southern Ethiopia. Cambridge Anthropology, Special Issue: Local Warfare in Africa. 1989; 13(2): 67–85.

UNDP. Draft. Position Paper of the Working Group on Operational Aspects of the Relief to Development Continuum. New York: UNDP; 1994 January 12.

——. Human Development Report 1996. New York: Oxford University Press and United Nations Development Programme; 1996.

UNHCR. The State of the World's Refugees: In Search of Solutions. Oxford : Oxford University Press for United Nations High Commission for Refugees; 1995.

UNHCU. Strategy for IDPs: Discussion Paper. Khartoum: United Nations Humanitarian Coordination Unit; 1997 August 16.

——. Displacement in Government Areas of Sudan. Khartoum: UN Humanitarian Coordination Unit; 1998a.

——. Minimal Operational Standards for Agencies in Wan. Khartoum: UN Humanitarian Coordination Unit; 1998b June.

——. Conditions for Relocation of Displaced Communities in Wan Town. Khartoum: UN Humanitarian Coordination Unit; 1998c July.

——. Evaluation of the UNHCU IDP Programme. Khartoum: UN Humanitarian Coordination Unit; 1998d October 6.

——. Population Estimates for IDPs in Government Areas in Sudan. Khartoum: UN Humanitarian Coordination Unit; 1998e October 10.

——. Confidential Annex to South Darfur Resettlement Proposal (for Donors). Protection of the South Darfur War-Affected Displaced: The Critical Role of Socio-Economic Factors in Protection – The South Darfur Resettlement Proposal. Khartoum: UN Humanitarian Coordination Unit; 1999.

UNICEF. A Human Rights Approach to UNICEF Programming for Children and Women: What it is, and some changes it will bring. New York: UNICEF; 1998 April 17.

——. Framework for Addressing the Problem of the Abduction of Children and Women in Sudan. Khartoum: UNICEF Sudan Country Office; 1999.

van Creveld, Martin. The Transformation of War. New York: Free Press; 1991.

van Niekerk, Phillip. Lust for Diamonds Undermines Hopes for Angola Peace. The Observer. 1995 September 17: 20.

Varese, Federico. Is Sicily the Future of Russia? Private Protection and the Rise of the Russian Mafia. Archives Europeennes De Sociologie. 1994 Summer; XXXV(2): 224–58.

Verdery, Katherine. What Was Socialism, and What Comes Next? Princeton, New Jersey: Princeton University Press; 1996.

Vines, Alex. CIIR Briefing Paper. One Hand Tied: Angola and the UN. London: Catholic Institute for International Relations; 1993 June.

——. Mercenaries and the Privatisation of Security in Africa in the 1990s. In: Mills, Greg and Stremlau, John, eds. The Privatisation of Security in Africa. Johannesburg: The South African Insitute of International Affairs; 1999; pp. 47–80.

Visvanathan, Shiv. A Carnival for Science: Essays on Science, Technology and Development. Delhi: Oxford University Press; 1997.

Von Hippel, Karin. Democracy by Force: US Military Intervention in the Post-Cold War World. Cambridge: Cambridge University Press; 1999.

Vulliamy, Ed. The Rape of Russia – Warnings No One Wanted to Hear. The Observer. 1999 September 5: 24.

Walker, Peter. Food for Recovery: Food Monitoring and Targeting in Red Sea Province, Sudan, 1985–1986. Oxford: Oxfam; 1987.

Wallerstein, Immanuel. The Modern World System. London : Academic Press; 1974.

—. The Global Picture, 1945–90. In: Hopkins, Terence K. and Wallerstein, Immanuel, eds. The Age of Transition: Trajectory of the World-System, 1945–2025. London: Zed Books Ltd; 1996; pp. 209–25.

Walton, John and Seddon, David. Free Markets and Food Riots: The Politics of Global Adjustment. Oxford: Blackwell; 1994.

Waters, Malcolm. Globalization. London: Routledge; 1995.

Weale, Sally. Once Were Warriors. The Guardian G2. 1999 November 9: 2–3.

Weiss, T. G. and Campbell, K. M. Military Humanism. Survival. 1991 September–October; 33(5):451–65.

Weiss, Thomas and Collins, Cindy. Humanitarian Challenges and Intervention: World Politics and the Dilemmas of Help. Boulder, Colorado: Westview Press; 1996.

Weiss, Thomas G., ed. Beyond UN Subcontracting: Task-Sharing with Regional Security Arrangements and Service-Providing NGOs. New York and London: St Martin's and Macmillan Press Ltd; 1998.

—. Military–Civilian Interactions: Intervening in Humanitarian Crises. Lanham, Maryland: Rowman and Littlefield Publishers, Inc.; 1999a.

—. Principle, Politics, and Humanitarian Action. Ethics and International Affairs. 1999b; 13:1–21.

Westlake, M. The Third World (1950–1990) RIP. Marxism Today. 1991 August:14–16.

Williams, Michael C. Civil–Military Relations in Peacekeeping. Adelphi Paper (International Institute for Strategic Studies). 1998; (321):1–93.

Wolpe, H. Capitalism and Cheap Labour Power in South Africa: From Segregation to Apartheid. Economy and Society. 1972; 1:425–56.

World Bank. Sub-Saharan Africa: From Crisis to Sustainable Growth. Washington DC: World Bank; 1989.

—. World Development Report 1990: Poverty. Oxford: Oxford University Press; 1990.

—. The State in a Changing World; The World Development Report, 1997. World Bank; 1997a.

—. A Framework for World Bank Involvement in Post-Conflict Reconstruction. Washington DC: World Bank; 1997b April 25.

World Bank and Carter Center. From Civil War to Civil Society: The Transition from War to Peace in Guatemala and Liberia. Washington DC and Atlanta: World Bank and Carter Center; 1997 July.

Zakaria, Fareed. Democratic Tyranny. Prospect. 1997 December; (25):20–5.

Zandee, Dick. Building Blocks for Peace: Civil Military Interaction in Restoring Fractured Societies. Study 4. The Hague: Netherlands Institute of International Relations; 1998 September.

Index

Abu Karinka 242, 244
Abu Matariq 241-2
Abyei 207
Addis Ababa 198
Adilla 238, 241, 244-5
Afghanistan 26, 94, 172, 188
Africa, Central 197; Horn of 26, 74, 77;
    North 62-3, 197; Southern 14, 26, 68,
    74, 157, 190; West 14, 63, 68, 112, 139,
    151-2, 157, 190, 197
African Rights 33
African, Caribbean and Pacific countries
    (ACP) 25
Aga Khan, Sadruddin 27, 29
agriculture 23, 29, 80, 117, 124, 142, 146,
    151-2, 168-9, 175, 205-7, 216-17, 220,
    224-5, 230-1, 233-43, 262
aid, aid farming 244-8, 256n; aid market
    54, 57; and bureaucracy 74, 76-7, 254;
    and civil society 57-9; and conflict
    11, 42, 54-5, 59, 105-6, 116, 120, 189,
    250-2, 254-5; and conflict resolution
    8; conditionality of 30, 94-5; and de-
    ethnicisation 215-21, 225, 228, 248-50,
    260; dependency on 80, 97, 100, 102-
    3, 105, 113, 209, 213, 217, 220, 223,
    231, 233, 236, 238, 246-7, 249-54;
    diversion of 180, 238-9, 246-8, 253-4,
    256n; ethics of 34, 85-6, 96; food 20,
    53, 80, 105, 119, 155, 188, 204, 209,
    217-20, 231-40, 246-9, 254; and
    human rights 215, 221-8, 230-1, 237,
    248-50, 255; and migration 217-19;
    and the military 57-61; narcissism of
    98; natural economy approach of
213-21, 248-9, 251-2, 255; Newtonian
    approach of 84-5, 97, 161, 248, 252,
    263; and peacekeeping operations
    57-61, 119; policy 2, 8, 10-11, 38, 41-2,
    73-5, 80-1, 90, 96, 98, 100-2, 104, 109,
    116, 119, 121, 128, 131-2, 135, 139-41,
    148, 161-2, 202-29, 231-7, 244-55, 259,
    261-5; and political oppression 205,
    208, 230-56, 260; politicisation of 11,
    15-16, 18, 38, 42, 75-107; and popular
    culture 76; professionalisation of 82;
    reduction of 113-14, 118, 151, 153,
    167, 183, 231-7, 246-8, 252, 254;
    regulation of 81-2, 88, 91, 105-6;
    reinvention of 249-50, 255, 263-4;
    Scandinavian effect on 73-4; and
    security 35, 69, 194, 246; and steady-
    state solutions 254, 262-3; *see also*
    development, humanitarian aid,
    NGOs, UN, reconstruction, self-
    management, etc.
Albania 41, 142, 171
Algeria 64
Amnesty International 33, 62
anarchy 6, 13-14, 110-13, 115, 124, 130-1,
    138
Anderson, Mary 94, 128, 129, 134-5
Angola 25, 59, 64, 70, 77, 137-8, 141-2,
    172, 177, 182, 185-6, 188, 196-7, 200-1
Annan, Kofi 195
Antwerp 197
apartheid 66, 206
Ariwara 152
Armenia 189
Armor Holdings 66

arms control 172, 199-201
arms trade 14, 27, 36, 45, 61-2, 67, 69-70,
    113, 116, 137, 143, 150, 171-2, 176,
    178, 188, 190, 196-201, 260
Arua 152
Asia 7, 62, 143, 152, 198; East 2, 3, 29, 30,
    40, 149, 159; South 149, Southeast 63,
    66
asylum 110, 113
Atwood, Brian 119-20, 128
Aweil 218
Azerbaijan 189

Baggara Arabs 203
Bahr el Ghazal 211, 218; Northern 202-3,
    226, 231, 242-3
Balkans 5, 13, 31, 34, 54, 58-9, 69, 71, 89,
    107, 111-12, 119, 121, 170, 174, 189,
    211, 250-1; see also Albania, Bosnia,
    Croatia, Kosovo, Serbia, Yugoslavia
Baltic states 189
Band Aid trust 76, 81
Bank of New York 180-1
Barakaat 172
Belgium 197
Bentiu 207
Berlin Wall 119
bioculturalism 109-10, 114-15, 127
biodiversity 37
biotechnology 10, 84, 181
Bolivia 142
Bong Bank 176
Bonino, Commissioner 41
Bosnia 12, 32, 54, 59-60, 78-9, 82, 90, 111,
    130, 169-70, 189; see also Balkans,
    Yugoslavia
Boutros-Ghali, Boutros 13, 117, 126
BP 64, 66
Branch Energy 185
Britain see United Kingdom
Brown University 88
Buddhism 84
Buram 224
bureaucracy 3, 9, 12, 34, 44, 60-1, 72, 74,
    77, 139, 149-50, 163, 166-7, 169-72,
    176, 183, 210, 245-6, 254, 262-4; de-
    bureaucratisation 166-7, 172, 175-6,
    178, 183-4, 188, 210
Burkino Faso 152
business 1-2, 12-13, 17, 31, 45-6, 48, 52,
    62-4, 172, 179, 193-5; see also capital-
    ism, foreign companies, multi-
national companies, private
    companies

Cambodia 178
Cameroon 151
Camesia 64
Canada 94, 198-9
Cancun 29
capitalism 2, 3, 7, 17, 22-5, 33, 47, 168
Capra, Fritjof 84-5
CARE 214-15, 217, 220-3, 234, 255
Carey, Dr George 33
Carnegie Commission on Preventing
    Deadly Conflict 127
Carr-Smith, Major General Stephen 66
Carter Center 39
Carter, Jimmy 78
Castells, Manuel 4-7, 144, 146-7, 179
Caucasus 62, 110, 189
Cayman Islands 181
Central African Republic 151, 171-2, 177,
    197
Central America 63
Cerny, Philip G. 164
Chad 133, 150, 171, 175, 206; Chad Basin
    150-1, 153, 171-3, 177, 180
Chechnya 110, 174, 178
Chevron 198
children 32, 62, 207, 228, 240-1, 251, 255
China 175, 198
China National Petroleum Company
    (CNPL) 198
Chingono, Mark 125
Chomsky, Noam 33-4
CIA 180
Cilliers, Jakkie 186-7
civil society 57-8, 64, 71, 115, 141, 258
civilian organisations 45
Civil–Military Cooperation (CIMIC) 59
Civil–Military Operations Centres
    (CMOCs) 59
Clinton, Bill 111, 120, 180
codes of conduct 56, 61-2, 70, 73
coffee 152-5, 177, 190
COLA 176, 196
Cold War 1, 4, 13, 15-17, 22, 31, 35-6, 39,
    44-5, 52, 54, 57-8, 66, 70-1, 76-9, 88,
    91, 93, 112, 116, 119-21, 126, 128, 137,
    150, 166-7, 171-2, 179, 183, 192, 194,
    257, 259
Collier, Paul 132-5
Colombia 64, 66

colonialism 3, 25, 27, 115, 148, 165-6, 185, 205-6; decolonisation 25-6, 93; postcolonial 23, 28
Committee for the Coordination of Humanitarian Assistance (CCHA) 55
communism 111-12
complex emergencies 12, 14, 52, 65, 71, 86, 89, 95-6, 161-3, 244, 250, 252, 254-5
complexity 10-12, 20, 80, 83-5, 87-90, 92-3, 96-7, 100, 145-6, 155-6, 208-9, 212-14, 217, 222, 224-8, 246-9, 251-5, 257-65
comprador class 24, 42, 43n, 47
conditionality 8, 29, 94-5, 106-7, 162; see also structural adjustment
Confederation of British Industry (CBI) 64
conflict, causes of 17-18, 26-8, 32, 73, 75-7, 86, 89, 91, 97, 99, 108-40, 165; civil war 118-19, 122-6, 132-4, 137, 174, 197, 202-56 passim; civil–military networks 57-61; Clausewitzian warfare 45; and commercialisation of politics 193-4; and complexity 87-8, 93; 'cooperative conflict' 177-8; cost of 31; conventional 61; and crime 173; criminalisation of 127-36, 139-40, 148, 159, 162, 190, 193, 201; and culture 36, 109-12, 118, 123-6, 136, 164, 192, 207, 228, 259-60; and democracy 116; and development 18, 27-8, 35, 39, 55, 71, 98-100, 102, 105-6, 114-27, 129-31, 137-41, 159, 162, 189-90, 202-56 passim, 250-2, 254-5; and displaced people 202-56 passim; 'durable disorder' 165; and economic growth 117, 133; and education 117; and emerging political complexes 131, 163; and ethnicity 110-11, 114, 118-25, 133, 164, 170, 191, 202-56 passim, 243, 246, 248-50, 255; and everyday life 159; and extractive industries 182-3; and food aid 232, 237-40, 246, 248-9, 254; and former socialist republics 170; and global economy 6, 120; and global liberal government 13, 20, 108-36, 139, 148, 159, 174, 193, 213, 222; and

greed 132-40; and health 113, 117; Hobbesian view of 102, 123-4; and human rights 116, 129, 222-8; and humanitarian aid 4-5, 11-12, 51, 75-7, 80, 88, 91-108, 155, 161, 194, 202-56 passim; just causes 129-30; and law 116; local perceptions of 214; management of 60, 94; merging of war and peace 187-9, 193; and migration 207, 211, 217-19; and multinational companies 62-3; of nation states 2, 7, 13, 16, 18, 36, 60, 118, 170, 257, 260; network wars 14, 19, 80, 85, 160, 172, 187-201, 258-60; new barbarism approach to 110-11, 113, 123, 164; new wars 9-10, 13-20, 27, 36, 45-6, 51-2, 57-8, 60-2, 66, 73, 80, 82-3, 85, 87-8, 92-3, 97-8, 100, 102, 114, 118-21, 124, 129-41, 145, 156, 159-60, 163, 177, 187, 189-201, 252, 257-60, 262-3; NGOs 1, 54, 56, 117, 125, 250; nuclear 61; orphan wars 13; pan-European approach to 74; peacekeeping 57-60, 119; post-Cold War 1, 4, 13; and poverty 18, 37, 117, 120-8, 133, 135-6, 149, 162, 196, 254; prevention of 58, 64, 117, 120-2, 126; and private military companies (PMCs) 62, 65, 68, 183-7; race 191; and refugees 26; regional 118-19, 125; reification of violence 189; religious 118, 133, 191; resolution of 1-2, 8-9, 11, 15, 18, 34, 38-9, 41-2, 57, 59, 62, 64, 68, 75, 82, 85, 94, 99, 117, 128-9, 135, 141, 228, 261, 263; and social reconstruction 117, 123-4, 128, 135, 189; stakeholder analysis of 259-60; state–non-state links in 177; and sustainable development 38; and trade 134; and transborder shadow economy 154-5, 159, 163, 190; as transformation 6, 121-3, 125, 127, 131-2, 136-41, 159-60; and underdevelopment 7, 18, 37-8, 45, 80-1, 99, 113-17, 127-8, 133; US 119; and values 40-2; war crimes 95, 129; war economies 80, 95, 130-9, 147, 160, 193, 200-1; war taxes 62; warlords 138-9, 165, 167, 175-8, 184-5, 190; wars of liberation 26, 93, 118; Western casualties of 51-2, 70
Congo, see Democratic Republic of

Congo and Zaïre (former)
consumerism 168, 191
Control Risks Group 66
Cook, Robin 41
Cornwell, Richard 186-7
corruption 30, 64, 113, 115, 122, 127, 129, 131-5, 148, 156, 162, 166
Côte d'Ivoire 176, 197
Cox, Robert 4, 8-9
crime 2, 6-7, 13, 16, 19, 36-7, 51, 61, 112, 114, 127-36, 139-46, 148, 156, 173, 179-81, 187-8, 190, 194-6, 201; war crimes 95, 129
Croatia 67, 70, 170, 189, 192; *see also* Balkans, Yugoslavia
Cuba 137
culture 109-15, 122-4, 136, 146, 157-8, 191-2, 207, 209, 211-12, 215-16, 221-2, 225, 228, 231, 248, 253, 259-60, 262-5
Cutts, Mark 87-8
Czech Republic 170

Darfur 206, 219-20, 225, 231; Northern 218, 220; South 202, 204, 213, 216-18, 230, 233, 237-8, 242-5, 247, 256n
Dayton peace process 32
De Beers 197
debt 28-9, 119, 151, 154, 213, 234, 236-43, 246-9
debureaucratisation *see* bureaucracy
decentralisation 44, 60-1, 164-5, 167, 175, 178
Defence Systems Limited (DSL) 66, 70, 184
deforestation 37, 175-6, 182, 190, 196
democracy 30, 38, 50, 67, 71, 116, 118-20, 129, 133, 161-2, 165, 251
Democracy Transition Assistance Programme (DTAP) 67
Democratic Republic of Congo 64, 81-2, 94, 106, 140, 197; see also Zaïre (former)
Democratic Unionist Party (DUP) 154
dependency 20, 24, 43n, 80, 97, 101-3, 105, 113, 158, 161, 169, 204, 208-9, 217, 220, 223, 231, 233, 236, 238, 246-7, 249-54; dependency theory 3-6, 17, 43n
deregulation 5, 14, 19, 30, 49, 61, 66, 148-50, 158-9, 167, 171, 182, 193-5, 198, 200-1, 250; *see also* regulation
Derlugian, Georgi 44

desertification 27
development, approach built on past failures 161-2; business involvement in 62-4, 193, 195; and Cold War 119; and conditionality 30, 34; and conflict 18, 35, 39, 55, 71, 92-3, 98-100, 102, 105-6, 114-31, 137-41, 159, 162, 189-90, 202-56 *passim*; and consequential ethics 75, 87, 90-9, 105-7, 204, 221-2, 251; on conventional economic base 141; and crime 114; and criminalisation of conflict 131; crisis of 247-8; and culture 114, 122-6; cuts in spending 113-14, 118, 151, 153, 167, 183, 231-7, 246-8, 252, 254; and democracy 24; development economics 23; developmental state 165-7, 172, 175-6, 178, 183, 194; developmentalism 114; discourse 1-2, 39, 82-3, 85-7, 92-3, 96, 114-15, 121, 126-7, 129, 130, 139-41, 144-5, 147, 161-2, 164-5, 174, 189, 208-13, 216, 222, 225, 248-9, 251, 253, 255, 264; early hopes for 119; in East Asia 40; and economic growth 82; and emerging political complexes 20, 163; ethics of 85-6, 92, 97, *see also* consequential ethics; and food security 101; and gender 83, 102; and global liberal governance 11, 34, 121, 129, 135, 159, 195; human emphasis in 57; and human rights 221-8, 230-1, 237, 248-50, 255; and humanitarian aid 11, 18, 38, 52, 54, 75, 80-2, 92-3, 98-106, 108, 202-29, 248-9, 251-3; long-term 244; 'lost decade' of 119, 149-50, 152, 159; and market system 195; and modernisation 39; and multiculturalism 114; and multinational companies 62-4; networks 114-116; and new wars 16, 82-3, 86, 92-3, 118, 120; Newtonian approach of 84-5, 97, 161, 248, 252, 263; and political oppression 230-56, 260; politicisation of 11, 15-16, 18, 38, 42, 75-107; and poverty 23-4, 35, 40, 119, 121-7, 147-8, 150, 153; and power 15, 83; privatisation of 15; radicalisation of 2, 15-16, 18-19, 22-43, 80, 82, 96-7, 99, 118, 121-3, 125, 150; reinvention of 30, 42, 249-50, 255, 263-4; and security 1-2, 4, 7, 9,

11-12, 15-19, 22-43, 45, 52, 88, 94, 99, 116, 118, 120, 122, 132, 195, 249, 252, 259-60; as self-management 20, 30, 34, 36, 42, 101-2, 169, 204, 209-10, 215-21, 223-8, 230-2, 234, 236, 241, 247-52, 255, 263; and social evolutionism 162-5; and social reconstruction 123, 189, 192; state-led 47; steady-state solutions in 254, 262-3; and structural adjustment 149-51, 159; sustainable 38, 42, 64, 101-3, 119; and technicism 82, 92; and terrorism 114; and transborder shadow economy 9, 141-3, 147-8, 150-3, 156-7, 159; as transformation 22, 30, 39-42, 46, 77, 82-3, 85, 121-3, 125, 127, 131-2, 136-41, 150, 159-60, 165, 167, 250, 252, 259, 261; UK programme of 72; underdevelopment 2, 7, 16, 18, 22-4, 26-8, 30, 32, 36-8, 42, 80-2, 99, 113-18, 121, 126-8, 133, 148, 159, 194, 259; unpredictability of 161; *see also* aid, humanitarian aid, NGOs, UN

diamonds 175, 177, 182, 184-5, 197-201

Dinka people 174, 203-4, 207, 211-13, 215-20, 224-8, 230-56

displaced people 19-20, 86, 123-5, 154-5, 174, 188, 191, 202-56

donor governments 1, 6, 8, 12, 15, 17-19, 25, 38, 50, 52, 54-8, 68, 72-3, 76, 81-2, 87-9, 94, 98, 99-101, 105-6, 114, 146, 155, 167, 208, 210, 212, 218, 221, 224, 230-2, 242, 244-6, 250, 255, 260, 262-3

drought 123, 214, 244

drugs trade 131, 142-3, 146, 148, 172, 196, 201

Dyachenko, Leonid 181

economic growth 23, 28, 39-40, 42, 48-50, 82, 101, 117, 119, 133, 159

Ed'Dien 216, 220, 224, 232-9, 241, 243-7

Ed Nahud 234

education 5, 29, 47-8, 64, 83, 102, 115, 117, 133, 149, 151, 173, 175, 195, 209, 211, 214, 222, 225, 234, 244, 250, 255

Egypt 198

El Fasher 218, 220

El Goura 238, 241-2

El Obeid airport 226

El Salvador 188

elite 24, 29, 39, 43n, 130, 163, 166, 169,

171, 173, 181-2, 184, 187

Ellis, Stephen 165, 167

emerging political complexes 14-15, 19-20, 32, 52, 97, 125, 131, 144-5, 159-201, 252-4, 260-1

employment 48, 102, 169, 188, 191, 234, 236-7, 240, 243

empowerment 42, 121, 126-7, 225

En Nahud 215, 234

energy industry 4, 64, 66, 180-1, 188

environment 36, 44, 62-4, 112-13, 115, 148, 214, 219, 244, 258

Environmental Liaison Committee (ELC) 56

Escobar, Arturo 83

Estonia 189

ethics 75, 85-7, 89, 90-9, 105-7, 200, 204, 221-2, 251, 259

Ethiopia 25, 76-7, 81

ethnicity 7, 18-20, 26, 38, 41, 110-11, 114, 118, 122-4, 127, 133, 156, 169-70, 174, 189, 191, 198, 202-56 *passim*, 260; ethnic cleansing 41, 90, 95, 170, 174, 211; ethno-nationalism 169, 174, 189

Europe 26, 54-6, 62, 74, 111, 162, 197-8; Eastern 28-30, 54, 142-3, 157, 161-2, 165, 170-2, 178, 181, 200; Western 2, 3, 172, 181

European Commission Humanitarian Office (ECHO) 56, 71, 104-5, 204, 233, 239, 262

European Council on Refugees and Exiles (ECRE) 56

European Union (EU) 25, 36, 38-9, 41, 54, 56, 71, 74, 76, 100, 103-7, 197, 199-200, 219, 246, 250, 262; Council of Europe 56

exclusivity 2, 4-8, 13-14, 18-19, 22-3, 25, 28, 33-4, 115, 118, 126-7, 170, 173-4

Executive Outcomes (EO) 65-70, 184-7

exports 29, 142, 182-3

extractive industries 182-6, 190, 193, 196-7

Exxon 64

famine 17, 76-7, 99, 207, 211, 218, 226, 232, 256n

fascism 41

Federation of Bosnia-Herzegovia Armed Forces (FAF) 68

Federation of Semi-Official and Private International Institutions 56

Fellata 206-7

finance 2, 3, 5, 28-30, 46, 148, 173, 181, 185, 188, 195-6; speculation 158-9

Firestone Tyre and Rubber Corporation 176, 196

fisheries 37, 236, 262

food 29, 105, 123, 148-9, 152, 154-5, 188, 204, 214, 217-20, 225; food aid 20, 53, 80, 105, 119, 155, 188, 204, 209, 217-20, 231-40, 246-9, 254; food for work 233; food security 9, 100-1, 204, 214, 217-20, 225, 232-40

Food Economy Approach 235, 240

foreign companies 165, 170-1, 175-6, 178, 184, 192, 194-5, 198; *see also* business, multinational companies, private companies

foreign exchange 142, 147, 152-4, 176

Fourth World 7

Framework Partnership Agreement (FPA) 56-7

France 78, 176, 250

Freetown (Sierra Leone) 185

Fulani people 146

fundamentalism 154

G8 group of countries 199

Gaia 84

Gambia 157

Gasper, Des 85-6

Geldof, Bob 76

gender 42, 83, 102, 125, 138, 156, 214, 216, 223, 228, 240, 255, 258

Geneva Conventions 69, 93

genocide 7, 81, 90, 111-12, 127, 191-2, 211

George, Susan 143

Georgia 189

Germany 55, 250

Gezira cotton scheme 206

Ghana 152

global economy 2, 4-8, 14, 17, 19, 24-6, 61, 120, 137-8, 141-2, 145-7, 149-50, 157-9, 175-7, 181-4, 187, 190, 193-200, 261

global warming 37

Global Witness 197

globalization 3-4, 11, 13-14, 30-31, 46-7, 51, 72-3, 127, 131, 138, 144, 148-9, 158-9, 163-4, 167, 170, 175-6, 192-5, 257

GOAL 221

Gogrial 243

gold 152, 182, 196

Goldberg, Jeffrey 113-15

Goma 82

governance, global liberal 2-3, 5-10, 12, 15, 17-18, 22, 30-1, 33-4, 37, 40, 44-6, 53, 78-9, 81, 87-8, 93, 98-100, 102, 104-5, 107-36, 140, 142, 146-7, 150, 153, 187, 189, 195, 200, 222, 226, 228, 247, 252, 257-65; and aid 8, 226, 228; and complex emergencies 162-3; and complexity 264; and conflict 13, 20, 108-36, 139, 148, 159, 174, 193, 213, 222; criminalises conflict and extreme leaders 127-36, 139, 148, 159, 174, 193; and development 11, 34, 121, 129, 135, 159, 195; and emerging political complexes 144, 163; and grassroots 130; and human rights 222; inclusivity of 259-61; and international standards 8; and local structures 8, 246-7; and multinational companies 62-3, 193; and nation state 164; networks of 6, 8, 44, 108-9, 136, 146-7, 247, 252, 264; policy making of 73, 108-9; and poverty 126-8, 132-3, 135, 150, 159; and security 195, 265; and state–non-state linkages 163; strategic complexes of 12-18, 34, 37, 42, 44-74, 109, 115-16, 122, 140-1, 145-7, 163-4, 193, 226, 252-3, 258, 261, 264; and transborder shadow economy 136-60, 156-7; and underdevelopment 126, 159; *see also* liberalism

Gozprom 181

Great Lakes region 90

Greater Nile Oil Project 198

Greek traders 166

gross national product (GNP) 141-3

Group of 21 countries 199

Guinea Bissau 152

Gulf War (1991) 57, 71, 77, 119

Gurkha Security Guards (GSG) 184

Hausa people 146

health 29, 47-8, 72, 83, 112-13, 117, 149, 151, 195, 204, 225, 230, 233-6, 240, 244-6

Heritage Oil 185

hierarchy 2, 12, 17, 34, 49-50, 60, 174

Hobbes, Thomas 213, 228

Hoogvelt, Ankie 3

human development indicators 27
human rights 14-15, 17-18, 20, 26-7, 32-
    3, 35, 37, 41, 58, 62-4, 66, 71, 76-8, 82,
    86, 89-92, 95, 104, 107, 116, 118, 126-
    7, 129, 131, 191, 199, 204-5, 208-10,
    215, 221-8, 230-1, 237, 248-50, 255,
    258
Human Rights Watch 33
humanitarian aid, access to unstable
    regions 31; and CCHA 55; classical
    form 87, 93; and complex
    emergencies 12; and complexity 92-
    3, 96-7; and conditionality 94-5, 106-
    7, 162; and conflict 5, 11, 51, 75-7, 80-
    1, 88, 91-4, 96-100, 102-8, 155, 161,
    194, 202-56 *passim*; conflict caused
    by 75-7, 80, 97; and conflict
    resolution 75; and consequentialist
    ethics 75, 87, 89, 90-9, 105-7, 204,
    221-2, 251; critique of 75-107; and
    debureaucratisation 166; and
    dependency 97, 102-3, 105, 161; and
    development 11, 18, 38, 52, 54, 75,
    80-2, 92-3, 98-106, 108, 202-29, 248-9,
    251-3; and ECHO 56, 71; and
    erosion of public goods 244-5; and
    ethnicity 205; EU policy on 41, 105,
    107, 219; as food 155; funding of
    106; harm–benefit analysis of 217,
    222-3, 225-8, 251; and human rights
    76-8, 82, 86, 89-92, 104, 107, 204, 208-
    9, 215, 221-8; and ICRC 77, 87; and
    ICVA 55-6; ideal form 87; and local
    structures 79, 94, 106; and market
    system 102; maximalist 93-4, 97;
    military involvement in 59-60;
    minimalist 93-4; and network war
    191; networks of 55-7, 98; neutrality
    of 75, 77-81, 87-93; new 75-107, 162,
    202-29; and new imperialism thesis
    33; and new wars 80, 92-3, 97, 98,
    100, 102; Newtonian approach to
    84-5, 97, 161, 248, 252, 263; OCHA
    55, 71; politicisation of 11, 15-16, 18,
    38, 42, 75-107; post-Cold War
    interventions 4-5; and poverty 102-
    3; problematised 194; 'prophetic' 77-
    82, 88, 92, 98, 259-60; Red Cross
    code of conduct in 70; and SCHR 56;
    and security 259; and social recon-
    struction 75, 88, 94; solidarist 93;
    and state 245; and transborder

shadow economy 155; UN 54, 71;
    and underdevelopment 80-1; and
    UNHCR 59; and VOICE 56
Humanitarian Aid Committee (HAC)
    105, 237, 245-6, 256n
Humanitarianism and War Project 88
Hungary 170
Huntington, Samuel P. 111-12
Hussein, Saddam 140
Hutu people 81-2

Ibis Air 186
Ibo people 146
identity 38, 41, 49, 51-2, 110-14, 123, 125,
    165, 174, 191, 210, 212-13, 215-16,
    218, 224-5, 230-1, 248
inclusivity 7-8, 14, 17, 22-4, 26, 33-4, 170,
    174, 259-61
Indonesia 64
industry 62, 64, 180
informal economy *see* transborder
    shadow economy
information 3-5, 7, 10, 45, 55, 64, 85, 158,
    181, 251, 254, 262-5; information
    economy 46, 150; information
    technology 158, 181
InterAction 57
inter-governmental organisations
    (IGOs) 1, 12, 18, 49, 54, 57, 82, 99,
    105, 258, 262
internally displaced people (IDPs) *see*
    displaced people
International Alert 124
International Chamber of Commerce
    199
International Committee of the Red
    Cross (ICRC) *see* Red Cross
International Council of Voluntary
    Agencies (ICVA) 55-6
International Federation of Red Cross
    and Red Crescent Societies (IFRC)
    see Red Cross (IFRC)
international financial institutions (IFIs)
    1, 12, 29, 46, 49-50, 101, 104-5, 118,
    142, 147, 149-50, 226
International Labour Organisation
    (ILO) 56, 147
International Monetary Fund (IMF) 29,
    48, 143, 162, 167, 180
investment 3-6, 23, 28-9, 49, 62, 82, 101,
    141, 150, 170, 180-2
Iran 198

Iraq 57, 140
Islam 32-3, 59, 154, 204, 206, 209, 211, 212, 216, 237, 250
isolationism 113-14, 118, 120
Israel 197
Italy 60
ivory 177, 196

Japan 3
Jaspars, Susan 213-14
Juba 154-5

Kampala 152
Kandahar 188
Kaplan, Robert 111-15, 164
Keen, David 139, 177
Kenya 141, 152
Khartoum 155, 198, 202, 209-10, 221, 224, 231-2, 237, 241, 244-5, 247, 250-1, 256n
Khatmiyya sect 154
Khor Omer 237, 239, 256n
Kingham, Tess 94
Kordofan 214-15, 219-20, 225; Southern 207; West 234, 237
Kosovo 33, 41-2, 59-60, 65, 94, 189
Kouchner, Bernard 78
Kurds 57
Kwaja Yai Kuol 203

labour 2-6, 24, 51, 102, 205-9, 220, 223-4, 230-1, 233-43, 247-8, 252, 255, 256n; child 62; migrant 23
Lake Chad 172
land 37, 117, 169, 171, 207, 217-18, 224, 234-7, 241, 243-4, 247
Latin America 7, 26, 143, 149, 201
Latvia 189
law 11, 34, 41, 61, 67, 69-71, 91, 116, 130, 165, 169-71, 175, 179, 186-7, 196, 221-2, 224, 226-7, 251, 258
Lebanese traders 166, 176
Liaison Committee of Development NGOs to the European Union 56
liberalism, alternatives to 22; and consumerism 51; and democracy 41, 165; discourse 28, 261 see also development discourse; as economic reform 5, 9, 11, 29-30, 46-8, 61, 101, 108, 141, 147-52, 157, 159, 164, 179-83, 188, 193-4; and ethics 259; liberal peace 11-20, 31, 34, 37, 45-6, 52-3, 57,

61-2, 65, 72-3, 79, 87-8, 93, 100, 107, 116-18, 121-3, 125-32, 135-6, 139-41, 145-6, 162, 189, 193-4, 202, 213, 253-5, 258-61, 264-5; liberal war 14-15, 261, 264; liberalisation see liberalism, economic reform; neoliberalism 8, 17, 29-30, 46, 57, 108, 260; as new imperialism 31-4, 93; and transformation 261; see also governance, global liberal
Liberia 90, 133, 139, 167, 175, 178, 184, 196
Libya 151, 198
Lithuania 189
Living Marxism 32-3
local structures 8, 53, 79, 91, 94-5, 100, 104, 106-7, 128, 135, 147, 156-8, 169, 173, 206, 214, 226-7, 230-1, 236-7, 243, 245-7
local–global linkages 5, 9, 14, 46, 72, 131, 138, 140, 146-7, 153, 159, 164-5, 175, 258, 261
Logging International Timber Inc. 176
Lomé Convention 25, 39, 104-6
London 66
looting 80, 241-2, 248

Macedonia 189
Macrae, Joanna 98
mafia 19, 150, 162, 174, 178-81, 187, 196
Mahdist regime 205
Mahliyya Arabs 203, 243
Malawi 122
Malaysia 198
Mali 152
malnutrition 149, 239-40
Malthus, Thomas 112
Maputo 153
market system 5, 6, 11, 14, 19, 28-30, 34, 39-41, 46-7, 49-50, 54, 61, 66, 69-70, 93, 101-2, 113, 119-120, 141, 145, 148-50, 152-5, 157-9, 161-2, 164, 167, 176-7, 182-4, 187, 190-1, 193-5, 198-201, 207, 217, 250, 256n, 259-60
Meagher, Kate 147, 151-2, 155-6
Médecins sans frontières (MSF) (Belgium) 204
media 76, 78, 82, 111, 113, 146, 250, 259
mercenaries 69-70, 143, 182
Mexico 192
Middle East 25, 62, 119, 149, 154
migration 4, 23, 110, 113, 124, 127, 169,

207, 211-12, 217-18; seasonal 239-40,
242, 256n
military 2, 8, 12-14, 16-20, 36, 45, 50-2,
54, 57-61, 65-72, 77-8, 87, 92, 100,
119, 136, 146, 150, 153-5, 163, 166,
170-5, 177, 182-7, 194, 220, 230-1,
236-7, 246-9
Military Professional Resources
Incorporated (MPRI) 67, 70, 184
military stabilisation programme
(MSP) 68
Minimum Operational Standards
(MinOps) 106, 226-8
mining 63, 66
Mitterrand, President 78
Mobil 64
modernisation 39-40, 67, 124, 140, 148,
166, 169-70
modernity 22, 25, 28, 30, 41-2, 47
Mogadishu 172
Mohonk Criteria for Humanitarian
Assistance in Complex Emergencies
(1994) 88
Moldovia 189
money laundering 146, 158, 162, 180-1,
187, 190, 199, 254
Monrovia 176
Monsanto 84
Morocco 197
Moscow 110
Mozambique 25, 122-5, 141-2, 153, 172,
196; Participatory Poverty
Assessment 123
MPLA (People's Movement for the
Liberation of Angola) 137
Mubarak, President 198
multiculturalism 109, 114
multinational companies (MNCs) 1-2,
48-9, 51, 62-3, 169-70, 193-4, 196, 199
Mulwal clan 203, 243
Muwafaq 236

Namibia 137
National Islamic Front 154
National Oil Company 198
National Patriotic Front of Liberia
(NPFL) 175-6
nationalism 32, 118, 169, 174, 189
natural resources 68, 148, 219-20
Netherlands 59, 78, 94, 250
networks, arms supply 62; commercial
231, 236-9, 246-9, 252-3;

communication between 73; and
conflict 160, 172, 187-201; corrupt
238, 246; criminal 7, 144, 180-1, 190,
194; cultural 146, 157-8, 191;
development 83, 114, 116;
development–security 16, 35-6; of
dominant groups in Sudan 20, 230-1,
237-8, 246, 248-9, 252-3; emerging
political complexes 165; ethnicity 7,
156-8, 169, 213, 216-18, 246, 249, 252-
3; everyday life 190; financial 2-3,
181, 198; global economy 6, 25, 138,
199, 258; global liberal governance 2,
6, 8-13, 18, 30, 34, 44-5, 49-50, 72-3,
100, 108-9, 136, 146-7, 247, 252, 257-8,
263-4; growth of 1-3; household 123;
humanitarian 55-7, 98; identity 191;
informational economy 142; kinship
207, 214, 243; liberal peace 12, 14, 34,
136; local 156-8, 169, 214; local–global
5, 14, 46, 131, 140, 147, 153, 159, 164-
5; mafia 150, 162; military 20, 60, 186-
7, 231, 236-7, 246-9, 252-3, 259; money
laundering 181; multi-level 11; multinational companies 64; nation states
72-3; network wars 14, 19, 80, 258-60;
new social morphology 146-7; NGOs
53, 55-7, 64, 90, 146; patronage 150;
private military companies 186-7;
public–private 17-18; regional 2-3, 5-
6, 201; religious 158; security 16, 35-
6, 116; social 11, 125, 214; state–non-
state 8, 13-14, 46, 153; strategic
complexes 12, 52-3, 109; subsistence
239-40, 243; technological 198; trade
2-3, 145-8, 151-2, 154, 155-9, 175, 177,
183, 188; transborder shadow
economies 5, 7, 19, 145-8, 150, 152,
154-9, 163-4, 171-3, 175-7, 179-81,
187-8, 190-1, 194, 196-201; war
economies 160; warlords 176
new barbarism 109-15, 118, 120, 122,
127, 130, 164, 170
new imperialism 31-4, 93
New International Economic Order
(NIEO) 25-6
Newtonian world view 9, 84-5, 97, 161,
248, 252, 263
Niger 151, 171
Nigeria 64, 146, 151-2, 172, 177, 206
Niles region 205
nomenklatura 178, 180

non-formal economy *see* transborder shadow economy

non-governmental organisations (NGOs), in Africa 216; as aid channel 53-4; and arms trade 200; bureaucracy in 77; codes of conduct for 56, 61-2, 70; competition from small private firms 64; complex emergencies needed by 250; and complexity 212-13; complicity in political oppression 208, 230, 234, 238, 252-3, 256n, 258-60; at conference fora 55, 74a; and conflict 1, 13, 31, 54, 56, 82, 117, 125, 250-1; and cultural breakdown 125; de-ethnicisation policy of 215-21, 225, 228; development role of 39, 53; and displaced people 243; dominant groups manipulate 230-1, 237-8, 244-9, 256n; and donor governments 54-5, 72, 81; and exclusion 127; and food aid 234-40, 246-9, 254; and global liberal governance 2, 11-13, 15-16, 18, 31, 45, 49-50, 52-3; growth in 53; and human rights 15, 20, 32; humanitarian aid role 52-7, 77, 155; and ICVA 55-6; and inter-governmental organisations (IGOs) 54-6; independence of 82; instrumental view of 97; Islamic 204, 211, 236, 246; and liberal peace 11-13, 15-16, 18, 31, 52-3; and local structures 53, 107, 130; and migration 217-19; and military 54, 57-61; and multinational companies 62-4; and nation state 49-50, 77, 130, 209-28, 230-9, 242, 244-51, 255, 256n; natural economy approach of 213-21; in networks 16, 18, 36, 52-3, 55-6, 90, 146; and neutrality 90; and new humanitarianism 96, 103-4; and new imperialism 32; and objectification of South by North 83; and Operation Lifeline Sudan 203-4; organisational structure of 265n; and poverty 127; professional standards of 90; protection for 65, 69-70, 172; regulation of 105-6; reinvent themselves 249-50, 255, 263-4; SCHR 56; and security 1, 36, 259; and self-management 215-21, 223-8; and self-sufficiency 9; and social movements

129; and social reconstruction 82, 123, 189; and social welfare 54; and steady-state solutions 254, 262; and strategic complexes 45, 49-50, 97, 52-3; and subcontracting 53-5; and transborder shadow economies 142; transformational policies of 42; and transnational politics 258; and UN 54, 71, 77-8; and UNICEF 55; and World Bank 55

Nord Resources 184

Nordstrom, Carolyn 142-3, 157, 188

North America 2-3, 62

North Atlantic Treaty Organisation (NATO) 41, 57-9, 61, 172, 258

North–South relations, aid impact on 253; and arms trade 172; Cancun conference on (1981) 29; and commercialisation of politics 193-4; conflict as legacy of South 79, 115; and control of humanitarian agenda 82; and criminalisation of conflict 132-3; and dependency 22-4, 158; and enforcement of peace 81; exclusion of South 4-8; and global liberal governance 50, 258; and globalisation 47-8, 144-5, 194; as instrumental relationship 97-8; and liberal economic reform 149; liberalism vs non-liberalism in 150, 156, 158-9; as mirror relationship 264; nation-state competence in 46-8, 50, 163-4; and network wars 14, 160; and New International Economic Order 25; and NGOs 53; 'new barbarism' approach to 109; and new imperialism 31-4; and non-state linkages 18; and normalisation of conflict 260; Northern country interests conflict 89; and poverty 127; and regulation of aid 105; security reproblematised in 36-7; shift in relationship 2; South objectified 83, 92-3, 96; and structural adjustment 108, 147-8; as Third Worldism declines 26-9; and transborder shadow economy 142, 150, 156, 158-9

Northern Ireland 64

Norway 199

Nuba Mts 206, 231

Nuba people 206-7

nuclear power 36, 61, 84, 119, 200
Nyala 224, 242-3, 245

Observer 76
OCHA *see* under UN
oil 25, 28, 63, 66, 119, 142, 180, 182, 185, 196, 198, 207, 255
Ombudsman for Humanitarian Assistance 90
Operation Lifeline Sudan (OLS) 77, 203-4, 210-11, 216, 218, 221, 227-8, 231-6, 238, 244-7
Organisation for Economic Cooperation and Development (OECD) 27, 48, 56, 74, 121, 199
Organisation for Security and Cooperation in Europe (OSCE) 71, 258
Organisation of African Unity (OAU) 56
Organisation of Petroleum Exporting Countries (OPEC) 25, 28
Owen, David 78
Oxfam 117, 200, 204, 217-18, 223-4, 236, 241-2, 255, 256n

Papua New Guinea 69
parallel currency market 153-5
participation 8, 34, 40-2, 91, 104, 123, 261
partnership 8, 34, 42, 126, 130, 228, 261
patrimonialism 30, 139, 148, 156, 175-6, 183; *see also* patronage, patron–client relationships
patron/client relationships 165-70, 174, 213, 230, 236-43, 246, 248; *see also* patronage, patrimonialism
patronage 207, 212, 218, 220; *see also* patrimonialism, patron–client relationships
Peru 64, 178
Petronas Carigali 198
planned economies 168, 180
pluralism 30, 41, 141
polyarchy 2, 12, 49-50
population 4, 27, 36, 37, 72, 112-13, 115, 133, 211-12, 239, 247
Port Sudan 198
poverty 4, 6-8, 13, 16, 18, 23-4, 27-8, 35-7, 40, 47, 63, 86, 101-2, 115-17, 119-27, 132-3, 135-6, 147-50, 153, 159, 162, 174, 195-6, 219, 250, 254

power 8-9, 14-15, 17, 28, 33-4, 36, 39, 42, 72-3, 83, 103, 108, 122, 126, 128, 135-6, 139, 146-7, 157, 168, 212, 220, 257, 260-1
Prince of Wales Business Leaders Forum 62-3
private companies 45, 49, 52, 61-2, 64, 72, 114, 116, 146, 193-4; *see also* business, capitalism, foreign companies, multinational companies
private military companies (PMCs) 65-8, 183-7; *see also* security, private companies
private security companies *see* security, private companies; *see also* private military companies (PMCs)
privatisation 12, 14-15, 17, 29, 45-6, 48-50, 52, 58, 65-7, 150-1, 161, 167, 170-1, 176-80, 182-4, 193, 195, 198
profit 23, 52, 62, 65, 67, 158
Pronk, Jan 78
property rights 165, 170, 179
protection 167, 170-4, 177-9, 180-7, 190, 192-3, 199, 224-8, 230, 243, 251, 260
protectionism 9, 14-15, 19, 46, 157-8, 174
Providence Principles (1993) 88

quantum theory 10, 84

racism 41, 83, 109-11, 113-15, 191, 206, 220
Ranger, Terence 185
raw materials 2, 3, 4, 5, 24, 25, 146, 180, 182
Reagan, Ronald 29
reconstruction *see* social reconstruction
Red Crescent 89; Sudanese 246
Red Cross 56, 60, 70, 77, 87, 89, 93, 188, 192; Code of Conduct (1994) 89
refugees 4-5, 12, 26-7, 29, 36-7, 58, 71, 81-2, 86, 119, 202; *see also* displaced people
regionalisation 1, 3-4, 8, 17, 36, 44, 48-9, 58, 71, 79, 82, 87-8, 104, 114, 118-19, 125, 144-5, 150-2, 157-8, 168, 171, 173, 177, 190, 201
regulation 9, 15, 19, 44, 47, 49, 52, 55, 62, 68-71, 73, 147-8, 156, 173-5, 177-8, 181-4, 190-1, 222, 228, 231, 239, 246, 249, 252, 257-8, 261
Regulation of Foreign Military Assistance Act (South Africa) 69-70

religion 38, 133, 158, 191
Reno, William 139, 162, 165, 175, 182-3, 194
research 259-65
resource competition 6, 13, 16, 36, 86, 95, 112, 115
Revolutionary United Front (RUF) 185
Richards, Paul 138
Rizegat Arabs 203-4, 224, 231, 241-3
rogue states 8, 140
Roitman, Janet 173, 194
Romania 157
Royal Dutch/Shell 64
Russia 19, 61, 110, 141, 150, 162, 178-82, 187, 189, 200
Rwanda 60, 81, 90, 111, 130, 182
Ryle, John 203, 212, 216, 256n

Saferworld 116-17, 126, 128
Saladin Security 66
sanctions 8, 128, 138, 196-8, 200-1
Sandline International 66, 69-70, 186
Sarajevo 78
Savimbi, Jonas 185
Scandinavian countries 60, 73-4
SCF (UK) 204, 213, 220, 224-5, 232-5, 239, 246; (US) 221
Schierup, Carl-Ulrik 165, 169
Schumacher, E. F. 35
Second World 47
Second World War 26, 39, 41, 47, 93, 121
security, and aid 35, 194, 246; and arms proliferation 113; biological 113; business sector involvement in 193, 195; and Cold War 257; and development 1-2, 4, 7, 9, 11-12, 15-19, 22-43, 45, 52, 88, 94, 99, 116, 118, 120, 122, 132, 195, 249, 252, 259-60; and human rights 64; and humanitarian aid 259; and legitimacy 69; and market system 195; and multinational corporations 62-6, 69-70; and nationalism 173; networks of 16, 35-6, 116; and new wars 52, 257; and NGOs 259; political 204; and poverty 35; private companies provide 12, 16, 19, 36, 45, 52, 61-2, 65-70, 150, 182, 184-7, 194; private military companies (PMCs) provide 65-6, 68-70; and privatisation 50-1, 62, 68, 170-1, 182-4, 198; protection services provide 179; and

regionalisation 44; regulation of 69, 182; reproblematisation of 2, 7, 16, 18, 22, 26-8, 35-8, 42, 45, 82, 99, 113-18, 126-8, 133, 148, 159, 194, 259; shadow structures of 166; studies of 1; and terrorism 113; and underdevelopment 2, 7, 16, 18, 22, 26-8, 35-8, 42, 45, 82, 99, 113-18, 126-8, 133, 148, 159, 194, 259; and UN vulnerability 71; of weak states 192
self-management 20, 30, 34, 36, 42, 101-2, 169, 204, 209-10, 215-21, 223-8, 230-2, 234, 236, 241, 247-52, 255, 263
self-organisation 10, 85
Senegal 152, 157
Serbia 41, 140, 170, 189
Short, Clare 94
Sicily 178
Sierra Leone 70, 94, 167, 175, 178, 184-5
Sierra Rutile 184
slavery 205, 207
Slim, Hugo 76, 98, 259-60
Slovakia 189
smuggling 137, 142, 146, 157, 180, 196
social evolutionism 162-5
social reconstruction 1-2, 8-9, 11-12, 15, 34, 58-9, 63-5, 69, 73-5, 82, 85, 88, 94, 99, 117, 119, 123-4, 128, 135, 141-2, 174, 178, 189, 192, 250, 261
social welfare 47-50, 54, 149, 163-4, 166-9, 173, 193
socialism 22, 25-6, 28-31, 47, 115, 162, 167-9
solidarity 33, 101, 106
Somalia 12, 59, 78, 90, 141, 152, 171-2, 176, 178
South Africa 4, 66, 69-70, 137, 183-4, 186, 188, 197, 206
South America 66
sovereignty 30-1, 49, 57, 77, 93, 118, 139, 148, 164-6, 170, 175-6, 178, 184, 222
Soviet Union, former 4, 26, 54, 111, 168, 170, 180
Spanish Civil War (1936–9) 93
Sphere Project 90
Srebrnica 59
Sri Lanka 64, 178
state–non-state linkages 8, 12-14, 18, 34, 42, 45-7, 49-51, 72, 74, 109, 141, 153, 163-5, 176-87, 190, 197, 226, 252, 259
Steering Committee for Humanitarian Response (SCHR) 56

Stewart, Colonel Bob 60
Stiglitz, Joseph 40
Strasser, Valentine 184-5
strategic complexes 12-18, 37, 42, 44-74, 78-9, 87-8, 93, 97, 109, 114-16, 122, 140-1, 145-6, 163-4, 193, 226, 252-3, 258, 261, 264
strongmen 14-15, 47, 166-7, 175-8, 183-4, 190, 192, 243; *see also* warlords
structural adjustment 9, 13, 19, 29, 40, 71, 108, 141, 147-53, 159, 167, 172, 190, 194-5
subcontracting 44-5, 53-5, 64-7, 81, 99
Sudan 19-20, 33, 54, 76-7, 89-90, 94-5, 100, 104-6, 124, 133, 140, 151-5, 167, 171, 174, 177, 182, 189-90, 198, 202-56, 258
Sudan Defence Force 199
Sudanese People's Liberation Army (SPLA) 140, 154, 207, 211-12, 226-7, 237, 242
Sudanese Society for Environmental Protection 246
superpowers 22, 31, 93, 119, 129, 131, 137-8, 166, 196
Sweden 36, 94
systems theory 84-5, 97

Tajikistan 172
Talisman Energy 198
Taylor, Charles 139, 175-6, 178, 184, 196
technicism 2, 75-6, 83, 86, 92
technology 2, 8, 23, 25, 46, 48, 75-6, 83, 158, 181, 199; transfer 101, 169
terrorism 2, 16, 37, 113-14, 118, 191, 209
Total Oil 198
trade, agricultural 151; arms 171-2, 176, 178, 188, 190, 196—201; colonial patterns of 25, 115; in dependency theory 17, 24; deregulation of 148; diamond 137-8; dollar 154-5; drugs 131, 142-3, 146, 148, 172, 196, 201; and EU Code of Conduct 199; Greek traders 166; Hausa–Fulani 146; illegal 134, 145-6; and import substitution 24; internal 244; intra-firm 158; ivory 172; Lebanese traders 166; liberalisation of 29, 48-9, 51, 149; local–global 146; and military 177; and network wars 196; networks of 3, 145-8, 151-9, 188; preferential 25; protectionism 9, 14-

15, 19, 46, 157-8, 174; reform 24-5; regionalisation of 2-3; sanctions 8, 128, 138, 196-8, 200-1; and subsistence in Sudan 235; terms of 24-26, 29, 115; transborder shadow economy 14, 19, 141-2, 145-8, 151-2, 154-9, 174-5, 178, 180-2, 188; unequal 17, 24; and warlords 175
transborder shadow economy 5, 9, 14, 19, 46, 85, 136-60, 163-4, 167, 171-201, 223, 246, 252, 254, 259-61
Trnopolje 32
Truman, Harry 35
Turco-Egyptian rulers 205
Turkmenistan 198
Third World/Third Worldism 17, 22-30, 35, 47, 54, 115

Uganda 113, 151-2, 154-5, 188
Ukraine 176, 196
Um Kaddada 220
Umma Party 154
unemployment 27, 36, 149-51, 172, 188
UNITA (National Union for the Total Independence of Angola) 137-8, 185, 188, 197, 200
United Kingdom 37, 62-3, 68-70, 72, 76, 78, 94, 184, 186, 250; Department for International Development (DFID) 91, 94, 105, 119, 124; International Development Committee (IDC) 94, 116-17, 126; National Criminal Intelligence Service 181; Overseas Development Administration (ODA) 78
United Nations, and Angolan peace process 137-8; and arms control 199-201; arms embargoes by 67, 70; Band Aid shows up 76; bureaucracy in 262; and business sector 63; casualties among staff 52; and complex emergencies 12, 71; and complexity 212-13; complicity in political oppression 208, 230, 234, 238, 252-3, 256n, 258-60; and conflict 1, 4-5, 12, 31, 57-9, 66, 68-9, 100; and conflict resolution 82; and corruption 78; and culture 264; Declaration of Human Rights 27, 223; Declaration on the Rights of the Child 32; demise of 90; diplomatic embargo by 198; and displaced

people 202; General Assembly 86, 244; and global liberal governance 1, 4-5, 12, 16, 31, 44, 77, 86, 89-90, 106; humanitarian operations by 3-4, 54, 71, 76-8, 81-2, 89, 100; and ICVA 56; Inter-Agency Standing Committee 55; and military 57-9, 66, 68-9; and nation state (Sudan) 209-28, 230-56; and NGOs 53-6, 77-8; and Operation Lifeline Sudan (OLS) 203-4; operational capacity of 54; as peace broker 188; peacekeeping role 58-9, 66, 68, 78; and private military companies 66, 68-9; reform of 264; and refugees 26-7, 36, 81-2; reorganisation for complex emergencies 71; and rights-based development 222-5; role changes post-Cold War 79; and Rwanda 81-2, 111; 'safe area' policies of 78; sanctions by 197, 200-1; and SCHR 56; Secretariat 111; Secretary-General 117, 195; Secretary-General's Special Envoy for Humanitarian Affairs in Sudan 227; Security Council 111, 255; and social reconstruction 82; and sovereignty 77; Special Political Committee 26; subcontracting by 54; and transborder shadow economy 142; and underdevelopment 26-7, 36
United Nations Children's Fund (UNICEF) 32, 55-6, 69, 149, 223, 228, 255
United Nations Conference on Trade and Development (UNCTAD) 56
United Nations Department of Humanitarian Affairs (DHA) 71, 78, 86, 100
United Nations Development Programme (UNDP) 56, 100, 143
United Nations Economic and Social Commission (ECOSOC) 55-6
United Nations High Commissioner for Refugees (UNHCR) 26, 59-61, 63, 69, 71, 81, 88, 202, 222, 224
United Nations Humanitarian Coordination Unit (UNHCU) 224
United Nations Organisation for the Coordination of Humanitarian Assistance (OCHA) 55, 59, 71

United States (US) 53, 57, 60, 66-8, 70, 78, 113, 119-20, 137, 162, 184, 198, 201, 250
United States Agency for International Development (USAID) 119-21
UNPROFOR military force 59
urbanisation 27, 124, 169
US Institute for Peace 60

Varese, Federico 178-9
Verdery, Katherine 157, 165
Vietnam 25-6
Vietnam Solidarity Campaign 129
Virginia 67
Voluntary Organisations in Cooperation in Emergencies (VOICE) 56

warlords 47, 175-8, 183-5, 190, 196
wars see conflict
Warsaw Pact (former) 172
Washington consensus 40
water 37, 64, 214, 240-1, 244-6
Wau 246
weak states 139-40, 163-8, 175-6, 184, 187, 192, 194, 196
Weiss, Thomas 88, 93, 97, 106
workers 168-9
World Bank 29, 39-40, 48, 55-6, 63, 122-3, 132, 143, 148, 150, 167; Operation Policy Group 55
World Conference on Religion and Peace 88-9
World Food Programme (WFP) 56, 213-14, 235, 239-40
World Health Organisation (WHO) 56, 63
World Trade Organisation (WTO) 199
World Vision 124

xenophobia 113

Yeltsin, Boris 180-1
Yugoslavia 41, 66, 111, 157, 165, 169-70, 178; see also Balkans, Bosnia, Croatia, Kosovo, Serbia

Zaïre 133, 152, 154-5, 197; see also Congo, Democratic Republic of
Zambia 122
Zapatistas 192